Palgrave Executive Essentials

Today's complex and changing business environment brings with it a number of pressing challenges. To be successful, business professionals are increasingly required to leverage and spot future trends, be masters of strategy, all while leading responsibly, inspiring others, mastering financial techniques and driving innovation.

Palgrave Executive Essentials empowers you to take your skills to the next level. Offering a suite of resources to support you on your executive journey and written by renowned experts from top business schools, the series is designed to support professionals as they embark on executive education courses, but it is equally applicable to practicing leaders and managers. Each book brings you in-depth case studies, accompanying video resources, reflective questions, practical tools and core concepts that can be easily applied to your organization, all written in an engaging, easy to read style.

V. Kumar · Philip Kotler

Transformative Marketing

Combining New Age Technologies and Human Insights

V. Kumar
Goodman School of Business
Brock University
St. Catharines, ON, Canada

Philip Kotler
Kellogg School of Management
Northwestern University
Evanston, IL, USA

ISSN 2731-5614 ISSN 2731-5622 (electronic)
Palgrave Executive Essentials
ISBN 978-3-031-59636-0 ISBN 978-3-031-59637-7 (eBook)
https://doi.org/10.1007/978-3-031-59637-7

© The Editor(s) (if applicable) and The Author(s), under exclusive license to Springer Nature Switzerland AG 2024

This work is subject to copyright. All rights are solely and exclusively licensed by the Publisher, whether the whole or part of the material is concerned, specifically the rights of translation, reprinting, reuse of illustrations, recitation, broadcasting, reproduction on microfilms or in any other physical way, and transmission or information storage and retrieval, electronic adaptation, computer software, or by similar or dissimilar methodology now known or hereafter developed.
The use of general descriptive names, registered names, trademarks, service marks, etc. in this publication does not imply, even in the absence of a specific statement, that such names are exempt from the relevant protective laws and regulations and therefore free for general use.
The publisher, the authors and the editors are safe to assume that the advice and information in this book are believed to be true and accurate at the date of publication. Neither the publisher nor the authors or the editors give a warranty, expressed or implied, with respect to the material contained herein or for any errors or omissions that may have been made. The publisher remains neutral with regard to jurisdictional claims in published maps and institutional affiliations.

Cover illustration: Jolene Zigarovich

This Palgrave Macmillan imprint is published by the registered company Springer Nature Switzerland AG
The registered company address is: Gewerbestrasse 11, 6330 Cham, Switzerland

If disposing of this product, please recycle the paper.

Dedicated with Love
To my parents, Patta and Viswanathan, my uncle, Kannan
My wife, Aparna
my daughters' family—Anita, Rohan, Ryan, Devin & Prita, Matt, Stephen and Austin
my sister Shanti, brother-in-law Prasad, and their family,
my in-laws, Dr. Lalitha and Ramamurthy, and my spiritual guru, M. Karthikeyan

—V. Kumar

Dedicated with Love
To my wife Nancy in celebration of our
69 wonderful years of marriage, love
and happiness.

—Philip Kotler

Preface

The realm of new-age technologies is captivating and profound about their influence on the constantly evolving marketing landscape and human understanding. In continuing with the ongoing evolution of digital technologies, we stand at the intersection of innovation and interconnectedness, where state-of-the-art technologies are revolutionizing the methods through which businesses engage, comprehend, and establish connections with their customer bases.

Progress in technology has a significant impact on the way consumers establish connections with companies. With the rise of tech-savvy customers, there is a growing demand for quick and effortless digital experiences, along with an expectation for immediate solutions to their requirements. Consequently, businesses are adapting their practices by embracing technology at a faster pace, revamping their procedures, creating new organizational frameworks, and introducing innovative business models. By allocating more resources to technological advancements, companies can reap the advantages of reduced expenses, improved efficiency, and a better ability to meet the expectations of stakeholders.

Welcome to a new marketing era, one that is powered by technologies of the modern age—the likes of artificial intelligence, machine learning, drones, robotics, and many more. This book serves as a valuable guide to navigating this new world, where the marketing function takes on various roles in shaping, creating, executing, and influencing both human minds and technological advancements in the rapidly evolving marketplace.

The emergence of cutting-edge technologies like AI, metaverse, drones, and IoT has paved the way for a fresh wave of marketing opportunities. This signifies the commencement of a transformative journey that explores the complexities of these technologies, their role in driving innovation, how they reshape customer interaction, and how they enhance the effectiveness of marketing endeavors. From the tailored experiences enabled by machine learning algorithms to the captivating encounters made feasible by the metaverse, this book will guide readers through the technological terrain that is propelling marketing through interesting times.

Significantly, this book delves into more than just the visible technological progress that surrounds us. By delving into these advancements, this book uncovers the interconnectedness between technology and human emotions and understanding. In the age of extensive data, comprehending the intricacies of consumer behavior has become more complex and nuanced than ever before. Modern technologies not only enable the gathering of massive data sets but also empower marketers to extract valuable insights that can guide strategic choices and foster business expansion. In essence, this book commemorates the essence of the human spirit within the realm of technology.

Moreover, this book delves into the challenges that marketing departments face when dealing with new-age technologies. It emphasizes the need for knowledge on which technology to use, how to use it, and when and why it should be used. Additionally, it highlights the significance of the data generated from successful technology deployment, which provides valuable feedback to marketers. The book also addresses the handling of this abundant data and the insights it offers for developing solutions and designing growth strategies that align with both firm profitability and stakeholder well-being.

This book is aimed at the top-level and mid-level management, who have the power and resources to change the design, development, and implementation of marketing strategies in their organization. This book also serves as a guide for executives on the rise to understand how new-age technologies interface with conventional and emerging marketing practices in the marketplace. Further, graduate /undergraduate/honors students in Business and Marketing programs will also stand to gain from this book as it covers emerging topics in technology and marketing. Therefore, this book can be adopted as a required/ supplemental/ recommended reading for courses including Customer Relationship Management (CRM), Customer Engagement, Technology Marketing, Technology Management, Social Media Marketing, Digital Marketing, Marketing Analytics, and Marketing Strategy.

St. Catharines, Canada   V. Kumar
Evanston, USA   Philip Kotler

Acknowledgments

We thank Bharath Rajan, Namrata Manchiraju, and Ben deHooge for their assistance in the preparation of this book. Many thanks to our colleagues, who stimulated us and brought new ideas and approaches to our attention in writing this book.

We also thank our coauthors in each of the studies referenced in this book for their contributions. Additional thanks are also to the practitioner community who gave us many opportunities to put ideas into practice and thus broaden our understanding of new-age technologies as it is currently evolving.

We are grateful to the students who, through constant interaction, provided valuable input and feedback from the consumer's perspective.

We are thankful to Renu for copyediting the book content.

Dr. V. Kumar, who is also the Distinguished Scholar of Research, We School, India; Distinguished Fellow, MICA, India; and Chang Jiang Scholar, Huazhong University of Science and Technology, Wuhan, China, thanks the generous support from these institutions for his ongoing research.

Praise for *Transformative Marketing*

"This is an important book from two of the most influential thought leaders the marketing profession has produced. They welcome you, the reader, as follows: 'Welcome to a new marketing era.... powered by technologies of the modern age...artificial intelligence, machine learning, drones, robotics, and...more. This book [is a] guide to navigating this new world...'. A world traveler who arrives in unfamiliar country needs a reliable guidebook. All marketing executives are now on a journey to an unfamiliar, rapidly changing, technological world. They need this guidebook. A must read."

—Gary L. Lilien, *Distinguished Research Professor of Management Science, Penn State*

"I consider Prof. Kotler as my Marketing Guru. Partnering with Prof. Kumar, he has produced yet another groundbreaking book, which is a must-read for anyone looking to understand the dynamic interplay between cutting-edge technologies and modern marketing practices, deftly integrated with human insights. Whether you're a top-level executive, a rising leader, or a student in the field of business and marketing, this book will equip you with the knowledge and strategies needed to thrive in today's rapidly evolving marketplace."

—Raja Rajamannar, *Chief Marketing Officer of Mastercard*

"Technology always transforms businesses by changing customer behavior, which, in turn, influences marketing strategies to attract new customers. V. Kumar and Philip Kotler's outstanding book is an excellent guide for businesses looking to embrace the right technologies in the Marketing 5.0 era."

—Hermawan Kartajaya, *Founder and Chairman of MCorp (MarkPlus), Indonesia*

"This book is a breakthrough because it identifies the enormous breakthrough technologies for marketing. The book is a must read for every marketer who wants to stay on the ball."

—Hermann Simon, *Founder and honorary chairman of Simon-Kucher*

"Marketing leaders that mindfully apply the capabilities of New Age Technologies ahead of rivals give their firms a durable advantage. Kotler and Kumar give these leaders a valuable guide to the transformative potential of these technologies."

—George Day, *Professor of Marketing, Wharton School, University of Pennsylvania*

"In their groundbreaking book, Kumar and Kotler provide a comprehensive and insightful guide to the future of technology-powered marketing. By expertly weaving together the latest advancements in technology with timeless marketing principles, they offer a roadmap for businesses to stay ahead in an increasingly competitive landscape. This book is a must-read for anyone looking to transform their marketing capabilities by leveraging the full potential of new age technologies."

—Mohan Sawhney, *Associate Dean for Digital Innovation, Director, Center for Research in Technology & Innovation, Northwestern Kellogg School of Management*

"*Transformative Marketing* brilliantly navigates the evolving landscape of marketing, offering a comprehensive guide to harnessing new-age technologies for success. In this groundbreaking work, the authors navigate the dynamic landscape of modern marketing, skillfully dissecting the impact of new-age technologies like AI, GAI, metaverse, robots, ML, drones, IoT, and blockchain. This book is a must-read for marketers seeking to not only survive but thrive in the dynamic, technology-driven future of the industry."

—Prof. Dr. Marc Oliver Opresnik, *Distinguished Professor of Marketing, Luebeck University of Applied Sciences, Germany*

"It is a New Age. Advances in technology have forced us to change the way we make marketing decisions. It brings exciting opportunity for what we produce, how we market our products and services, how we understand our customers, and how customers connect with us and others. Kumar and Kotler are at the forefront of the marketing impact brought to us by cutting edge technology. *Transformative Marketing* is a must read—the alternative is to be left behind."
 —David J. Reibstein, *William Stewart Woodside Professor of Marketing, Wharton, University of Pennsylvania*

"Professor Kotler's legacy in marketing is unparalleled, and *Transformative Marketing* cements his position as a thought leader for the digital age. Don't just adapt to change; embrace it with the transformative insights offered within these pages. Highly recommended!"
 —Waldemar A. Pfoertsch, *Senior Marketing Professor, CIIM Business School, University of Limassol, Cyprus*

"If you want to know how far behind you are in marketing technologies – read this book!"
 —Professor Hooi Den Huan, *Nanhang Technological University, Singapore*

"*Transformative Marketing* offers marketing managers a much needed roadmap of how to utilize eight new technologies to deliver superior customer experience and value while simultaneously increasing marketing efficiency."
 —V. "Seenu" Srinivasan, *Adams Distinguished Professor of Management, Emeritus, Stanford University*

"With technological advances profoundly changing the marketing world, there is a critical need for top marketers to develop new skills and thinking. Thankfully, *Transformative Marketing* delves into the eight most important new-age technologies to offer clarity and invaluable insight and inspiration to front-line marketers of all ranks."
 —Kevin Lane Keller, *E.B. Osborn Professor of Marketing, Tuck School of Business at Dartmouth College*

"Professors Kotler and Kumar are ideally placed to describe the "marketing of the future" and do so with remarkable clarity and prescience. A must read for marketing practitioners and students alike!"
 —Dominique M. Hanssens, *Distinguished Research Professor of Marketing, UCLA Anderson School of Management*

Contents

1	**Transformative Marketing Has Begun**	1
	Introduction	1
	A Brief Overview of NATs	4
	Looking Beyond the Digital Frontier of NATs	11
	Organization of the Book	13
	Notes and References	15
2	**Transformative Marketing: A Marketing 5.0 Perspective**	19
	Introduction	19
	Meaningful Connections Using Human Insights	20
	Convergence of NATs and Marketing	22
	Understanding Resources, Capabilities, and Strategies of NATs	23
	Notes and References	26
3	**Transformative Marketing with Artificial Intelligence**	29
	Overview	29
	Origin, Definition, and Components of AI	32
	The Rise of the Transformative Home	34
	Personalized Education	35
	The World of Wearables	36
	AI in the Marketing 5.0 World	38
	Data-Driven Marketing Using AI	39
	Predictive Marketing Using AI	39
	Contextual Marketing Using AI	40

xvii

Augmented Marketing Using AI	41
Agile Marketing Using AI	42
Current AI Applications in Marketing	43
Understanding Customer Needs to Deploy AI	44
Revisiting Firm's Capabilities to Integrate AI	45
Designing Marketing Mix Strategies with AI	46
Driving Customer Engagement Through AI	47
Designing Digital Strategies with AI	48
Future of AI in Marketing	49
AI in Social Media	51
Marketing Tools for AI	52
Seamless Integration of AI with Marketing—The New Marketing Culture	52
Notes and References	55

4 Transformative Marketing with Generative Artificial Intelligence — 65

Overview	65
Origin, Definition, and Classification of Generative AI	67
Origin	67
Definition	68
Classification	69
Some Commercial Applications of GAI	71
Generative AI in the Marketing 5.0 World	75
Data-Driven Marketing Using GAI	75
Predictive Marketing Using GAI	76
Contextual Marketing Using GAI	77
Augmented Marketing Using GAI	78
Agile Marketing Using GAI	79
Current Generative AI Applications in Marketing	79
Understanding Customer Needs to Deploy GAI	81
Revisiting Firm Capabilities to Integrate GAI	82
Designing Marketing Mix Strategies with GAI	83
Driving Customer Engagement Through GAI	87
Designing Digital Strategies with GAI	88
Future of Generative AI in Marketing	89
Ultra-Personalized Experiences	90
Personalized Marketing at Scale	90
New Forms of Creative Content	91

		Ethical Considerations for Developing Marketing Campaigns	92
		Notes and References	94
5		**Transformative Marketing with Machine Learning (ML)**	103
		Overview	103
		Origin, Definition, and Components of ML	104
		Analytics-Oriented Technology	108
		Link to Artificial Intelligence	110
		Machine Learning Models	112
		Machine Learning in the Marketing 5.0 World	114
		Data-Driven Marketing Using ML	114
		Predictive marketing using ML	115
		Contextual Marketing Using ML	116
		Augmented Marketing Using ML	117
		Agile Marketing Using ML	117
		Current ML Applications in Marketing	118
		Understanding Customer Needs to Deploy ML	119
		Revisiting Firm Capabilities to Integrate ML	120
		Designing Marketing Mix Strategies with ML	121
		Driving customer engagement through ML	124
		Designing Digital Strategies with ML	125
		Future of ML in Marketing	126
		ML and Customer Churn Analytics	127
		Improvement to demand forecasting	128
		Strategy Development for Customers and Products	130
		Notes and References	133
6		**Transformative Marketing with Metaverse**	141
		Overview	141
		Origin, Definition, and Classifications of the Metaverse	142
		Origin	142
		Definition	144
		Classification	145
		Metaverse in the Marketing 5.0 World	145
		Data-Driven Marketing Using the Metaverse	148
		Predictive Marketing Using the Metaverse	149
		Contextual Marketing Using the Metaverse	150
		Augmented Marketing Using the Metaverse	151
		Agile Marketing Using the Metaverse	151
		Current Metaverse Applications in Marketing	152

	Understanding Customer Needs to Deploy in the Metaverse	153
	Revisiting Firm Capabilities to Integrate in the Metaverse	154
	Designing Marketing Mix Strategies in the Metaverse	155
	Driving Customer Engagement Through the Metaverse	158
	Designing Digital Strategies Within the Metaverse	159
	Future of Metaverse in Marketing	160
	Technical Considerations	161
	Social/Ethical Considerations	162
	Economic Considerations	163
	Notes and References	164
7	**Transformative Marketing with the Internet of Things (IoT)**	**171**
	Overview	171
	Origin, Definition, and Classifications of IoT	172
	Individuals	173
	Organization	174
	Industry	174
	National	175
	IoT in the Marketing 5.0 World	181
	Data-Driven Marketing Using IoT	181
	Predictive Marketing Using IoT	182
	Contextual Marketing Using IoT	183
	Augmented Marketing Using IoT	184
	Agile Marketing Using IoT	185
	Current IoT Applications in Marketing	186
	Understanding Customer Needs to Deploy IoT	186
	Revisiting Firm Capabilities to Integrate IoT	187
	Designing Marketing Mix Strategies with IoT	188
	Driving Customer Engagement Through IoT	190
	Designing Digital Strategies with IoT	191
	Future of IoT in Marketing	192
	IoT and Transportation	193
	Smart Cities	194
	Real-Time Buying Process and Purchasing	196
	Notes and References	199
8	**Transformative Marketing with Robotics**	**211**
	Overview	211
	Origin, Definition, and Classifications of Robotics	212
	Origin	212
	Definition	213

Classification of Robots	214
Industrial and Business Applications	216
Domestic-Oriented Technology	219
Humanoid Robots	221
Robotics in the Marketing 5.0 World	222
Data-Driven Marketing Using Robotics	223
Predictive Marketing Using Robotics	224
Contextual Marketing Using Robotics	224
Augmented Marketing Using Robotics	225
Agile Marketing Using Robotics	226
Current Robotics Applications in Marketing	227
Understanding Customer Needs to Deploy Robotics	227
Revisiting Firm Capabilities to Integrate Robotics	228
Designing Marketing Mix Strategies with Robotics	229
Driving Customer Engagement Through Robotics	232
Designing Digital Strategies with Robotics	233
Future of Robotics in Marketing	234
Robotics and the Interactive Service Industry	235
Interactive Marketing	236
Creative Content Curation	238
Notes and References	241

9 Transformative Marketing Using Drones

Overview	255
Origin, Definition, and Classification of Drones	256
Origin	256
Definition	257
Classification of Drones	257
Military-Oriented Technology	262
Consumer Applications	263
Business Applications	265
Disaster Response	268
Drones in the Marketing 5.0 World	269
Data-Driven Marketing Using Drones	269
Predictive Marketing Using Drones	270
Contextual Marketing Using Drones	271
Augmented Marketing Using Drones	272
Agile Marketing Using Drones	273
Current Drone Applications in Marketing	274
Understanding Customer Needs to Deploy Drones	275
Revisiting Firm Capabilities to Integrate Drones	276

Designing Marketing Mix Strategies With Drones 277
Driving Customer Engagement Through Drones 278
Designing Digital Strategies With Drones 280
Future of Drones in Marketing 281
The "Good," "Bad," and "Ugly" of Drones 282
Enhanced Customer Experience 283
Customer Contact Solutions 284
Notes and References 287

10 Transformative Marketing Using Blockchain 299
Overview 299
Origin, Definition, and Classification of Blockchain 300
Origin 300
Definition 302
Classification of Blockchain 304
Security-Oriented Technology 306
Link to AI and ML 308
AI/ML Improving Blockchain's Effectiveness 309
Blockchain in the Marketing 5.0 World 310
Data-Driven Marketing Using Blockchain 310
Predictive Marketing Using Blockchain 311
Contextual Marketing Using Blockchain 312
Augmented Marketing Using Blockchain 314
Agile Marketing Using Blockchain 314
Current Blockchain Applications in Marketing 316
Understanding Customer Needs to Deploy Blockchain 316
Revisiting Firm Capabilities to Integrate Blockchain 317
Designing Marketing Mix Strategies with Blockchain 318
Driving Customer Engagement Through Blockchain 321
Designing Digital Strategies with Blockchain 322
The Future of Blockchain in Marketing 324
Data and Transaction Security 325
Impact on Advertising Transparency 325
Online Marketing Campaign Management 327
Notes and References 331

11 Putting It All Together 345
New-Age Technologies for Better Marketing: A Strategic Framework 346
New-Age Technologies 346
Generation of Firm Capabilities 351

Strategic and Tactical Marketing Actions 353
Customer Experience 354
Stakeholder Engagement/Benefits 355
Value and Social Well-being in a New-Age Technology World 359
Notes and References 360

Index 365

List of Figures

Fig. 2.1	The Marketing 5.0 concept	21
Fig. 3.1	Role of AI in personalized engagement marketing	50
Fig. 3.2	Popular and emerging applications of AI	51
Fig. 4.1	Amazon's customer review highlights feature developed by GAI	81
Fig. 5.1	Data mining process for marketing purposes	106
Fig. 11.1	NATs for transformative marketing: A strategic framework	347
Image 3.1	Smart locks for homes. A smart lock device used for home protection	34
Image 3.2	Wearable devices. A smartwatch is a wearable device that provides several features such as local weather, to-do lists, appointments, personal communications, personal health-related information, and much more	37
Image 5.1	Shopify. Shopify facilitates businesses through its machine-learning capabilities	109
Image 5.2	Ride-sharing Applications. Ride-sharing apps such as Uber and Lyft use a combination of AI and ML to provide the most relevant route results	111
Image 5.3	Video and Music Editing Software. Video and music editing software work in tandem with humans to create content that can be personalized and highly engaging	129

Image 5.4	Machine Learning-powered Warehousing Solutions. Machine learning solutions deployed at warehouses aid in demand fulfillment, warehouse automation, and route optimization for maximum efficiency	130
Image 5.5	Chatbots and intelligent agents. Chatbots and intelligent agents use ML capabilities to assist customers in making informed choices	131
Image 6.1	Fortnite. A person playing Fortnite on a mobile device	143
Image 6.2	Pokémon Go. A person playing Pokémon Go on a mobile device	143
Image 6.3	Product design using Metaverse. Product design and ergonomic features can be configured on the metaverse	155
Image 6.4	Metaverse in public spaces. Metaverse can be used in public spaces such as museums to blend physical and virtual worlds	158
Image 7.1	Wearable. Personal wearables such as the Apple Watch can perform and monitor a wide range of actions	177
Image 7.2	Smart Homes. Consumers can connect and control their devices via Google Home	178
Image 7.3	Smart Thermostats. Smart home energy management systems such as Nest can automatically regulate room temperature based on learning energy usage patterns over time	191
Image 7.4	IoT Warning Applications. IoT applications for smart cities such as this one, LOCUS, provide a direct connection between the citizens and the information system of the city in a visualized form	195
Image 7.5	Amazon Go store. An Amazon Go store that uses a combination of machine vision, IoT sensors, and a mobile app to facilitate contactless retail customer transactions	197
Image 8.1	Robots in manufacturing. Robots in an automobile manufacturing plant	217
Image 8.2	Service robots. Robots serving drinks at a bar	220
Image 8.3	Interactive robots. Robots can be used in interactive settings in social spaces	237
Image 8.4	Robots in airports. A robot assisting passengers at Incheon airport, South Korea	238
Image 8.5	Collaborative robots in manufacturing. Collaborative robots are used alongside humans in an industrial setting	239
Image 9.1	Fixed-wing drone	259
Image 9.2	Multirotor drone	259
Image 9.3	Drones used in Aerial Photography	264
Image 9.4	Drone Racing. First-person view drone racing	265

Image 9.5	Drones used in spraying farms	267
Image 9.6	Drones used in construction	268
Image 9.7	Drones used in apple-picking	274
Image 10.1	Bitcoin. Bitcoins are used widely as a reliable means of digital currency	301
Image 10.2	Tracking food origin using blockchain. Nestlé allows users to trace the coffee origins of their Zoégas coffee brand through blockchain-recorded data	315
Image 10.3	Blockchain for advertising effectiveness. Blockchain is used to improve efficiencies in ad buying and ad development	327
Image 10.4	Blockchain for managing influencer marketing. Blockchain can be used to manage influencer marketing programs efficiently	329

List of Tables

Table 1.1	Understanding new-age technologies for transformative marketing	5
Table 3.1	AI adoption worldwide 2022, by industry and function	30
Table 3.2	Selected companies in the AI ecosystem	31
Table 4.1	Representation of how GAI is used by industry worldwide	66
Table 4.2	Definition of Generative AI offered by various organizations	69
Table 4.3	Classification of GAI	70
Table 4.4	Types of GAI models	71
Table 4.5	A comparison of the popular GAI models—ChatGPT, DALL-E, & Bard	73
Table 4.6	Top 10 professions that show the most automation potential for GAI	80
Table 6.1	Types of metaverses	146
Table 8.1	Select definition of robotics	214
Table 8.2	Select conceptualization of robots	214
Table 8.3	Classification of robots	215
Table 8.4	Select conceptualization of social robots	221
Table 9.1	Similar terms relating to drones	258
Table 9.2	Changing nature of user demographics in the United States	281
Table 10.1	Select conceptualizations of Blockchain	302
Table 10.2	Classification of Blockchain	305

1

Transformative Marketing Has Begun

Introduction

Avant-garde. This is a term that can be used to describe the current state of business and marketing. In the vast canvas of human history, there have been pivotal moments that have redefined the way we live, work, and connect. Today, we find ourselves at the cusp of such a transformative era, where the convergence of new-age technologies is reshaping the world as we know it. The rapid and relentless march of innovation, fueled by advances in technology has ushered in a new chapter in the human story.

Essentially, everything we know, have, and see today is different from what it was a decade ago. There may have been signs of technology penetrating our daily lives in popular culture, but the rate at which it is taking place is both scary and exciting. As with many things, marketing has also adapted to these technological advancements. Originally, marketing was product-driven (1.0), which then evolved to be customer-oriented (2.0), and then human-centric (3.0). These phases have taken seven decades to come into place.

In this era of unprecedented change, traditional boundaries are dissolving, and established norms are being upended. The impact of these technologies reaches into every corner of our lives, from the way we communicate and access information to the way we address global challenges, including climate change and healthcare. Just as we currently reflect on past transformative periods, such as the Industrial Revolution or the rise of the Internet, future marketing experts will undoubtedly look back on this era as a pivotal moment in history. The impact of these technological advancements on marketing strategies, consumer behavior, and the overall business landscape will be analyzed and studied for years to come.

In this regard, while many thought that Marketing 3.0 (human-centric marketing) would be the last of the evolution; a new set of values and principles of Generation Y and Z have ushered in marketing with new frameworks to serve customers in the hybrid customer journeys. Thus, emerged Marketing 4.0, which discusses the use of technologies, digital media, and channels. Undoubtedly, technology's role in marketing extends beyond that—thus paving the carpet for Marketing 5.0.[1] Companies are unleashing technologies into their strategies, tactics, and operations, while also leveraging them for the good of humanity. In this phase, the human-centricity of marketing and technological empowerment are integrated, with the core intention of using new-age technologies to emulate the capabilities of human marketers.

At the heart of this transformation lies the exponential growth of data, which has become the lifeblood of innovation and progress. Our digital footprints, from the websites we visit to the products we purchase, are now meticulously analyzed by algorithms to understand our behaviors and preferences. These insights are then leveraged to create personalized experiences, from curated content recommendations to tailored personal solutions. Further, the rise of social media platforms, search engines, and e-commerce has fundamentally changed the way businesses reach and interact with their target audience. Traditional marketing channels, such as print advertisements or television commercials, are being supplemented, and in some cases replaced, by digital advertising methods that offer greater precision, personalization, and measurability.

Furthermore, the way we interact with our environment is evolving. Smart cities are emerging, harnessing the power of the IoT to enhance urban living, from intelligent transportation systems that reduce traffic congestion to energy-efficient buildings that reduce our carbon footprint. Recognizing the impact of new-age technologies on human lives and the environment, many organizations now track the performance of cities in their efforts to use technology to improve human lives.[2]

Moreover, the proliferation of smartphones and other mobile devices has further accelerated this shift towards digital marketing. Consumers now have constant access to the internet and are increasingly relying on their mobile devices to research products, compare prices, and make purchases. As a result, businesses must adapt their marketing strategies to effectively engage with consumers on these platforms, ensuring their brand message is accessible and compelling across various devices and channels.

In addition to digital marketing, emerging technologies such as artificial intelligence (AI), virtual reality (VR), and augmented reality (AR) are poised to have a profound impact on the marketing landscape. AI-powered chatbots and virtual assistants are already being used to enhance customer service and provide personalized recommendations. VR and AR technologies enable immersive brand experiences, allowing consumers to visualize products in their environment before purchasing.

Furthermore, the increasing emphasis on data-driven marketing is transforming the way businesses understand and target their audience. The vast amount of data generated by consumers' online activities, combined with advanced analytics tools, allows marketers to gain valuable insights into consumer preferences, behaviors, and purchasing patterns. This data-driven approach enables businesses to deliver highly targeted and personalized marketing campaigns, resulting in improved customer engagement and higher conversion rates.

Yet, as we stand on the edge of this brave new world, we must also grapple with profound questions about the ethical and societal implications of these advancements. Issues of data privacy, algorithmic bias, and the potential for job displacement loom large, calling for careful consideration and responsible regulation.

Here, new-age technologies (NATs) are expanding known marketing boundaries. It is the leveraging of these innovative, new-age technologies as we understand them when viewed through the lens of marketing that will both inform and redefine our approach to customers for many years to come.[3] Particularly, NATs such as artificial intelligence (AI), generative AI, metaverse, robots, machine learning (ML), drones, Internet of Things (IoT), and blockchain are just the beginnings of an infrastructure whereby marketing is both experiential and instantaneous, a constant loop that marketers will be able to tap into to shift perceptions, provide goods and services and satisfy consumers.

Academic research has defined transformative marketing as, "…the confluence of a firm's marketing activities, concepts, metrics, strategies, and programs that are in response to marketplace changes and future trends to leapfrog customers with superior value offerings over competition in exchange for profits for the firm and benefits to all stakeholders."[4] Considering the confluence of new-age technologies in the marketing function, we define transformative marketing in this context as, *the usage of new-age technologies and human insights to revolutionize how businesses and customers interact to create more personalized and immersive experiences to engage customers with superior value offerings over competition in exchange for profits for the firm and benefits to all stakeholders.*

How did we get here? What is the potential for new-age technologies in marketing? What strategies, capabilities, and resources can we explore to prepare? By examining the attributes of these eight key technologies, their larger impact on marketing management, and taking a closer look into countries currently making advancements, we can better understand how new marketing advancements in a digital world emerge.

A Brief Overview of NATs

As mentioned earlier, this book deals with eight rapidly emerging NATs. To better understand these technologies and what they offer to firms and users, a brief overview of these technologies is warranted. Table 1.1 presents a brief overview of these technologies.

As listed in Table 1.1, each of the eight NATs denotes specific contexts, serving tangible needs for firms and users through various marketing applications. A brief discussion of the NATs that can serve as a good starting point to illustrate their potential for marketing applications is presented here.

Artificial intelligence. AI operates in the domain of continuous learning and automation, acting as the intelligence that drives data-based analytics and enables automated decision-making. AI uses technologies like deep learning and natural language processing, to train machines to accomplish specific tasks by processing large amounts of data and recognizing patterns in the data. AI can analyze complex data to identify behavioral patterns and insights. This ability prepares a firm to implement AI solutions to learn from experience. As a result, AI can aid firms in making transformative decisions, with minimum error, and automatically trigger responses based on prior experiences.

Generative AI. Generative AI refers to a category of artificial intelligence (AI) algorithms that generate new outputs based on the data they have been trained on.[13] This data can take many forms, including text, images, music, and even entire virtual worlds. The goal of generative AI is to create machines that can not only replicate human creativity but, in some instances, also surpass it, producing content that is both novel and high-quality. One of the key techniques used in generative AI is deep learning, a type of machine learning that involves training neural networks on large datasets. These networks can then be used to generate new content by sampling from the learned distribution. Other techniques used in generative AI include reinforcement learning, evolutionary algorithms, and Bayesian networks. Generative AI has the potential to transform the way businesses

Table 1.1 Understanding new-age technologies for transformative marketing

	AI	Generative AI	Machine Learning	Metaverse
Definition	• A system's ability to interpret external data correctly, to learn from such data, and to use those learnings to achieve specific goals and tasks through flexible adaptation.[5]	• A category of artificial intelligence (AI) algorithms that generate new outputs based on the data they have been trained on.[6]	• Computational methods using experience to improve performance or to make accurate predictions.[7]	• A fully immersive, hyper spatiotemporal, and self-sustaining virtual shared space blending the ternary physical, human, and digital worlds.[8]
Fields of origin	• Philosophy • Cognitive Science • Computer Science	• Philosophy • Cognitive Science • Computer Science	• Mathematics • Computational Statistics • Computer Science	• Computer Science • Virtual Reality • Augmented Reality • Sensors
Popular marketing uses	• Digital Marketing • Content Marketing • Interactive Marketing	• Email Marketing • Digital Marketing • Social Media Marketing • Predictive Analytics	• Digital Marketing • Content Marketing	• E-commerce • Test marketing • Content Marketing • Digital Marketing
Types of data used	• Text • Audio • Video	• Text • Audio • Video • Images • Code	• Numerical data • Categorical data • Time series data • Text	Structured, semi-structured, or wholly unstructured
Types of human/technology interaction	• Direct/Visual • Mobile • Web-based	• Direct/Visual • Mobile • Web-based	• Mobile • Web-based	• Mobile • Web-based • AR/VR headsets
Key end user benefits	• Continuous learning • Automation of non-routine tasks • Decision support aid • Personalization	• Personalized results • Solution to complex inquiries • Humanlike conversations	• Automation of learning • Decision-making support	• Entertainment • Interactivity • Easier to try out new offerings
Key user challenges	• Requires a specialist level of understanding • Importance of trust in results	• Inaccurate results • Potential intellectual property violations	• Understanding potential benefits • Managing user expectations of the results	• Privacy/Data concerns • Early stages of technological know-how • Relatively higher cost of usage

(continued)

Table 1.1 (continued)

	AI	Generative AI	Machine Learning	Metaverse
Key firm benefits	• Customer strategy development • Omnichannel marketing • Marketing intelligence capabilities	• Saving time and resources • Delivering superior customer experience • Enhancing user engagement • Create personalized offerings	• Pattern recognition • Data management • Integration with traditional job roles	• Virtual work environment and collaboration • Expanded learning spaces • E-commerce opportunities • Social media proficiency
Key firm challenges	• Employee training • Compliance with government regulations • Identifying and using relevant knowledge to drive the development of AI solutions	• Bias and accuracy issues • Ethical and legal uncertainties • Integration with existing infrastructure	• Security concerns, especially with sensitive data • Infrastructure for testing, implementing, and managing of large data • Financial and operational planning regarding talent management, data management, and solutions development • Managing firm expectations • User education efforts	• Higher level of initial investment to set up the infrastructure • Limited clarity on the regulatory and compliance framework • Potential misuse of data
Key reasons for the breadth/depth of firm adoption	• Growing acceptance among users and marketers • Faster turnaround of data-driven decision-making • Elimination of human errors	• Quick response time to customers • Real-time insights • Scalable personalized marketing • Access to high-quality data	• Rapidly evolving • Early focus remains on improving customer service, with more promising areas of use in the future • Emphasis on efficient problem-solving	• Easy integration with other NATs • Ability to create digital twins • Enhance operational performance

	AI	Generative AI	Machine Learning	Metaverse
Nature of privacy concerns/ origin of concerns	• Collection and retention of personal data • Understanding the implications of using users' digital footprint to develop solutions • Balancing inference generation and maintaining anonymity • Dealing with personally identifiable information and quasi-identifiers	• Exposing private or proprietary information to the public • Ambiguities over the ownership of the generated content • Potential employee misuse	• Data-driven spear-phishing • Data poisoning	• Potential misuse of data, especially that of minors • High degree of intrusion into private lives • Misapplication and applicability of current privacy regulations (e.g., GDPR) • Issues concerning data rights and ownership

(continued)

Table 1.1 (continued)

	IoT	Robots	Drones	Blockchain
Definition	• A system of uniquely identifiable objects (things) and virtual addressability that would create an Internet-like structure for remote locating, sensing, operating, and/or actuating of entities.[9]	• Mechanical machines or intangible computer programs that perform rule-based work and tend to be configurable with basic features like authentication, security, auditing, logging, and exception handling.[10]	• Any aerial vehicle that does not rely on an onboard human operator for flight, either autonomously or remotely operated.[11]	• A distributed database solution that maintains a continuously growing list of data records that are confirmed by the nodes participating in it.[12]
Fields of origin	• Computer Science	• Philosophy • Industrial Engineering • Mechanics • Computer Science	• Mathematics • Physics • Engineering • Military defense • Computer Science	• Computer Science
Popular marketing uses	• Digital Marketing • Content Marketing • Interactive Marketing	• Interactive Marketing • Content Marketing • Digital (when combined with AI)	• Direct Marketing • Digital Marketing • Visual Marketing • Creative Marketing • Content Marketing	• Digital Marketing • Interactive marketing • Content marketing
Types of data used	• Combination of apps, wearables, sensors, devices, web, media, and location	• Programming languages • Mechanics	• Sensor data (Speed/Distance, Infrared/ Thermal) • Images • Chemical	• Inter-node communications • Text • Audio/video • Numerical
Types of human/technology interaction	• Mobile • Web-based	• Direct/Visual: person-robot	• Direct/Visual: person-drone	• Mobile • Web-based
Key end user benefits	• Enhanced functionality • Device integration • Real-time connectivity	• Task execution • Efficiency • Quicker and consistent responses	• Last mile solutions • Connectivity • Monitoring • Security	• Expedited processing of actions • Secure transfer of data and value
Key user challenges	• Establishing trust • Privacy/ Data concerns • Security of multiple devices • Adjusting to an environment of integrated devices	• Human-robot interaction/ communication can be tricky at times • Less accountability for problems that arise • Ethical issues	• Privacy • Legalities • Navigating no-fly zones • Accounting for physical damages to assets	• Unstandardized implementation • Potential liability and legal issues, and their recourse

	IoT	Robots	Drones	Blockchain
Key firm benefits	• Better sensing, tracking, and monitoring capabilities • Security of assets • Single point of data collection from integrating multiple assets • Enables easier communication between multiple assets	• Superior efficiency • Precision • Enhanced work capacity • Faster adaptability to procedural changes • Tolerance of severe and hazardous environments	• Content creation • Data collection and integration • Delivery solutions • Use in media uses for marketing campaigns	• Transparency in business operations • Faster processing of business operations • Better tracking of business processes
Key firm challenges	• Integration of multiple business functions responsible for developing, implementing, and maintaining IoT solutions • Data protection • Efforts towards determining security vulnerabilities within devices or networks • Compliance with IoT regulations	• Understanding mobility and dexterity needs • Integration with the development agenda of solutions • Clarity on when and where to use robots • Compliance with government regulations	• Operational concerns • Privacy management • Compliance with regulatory framework • Managing damages while in operation	• Estimating and managing the volume and speed of transaction traffic to develop and implement Blockchain solutions • Understanding liability and legal issues
Key reasons for the breadth/depth of firm adoption	• Rapidly gaining traction among users and firms, owing to a wide range of applications • Increased collaborations between technology companies enable the development of many IoT applications	• Still in the exploratory stages of development • Wide range of business and customer-facing applications • Future potential remains varied	• A new and promising way to reach consumers • Provides ample scope for marketing and promotion activities • Useful in data collection and targeting activities, especially when paired with IoT, virtual reality, augmented reality, and cloud services	• Formative stages of development • Early adopting firms are exploring uses and boundaries regarding potential uses and implementation
Nature of privacy concerns/origin of concerns	• Data or Network based hacking concerns	• Privacy concerns center around movement and surveillance	• Safety & surveillance concerns • Detecting and recording without explicit permission. • Staying informed of the distinction and classification of public and private spaces	• Data (private vs. public) • Jurisdiction concerns, HIPPA concerns, Federal and State Law concerns, GDPR • Threats from new-age hackers and hacking techniques

Source Adapted and extended from Kumar, V. (2021). *Intelligent marketing: Employing new age technologies*. Sage Publications approach marketing and customer service. From product design to personalization, and nurturing customer relationships to delivering superior customer experiences, this technology has the potential to transform the way businesses operate and interact with their customers.

Machine Learning. Machine learning refers to computational methods that use experience to improve performance or to make accurate predictions.[14] By considering past information (i.e., referred to as experience), machines gain the ability to learn while they perform, thereby showing performance improvement. Therefore, the quality of learning is dependent on the volume and quality of data; and the key outcome is predictions about key variables of interest. Simply put, ML is a subset of AI that trains a machine to learn. Thus, through ML, firms can develop algorithms that enable them to predict future behaviors and trends based on prior data and patterns in behaviors.

Metaverse. Metaverse refers to a fully immersive, hyper spatiotemporal, and self-sustaining virtual shared space blending the ternary physical, human, and digital worlds.[15] It can also be visualized as a virtual reality space where users can interact with a computer-generated environment and other users in real-time. It is a collective virtual shared space that encompasses the physical world and various virtual worlds, allowing users to engage in a wide range of activities, such as socializing, gaming, and conducting business. Metaverse is characterized by its immersive nature and interconnectedness. In this regard, the metaverse has the potential to revolutionize the way we work, learn, and entertain ourselves. In the business world, the metaverse holds important implications for productivity, content creation, and delivering experiences. Overall, the metaverse has the potential to reshape various aspects of our lives and open new possibilities for human interaction and creativity.

Internet of Things. The International Telecommunication Union (ITU) defines IoT as "a global infrastructure for the information society, enabling advanced services by interconnecting (physical and virtual) things based on existing and evolving interoperable information and communication technologies."[16] IoT is designed on a network of sensors that capture information about each device and are individually identifiable. IoT devices can sense, compute, and communicate wirelessly over short distances, and can interconnect to form a wireless sensor network. By interconnecting *things*, harvesting information from the environment, and interacting with the physical world through the Internet, IoT can provide services for information transfer, analytics, applications, and communications.[17] IoT devices can sense, compute, and communicate wirelessly over short distances, and can interconnect to form a wireless sensor network.

Robots. Robots are mechanical machines, systems, or programs that "perform rule-based work, and tend to be configurable with basic features like authentication, security, auditing, logging, and exception handling".[18] Robots made their first appearance in the industrial space in the 1970s by assisting in production activities. Recently, service robots (i.e., robots that are used for service applications) aid firms in performing a wide array of customer-oriented tasks. Intelligent robots, a specialized class of service robots (e.g., robotic waiters, robotic home cleaners), refer to "technology that can perform physical tasks, operate autonomously without needing instruction, and are directed by computers without help from people."[19] With intelligent robots, efficiency can be achieved using some human participation, or achieved totally by machines.

Drones. A drone refers to any aerial vehicle that does not rely on an onboard human operator for flight, either autonomously or remotely operated.[20] Drones and drone technology have significantly benefitted from the open-source developer market. The drone manufacturers have harnessed the passion and expertise of the open-source community by bringing together geographically distributed user communities. Such an initiative continues to pay rich dividends by developing solutions that serve specific use cases. In this regard, drones are used in a wide range of commercial applications such as surveillance, inspection, logistics, film production, and rescue efforts, among others.

Blockchain. Blockchain is a distributed database that allows for the permanent, immutable, and transparent recording of data and transactions.[21] The decentralized storage of records ensures that no single point of weakness exists, thereby lowering the likelihood of hacking and data breaches.[22] By specifying the conditions under which a transaction may be executed, a blockchain allows two or more parties to complete their transactions efficiently and more quickly, with greater security of data and assets.

Looking Beyond the Digital Frontier of NATs

Digitalization in marketing has revolutionized the way businesses interact with their customers. Social media marketing has enabled businesses to reach a wider audience and engage with them in real time. E-commerce has made it easier for customers to purchase products and services from the comfort of their homes. These advancements have made marketing more efficient, cost-effective, and personalized. One of the key benefits of digitalization in marketing is the ability to track customer behavior and preferences. With the help of analytics tools, businesses can gather data on customer interactions with their brand, including website visits, social media engagement, and purchase history. This data can be used to create targeted marketing campaigns that are tailored to the specific needs and interests of each customer.

Another benefit of digitalization in marketing is the ability to automate certain tasks. For example, businesses can use chatbots to provide customer support and answer frequently asked questions. This not only saves time and resources but also improves the customer experience by providing instant responses. Digitalization in marketing also allows businesses to create more engaging and interactive content. For example, augmented reality and virtual reality technologies can be used to create immersive experiences that allow customers to interact with products in a virtual environment. This can help businesses to showcase their products more engagingly and memorably.

The NATs individually and collectively are ushering in a business scenario that is markedly different from conventional practices.[23] Specifically, marketing activities and business tasks have seen the incorporation of NATs as individual implementations. More recently, firms are beginning to see the merits of an integrated implementation of NATs wherein multiple technologies are used in a specific area of operation. Further, an added focus on data-driven business and marketing strategies has allowed firms to harness the power of NATs in their firm-wide operations, particularly in marketing. The potential of NATs in integrating multiple sources of data and mining this data using sophisticated techniques geared towards the generation of insights has encouraged firms to view NATs in a new way.

Today, new-age technology is making its presence known in the marketing environment, right up to our doorsteps. Amazon, for instance, uses a confluence of AI, robots, ML, drones, IoT, and blockchain to offer, deliver, and develop solutions that are already changing the business landscape. A far cry from the humble homepage set up in 1995, Amazon has truly embraced an ever-evolving digital ecosystem. AI engages the moment you interact with the Amazon app, website, or Alexa-enabled device, robots zing through warehouses to identify and retrieve products, ML fuels a flurry of recommendations based on individuals' shopping and browsing behaviors, and drones stand ready to deliver PrimeAir packages (pending regulatory support). Amazon Web Services (AWS) offers AWS IoT, which presents a wide range of solutions to integrate devices and data collection for industrial, consumer, and commercial applications. Advances are being made into blockchain with Amazon Managed Blockchain providing a means to create and manage a scalable blockchain network using open-source frameworks, and the added ability to perform necessary analyses. This is but one example to note, how each technology in its own right—AI, robots, ML, drones, IoT, and blockchain—will continue to foster firm capabilities to address the ever-growing information pool.

The NATs form the foundation on which companies design their digitalization journey. For instance, AI enables marketers to forecast the outcomes of marketing campaigns, analyze past data to identify patterns and suggest optimized designs for future campaigns. This empowers marketers to be aware of potential market failures and navigate through them. Similarly, IoT empowers businesses to incorporate contextual touchpoints into physical locations, creating a seamless omnichannel experience. It also allows marketers to offer personalized experiences to their customers. Augmented and virtual realities assist companies in delivering captivating products with minimal human intervention.

Therefore, it is no wonder that marketers throw around these new technology buzzwords as they flock to capitalize on each of the above-mentioned NATs, adapting to the observable impacts taking place currently in the marketing arena and which will continue, no doubt, for decades to come. Overall, technology will drive marketing to be data-driven, predictive, contextual, augmented, and agile. The Marketing 5.0 concept revolves around three interconnected applications—predictive marketing, contextual marketing, and augmented marketing. These applications are built upon two organizational disciplines—data-driven marketing and agile marketing. Chapter 2 will discuss how these marketing applications contribute to enhancing human lives.

Organization of the Book

This book will adopt a humanistic applications perspective, based on the Marketing 5.0 concept, with specific reference to the marketing discipline regarding NATs. Particularly, the following eight NATs are covered in this book—AI, Generative AI, ML, Metaverse, IoT, Robotics, Drones, and Blockchain—with eight chapters devoted to each of the eight NATs. The eight NAT chapters are bookended by introductory and concluding chapters. All eight chapters on the NATs follow a similar four-part narrative structure that focuses on key areas of these technologies. The choice of keeping a similar narrative structure is in recognition of the interconnectivity and relatedness of these technologies, and how they often work in tandem in many organizations for the betterment of human lives.

The introduction chapter (this chapter) opens with a discussion about the Marketing 5.0 concept and how it can be viewed from the NATs perspective. Here, the eight NATs covered in this book are introduced. Further, this chapter sets up the case to look beyond the NATs as just technologies and view them as being critical in the digitization process of companies and in enriching human lives.

In Chapter 2, the case is made for how NATs can be used by companies in not only enhancing customer journeys but also improving human lives by making meaningful connections. This is done through the Marketing 5.0 concept that integrates several key marketing concepts relating to technology and humans. Subsequently, Chapters 3–10 are dedicated to each of the NATs.

Each NAT chapter (Chapters 3–10) begins with a discussion on the foundations of these technologies—i.e., origin(s), definition, and components. While the discussion of the foundations can be technical, it is kept to a minimum so that readers can follow the marketing discipline-specific discussion that subsequently follows.

In the second part of the NAT chapters, the components of Marketing 5.0 (i.e., data-driven marketing, predictive marketing, contextual marketing, augmented marketing, and agile marketing) are discussed concerning the NAT covered in that chapter. This approach would allow readers to see how each of the NATs works towards enhancing value across the customer journey while devoting attention to creating a better living for humanity.

In the third part of the chapters, the five components of Marketing 5.0 are dwelled upon in detail. Here, the five components are envisaged from a customer experience and customer engagement perspective as follows: (a) understanding customer needs to deploy the NAT, (b) revisiting firm capabilities to integrate the NAT, (c) designing the marketing mix strategies with the NAT, (d) driving customer engagement through the NAT, and (e) designing digital strategies with the NAT. In doing so, the discussion is firmly centered around how the resources, capabilities, and strategies that the NATs present and sustain can be used to improve human living. By drawing upon marketplace examples, trends, and business practices, this section of the chapters presents the marketing applications of NATs as it currently stands.

In the final part of the chapters, the future of these technologies is discussed, along with early indications of how these technologies are likely to progress. It presents a range of upcoming developments that can signify future business practices and marketing uses of the NATs.

Subsequently, the concluding chapter (Chapter 11) presents largely organizational issues driving and challenging the implementation and development of NATs, and the Marketing 5.0 concept. Further, a discussion on the next developments in the world of NATs is presented and discussed.

Key Terms and Related Conceptualizations

Artificial intelligence	A new-age technology that uses deep learning and natural language processing to train machines to accomplish specific tasks by processing large amounts of data and recognizing patterns in the data.
Blockchain	A distributed database that allows for the permanent, immutable, and transparent recording of data and transactions.
Drones	Aerial vehicles that do not rely on an onboard human operator for flight, either autonomously or remotely operated.
Generative artificial intelligence	A category of artificial intelligence (AI) algorithms that generate new outputs based on the data they have been trained on.
Internet of Things	A global infrastructure for the information society, enabling advanced services by interconnecting (physical and virtual) things based on existing and evolving interoperable information and communication technologies.
Machine learning	A subset of AI that trains a machine to learn.
Metaverse	A collective virtual shared space that encompasses the physical world and various virtual worlds and allows users to engage in a wide range of activities.
Robots	Mechanical machines, systems, or programs that perform rule-based work, and tend to be configurable with basic features like authentication, security, auditing, logging, and exception handling.
Transformative marketing	The usage of new-age technologies and human insights to revolutionize how businesses and customers interact to create more personalized and immersive experiences to engage customers with superior value offerings over competition in exchange for profits for the firm and benefits to all stakeholders

Notes and References

1. Kotler, P., H. Kartajaya, & . Setiawan (2021). *Marketing 5.0: Technology for humanity*. John Wiley & Sons.
2. The Smart City Index created by IMD in 2019 adopts a balanced focus on the economic and technological aspects of global smart cities on the one hand, and the "humane dimensions" of the global smart cities (quality of life, environment, inclusiveness) on the other. According to the 2023 Smart City Index, the top five global smart cities are Zurich, Oslo, Canberra, Copenhagen, and Lausanne, respectively. [*Source*: "IMD Smart City Index 2023," *IMD*, April, accessed from https://www.imd.org/wp-content/uploads/2023/04/smartcityindex-2023-v7.pdf.]

3. Kumar, V. (2021). *Intelligent marketing: Employing new age technologies.* Sage Publications.
4. Kumar, V. (2018). "Transformative marketing: The next 20 years," *Journal of Marketing, 82*(4), 1–12.
5. Kaplan, A., & M. Haenlein (2019), "Siri, Siri, in my hand: Who's the fairest in the land? On the interpretations, illustrations, and implications of artificial intelligence," *Business Horizons, 62*(1), 15–25.
6. Routley, N. (2023), "What is generative AI? An AI explains," *World Economic Forum*, February 6, accessed from https://www.weforum.org/agenda/2023/02/generative-ai-explain-algorithms-work/.
7. Mohri, M., A. Rostamizadeh, & A. Talwalkar (2018). *Foundations of machine learning.* Cambridge, MA: MIT Press.
8. Wang, H., H. Ning, Y. Lin, W. Wang, S. Dhelim, F. Farha, J. Ding, & M. Daneshmand (2023), "A survey on the metaverse: The state-of-the-art, technologies, applications, and challenges," *IEEE Internet of Things Journal, 10*(16), 14671–14688. https://doi.org/10.1109/JIOT.2023.3278329.
9. Ng, I. C. L., & Y. L. W. Susan (2017), "The Internet-of-Things: Review and research directions," *International Journal of Research in Marketing, 34*(1), 3–21.
10. Wilson, H. J. (2015), "What is a robot, anyway?" *Harvard Business Review*, April 15, available at https://hbr.org/2015/04/what-is-a-robot-anyway.
11. Newcome, L. R. (2004), *Unmanned aviation: A brief history of unmanned aerial vehicles.* American Institute of Aeronautics and Astronautics.
12. Yli-Huumo, J., D. Ko, S. Choi, S. Park, & K. Smolander (2016), "Where is current research on blockchain technology?—A systematic review," *PloS One, 11*(10), e0163477.
13. Routley, N. (2023), "What is generative AI? An AI explains," World Economic Forum, February 6, accessed from https://www.weforum.org/agenda/2023/02/generative-ai-explain-algorithms-work/.
14. Mohri, M., A. Rostamizadeh, & A. Talwalkar (2018). *Foundations of machine learning.* Cambridge, MA: MIT Press.
15. Wang, H., H. Ning, Y. Lin, W. Wang, S. Dhelim, F. Farha, J. Ding, & M. Daneshmand (2023), "A survey on the metaverse: The state-of-the-art, technologies, applications, and challenges," *IEEE Internet of Things Journal, 10*(16), 14671–14688. https://doi.org/10.1109/JIOT.2023.3278329.

16. ITU (2012), "Overview of the Internet of things," *International Telecommunication Union*, June, accessed from http://handle.itu.int/11.1002/1000/11559.
17. Gubbi, J., R. Buyya, S. Marusic, & M. Palaniswami (2013), "Internet of Things (IoT): A vision, architectural elements, and future directions," *Future Generation Computer Systems, 29*(7), 1645–1660.
18. Wilson, H. J. (2015), "What Is a Robot, Anyway?" *Harvard Business Review*, April 15, available at https://hbr.org/2015/04/what-is-a-robot-anyway.
19. Colby, C. L., S. Mithas, & A. Parasuraman (2016) "Service robots: How ready are consumers to adopt and what drives acceptance," The 2016 Frontiers in Service Conference. Norway: Bergen.
20. Newcome, L. R. (2004), *Unmanned aviation: A brief history of unmanned aerial vehicles*. American Institute of Aeronautics and Astronautics.
21. McKinsey (2022). What is blockchain? *McKinsey*, December 5, accessed from https://www.mckinsey.com/featured-insights/mckinsey-explainers/what-is-blockchain#.
22. While new blocks of information can be appended to the existing blockchain ledger, previous data cannot be overwritten or erased, thereby creating a permanent, verifiable, and traceable trail of transactions (Giordani 2018).
23. Kumar, V. (2021). *Intelligent marketing: Employing new age technologies*. Sage Publications.

2

Transformative Marketing: A Marketing 5.0 Perspective

Introduction

Transformative marketing aims to leverage the potential of cutting-edge NATs to revolutionize the way businesses connect with their target audience. By harnessing the capabilities of new-age technologies, companies can create innovative and impactful marketing campaigns that drive significant results. These technologies encompass a wide range of tools and platforms, including AI, drones, metaverse, robotics, and other NATs introduced in Chapter 1. The term "transformative" suggests that these technologies have the potential to significantly change the way marketing is conducted. These technologies can revolutionize how businesses interact with their customers, allowing for more personalized and immersive experiences.

One of the key aspects of transformative marketing is its ability to adapt and evolve with the ever-changing digital landscape as it combines new-age technologies and human insights. With the rapid advancements in technology, businesses need to stay ahead of the curve to remain competitive. By embracing NATs, companies can stay relevant and effectively engage with their customers in a dynamic and personalized manner. For instance, AI can be used to analyze vast amounts of customer data, enabling businesses to gain valuable insights into consumer behavior and preferences. This information can then be utilized to create targeted marketing campaigns that resonate with the target audience on a deeper level.

Moreover, transformative marketing using NATs enables businesses to enhance customer experiences and build stronger brand loyalty. Virtual reality and augmented reality, for example, can be utilized to create immersive and interactive experiences for customers. This can range from virtual showrooms that allow customers to explore products in a lifelike environment to augmented reality apps that enable users to visualize how a product would look in their own space. By providing such engaging experiences, businesses can leave a lasting impression on customers and foster a sense of loyalty and trust. Going by industry developments, transformative marketing appears to be a game-changer for businesses looking to stay ahead in the digital era.

Meaningful Connections Using Human Insights

In their quest for market expansion, companies are focusing on development (of themselves, and society), not just on growth. When a society moves toward greater literacy and better incomes, the untapped segments become new sources of growth. Further, brands are recognizing the need to develop and nurture the markets they are competing in. With the advancements due to the internet and technology, companies are under constant scrutiny and their ethical aspects are being monitored. Adopting an inclusive and sustainable marketing approach would help mitigate the problem. Utilizing technologies to invest back into society accelerates progress and opens opportunities for everyone. This has opened a whole new realm of possibilities for building relationships and fostering connections with people who share similar interests or goals. Now, new-age technologies offer unique opportunities to foster meaningful human connections.[1] While it may seem paradoxical that technology, often accused of isolating people, can bring them closer together, the potential lies in how these tools are harnessed.

In this regard, Marketing 5.0 has been presented as a concept that can foster togetherness and connections for humanity. Here, Marketing 5.0 is defined as "...the application of human-mimicking technologies to create, communicate, deliver, and enhance value across the customer journey" (p. 6).[2] It has the potential to assist marketers in effectively tackling contemporary obstacles, including the generation gap, prosperity polarization, and the digital divide. Through its implementation, marketers can successfully generate, convey, distribute, and augment value throughout the customer journey, all while maintaining a harmonious equilibrium between human intellect and computer intelligence. The deployment of Marketing 5.0 calls for the use of NATs (such as AI, generative AI, metaverse, robots, ML, drones, IoT, and blockchain) that aim to emulate the capabilities of human marketers. The Marketing 5.0 concept revolves around three interconnected applications, namely predictive marketing, contextual marketing, and augmented marketing. These applications are further grounded in two fundamental organizational disciplines, namely data-driven marketing, and agile marketing (p. 12).³ Figure 2.1 illustrates the Marketing 5.0 concept.

Accordingly, the two disciplines in the Marketing 5.0 concept can be understood as follows. First, data-driven marketing involves the systematic gathering and examination of extensive data obtained from both internal and external sources. Additionally, it entails the establishment of a comprehensive data ecosystem aimed at facilitating and enhancing marketing decision-making processes. Second, agile marketing entails the utilization of decentralized, cross-functional teams to swiftly conceptualize, design, develop, and validate products and marketing campaigns. These two disciplines form the foundation for the implementation of the Marketing 5.0 concept.

The three disciplines in the Marketing 5.0 concept are explained as follows. First, predictive marketing refers to the systematic approach of constructing

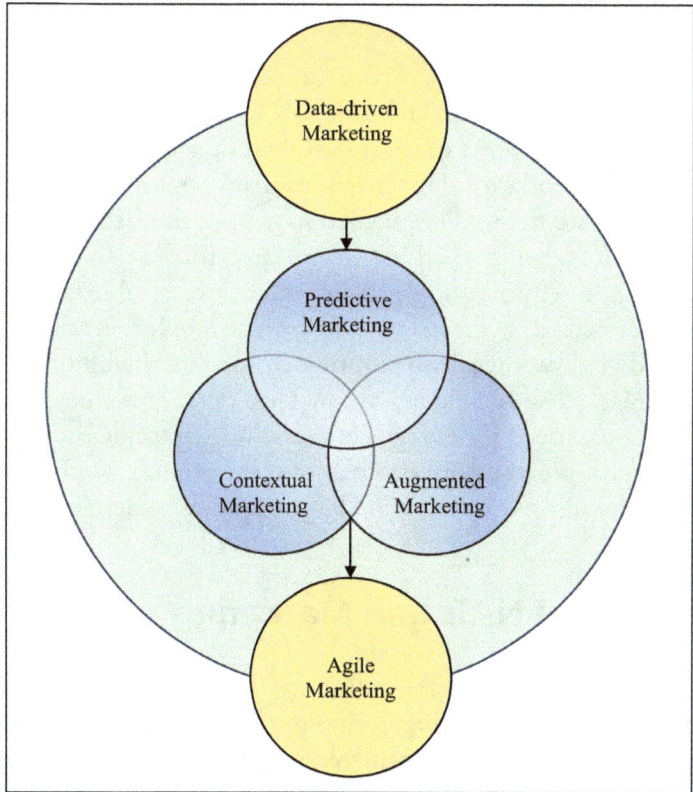

Fig. 2.1 The Marketing 5.0 concept
(*Source* Kotler, P., Kartajaya, H., & Setiawan, I. (2021). *Marketing 5.0: Technology for humanity*. John Wiley & Sons)

and employing predictive analytics, occasionally incorporating ML techniques, to anticipate the outcomes of marketing endeavors before their commencement. Second, contextual marketing refers to the process of recognizing and characterizing customers and delivering tailored experiences using sensors and digital interfaces in the physical environment. Finally, augmented marketing refers to the utilization of digital technology to enhance the efficiency of customer-facing marketers through the integration of humanlike technologies, including chatbots and virtual assistants.

The adoption of Marketing 5.0 necessitates a data-driven approach, which can be achieved through the establishment of a comprehensive data ecosystem. This ecosystem enables marketers to engage in predictive marketing, deliver personalized marketing messages, and create seamless interfaces with customers using augmented marketing. However, to fully leverage these execution elements, companies must also possess corporate agility, allowing them to respond promptly to market changes. By embracing these principles, companies can effectively implement Marketing 5.0 and maximize their marketing efforts.

The NATs offer tremendous opportunities for society and bring value through Marketing 5.0. It allows businesses to build platforms and ecosystems that are capable of processing large-scale transactions without geographical and industry boundaries. This helps companies meet customers' growing expectations, increase their willingness to pay, and drive better value creation. For instance, AI is being used in healthcare, thanks to its potential in accelerating drug discovery and precision medicine. Health tracking devices (wearables), connected with IoT are being used in preventive healthcare. Additionally, digitalization is contributing to the sustainability initiatives of global companies. Electric vehicles are picking up momentum, solar energy trading is being practiced for energy conservation. To tackle the digital divide and the issues with polarization, companies need to apply NATs in all aspects of our lives—extending it to serve the larger good of society.

Convergence of NATs and Marketing

The age of technological transformation has begun. However, this was not always the case. Despite technology's vital role in driving marketing objectives and firm outcomes, it was not considered a key component of the marketing practice.[4] Recent developments in marketing practices have embraced technology and firmly placed it at the center of business operations. Using technology, firms are now able to interact with users through various touch points and often at several points in a day. Further, technology also enables firms to facilitate and monitor interactions among users. Such technology-focused actions allow firms to collect real-time data about users and their needs. Subsequently, this knowledge can be used in developing personalized offerings and implementing customer-centric marketing strategies that can result in the creation of customer engagement with firms.

The origins of the NATs are entwined with long-established disciplines (e.g., philosophy, mathematics, engineering, etc.) and of course with more recent disciplines such as computer science. Understanding the origins and evolution of NATs is therefore important given their ever-increasing presence in our lives and, in turn, the rules of marketing. IoT and blockchain, by far the youngest of the eight technologies, are considered to have grown because of knowledge gleaned from computer science. Considering each technological advancement respective to its historical context with society is important to modern marketers as they represent platforms for customer engagement. Knowledge of what technology to employ, how to employ it, and when and why it should be employed across countries and cultures is critical. Also, it stands to reason that once these platforms are effectively harnessed, the resultant data generated will provide a continuous stream of feedback to marketers with potential implications for developing solutions and firm growth strategies. In other words, a clear understanding of how the eight NATs will help firms develop strategies, build capabilities, and deploy resources is of utmost need.

Understanding Resources, Capabilities, and Strategies of NATs

The convergence of NATs and the marketing discipline can best be understood via resources, capabilities, and strategies.[5] Resources[6] refer to something an organization can draw on to accomplish its goals and are conceptualized as a firm's physical, human, and organizational capital that enable a firm to conceive and implement strategies that improve its efficiency and effectiveness.[7] Originally conceptualized as part of the resource-based view (RBV) of the firm, resources are viewed as integral to the sustained competitive advantage (SCA) of the firm.[8] Research has provided the VRIO framework (Value, Rarity, Imitability, and Organization) to understand the relationship between a resource and sustainable competitive advantage. It has been identified that SCA only results when the resources are simultaneously valuable, rare, imperfectly imitable, and exploitable by the firm's organization.[9]

Capabilities are subsets of the firm's resources and refer to "an organizationally embedded non-transferable firm-specific resource whose purpose is to improve the productivity of the other resources possessed by the firm" (p. 389).[10,11] Capabilities can be static or dynamic. While static capabilities denote "...well-honed and difficult-to-copy routines for carrying out established processes" (p. 185)[12]; dynamic capabilities refer to "the capacity of an organization to purposefully create, extend, or modify the resource base" (p. 4).[13] In essence, unlike static capabilities, dynamic capabilities enable the firm to stay informed of marketplace developments and prepare the firm to constantly update its approach of using resources to deliver value to all its stakeholders.

Research has also identified advancements to the *capabilities* theory in terms of the firm perspective. Specifically, the dynamic capabilities approach adopts an inside-out view wherein the firm looks at the outside market (i.e., external to the firm) and undertakes all necessary steps to prepare and perform its stated objectives. Adaptive capabilities, in contrast, recognize the need for an outside-in orientation (i.e., a perspective that begins with the market and flows inward to the firm), and prepare the management team to step outside the firm to understand customer needs (for strategy development).[14]

Strategy refers to "...a firm's theory of how it can gain superior performance in the markets within which it operates" (p. 140).[15] Further, strategy is also seen as a plan, ploy, pattern, position, and perspective adopted by firms in managing their business relationships[16] that ultimately deliver value to customers.[17] Overall, strategy binds firms through collective perception and action, rather than discrete steps aimed at solving specific issues. While from a definition standpoint strategies, capabilities, and resources refer to discrete firm-related concepts, the current NAT-driven environment has ushered in a medium to integrate various technologies and how firms utilize them.

Any successful implementation of a NAT will need firms to unify resources, capabilities, and strategies. Netflix is a faithful illustration of this process in action in a firm using NATs. Netflix's corporate strategy is centered around people (i.e., employees, customers, etc.). Despite not having a stated mission statement, we can find information on their firm strategy from how they speak of their current corporate culture. Specifically, their core philosophy is "people over process" and focuses on a list of values such as judgment, communication, curiosity, passion, selflessness, innovation, inclusion, integrity, and impact.[18] Netflix's capabilities include a well-built technology infrastructure with strong data management and the ability to source talent and content effectively.

We can observe Netflix's capabilities in action from a consumer standpoint when users log into the Netflix app via internet-enabled devices (computers, TVs, tablets), or using cellular data via mobile phones. Once logged in they make selections based on their interests. The proprietary machine learning algorithms get to work and soon curate the shows and previews specifically for the user. A wealth of information is generated over time capturing not only preferences but behaviors also. What they watch, when they watch, how often they watch, and where and how they watch, are only some of the information that is captured, in addition to a host of other user-specific details. The information generated ties into Netflix's firm resources and to those tangible and intangible benefits. As a result, Netflix can procure more titles their consumers are genuinely interested in saving both time and money, and create targeted marketing campaigns to gain new users given what they learn from current consumers. Understanding the implications of firm strategies, resources, and capabilities is an integral part of utilizing new technologies for marketing management potential. It certainly is a win-win for Netflix and its subscribers.

Key Terms and Related Conceptualizations

Agile marketing	The utilization of decentralized, cross-functional teams to swiftly conceptualize, design, develop, and validate products and marketing campaigns
Augmented marketing	The utilization of digital technology to enhance the efficiency of customer-facing marketers through the integration of humanlike technologies, including chatbots and virtual assistants
Capabilities	Subsets of the firm's resources that belong to an organizationally embedded non-transferable firm-specific resource whose purpose is to improve the productivity of the other resources possessed by the firm.
Contextual marketing	The process of recognizing and characterizing customers and delivering tailored experiences using sensors and digital interfaces in the physical environment
Data-driven marketing	The systematic gathering and examination of extensive data obtained from both internal and external sources
Dynamic capabilities	The capacity of an organization to purposefully create, extend, or modify the resource base
Marketing 5.0	The application of human-mimicking technologies to create, communicate, deliver, and enhance value across the customer journey
Predictive marketing	The systematic approach of constructing and employing predictive analytics, occasionally incorporating ML techniques, to anticipate the outcomes of marketing endeavors before their commencement.

(continued)

	(continued)
Resources	Something an organization can draw on to accomplish its goals and is conceptualized as a firm's physical, human, and organizational capital that enables a firm to conceive and implement strategies that improve its efficiency and effectiveness
Static capabilities	Well-honed and difficult-to-copy routines for carrying out established processes
Strategy	A firm's theory of how it can gain superior performance in the markets within which it operates

Notes and References

1. Barney, J. (1991), "Firm resources and sustained competitive advantage," *Journal of Management, 17*(1), 99–120.
2. Kotler, P., H. Kartajaya, & I. Setiawan (2021). *Marketing 5.0: Technology for humanity*. John Wiley & Sons (p. 6).
3. Kotler, P., H. Kartajaya, & I. Setiawan (2021). *Marketing 5.0: Technology for humanity*. John Wiley & Sons (p. 12).
4. Brady, M., M. Saren, & N. Tzokas (2002), "Integrating information technology into marketing practice–the IT reality of contemporary marketing practice," *Journal of Marketing Management, 18*(5–6), 555–577.
5. Kumar, V. (2021). *Intelligent marketing: Employing new age technologies.* Sage Publications.
6. Barney and Arikan (2001). Define resources as the tangible and intangible assets firms use to conceive of and implement their strategies (p. 138).
7. Barney, J. (1991), "Firm resources and sustained competitive advantage," *Journal of Management, 17*(1), 99–120; Wernerfelt, B. (1984), "A resource-based view of the firm," *Strategic Management Journal, 5*(2), 171–180.
8. The RBV proposes that if a firm possesses valuable resources that are not normally possessed by other firms, and if other firms find it too expensive or challenging to imitate the resources, the firm owning the resources can create a sustainable competitive advantage (Barney and Hesterly 2012).
9. Barney, J. & W. Hesterly (2012). *Strategic management and competitive advantage: Concepts and cases* (4th ed.). New Jersey: Pearson.
10. Makadok, R. (2001), "Toward a synthesis of the resource-based and dynamic-capability views of rent creation," *Strategic Management Journal, 22*(5), 387–401 (p. 389).

11. From a knowledge standpoint, capabilities are conceptualized by Day, G. S. (1994), "The capabilities of market-driven organizations," *Journal of Marketing*, *58*(4), 37–52, as complex bundles of skills and accumulated knowledge, exercised through organizational processes that enable firms to coordinate activities and make use of their assets (p. 38).
12. Day, G. S. (2011), "Closing the marketing capabilities gap," *Journal of Marketing*, *75*(4), 183–195.
13. Helfat, C. E., Finkelstein, S., Mitchell, W., Peteraf, M., Singh, H., Teece, D., & Winter, S. G. (2007). *Dynamic capabilities: Understanding strategic change in organizations*. Blackwell (p. 4).
14. Day, G. S. (2011), "Closing the marketing capabilities gap," *Journal of Marketing*, *75*(4), 183–195 (p. 185).
15. Barney, J. & A. M. Arikan (2001). The resource-based view: Origins and implications. *The Blackwell handbook of strategic management*, 124–188 (p. 140).
16. Mintzberg, H. (1987), "The strategy concept I: Five Ps for strategy," *California Management Review*, *30*(1), 11–24.
17. Varadarajan, R. (2010), "Strategic marketing and marketing strategy: Domain, definition, fundamental issues and foundational premises," *Journal of the Academy of Marketing Science*, *38*(2), 119–140.
18. Netflix (2020), "Netflix Culture," *Netflix.com*, accessed from https://jobs.netflix.com/culture.

3

Transformative Marketing with Artificial Intelligence

Overview

Artificial intelligence (AI) is ubiquitous in our everyday lives. By utilizing data analysis, machine learning, algorithms, and natural language processing, AI influences the marketing industry by giving companies a competitive advantage for the present and the future.[1] Currently, nearly all industries and business functions use AI to varying degrees. Table 3.1 provides the adoption of AI by industry and function in 2022.

As provided in Table 3.1, the business function deploying AI the most was risk management in the high-tech/telecom industry (38%), followed by service operations for consumer goods/retail (31%), and product and/or service development for financial services (31%). Notably, the use of AI in marketing is low. This is perhaps due to the relatively higher levels of individual human instincts and interventions required in the marketing function, compared to the other functions. Looking ahead, this also represents areas of potential growth and opportunities for companies to develop AI applications in marketing. Companies have already started to use AI for initiating personalized customer actions. In this regard, the importance of AI for businesses can be seen in the varied uses of AI such as automating customer interactions, personalizing customer journeys across channels, and predicting customer/prospect behavior, among others.[2] Other growing applications of AI in marketing include conducting survey research, writing and publishing, interpretation and translation services, and public relations management, among others. As the number of AI applications increases, the AI ecosystem is also

Table 3.1 AI adoption worldwide 2022, by industry and function

	Human resources (%)	Manufacturing (%)	Marketing and sales (%)	Product/service development (%)	Risk (%)	Service operations (%)	Strategy and corporate finance (%)	Supply chain management (%)
All industries	11	8	5	10	19	19	21	9
Business, legal, and professional services	11	10	9	8	16	20	19	12
Consumer goods/retail	14	4	3	4	15	31	29	11
Financial services	1	8	7	31	17	24	23	2
Healthcare/Pharma	15	7	2	4	22	12	8	8
High-tech/telecom	6	6	4	7	38	21	25	8

Source Stanford University. (March 15, 2023). AI adoption by industry and function, 2022 [Graph]. In *Artificial Intelligence Index Report 2023*. Retrieved September 4, 2023, from https://aiindex.stanford.edu/wp-content/uploads/2023/04/HAI_AI-Index-Report_2023.pdf

Table 3.2 Selected companies in the AI ecosystem

Selected AI applications	Key players
Data Science Platforms	SAS, IBM Watson, Rapidminer, Anaconda
Data Generation & Labelling	Hive, Upwork, Amazon MTurk, Unity
Machine Learning Operations (MLOPS)	Fiddler, Arize, Neural Magic, Evidently AI
Computer Vision	Amazon SageMaker, Matroid, clarifai
Speech	Siri, Alexa, Cortana, PolyAI
Natural Language Processing (NLP)	Google Cloud Natural Language AI, Hugging Face, Amazon Translate
Edge AI	Hailo, Deeplite, Edge Impulse
Horizontal AI/AGI	Google Research, Microsoft Research, Meta Research, OpenAI, stability.ai, Midjourney
AI Hardware	Google Cloud, Nvidia, Intel, Graphcore, Cerebras
Closed Source Models	OpenAI (ChatGPT), OpenAI (DALLE2), OpenAI (GPT-4), DeepMind, Midjourney, Google Bard, Google LaMDA

Source Insights Compass 2023—Unleashing Artificial Intelligence's true potential. In *Statista*. Retrieved September 4, 2023, from https://www.statista.com/download/MTY5MzcONjk0MiMjMjIwMjY0OCMjMTM4OTcxIyMxIyNudWxsIyNTdHVkeQ==

expanding with more companies developing AI offerings and applications. Table 3.2 presents a list of selected companies in the AI ecosystem.

As listed in Table 3.2, AI solutions are dominant in many user-facing interactions. For instance, AI-powered chatbots influence the online shopping experience by personalizing the experience based on the customer's previous shopping data. Everyday uses of AI include automated customer support for customer queries and requests, and travel assistance wherein chatbots provide users with travel recommendations, ticket booking, and landmarks recommendations. The growth of AI and its prospects for the marketing industry are immense.

This chapter is organized in the following manner. First, a brief history of the origin of AI is presented, followed by a definition of AI (from a marketing standpoint), and a discussion on related processes that are linked to AI such as neural networks, and deep learning, among others. In this regard, some practical applications of such AI processes are presented. Next, some marketing applications of AI focusing on understanding customer needs, revisiting firm capabilities to integrate AI, designing AI-focused marketing mix strategies, driving customer engagement through AI, and designing digital strategies with AI are discussed. Finally, the future of AI for the marketing industry is envisioned through specific customer-facing tasks such as the inclusion of robotics, user experience, and seamless integration of various customer interaction points with the company.

Origin, Definition, and Components of AI

The quest for AI over the years has not been smooth sailing. In this regard, Alan Turing was a pioneer in identifying the possibility of AI as a field of study. Turing believed that computers can assess and solve problems like humans. He published how to build and test machines with intelligence in his 1950s paper titled "Computing Machinery and Intelligence".[3] This seminal research laid the foundation for the field of AI and spurred research in this area. In 1956, John McCarthy and Marvin Minsky hosted the Dartmouth Summer Research Project on Artificial Intelligence. This event marked the first AI program, and it was where the term "artificial intelligence" originated. In the following years, computers were able to become more accessible and less costly, leading to more advances in AI. Computers' memory and speed improved, as well as more knowledge was gained on the usage of algorithms. Today, our lives encompass several elements of AI through technology. The entertainment, banking, and marketing industries all use AI. From voice assistants such as Siri, Cortana, and Alexa to generative AI tools like ChatGPT, Bard (Google's chatbot and content generative tool), DALL-E (Open AI's tool for image and art generation), AI continues to affect our everyday lives.

In establishing the concept of AI, John McCarthy described AI as "the science and engineering of making intelligent machines, especially intelligent computer programs".[4] The idea of intelligence comes from the framework of the human brain, such as the ability to solve problems, reason, and learn. In marketing, AI is defined as "a system's ability to interpret external data correctly, to learn from such data, and to use those learnings to achieve specific goals and tasks through flexible adaptation".[5] Now, with the integration of AI, marketers can automate tasks (lead generation, scoring, customer retention). By leveraging AI, they can identify potential customers and engage with them at times they are most likely to respond to marketing messages. Additionally, AI technologies can create customer profiles based on the purchase history and interactions customers have had with the brand. Through these profiles, marketers can generate targeted marketing campaigns, and enhance customer engagement and conversion rates. And lastly, AI is an essential component of predictive analytics and forecasting. Harnessing its ease in navigating through large and complex datasets, AI can forecast customer responses, as well as business metrics like revenues, returns on investments, etc. to guide strategic decision-making.[6]

The power of AI stems from various subfields like natural language processing, neural networks, and deep learning. Specifically, AI operates in the field of automation and continuous learning, acting as the intelligence that drives data-focused analytics and decision-making using data science.[7] That is, AI can assist in programming many of the processes in handling information that pertains to storing, retrieving, and using relevant information for the marketing activities of firms. Further, AI can be used to teach machines and generate insights to accomplish specific tasks by processing large amounts of data and recognizing patterns in the data.

The language used by AI scientists is like that used by humans. While computer programs are developed using specific codes, the codes are not easily understood by all people. Therefore, when machines go through natural language processing (i.e., the natural way humans communicate), it results in the development of value-rich human-focused solutions. Natural language processing (NLP) consists of natural language understanding and natural language generation. Ambiguity is a phenomenon in natural language and pertains to understanding a linguistic structure in multiple ways. This is because many words, phrases, and sentences can have multiple meanings or even similar meanings, addressing ambiguities in NLP is essential for understanding and comprehending that the understanding of the natural language aims for analyzation and comprehension of the text in the intended manner. Ambiguities can be classified into four types, depending on where the source of ambiguity lies in the text. The ambiguity may arise at the level of words (lexical ambiguity), syntax (syntactic ambiguity), semantic interpretation (semantic ambiguity), and the interaction between interpretation and context (pragmatic ambiguity).[8] By adequately addressing ambiguities, NLP can help to understand and make sense of the spoken word in a manner that is valuable. However, as mentioned earlier, owing to the complexities of the human language and how computers interpret it, NLP continues to be a challenge for machines to implement.[9]

In machine learning (ML), machines realize specific patterns and improve their performance for the future. Specifically, by considering past information (i.e., referred to as experience), machines gain the ability to learn while they perform, thereby showing performance improvement. The past information can be in the form of collected data or information actively sourced through interaction with the environment. The quality of learning is dependent on the volume and quality of data, and the key outcome is predictions about key variables of interest.[10] To facilitate deep learning, AI uses neural networks, like the way a human brain functions. Artificial neural networks (ANNs) consist of a regular neural network and a deep neural network. Their differences relate to the number of neurons. A deep neural network contains several hidden layers of neurons, which is where information is processed. The more the layer of neurons, the more connections occur. In general, ML focuses on learning that is inherently based on data analysis and statistics, with an added emphasis on predictions (and higher-order interactions that are not pre-specified).[11] As a result, ML can produce predictions that can also be used to (in)validate theories and calibrate data.[12]

Following deep learning, inference is possible. Inference takes place when abilities gained from training are used to understand new data. An example of deep learning and inference in use today is the facial recognition tool that allows Facebook to tag known family and friends in photos. In conclusion, the overview of AI, the following three vignettes present the possibilities of AI and how companies and users are deriving value from such offerings.

The Rise of the Transformative Home

The use of transformative devices is constantly increasing as consumers seek devices that can perform small tasks within the home.[13] Alexa, developed by Amazon to accompany an Echo device, comes with the ability to answer questions and requests, such as forecasting the weather, playing music, dimming the lights, or locking doors (see Image 3.1). Activation of the device follows the term "Alexa," and a cloud-based service will do the job of answering the requests.[14] Other popular tools in the transformative home include solutions for travel planning (e.g., Mezi), music (e.g., Pandora), financial planning (e.g., Olivia), language translation (e.g., Liv), and smart-home solutions (e.g., Nest), among others. Due to the popularity of mobile devices, consumers use Siri and Google Assistant more frequently than Amazon's Alexa.

Image 3.1 Smart locks for homes. A smart lock device used for home protection (*Source* Photo by *Sebastian Scholz (Nuki)* on *Unsplash*)

In 2019, there were an estimated 3.25 billion voice assistants in use worldwide, which is expected to reach 8.4 billion active devices in 2024.[15] Virtual assistants have become an important part of the smart device business, playing an important role in how users engage with their devices. Companies are increasingly looking for bigger and better uses of "smart" technology as the business grows and its technology advances. Tech-savvy consumers may now communicate with their connected homes and automobiles in the same manner that they can with their smartphones. The popularity of voice assistants continues to grow, which contributes to the market of AI, among others. Similarly, Amazon, Google, and Apple continue to work on advancing their AI devices. Amazon aims to allow conversations with Alexa to last longer without having to repeat the wake word "Alexa" before every request. Google's Duplex on the Web allows Google Assistant to book appointments, make reservations, and even book car rentals using autofill. Apple plans to update Siri with voice-recognition ability to provide the user with customized recommendations. Overall, the future of voice assistant devices is expected to have a more natural dialog and human-sounding voice.

Personalized Education

AI is also making strides in the field of education. Particularly, AI is used in educational applications such as intelligent tutoring, simulation activities in science, personalized learning, educational resources and courses, and educational games. The standard model of education has largely stayed unchanged, with one instructor giving the same content to an entire class of students but paying limited attention to their individual growth. The need to design personalized learning programs for each student is currently the most powerful motivating factor for AI in education and learning. When instructors think of testing students' knowledge, exams and tests are the main factors for them to analyze. This aspect can change as AI tools can be used to analyze students' educational data to assist teachers in creating personalized learning plans. For example, Brightspace Insights by D2L can analyze data from online sources, publishers, and learning apps to come up with a student's learning behavior. Brightspace Insights provides teachers with information for them to decide how to teach, and it predicts the learner's current issues allowing teachers to address the problem right away.[16] Similarly, Georgia State University introduced an AI chatbot, Pounce, that reduced "summer melt" (i.e., students enrolled in spring dropping out of college in fall) by 22%. Using conversational AI technology, the chatbot was able to guide students in getting their queries answered in a timely and relevant manner, thereby helping them stay in college.[17] At the K-12 level in the United States, Cognitive Tutor®, an AI-based application developed by Carnegie Learning, is a secondary mathematics program with an emphasis on how learners understand and absorb mathematics. Teachers help students learn by letting them acquire and apply new material while discussing their work. A textbook, adaptive software, or a combination of textbook and software activities can be used to implement the curriculum.

Similar tools are also developed for younger kids, as part of developmental learning aids. Pillar Learning created an AI interactive toy, Codi, for children with customized content based on the child's age, ability, and interest. Codi contains songs, lessons, and stories that can be regulated by parents through a coordinating mobile app. According to the CEO of Pillar Learning, Dayu Yang, "Unlike other children's toys, Codi is development-focused, over purely comfort or entertainment-focused".[18] Other examples of such applications include Querium Corporation using an AI platform called Stepwise to help students with personalized lessons on STEM, and Hubert.ai creating an assessment system that can analyze a child's skills, such as imagination, background reasoning, and creativity.[19] These programs are all made possible by AI's ability to augment personalized learning.

The World of Wearables

Wearable devices (popularly referred to as wearables) are electric technology or devices incorporated into items that can be worn on a body. These devices are used for tracking information (sleep schedules, heart rates, activity) on a real-time basis (see Image 3.2). While wearable technology entered the consumer market in recent years, they have been widely used for military, medical, and healthcare purposes. Smartwatches, fitness trackers, head-mounted displays, sports watches, and smart jewelry are a few of the wearables that are trending in today's consumer markets.[20]

Wearables consist of MEM (Micro-Electric-Mechanic) sensors that are designed to sense and measure a diverse range of environmental and physical parameters such as motion, temperature, humidity, etc. The different types of MEM sensors in wearables include accelerometers (track movements, distance traveled, sleep patterns), gyroscopes (detecting gestures, measuring orientation), and barometric pressure sensors (for weather prediction, and altitude tracking). The sensors make wearables accurate and also strengthen their capabilities in offering valuable insights into users' health and daily activities. The popular applications of wearables are discussed below.

Image 3.2 Wearable devices. A smartwatch is a wearable device that provides several features such as local weather, to-do lists, appointments, personal communications, personal health-related information, and much more
(*Source* Photo by *Fabian Albert* on *Unsplash*)

Smartwatches and Fitness Trackers. As the industry competition intensifies with new entrants, brands such as Apple, Fitbit, Garmin, Samsung, and others are increasing efforts to gain market share. For instance, the Apple Watch Series 8 can now detect skin temperatures, track menstrual cycles, detect falls, and call for help using its fall detection feature. Smartwatches and fitness trackers are seeing a surge in new users (including people from older populations), to cater better to this new segment by adding abilities such as glucose monitoring for people with diabetes. Similarly, Fitbit added a feature to detect sleep apnea, while also offering features that track activity, steps taken, sleep patterns, etc.

Head-Mounted Displays: Ten years ago, Google ventured into the Head-mounted Displays space with their invention—the Google Glass. Their wearable smart glasses were pulled from the market in 2015 due to reasons that included high price and safety and privacy concerns. While Google still may explore the area further, other industry leaders like Microsoft and Apple are taking the space by storm. Microsoft's HoloLens, Microsoft's mixed-reality headset, combines the best of augmented reality (AR) and virtual reality (VR) and can boost an organization's productivity (specifically across manufacturing, healthcare, and education). Through multiple sensors, advanced optics, and holographic processing that melds seamlessly with the environment—holograms can be used to display information, blend with the world, and simulate a virtual world. The main features of this device include Holograms (create photographic images of objects without using a lens), Cortana (Microsoft's Virtual Assistant), and Cloud (the device works seamlessly with Microsoft Azure).

Smart Jewelry: Searches for health-tracking jewelry were up 200% year over year, with millions of these devices being sold globally. In 2023, customers are seeing a new era of smart jewelry—sleek, stylish, technologically advanced, and discreet. Smart jewelry has expanded its focus on sleep data, fertility, and mental health—thus providing a holistic picture of well-being. For instance, Oura, the Finnish health technology company known for launching the Oura Ring in 2015, collects data on heart rate, body temperature, respiratory rate, sleep data, etc. from the user's finger. They launched the third-generation Oura Ring in 2021, with new features such as heart rate monitoring, blood oxygen monitoring, period predictions, etc. As of 2022, the company sold more than one million rings, with celebrities like Jennifer Aniston, Prince Harry, and Gwyneth Paltrow using it. Other examples of smart jewelry include Bellabeat's Leaf Urban, which is a bracelet, necklace, or brooch, Ringly's Aries smart ring, Fossil's Q Tailor analog watch, and Ringly's Aries bracelet, among others. While these products are receiving critical acclaim, companies continue to develop designs and accuracy to offer the best customer experiences.

AI in the Marketing 5.0 World

The utilization of AI in marketing has become increasingly significant in recent years. AI has revolutionized the way businesses approach marketing by providing valuable insights into consumer behavior and preferences. With the help of AI, marketers can analyze vast amounts of data and gain a deeper understanding of their target audience, allowing them to create more personalized and effective marketing campaigns. Companies that are adopting AI into their business processes are gaining a competitive advantage that will augur well in the future. Expanding on the Marketing 5.0 concept discussed in Chapter 2, this section presents how AI operates in the Marketing 5.0 world. Particularly, this section discusses five examples of where AI is applied through the lens of Marketing 5.0 and establishes how such actions can also bode well for humanity.

Data-Driven Marketing Using AI

The significance of technology in delivering customized experiences for customers is being extensively documented. In this context, it is intriguing to examine how Spotify, a digital native company, utilizes artificial intelligence (AI) and implements data-driven marketing. Spotify's AI models suggest audio content to users by harnessing user data, such as playlist creation, listening history, and interactions with the platform, to predict their preferences for future listening. Spotify heavily relies on reinforcement learning, which optimizes long-term user satisfaction, to provide highly personalized recommendations that enhance user happiness and encourage continued engagement. While each player in the music streaming platforms industry has its unique characteristics, Spotify's ability to offer hyper-personalized recommendations positions it at the forefront. By leveraging AI, they have revolutionized their service, generating unparalleled value in the market. According to the company, they process an astounding half a trillion events daily to train their models, enabling them to provide recommendations of superior quality as they accumulate more data.[21]

Recently, Spotify introduced a new AI DJ that acts as a personalized guide for users based on their music data.[22] This feature was initially launched as a beta version and offers a curated selection of music and commentary on tracks and artists in a realistic voice. The AI guide can sift through the latest music, revisit users' old favorites, and bring back albums they have not listened to in years. The DJ is a combination of Spotify's personalization technology, Generative AI, and a dynamic AI voice that brings text to life with realistic voices.

Predictive Marketing Using AI

As technology continues to evolve and our interactions with it become more extensive, it becomes crucial to establish a series of procedures that allow us to effectively analyze data and stay focused on the objectives that organizations initially set. To assist organizations in making informed decisions, technology companies are developing various AI-based tools that enable them to extract valuable insights from data. A notable example is Salesforce's Einstein Analytics.

Salesforce Einstein Analytics is a cloud-based analytical solution designed to help Salesforce users gain insights from data collected from various sources such as ERPs, data warehouses, and log files.[23] The main objective of this platform is to address the challenge of consolidating data from different locations and generating valuable insights. By leveraging AI, the tool is capable of generating reports, building predictive models, and even providing chatbot functionalities. With its data exploration and predictive analytics capabilities, businesses can find answers to critical business questions and make smarter decisions to meet customer needs. Additionally, the tool offers AI forecasting, empowering the sales team to assess risks, provide interactive deal guidance, identify potential missed opportunities, and offer recommendations to improve performance. Lastly, the platform provides complete visibility into the sales pipeline, enabling a transparent evaluation of each sales metric throughout the process.

The predictive capabilities of Einstein Analytics have made it a popular tool across various industries. For instance, in the healthcare sector, Einstein Analytics for Healthcare leverages AI to provide care coordinators, utilization managers, and referral managers with valuable insights and metrics related to their patient populations. By using this tool, healthcare coordinators can quickly identify patients who are not following their care plans and take proactive measures to prevent unnecessary hospital admissions. Utilization managers can also benefit from insights into the care request process, which can help them reduce cycle times and increase approval rates. Additionally, referral coordinators can use patient referral management insights to better understand referral sources, identify areas for improvement, and increase patient conversions.

Contextual Marketing Using AI

Contextual marketing using artificial intelligence involves the use of sophisticated algorithms and machine learning techniques to understand the context in which consumers interact with brands. This includes analyzing factors such as location, time of day, device used, and even the weather to deliver tailored marketing messages. AI-powered systems can also analyze social media posts, online reviews, and customer feedback to gain deeper insights into consumer sentiment and preferences. The integration of artificial intelligence in contextual marketing has not only improved the efficiency and effectiveness of marketing campaigns but has also enhanced the overall customer experience. AI-powered chatbots and virtual assistants further enhance the customer experience by providing instant and accurate responses to queries, offering personalized recommendations, and even assisting with purchases.

Starbucks is a prime example of how AI can revolutionize contextual marketing. The company firmly believes in the power of innovation, emphasizing the need for swift action rather than lengthy timelines. This allows for constant improvement in the customer experience and the lives of employees.

By utilizing AI and data science, Starbucks can inform its processes and product development. They take both quantitative and qualitative feedback from customers, empowering their partners and exploring ways to add more value to the organization.

In 2019, Starbucks launched Deep Brew, which uses AI and IoT technologies to optimize store labor allocations, drive inventory management, and personalize the customer experience.[24] This technology streamlines operations and humanizes the customer experience, making it easier for customers to get what they want and for employees to provide it. By embracing AI, Starbucks can stay ahead of the curve and provide a unique and personalized experience for its customers. Furthermore, by analyzing customer purchase history, preferences, and behaviors, Deep Brew generates personalized recommendations for customers through the mobile app. This enhances user experiences and drives engagement. In addition to this, Deep Brew also helps Starbucks create targeted promotions and offers by identifying trends and patterns. This allows Starbucks to launch campaigns that resonate with specific customer segments, driving sales and engagement.

Starbucks is not only using Deep Brew to create contextually relevant experiences for its customers.[25] The company is also exploring other initiatives such as location-based targeting. The Starbucks app uses geolocation to provide location-specific promotions and features to users. When a customer is near a store, the app can send notifications about ongoing offers or personalized discounts to encourage visits. By leveraging AI and other technologies, Starbucks can create a more personalized and engaging experience for its customers, ultimately driving sales and loyalty.

Augmented Marketing Using AI

Augmented marketing is a powerful tool that can help businesses improve their marketing efforts in two critical ways. First, it allows marketers to create more targeted and personalized marketing campaigns. By analyzing customer data, AI algorithms can identify patterns and preferences that can be used to create more effective marketing messages. Second, augmented marketing can help businesses save time and money. By automating certain marketing tasks, businesses can reduce the time and resources required to create and execute impactful campaigns.

AI plays a crucial role in enhancing human efforts, particularly in the field of cancer research and treatment. The shortage of pathologists, especially in cancer treatment, has become a significant concern in recent years, mirroring the challenges faced by various sectors of healthcare. Additionally, the aging population has led to an increase in the workload of pathologists. Pathologists must allocate an appropriate amount of time to each case, as the consequences for patients can be severe if too much or too little time is spent. Although digitization is being explored as a means to enhance the efficiency of pathologists' workflow, it presents significant challenges. For example, the process of digitizing a single slide can consume a substantial amount of storage, exceeding a gigabyte. Consequently, this places immense pressure on the technology infrastructure and incurs substantial costs for data collection and storage.

Google and the US Department of Defense have collaborated to tackle this challenge by creating the Augmented Reality Microscope (ARM).[26] This microscope, resembling the ones commonly used in high school labs, is connected to a computer equipped with AI models. By placing a prepared glass slide under the microscope, the AI can accurately outline the location of the cancer. Pathologists can observe this outline as a bright green line through their eyepieces and on a separate monitor. Additionally, the AI provides information on the severity of the cancer and generates a black-and-white heat map on the monitor, displaying the cancer's boundaries in a pixelated format. Moreover, the ARM software's ability to capture screen grabs of slides is expected to bring significant cost savings to healthcare organizations.

Although the ARM is not intended to substitute digital pathology systems, its uncomplicated design can aid healthcare institutions in obtaining speedy diagnoses. At present, there are only 13 ARMs in existence, and they are not yet utilized to assist in diagnosing patients. Nevertheless, experts suggest that it could be a valuable resource for pathologists who do not have convenient access to a second opinion. All things considered, due to the cost savings and enhanced workflow efficiencies, this technology has the potential to revolutionize cancer research and treatment globally.

Agile Marketing Using AI

As mentioned in Chapter 2, agile marketing involves the utilization of decentralized, cross-functional teams to swiftly conceptualize, design, develop, and validate products and marketing campaigns. When coupled with AI, agile marketing offers a dynamic and flexible approach to marketing that is unparalleled. With AI algorithms analyzing vast amounts of data, marketers can gain valuable insights into consumer behavior, preferences, and trends. This enables them to make data-driven decisions and tailor their marketing efforts to target specific audiences with precision. By leveraging AI, businesses can automate repetitive tasks, streamline processes, and optimize their marketing efforts for better results.

For instance, consider the case of Kraft Foods. The company recently announced plans to implement its Agile-based strategy—Agile@Scale—throughout all areas of its business operations, incorporating specialized pods of teams dedicated to addressing specific challenges and opportunities.[27] This expansion aims to enhance the company's ability to effectively compete with private label brands by efficiently managing increased promotional activities this year.

As part of its Agile@Scale approach, the organization has implemented multifunctional pods that consist of twelve individuals who concentrate on crucial opportunities, including revenue management and innovation. This strategy combines technology investments, such as artificial intelligence, with Agile methodologies to enhance the company's in-house capabilities while collaborating with vendors like Microsoft. As per the strategy, the pods are distributed across various departments such as innovation, logistics, manufacturing, sales, and finance. These pods are defined by ROI and consist of teams comprising both Kraft Heinz employees and external partners like Microsoft. Each team is dedicated to addressing a specific challenge or opportunity.

Through the partnership with Microsoft, a "Supply Chain Control Tower" was established to serve as an air traffic control for the company's entire product portfolio. This innovation provided the company with real-time visibility into plant operations and automated the supply chain distribution across Kraft Heinz's 85 product categories. By utilizing Azure's AI, IoT, and data analytics capabilities, the company was able to get its products efficiently and cost-effectively to its 2,500 US retailer and food service customers, as well as millions of consumers.[28] By implementing this program, Kraft successfully integrated AI into its supply chain visibility operations, resulting in a significant increase of $30 million in sales. Moreover, this initiative enabled the company to streamline its operational priorities and automate the identification of service risks and operator alerts. As a result, Kraft Heinz has effectively reduced its operator alerts by an impressive 42% through the utilization of this advanced technology.[29]

Current AI Applications in Marketing

Companies are increasingly using AI technology to develop customer-focused solutions.[30] Additionally, governments across the world are also keenly looking into AI investments to spur economic and technological growth.[31] When used correctly, AI can become a critical tool for boosting companies' productivity and increasing the speed of the decision-making process. It is critical to understand that AI-powered tools can enable managers to have a more in-depth insight into subjects such as segmentation and positioning without spending too much time.

Further, AI has achieved enhanced capabilities with the help of big data.[32] By analyzing vast sets of data of demographics and personal information, AI can suggest personalized products and services, which generally include advertisements and strategic discounts to influence consumers directly. AI allows product curation on a scale impossible for any human or group of humans to achieve. Machines are better at it, and the insights created as a result of their ability to slice and dice data are much better than the ones performed by humans. Additionally, companies can use AI to offer enhanced search engines, which are based on machine learning-based algorithms. For instance, Google, the leader in online search, also incorporates AI to provide elaborate and comprehensive results regarding search queries. Using a technology called Search Generative Experience, Google leverages large language models and generative AI to not only identify the most relevant information but also present it in neatly written text (along with the relevant search results) that the user can readily use.[33] Initially popularized by Google, many companies are trying to offer smarter search results. For instance, Carmax's AI tool sifts through choices regarding brands, mileage, and price ranges to fully customize options, acting as the customer's personalized dealer. This ensures that the consumer sees only the content and options that are relevant to their needs.[34] The section presents five specific application areas where AI continues to help companies in developing marketing initiatives.

Understanding Customer Needs to Deploy AI

A deep understanding of customers' needs and wants is critical to the success of any company. Following this, firms are collecting more data on various aspects of their business than ever before, which offers both significant opportunities and challenges as firms try to convert all this data into actionable insights. However, firms are facing a paradox of increasing information, yet decreasing knowledge and insight. This has been identified as quantity overpowering quality, thereby resulting in poor-quality information.[35] In other words, it is not a case of how much data firms possess, but a case of what data they have for decision-making. Further, analyzing and using that data in the decision-making process raises different types of challenges. In this regard, AI serves companies well in analyzing the volumes of data collected.

To speed up the process for simple procedures and daily responsibilities, chatbots, and virtual assistants can be beneficial tools. Companies can take advantage of these tools to increase customer satisfaction by optimizing the time spent on these routine tasks. By examining large data sets, AI can predict consumer needs and wants with a high degree of accuracy that can help firms develop timely and valuable offerings. An industry where AI is used for understanding customer needs is the fashion industry. Here, the popular use cases include Zara using AI algorithms to generate textures and patterns, Adidas and Nike allowing customers to design their shoes using AI algorithms, and Stitch Fix using AI to deliver a superlative online shopping experience, among others. Particularly, Stitch Fix utilizes AI extensively to drive several of its core functions. While they are known for the styling algorithm that picks out the best clothes for their clients based on their stated preferences and needs, the company also employs AI in other areas.[36] Examples of such uses include using algorithms to pair the right stylists with their clients, helping buyers predict future styles to better manage inventory, and identifying a buyer's 'latent style' and 'latent size', regardless of their explicitly stated preferences. Overall, these algorithms work together to deliver clothes that best-fit clients' distinctive needs.

Revisiting Firm's Capabilities to Integrate AI

As noted earlier, ML is one of the main driving forces of AI. Specifically, ML examines similar statistical patterns that computer systems use to perform a specific task based on models instead of precise instructions. For businesses that thrive in the fiercely competitive environment, it is vital to implement AI effectively in the solutions that have been offered to the customers. This implies that it is essential that the AI tool be in sync with firm objectives for the AI implementation to triumph. Further, it is important to set clear expectations for AI tools. In this regard, a key reason for companies to not adopt AI is the insufficient or unclear returns from an AI implementation.[37]

Furthermore, AI can help businesses to allocate their resources more efficiently. Many job functions currently contain several repetitive and time-consuming tasks, such as document processing, proofreading, and data collection, among others. The AI infrastructure enables businesses to tackle these time-consuming tasks with ease. Therefore, there is more time to spend on essential tasks, that are more important for the companies' future, such as creative thinking and decision-making. For instance, it has been estimated that 60% of occupations will have at least 30% of their work automated, in addition to the actual decline in certain occupations. Further, AI is also forecast to create new job roles previously nonexistent.[38] In this regard, AI is set to alter the workplace in terms of type of work and workforce management.

Designing Marketing Mix Strategies with AI

In a dynamic business environment where consumer preferences and demands change continuously, it can be challenging to determine a marketing strategy to execute. Today, AI allows businesses to examine these instant changes and adapt to the fast-paced environment. Breaking down AI's role in the marketing mix provides interesting insights into the extent to which it has permeated through the organization. This can be observed in how AI is included in the marketing mix strategies of companies, as discussed below.

AI in product decisions: AI in product decisions refers to the use of artificial intelligence tools to help designers and manufacturers create better products. With AI, designers can collect and analyze large amounts of data, understand customer needs, and create efficient, cost-effective products. It offers capabilities to customize offerings to suit the customer needs.[39] Another feature of AI in product design is its ability to generate designs based on a set of parameters (materials, costs, size, etc.). In this regard, generative design algorithms are becoming increasingly popular in the industry today; with it being used in aerospace, architecture, and manufacturing of consumer products. For instance, companies are increasingly using digital twins to design, manage, and update their products in real time. A digital twin is a virtual representation of a physical product available in real-time through new-age technologies such as AI and connected devices. Such a format allows companies to define, manage, and update product features and product design, in addition to monitoring the performance of the product and predicting potential performance issues. Examples of companies using digital twins include Microsoft, Boeing, and Mercedes-Benz, among others. In the future, as AI becomes more accessible and affordable, more companies are expected to adopt digital twins to manage their product development and management that can not only drive better product performance but also deliver immersive and engaging experiences to customers.

AI in pricing decisions: In today's competitive business environment, companies are constantly looking for ways to increase revenue, and maintain and gain a competitive advantage. In recent years, one approach that has gained attention is price optimization using AI algorithms. AI's capability to analyze large amounts of real-time data offers the potential to identify optimal pricing for products and services at any given time. For example, the ride-sharing app, Uber, uses dynamic pricing. Here, AI algorithms analyze real-time data to forecast demand, identify pricing trends, and adjust prices in real time. For Uber, this translates to adjusting prices based on real-time market demand and traffic conditions. Additionally, AI-based analytics help companies analyze customer data (purchase history, demographics, online behavior) to create a personalized pricing strategy for each customer. Through this approach, companies can increase customer loyalty, and boost sales by offering prices that match customer needs and their willingness to pay. Brands can also build stronger relationships with customers and improve customer satisfaction.

AI in place and promotion decisions: Product access and product availability are essential for maximizing customer satisfaction levels. Product distribution, as a process, relies on various other processes like logistics, inventory management, transportation, etc.—all of which are repetitive processes. AI offers solutions that automate these processes, through the integration of other new-age technologies like robots for packaging, drones for deliveries, and IoT (the Internet of Things) for order tracking and refilling.[40] Concerning promotions, AI plays a role in the personalization and customization of the message as per the customer profile. Emotive AI algorithms and content analysis could be deployed to track and understand customer sentiments. For instance, AI-based online writing tools such as CopyAI, Jasper, and QuillBot help users generate various types of content (blog headlines, emails, social media content). It provides tools and writing frameworks to aid marketers in generating content and is great for beginners to get familiar with generative AI.

Driving Customer Engagement Through AI

Having the advantage of AI allows companies to connect with their customers efficiently. Within AI, ML algorithms (e.g., collaborative filtering, deep learning, etc.) are increasingly being used to create tools that not only understand customer needs and expectations but also identify firm offerings that users are more likely to favor.[41] Such firm actions would likely result in solidifying the relationship between customers and marketers.[42,43]

Further, satisfied customer relationships that also have an emotional bonding have been identified to progress to a state of engagement,[44] and positive relationships play a role in influencing customer engagement behaviors.[45] Accordingly, engagement (with two stakeholders) has been defined as the attitude, behavior, the level of connectedness (1) among customers, (2) between customers and employees, and (3) between customers and employees within a firm.[46] Further, the more positive the attitude and behavior and the higher the level of connectedness, the higher the level of engagement.

Data allows AI to analyze, predict, and recommend personalized consumer needs and wants smartly and efficiently.[47] Consumers are always searching for products and services that make their lives better and easier. In this regard, offering personalized solutions via an AI tool in a curated manner can be considered by firms to improve customer engagement.[48] Curated offerings play a critical role for firms, especially in an environment where users have access to a high volume of information.[49] For instance, a recent survey found that 48% of consumers moved their purchase to a different provider (online or in-store) simply because the offerings were poorly curated.[50] Further, research has identified that customer engagement improved with curation.[51] Overall, the use of AI to curate and recommend products across industries continues to yield impressive results for companies.

Designing Digital Strategies with AI

Executing an online marketing campaign is an integral part of every marketing strategy. The possibility of reaching large masses of people with online campaigns is increasing every day. Pay-per-click advertisements, search engine optimization, content marketing, email, and social media marketing are the most practiced strategies of a digital marketing campaign. There is a possibility that AI will be integrated with digital marketing strategies.

AI can enable companies to expand into new platforms, that have not been discovered by competitors. Displaying relevant advertisements to the right people in the right place can become a valuable aspect of a successful digital marketing strategy. Specifically, using AI tools, companies can accurately ascertain and develop innovative offerings that otherwise may have been difficult to determine. For instance, in the United Kingdom, L'Oréal has incorporated AI tools to closely monitor social media regarding what users say about them. The brand's CMO Stéphane Bérubé says "By personalizing our interactions with consumers we get to understand them and react accordingly. More than ever before, we will be able to predict and forecast market-wide trends to serve the consumer".[52] Similarly, IBM Watson is implemented at McCormick Foods to develop new spice variations that are driven by monitoring customer feedback and social media.[53]

Natural language processing, linking similar products based on consumer research, semantic understanding, and relevance instead of optimization continues to drive the features of an AI-powered offering. Furthermore, it is possible to apply these aspects to content creation. For instance, AI enables the development of content-focused advertising as seen in the case of McCann's AI tool, wherein the tool aids the creative team to script and film commercials that resonate closely with the intended audiences.[54] Tools such as Grammarly can predict what the user wants to say and give recommendations to make the content concise and relevant. There are some areas where AI is better than humans in content marketing tasks such as writing e-mail subject lines and suggesting keywords. As a result, companies can design their digital marketing strategies more efficiently by using AI.

In short, the overarching theme of AI in marketing appears to center around personalization. Recent research has recognized that AI impacts a firm's marketing practices in a way that is significantly different from conventional and contemporary marketing practices. In this new technological age, it is proposed that personalization can deliver better marketing results when done using the AI tool through the strategy of curation. Subsequently, when firms use AI in the context of curation for personalization, significant enhancements to branding and customer management practices can be observed.[55] In this regard, Fig. 3.1 presents a framework to understand the role of AI in delivering personalized offerings via curation.

As illustrated in Fig. 3.1, two factors—(a) how consumers process their decision choices to arrive at credible decisions, and (b) how consumers store and use knowledge to make decisions—continue to influence the development of firm offerings. Specifically, the richness of information and the need for consumers to process publicly available information has been captured in academic research as the paradox of choice and digital cognitive load.[56] Collectively, the above-mentioned two factors prepare firms and users for a new era wherein AI neatly distills and curates wide-selection options for customers and an abundance of information in a format that is personalized to individual users. Additionally, it is expected that personalization will continue to drive firm offerings in the future, with the help of AI solutions.

Future of AI in Marketing

AI has made significant developments in the relatively short time that it has been used in businesses and marketing. More importantly, it has demonstrated its relevance and practicality to businesses and users in a wide range of settings. The future of AI is set to build on its current progress and gather momentum in doing so. Currently, the most important implication of AI in marketing appears to be building customer engagement by offering personalized experiences.[57] The automated decision-making of AI reduces manual guesswork from marketers who try to personalize a customer's experience. This presents various marketing opportunities in the areas of content strategy, campaign strategy, product delivery, sales strategy, sales intent, retargeting, and more. Specifically, AI aids users in making critical purchase decisions and accurately pairs the right firm offering(s) with the user's needs by looking into the data. This makes AI an influential force in ensuring consumers make

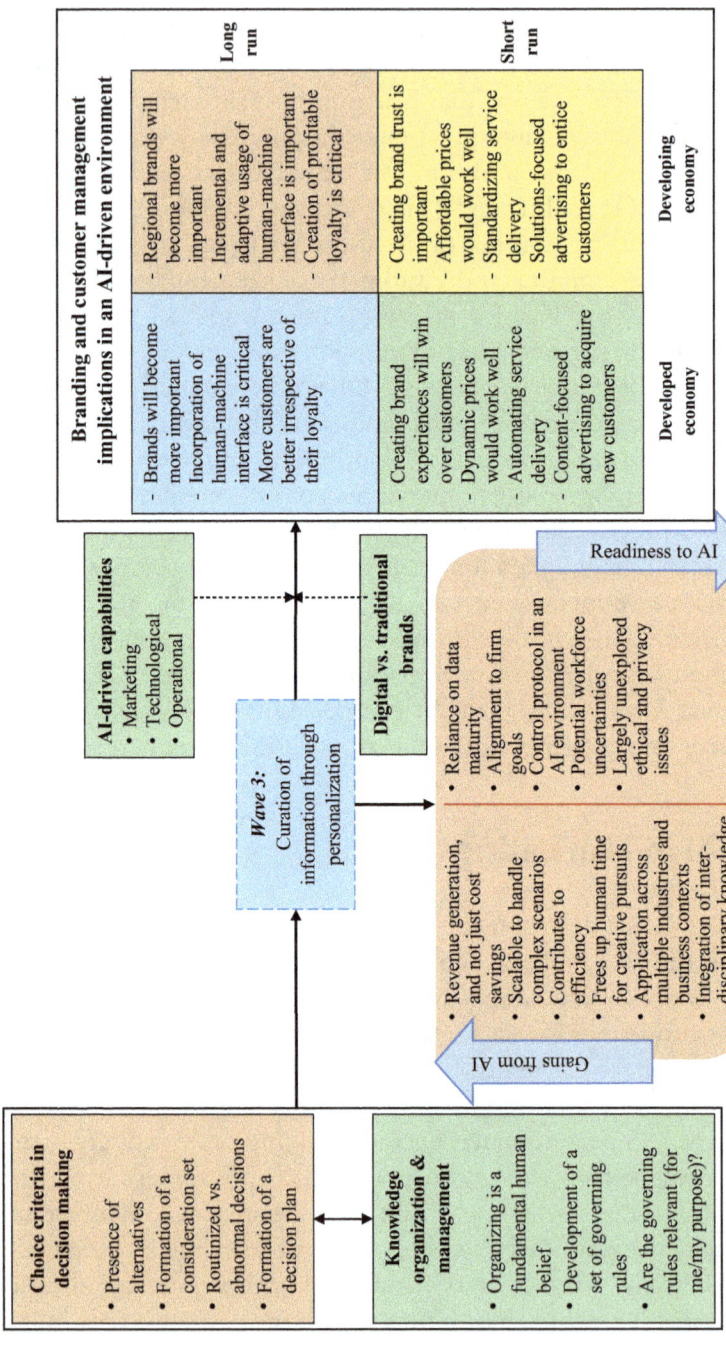

Fig. 3.1 Role of AI in personalized engagement marketing
(Source V. Kumar, Bharath Rajan, Rajkumar Venkatesan, & Jim Lecinski [2019], "Understanding the Role of Artificial Intelligence in Personalized Engagement Marketing," California Management Review, 61(4), 135–155)

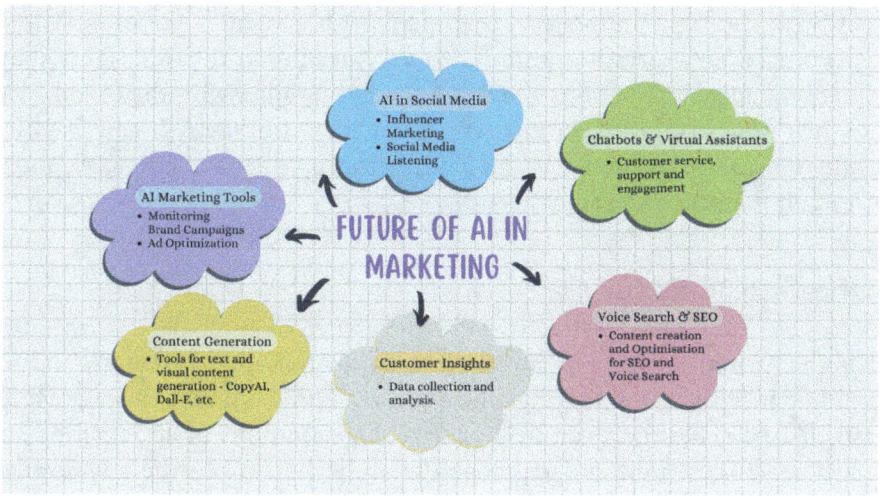

Fig. 3.2 Popular and emerging applications of AI
(*Source* Authors' own)

the right choices within a short time. Figure 3.2 presents an illustration of popular and emerging applications of AI.

A 2023 McKinsey report identifies that AI and related analytics can unlock $17.7 trillion of economic value.[58] Furthermore, AI-enabled marketing can unlock significant value for the firm by—aiding in offering better products and services, delivering higher satisfaction, and transforming the overall business operation.[59] Particularly, the future of AI in marketing can be viewed in two ways—(a) through the lens of data-driven marketing, and (b) through the lens of customer engagement and experience management. Data-driven marketing with AI begins with collecting data from a multitude of sources (social media, customer relationship management systems, website analytics). Upon collecting the data, AI-powered tools can be employed to analyze the data, identify the patterns and trends to aid decision-making, and uncover opportunities for optimization. Within data-driven marketing, we discuss three key areas where AI is expected to play a bigger role—AI in social media, marketing tools for AI, and content generation using AI.

AI in Social Media

The use of AI in social media is growing.[60] Within industries, it is observed that social media platforms are becoming popular as retail businesses are using them to strengthen customer relationships. AI in social media helps retail brands make their promotions more effective. In today's age of influencers, identifying the right influencers that align with a brand's values and offerings is crucial for successful promotions. AI can offer in-depth insights about influencers, make predictions about how well they align with the brand, evaluate their potential based on their engagement statistics, etc. It can also offer healthy returns on investments and aid in selecting the most effective content for each influencer campaign.

Marketing Tools for AI

AI-powered marketing tools are facilitating analysis for marketers, and are providing insights based on real-time data, at a faster and more accurate level. Firstly, AI-powered tools can help analyze large amounts of ad targeting and budget variations, find and segment the audiences, make the ads creative, test ads, and improve ad performance in the target audiences, etc. AI could also be used to make predictions—on which language would drive the best results in the customer segments, on the type of content to create based on the keywords customers use for searching the products and services, etc. Additionally, many companies are incorporating AI-powered logo detection systems to check how often their logos appear on social media networks, understand the customer sentiments about their brand, and identify areas they can improve their advertising, among others.

Seamless Integration of AI with Marketing—The New Marketing Culture

The possibility for AI to benefit the marketing industry remains immense, and businesses should consider how AI advancements can aid in their brand's goals. Companies are integrating AI in personalization, search engine optimization, content development, consumer decision-making, customer service, customer relationship management, and more. To ensure the success of AI implementations, it is vital to align with firm goals. That is, a successful AI implementation covers the entire organization and leaves no departments or interested parties behind. Since AI is interactive, a successful implementation is often one that is interdisciplinary, interactive, and integrative and ties in all firm operations, rather than in a siloed or even sequential manner. This would place firms in a better position to overcome the various challenges that arise in an AI implementation. Further, the identification of defined AI implementation is vital.[61]

In summary, the future looks to be firmly trending towards personalization, and curated offerings. Firms have taken notice of this trend and are progressing well along this path. As with many innovations on the rise, the future of AI is expected to undergo rapid changes. However, a certain facet of AI is the fundamental shift in the operation of business enterprises. This is true for companies operating in both developed and developing markets. As immediate changes, the developed market firms are already incorporating AI-driven changes, i.e., with specific reference to personalization in (a) delivering memorable usage encounters for users (e.g., Spotify's 'Discover Weekly,' a curated personalized playlist based on their listening history),[62] (b) real-time pricing information (e.g., online retailer Jet using AI to dynamically update pricing in real-time),[63] and (c) preprogrammed service delivery instances (e.g., Uber Eats' use of AI to optimize delivery times).[64]

The developing market firms, on the other hand, are focusing on actions such as (a) establishing a trusted image among users for the brand (e.g., mobile financial conversation platform, Juntos tailors personalized text messages in multiple local Latin American languages to help consumers achieve their financial goals),[65] (b) identifying firm offerings at reasonable price points (e.g., Amazon India's AI tool can study holiday purchase data and advise on the right pricing),[66] (c) regimenting service delivery options that ensure uniformity (e.g., Keeko robot that teaches kindergarten kids has been in 600 schools in China can bring in a uniform level of instruction),[67] and (d) developing commercials that focus on the solution (e.g., Ogilvy created a nutrition assistant for Nestle in China to help in the development of personalized meal preparation options).[68]

In terms of long-term impact, firms are likely to equip themselves better in delivering AI solutions that encompass all aspects of customer interaction with the firm, instead of being deployed at only specific usage instances often deployed in the short run. In this regard, research has identified that developed market firms' personalization approach is likely to focus on (a) strengthening their brand value, (b) incorporating human-machine interaction as a core feature, and (c) serving customers across varying profitability levels (rather than focus only on high-profit customers) to serve as the cornerstones of their marketing strategy.[69]

As expected, in the long term the developing market firms are likely to focus on different aspects from their developed market counterparts. Specifically, it is expected that developing market firms are likely to focus on (a) building brand value at the regional level (rather than at the national level), (b) incorporating the human-machine interaction on incremental and adaptive levels to supplement existing business practices, and (c) promoting and ensuring profitable customer loyalty among users.

Of course, both short and long-term firm initiatives (in developing and developed markets) would not be possible without building firm capabilities in AI. The AI-driven capabilities are comprised of capabilities about marketing, technology, and operational elements. The marketing capabilities (e.g., gathering and using customer-level data to drive firm marketing actions) impact how AI benefits a firm. The new-age technologies like AI enable firms to collect, integrate, and analyze large amounts of data at the individual level, giving firms access to granular insights but the volume, variety, and velocity of data available to firms could lead to information overload.[70] This enables corporations to identify and extract insights that can aid in ensuring superior marketing performance.

In terms of technological capabilities, organizations would have to reevaluate their technological infrastructure and ascertain how they would align with the new-age technologies. Further, the effort and time required to learn how to use and apply new-age technologies can be impacted by the extent to which new-age technologies are related to the existing knowledge base and skills of the firm and its employees.[71]

Finally, operational capabilities enable a firm to perform an activity on an ongoing basis using more or less the same techniques on the same scale to support existing products and services for the same customer population.[72] Further, they are conceptualized as geared towards the operational functioning of the firm, including both staff and line activities.[73]

The developments in AI indicate its strong potential in personalizing and curating offerings while providing valuable information to guide users in their decision-making process. With the power of robust algorithms, an AI tool can accommodate user requirements and specifications in developing targeted suggestions and offerings. Additionally, an AI tool can learn and improve over time, which further augments the accuracy of suggestions and offerings. Finally, the output of an AI tool is often designed to be user-friendly and easy to use. This serves as a strong point for users to adopt such offerings, and in turn, enjoy memorable usage experiences.

Key Terms and Related Conceptualizations

Ambiguity	A phenomenon in natural language that pertains to understanding a linguistic structure in multiple ways
Artificial intelligence	The science and engineering of making intelligent machines, especially intelligent computer programs

(continued)

(continued)

Artificial intelligence (in a marketing context)	A system's ability to interpret external data correctly, to learn from such data, and to use those learnings to achieve specific goals and tasks through flexible adaptation
Deep neural network	A component of artificial neural networks that contains several hidden layers of neurons where information is processed. The more the layer of neurons, the more connections occur
MEM (Micro-Electric-Mechanic) sensors	Sensors that are designed to sense and measure a diverse range of environmental and physical parameters such as motion, temperature, humidity, and so on

Notes and References

1. The global market for AI was estimated at USD 95 billion in 2021 and is projected to reach USD 1.07 trillion by 2028 (Next Move Strategy Consulting. [2023, July 26]. Artificial intelligence (AI) market size worldwide in 2021 with a forecast until 2030 (in million U.S. dollars) [Graph]. In *Statista*. Retrieved September 4, 2023, from https://www.statista.com/statistics/1365145/artificial-intelligence-market-size/). Particularly, the global market for AI applications in marketing is expected to reach USD 36 billion by 2024, and around USD 108 billion by 2028 (Statista, & The Insight Partners. [April 15, 2021]. Market value of artificial intelligence (AI) in marketing worldwide from 2020 to 2028 (in billion U.S. dollars) [Graph]. In *Statista*. Retrieved September 03, 2023, from https://www.statista.com/statistics/1293758/ai-marketing-revenue-worldwide/).
2. Salesforce Research found that (a) 87% of marketing professionals used AI for bridging online and offline experiences in 2022, compared to 71% in 2021, (b) 87% of marketing professionals used AI for resolving customer identity in 2022, compared to 82% in 2021, and (c) 88% of marketing professionals used AI for automating processes (such as reporting) in 2022, compared to 83% in 2021 (Salesforce 2023).
3. Turing, A. (1950), "Computing Machinery and Intelligence," *Mind*, *49*(236), 433–460.
4. McCarthy, J. (2007), "What is Artificial Intelligence?" accessed from http://jmc.stanford.edu/articles/whatisai/whatisai.pdf.
5. Kaplan, A., & M. Haenlein (2019), "Siri, Siri, in my hand: Who's the fairest in the land? On the interpretations, illustrations, and implications of artificial intelligence," *Business Horizons*, *62*(1), 15–25.

6. Salesforce (2023), "What is AI marketing and how to incorporate it in your marketing strategy," *Salesforce.com*. Retrieved from https://www.salesforce.com/in/resources/guides/role-of-ai-in-marketing/.
7. Kumar, V., B. Rajan, R. Venkatesan, & J. Lecinski (2019), "Understanding the role of artificial intelligence in personalized engagement marketing," *California Management Review*, 61(4), 135–155.
8. Yang, H., A. D. Roeck, V. Gervasi, A. Willis, & B. Nuseibeh (2011), "Analysing anaphoric ambiguity in natural language requirements," *Requirements Engineering*, 16(3), 163–189.
9. For a detailed reading on NLP, please see Nitin Indurkhya and Fred Damerau (2010), *Handbook of natural language processing*, Chapman and Hall/CRC; and Robert Dale, Hermann Moisl, and Harold Somers (Eds.) (2000), *Handbook of natural language processing*, CRC Press.
10. Kumar, V., & M. Vannan (2021), "It takes two to tango: Statistical modeling and machine learning," *Journal of Global Scholars of Marketing Science*, 31(3), 296–317.
11. Mohri, M., A. Rostamizadeh, & A. Talwalkar (2018), *Foundations of machine learning*. Cambridge, MA: MIT Press.
12. Levy, D. (2018), "Navigating statistical modeling and machine learning," May 14, available at http://www.fharrell.com/post/stat-ml2/.
13. In 2015, consumers spent USD 51 billion on smart home products and services worldwide. This amount is expected to increase to USD 173 billion by 2025 (Strategy Analytics. [2021, July 6]. Consumer spending on smart home products and services worldwide from 2015 to 2025 (in billion U.S. dollars) [Graph]. In *Statista*. Retrieved September 4, 2023, from https://www.statista.com/statistics/693303/smart-home-consumer-spending-worldwide/). The new-age technology devices have smart assistant capabilities and can respond to verbal prompts or command other smart home devices. Moreover, nearly 350 million units of smart home devices were shipped worldwide in 2020, which is expected to increase to over 1.7 billion units by 2025 (Juniper Research. [March 1, 2021]. Smart home device shipments worldwide from 2020 to 2025, by region (in millions) [Graph]. In *Statista*. Retrieved September 4, 2023, from https://www.statista.com/statistics/1223262/smart-home-device-shipments-worldwide-by-region/).
14. Rawes, E., & K. Wetzel (2019), "What exactly is Alexa? Where does she come from? How does she work?" *Digital Trends*, October 3, accessed from https://www.digitaltrends.com/home/what-is-amazons-alexa-and-what-can-it-do/.

15. Voicebot.ai, & Business Wire. (April 28, 2020). Number of digital voice assistants in use worldwide from 2019 to 2024 (in billions)* [Graph]. In *Statista*. Retrieved September 4, 2023, from https://www.statista.com/statistics/973815/worldwide-digital-voice-assistant-in-use/.
16. Loeffler, J. (2018), "Personalized learning: Artificial intelligence and education in the future," *Interesting Engineering*, December 24, accessed from https://interestingengineering.com/personalized-learning-artificial-intelligence-and-education-in-the-future.
17. Ravipati, S. (2017), "Using AI chatbots to freeze 'summer melt' in higher ed," *Campus Technology*, March 7, accessed from https://campustechnology.com/articles/2017/03/07/using-ai-chatbots-to-freeze-summer-melt-in-higher-ed.aspx.
18. Markets Insider (2018), "Pillar learning introduces Codi, an AI interactive children's toy," *Markets Insider*, August 14, accessed from https://markets.businessinsider.com/news/stocks/pillar-learning-introduces-codi-an-ai-interactive-children-s-toy-1027458352.
19. Lynch, M. (2019), "Artificial intelligence & machine learning in education: Top 5 companies," *The Tech Edvocate*, May 10, accessed from https://www.thetechedvocate.org/artificial-intelligence-machine-learning-in-education-top-5-companies/.
20. In 2022, there were an estimated 1.1 billion connected wearable devices worldwide, compared to 722 million in 2019 (Research and Markets [2023], "Artificial Intelligence (AI) in Social Media—Global Strategic Business Report," *ResearchandMarkets.com*, October, accessed from https://www.researchandmarkets.com/; Research and Markets. [April 15, 2023]. Number of connected wearable devices worldwide from 2019 to 2022 (in millions) [Graph]. In *Statista*. Retrieved September 11, 2023, from https://www.statista.com/statistics/487291/global-connected-wearable-devices/). Further, smartwatches accounted for nearly USD 39 billion in 2022 (expected to reach nearly USD 62 billion by 2027), and fitness/activity tracking wristwear accounted for nearly USD 16 billion in 2022 (expected to reach around USD 32 billion by 2027) (Statista. [June 1, 2023]. Revenue of the digital fitness & well-being device market worldwide from 2018 to 2027, by segment (in billion U.S. dollars) [Graph]. In *Statista*. Retrieved September 11, 2023, from https://www.statista.com/forecasts/1314353/worldwide-digital-fitness-and-well-being-device-market-revenue-by-segment).

21. Spotify (2021), "How Spotify uses ML to create the future of personalization," *Spotify*, December 2, accessed from https://engineering.atspotify.com/2021/12/how-spotify-uses-ml-to-create-the-future-of-personalization/.
22. Cavender, E. (2023), "How to get the Spotify AI DJ," *Mashable India*, March 1, accessed from https://in.mashable.com/apps-and-software/48173/how-to-get-the-spotify-ai-dj.
23. Golovtseva, V. (2023), "Salesforce Einstein analytics: A complete guide," *revenuegrid.com*, January 2, accessed from https://revenuegrid.com/blog/einstein-analytics/.
24. Warnick, J. (2020), "AI for humanity: How Starbucks plans to use technology to nurture the human spirit," *Starbucks.com*, January 10, accessed from https://stories.starbucks.com/stories/2020/how-starbucks-plans-to-use-technology-to-nurture-the-human-spirit/.
25. Starbucks (2023), "Starbucks announces triple shot reinvention strategy with multiple paths for long-term growth," *Starbucks.com*, November 2, accessed from https://stories.starbucks.com/press/2023/starbucks-announces-triple-shot-reinvention-strategy-with-multiple-paths-for-long-term-growth/.
26. Capoot, A. (2023), "Google and the Department of Defense are building an AI-powered microscope to help doctors spot cancer," *CNBC*, September 18, accessed from https://www.cnbc.com/2023/09/18/google-dod-built-an-ai-powered-microscope-to-help-doctors-spot-cancer.html.
27. Johnston, L. (2023), "Kraft Heinz expands Agile Pods across organization," *Consumer Goods Technology*, June 2, accessed from https://consumergoods.com/kraft-heinz-expands-agile-pods-across-organization.
28. Kraft Heinz (2022), "Kraft Heinz and Microsoft join forces to accelerate supply chain innovation as part of broader digital transformation," *Kraft Heinz*, April 21, accessed from https://news.kraftheinzcompany.com/press-releases-details/2022/Kraft-Heinz-and-Microsoft-join-forces-to-accelerate-supply-chain-innovation-as-part-of-broader-digital-transformation-/default.aspx.
29. Unglesbee, B. (2023), "Kraft Heinz leans on AI to boost its supply chain performance," *Supply Chain Dive*, May 11, accessed from https://www.supplychaindive.com/news/kraft-heinz-leans-on-ai-to-boost-its-supply-chain-performance/649762/.
30. For instance, Goldman Sachs Research estimates AI investment could approach $100 billion in the United States and $200 billion globally by 2025 (Goldman Sachs [2023], "AI investment forecast to

approach $200 billion globally by 2025," *Goldman Sachs*, August 1, accessed from https://www.goldmansachs.com/intelligence/pages/ai-investment-forecast-to-approach-200-billion-globally-by-2025.html).
31. The 2022 Government AI Readiness Index lists 181 countries and territories on a score of 0–10 (0—low, and 10—high), based on their preparedness to use AI in the delivery of public services. According to the survey, the United States of America ranks first, followed by Singapore, the United Kingdom, Finland, and Canada, comprising the top 5 ranks (Oxford Insights [2022], "Government artificial intelligence Readiness Index 2022," *Oxford Insights*, accessed from https://www.unido.org/sites/default/files/files/2023-01/Government_AI_Readiness_2022_FV.pdf).
32. Kumar, V. (2021). *Intelligent marketing: Employing new age technologies*. Sage Publications.
33. Reid, E. (2023), "Supercharging search with generative AI," *Google*, May 10, accessed from https://blog.google/products/search/generative-ai-search/.
34. Haviland, D. (2018) "CarMax innovates with omnichannel strategy," *Customer Strategist*, July, accessed from https://www.ttec.com/resources/articles/carmax-innovates-omnichannel-strategy.
35. Orman, L. V. (2015), "Information paradox: Drowning in information, starving for knowledge," *IEEE Technology and Society* (December), 63–73.
36. Pardes, A. (2019), "Need some fashion advice? Just ask the algorithm," *Wired*, September 12, accessed from https://www.wired.com/story/stitch-fix-shop-your-looks/.
37. Bughin, J., E. Hazan, S. Ramaswamy, M. Chui, T. Allas, P. Dahlström, N. Henke, & M. Trench (2017), "Artificial intelligence: The next digital frontier?" *McKinsey Global Institute*, accessed from https://www.mckinsey.com/~/media/McKinsey/Industries/Advanced%20Electronics/Our%20Insights/How%20artificial%20intelligence%20can%20deliver%20real%20value%20to%20companies/MGI-Artificial-Intelligence-Discussion-paper.ashx.
38. Manyika, J., S. Lund, M. Chui, J. Bughin, J. Woetzel, P. Batra, R. Ko, & S. Sanghvi (2017), "Jobs lost, jobs gained: What the future of work will mean for jobs, skills, and wages," *McKinsey Global Institute*, accessed from https://www.mckinsey.com/featured-insights/future-of-work/jobs-lost-jobs-gained-what-the-future-of-work-will-mean-for-jobs-skills-and-wages.

39. Kumar, V., B. Rajan, R. Venkatesan, & J. Lecinski (2019), "Understanding the role of artificial intelligence in personalized engagement marketing," *California Management Review*, *61*(4), 135–155.
40. Huang, M. H., & R. T. Rust (2021), "A strategic framework for artificial intelligence in marketing," *Journal of the Academy of Marketing Science*, *49*, 30–50.
41. Jordan, M. I., & T. M. Mitchell (2015), "Machine learning: Trends, perspectives, and prospects," *Science*, *349*(6245), 255–260; Ansari, A., Y. Li, & J. Z. Zhang (2018), "Probabilistic topic model for hybrid recommender systems: A stochastic variational Bayesian approach," *Marketing Science*, *37*(6), 987–1008.
42. Simonson, I. (2005), "Determinants of customers' responses to customized offers: Conceptual framework and research propositions," *Journal of Marketing*, *69*(1), 32–45.
43. Wind, J., & A. Rangaswamy (2001), "Customerization: The next revolution in mass customization," *Journal of Interactive Marketing*, *15*(1), 13-32.
44. Pansari, A., & V. Kumar (2017), "Customer engagement: The construct, antecedents, and consequences," *Journal of the Academy of Marketing Science*, 1–18.
45. Van Doorn, J., K. N. Lemon, V. Mittal, S. Nass, D. Pick, P. Pirner, & P. C. Verhoef (2010), "Customer engagement behavior: Theoretical foundations and research directions," *Journal of Service Research*, *13*(3), 253–266.
46. Kumar, V., & A. Pansari (2016), "Competitive advantage through engagement," *Journal of Marketing Research*, *53*(4), 497–514.
47. Kumar, V. (2021). *Intelligent marketing: Employing new age technologies*. Sage Publications.
48. Kumar, V., B. Rajan, R. Venkatesan, & J. Lecinski (2019), "Understanding the role of artificial intelligence in personalized engagement marketing," *California Management Review*, *61*(4), 135–155.
49. Beath, C., I. Becerra-Fernandez, J. Ross, & J. Short (2012), "Finding value in the information explosion," *MIT Sloan Management Review*, *53*(4), 18.
50. Accenture (2018), "2018 Personalization Pulse Check," *Accenture*, accessed from https://www.accenture.com/t20180503T034117Z__w__/us-en/_acnmedia/PDF-77/Accenture-Pulse-Survey.pdf%23zoom=50.
51. Karp, P. D. (2016), "Can we replace curation with information extraction software?" *Database*, 2016.

52. Campaign (2018), "Human creativity v machine creativity: When artificial intelligence gets creative," *Campaign*, June 14, 2018, accessed from https://www.campaignlive.co.uk/article/human-creativity-v-machine-creativity-when-artificial-intelligence-gets-creative/1485063.
53. Holt, K. (2019), "McCormick hands over its spice R&D to IBM's AI," *Engadget.com*, February 4, accessed from https://www.engadget.com/2019/02/04/ibm-ai-food-seasonings-mccormick/.
54. McEleny, C. (2016), "McCann Japan hires first artificially intelligent creative director," *The Drum*, March 29, accessed from https://www.thedrum.com/news/2016/03/29/mccann-japan-hires-first-artificially-intelligent-creative-director.
55. Kumar, V., B. Rajan, R. Venkatesan, & J. Lecinski (2019), "Understanding the role of artificial intelligence in personalized engagement marketing," *California Management Review*, 61(4), 135–155.
56. Brynjolfsson, E., Y. J. Hu, & M. D. Smith (2006), "From niches to riches: Anatomy of the long tail," *MIT Sloan Management Review*, 47(4), 67–71.
57. Kumar, V. (2021). *Intelligent marketing: Employing new age technologies*. Sage Publications.
58. Chui, M., R. Roberts, L. Yee, E. Hazan, A. Singla, K. Smaje, A. Sukharevsky, & R. Zemmel (2023), "The economic potential of generative AI: The next productivity frontier," *McKinsey*, June 14, accessed from https://www.mckinsey.com/capabilities/mckinsey-digital/our-insights/the-economic-potential-of-generative-ai-the-next-productivity-frontier#work-and-productivity.
59. Das, A. C., M. Gomes, I. L. Patidar, G. Phalin, R. Sawhney, & R. Thomas (2023), "The next frontier of customer engagement: AI-enabled customer service," *McKinsey*, March 27, accessed from https://www.mckinsey.com/capabilities/operations/our-insights/the-next-frontier-of-customer-engagement-ai-enabled-customer-service.
60. The global market for AI in social media in 2022 is estimated at USD 2.2 billion and is projected to reach USD 13.3 billion by 2030, growing at a CAGR of 25.1% (Research and Markets 2023). The fastest-growing geographic regions are the USA, China, Japan, and Canada.
61. A Deloitte global survey found that 35% of global companies in the developed markets already have a comprehensive, companywide AI strategy, with others planning to have such a strategy soon (Loucks, J., S. Hupfer, D. Jarvis, & T. Murphy [2019], "Future in the balance? How countries are pursuing an AI advantage," *Deloitte Insights*,

May, accessed from https://www2.deloitte.com/content/dam/Deloitte/lu/Documents/public-sector/lu-global-ai-survey.pdf). This shows that it is important to investigate and have ready the implementation specifics for a successful AI implementation.
62. Pasick, A. (2015), "The magic that makes Spotify's Discover Weekly playlists so damn good," *Quartz*, December 21, accessed from https://qz.com/571007/the-magic-that-makes-spotifys-discover-weekly-playlists-so-damn-good/.
63. Intelligence Node (2018), "3 retail leaders using big data & AI to drive efficiency," *Intelligence Node*, September 27, 2018, accessed from http://www.intelligencenode.com/blog/3-retail-leaders-using-big-data-ai-to-drive-efficiency/.
64. Williams, R. (2018), "Uber Eats harnesses AI for $6B in annual bookings," *Mobile Marketer*, October 3, accessed from https://www.mobilemarketer.com/news/uber-eats-harnesses-ai-for-6b-in-annual-bookings/538724/.
65. Estopace, E. (2018), "Beyond FIGS: How Juntos Localizes into Bemba, Swahili, Tagalog, Arabic and more," *Slator*, April 2, accessed from https://slator.com/features/localization-a-force-multiplier-in-juntos-financial-conversation-platform/.
66. Baruah, A. (2018), "Artificial intelligence at India's top eCommerce firms—Use CASes from Flipkart, Myntra, and Amazon India," *techemergence*, February 1, accessed from https://www.techemergence.com/artificial-intelligence-at-indias-top-ecommerce-firms-use-caes-from-flipkart-myntra-and-amazon-india/.
67. Low, A. (2018), "China is using adorable robot teachers in kindergartens," *cnet*, August 29, accessed from https://www.cnet.com/news/china-is-using-adorable-robot-teachers-in-kindergartens/.
68. Lyall, N. (2018), "Where does AI fit into the future of advertising and marketing?" *Ogilvy*, September 14, accessed from https://www.ogilvy.com/feed/where-does-ai-fit-into-the-future-of-advertising-and-marketing/.
69. Kumar, V., B. Rajan, R. Venkatesan, & J. Lecinski (2019), "Understanding the role of artificial intelligence in personalized engagement marketing," *California Management Review*, 61(4), 135–155.
70. Day, G. S. (2011), "Closing the marketing capabilities gap," *Journal of Marketing*, 75(4), 183–195; Martin, J. E. & M. Jeanne (2004), "The concept of information overload: A review of literature from organization science, accounting, marketing, MIS, and related disciplines," *The Information Society*, 20(5), 325–344.

71. Cohen, W. M. & D. A. Levinthal (2000), "Absorptive capacity: A new perspective on learning and innovation," *Administrative Science Quarterly*, *35*(1), 128–152.
72. Helfat, C. E. & S. G. Winter (2011), "Untangling dynamic and operational capabilities: Strategy for the (N) ever-changing world," *Strategic Management Journal*, *32*(11), 1243–1250.
73. Cepeda, G. & D. Vera (2007), "Dynamic capabilities and operational capabilities: A knowledge management perspective," *Journal of Business Research*, *60*(5), 426–437.

4

Transformative Marketing with Generative Artificial Intelligence

Overview

Generative Artificial Intelligence, Generative AI (or GAI), is a form of AI that creates new content in text, imagery, audio, video, or synthetic data based on what it learned from the existing content. The process of learning from the existing content is training, which results in creating a statistical model. Generative AI uses the statistical model to predict an expected response, thus generating new content. The world today has come a long way since traditional programming, where one had to write hard code the rules for the model. Since then, there has been the advent of neural networks, which consist of many layers of neurons that help them process more complex patterns and provide outputs. Generative AI is a subset of deep learning, that uses supervised, unsupervised, and semi-supervised machine learning methods to generate new data instances based on the learned probability distribution of existing data. The output is natural language like speech, text, image, audio, and video. Interestingly, previous models were not flexible with the input type, whereas GAI takes prompts in the form of text, speech, etc.

Relatively new to the marketing landscape, GAI's market is expected to rise significantly, from 14 billion US dollars in 2020 to nearly 900 billion US dollars in 2023 and more than 1.3 trillion US dollars in 2032.[1] This is due to an explosion of generative AI tools in recent years such as Bard by Google, ChatGPT by OpenAI, and Midjourney by Midjourney, Inc., among others. GAI is receiving increasing attention from all business industries and functions, with nearly all industries around the world having tried a generative AI tool at least once in 2023.[2] Table 4.1 presents how GAI is used by industry worldwide.

The employment of GAI tools has become increasingly pervasive in various business functions. As is the case with AI, the business functions that exhibit the most common use of GAI are marketing and sales, product, and service development, and service operations, which include customer care and back-office support. For instance, within the marketing function, the common uses of GAI include developing copies for emails and social media messages, images for social media and websites, scripts for chatbots and marketing materials, creating early drafts of marketing documents, messaging for personalized marketing campaigns, and summarizing text documents, among others.[3] As the adoption of newer GAI tools gains momentum, reports indicate that these same business functions exhibit the highest usage of these tools.

Table 4.1 Representation of how GAI is used by industry worldwide

Characteristic	Regularly used for work (%)	Regularly used for work and outside of work (%)	Regularly used outside of work (%)	Have tried at least once (%)	No exposure (%)	Don't know (%)
Advanced industries	5	11	16	47	15	5
Business, legal, and professional	7	16	13	41	21	2
Consumer goods/retail	7	11	12	40	26	4
Energy and materials	6	8	15	50	19	3
Financial services	8	16	18	41	14	4
Healthcare, pharma, and medical products	6	10	17	44	15	7
Technology, media, and telecom	14	19	19	37	9	3

Source McKinsey & Company. (August 1, 2023). Share of respondents using generative AI at work or outside of work in 2023, by industry [Graph]. In *Statista*. Retrieved October 10, 2023, from https://www.statista.com/statistics/1407402/generative-ai-use-by-industry/.

The above trends indicate that the rise of GAI has undoubtedly imprinted its transformative footprint in the evolving landscape of organizational functions. Among the numerous domains witnessing this transformation, marketing emerges as a standout beneficiary of this cutting-edge innovation. This chapter will investigate the multifaceted effects of GAI on marketing paradigms.

This chapter is organized in the following manner. First, a brief history of the origin of GAI is presented, followed by a definition of GAI (from a marketing standpoint), and a discussion of related processes that are linked to GAI. In this regard, some practical applications of such AI processes are presented. Next, some marketing applications of GAI focusing on understanding customer needs, revisiting firm capabilities to integrate GAI, designing GAI-focused marketing mix strategies, driving customer engagement through GAI, and designing digital strategies with GAI are discussed. Finally, the future of GAI for the marketing industry is envisioned through specific marketing actions and initiatives that show a lot of promise.

Origin, Definition, and Classification of Generative AI

Origin

Generative AI finds its roots in the broad areas of AI and machine learning (ML). Whereas AI and ML have been in existence since the mid-20th century, GAI began its journey in the 1960s. An early development of a GAI tool was the ELIZA chatbot which could simulate conversations with humans based on prior text received. The introduction of Generative Adversarial Networks (GANs) by Ian Goodfellow and colleagues in 2014 was a watershed moment in the evolution of generative models. This novel framework pits two neural networks against each other, one to generate data and the other to distinguish between generated and real data, resulting in highly realistic outputs. Since then, the field has grown to include a wide range of approaches and models that contribute to the generative aspect of AI.[4] Subsequent advancements in computing power and data availability led to the development of GAI models such as Markov chains and neural networks.

During the late 1990s and early 2000s, with the availability of diverse datasets, improved computing processes, and an increased body of knowledge, GAI saw developments such as generative adversarial networks (GANs) that can be used to generate realistic images, text, and other forms of content.

More recently, additional research and development in this area have led to the development of richer and more advanced GAI tools such as DALL-E, and GPT (Generative Pre-trained Transformer) models. These models can generate incredibly realistic and creative content, which has led to a wide range of new applications for GAI.

In recent academic discourse, the rise of GAI has been recognized as a pioneering catalyst for a comprehensive embracement of AI within corporate spheres.[5,6] Marketing emerges as a particularly favored beneficiary as organizations embrace this cutting-edge innovation across all functional terrains.[7] One could argue, with substantial evidence, that the brilliance of GAI truly shines in industries such as marketing and advertising, where impeccable content becomes an essential bridge between corporations and their various stakeholders.

Additionally, literature has established that digital intervention enables firms to curate communications, ultimately enriching the customer journey.[8] Such enhancements are precursors to improved brand interactions[9] and associated increases in allegiance and institutional performance. Anisin[10] offers a compelling argument contending that GAI's impact dwarfs that of its digital predecessors, owing primarily to its ability to simulate humanlike content, providing marketers with a plethora of powerful tools for content refinement.

To marketers, GAI is more than just an efficiency tool; it is a transformative ally.[11] Beyond mere financial prudence and accelerated tasks, the wonders of GAI enable brands to transcend traditional boundaries, providing unparalleled personalization unfathomable by manual endeavors alone. With its ability to communicate dynamically, GAI provides a combination of tailored visuals, text, and predictive insights, paving the way for cost-effective, moment-specific customization.

Definition

Generative AI is a subset of artificial intelligence algorithms and models that can generate new content that is like but not identical to the data on which they were trained. These algorithms do more than just analyze input data; they can also generate entirely new data instances—whether text, images, sound, or even video—that can be difficult to distinguish from genuine human-generated data. The term "generative" refers to the creation of something new rather than the processing or analysis of existing data. GAI has been defined on similar lines by various organizations (see Table 4.2).

We asked ChatGPT to define GAI, it provided the following definition— "Generative AI, short for Generative Artificial Intelligence, refers to a subset

Table 4.2 Definition of Generative AI offered by various organizations

Organization	Definition
Gartner	"...AI techniques that learn a representation of artifacts from data, and use it to generate brand-new, unique artifacts that resemble but don't repeat the original data."[12]
IBM	"...deep-learning models that can generate high-quality text, images, and other content based on the data they were trained on."[13]
Marketing Accountability Standards Board (MASB)	"...broad category of artificial intelligence (AI) that is meant to generate something new based on preexisting materials and user-defined parameters. The output of generative AI can be in the form of new text, images, audio, video, and combinations of these."[14]
World Economic Forum	"...a category of AI algorithms that generate new outputs based on the data they have been trained on."[15]

of artificial intelligence (AI) techniques and models that can generate new data that is like, or in some cases indistinguishable from, data that could have been created by humans. Generative AI models are designed to understand patterns and structures within existing data and then generate new data samples that adhere to those patterns. These models can produce various types of content, including text, images, audio, and more."

Despite the variations in the definitions, all the definitions seem to agree that GAI is a type of AI that can create new things. Further, GAI is a powerful tool with a wide range of potential applications, and based on subsequent advancements in technology more innovative and exciting uses for GAI can emerge in the future.

Classification

Generative AI is classified broadly based on the type of content it generates and the methods it employs to generate this content. Table 4.3 provides some examples of classifications.

Based on the classification of GAI, different types of GAI models vary on the inputs and outputs of the model. We discuss four broad types of GAI models here. First, text-to-image models are trained on a large set of images

Table 4.3 Classification of GAI

Classification	Meaning
By type of content	
Text	Models such as the GPT (Generative Pretrained Transformer) series, can write essays, code, poetry, or translate languages
Images	GANs (Generative Adversarial Networks) are well-known for producing realistic images ranging from human faces to art
Audio	Models that can generate music, mimic voices, or create sound effects are known as audio models
Video	AI can create video clips or modify existing footage to create new scenes or effects
By methodology	
Generative Adversarial Networks (GANs)	Composed of two networks, a generator, and a discriminator, that improve through competition with one another
Variational Autoencoders (VAEs)	Generate data using a probabilistic approach by learning a latent space
Transformer Models	By leveraging attention mechanisms, these models are especially effective at generating coherent and contextually relevant text sequences
Autoregressive Models	Learn to generate data one piece at a time and predict the next item in a sequence
By application	
Content Creation	For the creation of creative design, literature, and digital art
Data Augmentation	When data is scarce or imbalanced, data augmentation is used to improve datasets in machine learning
Simulation and Modeling	Simulation and modeling are techniques for creating realistic environments for training and research

Source Authors' compilation

Table 4.4 Types of GAI models

Generative AI models	Applications	Examples
Text-to-image	• Image generation • Image editing	• Stable Diffusion • LimeWire • Jasper • Canva
Text-to-text	• Translation • Content editing/Writing	• Quillbot • GPT-3 • Byword • HiveMind
Text-to-video, text-to-3D	• Video generation • Video editing • Game assets	• Synthesys • Synthesia • InVideo • Colossyan
Text-to-task	• Software agents • Virtual assistants • Automation	• Taskade • TextCortex • Otter • Alexa

Source Authors' compilation

and each image is captioned with a short text description. These models are applied for image generation and image editing. Open AI's Dall-E is an example of the text-to-image model. Second, text-to-text models take a natural language input and produce a text output. The models are trained to learn the mapping between a pair of texts. Third, text-to-video models generate a video representation from a text input, where the input can range from a single sentence to a full script. Relatedly, text-to-3D models are models that create three-dimensional objects that correspond to a user's text description. Finally, text-to-task models are trained to perform a specific task or action based on text input. The task could range from answering a question, performing a search, making a prediction, etc. The applications of these models are presented in Table 4.4.

As new models and applications are developed, generative AI's classification is likely to become more nuanced. It represents not only a technical accomplishment but also a paradigm shift in how we think about machines' creative capacities and their potential to emulate—and sometimes even enhance—human creativity.

Some Commercial Applications of GAI

The commercial applications of GAI tools find their origins with the commencement of Open AI. Open AI is an AI research and deployment company that focuses on ensuring that AGI, or artificial general intelligence (i.e., systems that are generally smarter than humans), benefits all of humanity. Founded in 2015 by notable entrepreneurs from the technology industry, Open AI is involved in building safe and beneficial AGI and has been transforming work and creativity with AI. Open AI offers a variety of models, such as ChatGPT (Chat Generative Pre-Trained Transformer), Dall-E, Whisper, etc. ChatGPT is an AI chatbot technology that can process natural human language and generate a response. It interacts with the users in a conversational way—a dialogue format that makes it possible to answer follow-up questions, admit mistakes, and reject inappropriate requests.

OpenAI has been making significant advancements in natural language processing technology.[16] OpenAI is currently working on GPT-4, which is based on a model trained on 1.7 trillion parameters. GPT-4 is expected to have advanced reasoning, complex instruction, and enhanced creativity. It will also be able to adapt to user intention and requests to reduce the likelihood of harmful output.

Another innovation from Open AI is DALL-E, which is a text-to-image generative AI model. DALL-E allows users to create images by giving text-to-graphic prompts. It is a neural network that can produce new and often surreal images in different styles as per the user's prompts. The name 'DALL-E' is a combination of Spanish surreal artist Salvador Dali and the fictional robot Wall-E from Disney. The technology uses deep learning models alongside GPT-3 to understand natural language prompts and generate new images. Initially, DALL-E generated images using Discreet Variational Auto-Encode (dVAE). However, DALL-E 2 improved on the methods used and was able to generate more high-end, photorealistic images.[17] DALL-E 3 is built on ChatGPT and is currently available to ChatGPT plus subscribers.

Google AI developed its large language model (LLM) chatbot, Bard. This model is based on the Language Model for Dialogue Applications (LaMDA), an AI language model that can allow users to engage in conversational AI. This model is trained on a massive dataset of text and code—it can generate text, translate languages, and write different kinds of creative content. Bard's first version, launched in February 2023, uses a lighter model of LaMDA, requiring less computing power to handle more concurrent users. In addition to LaMDA, Bard extracts data from the web to provide its users with various services, including creating different types of content, summarizing texts, and translating between multiple languages. All of this is offered in a minimalist interface through a text-based chat. Bard possesses a remarkable ability to participate in multi-turn conversations, in which the AI can sustain a consistent topic and persona throughout multiple interactions with a human user. This quality makes Bard especially valuable for applications like chatbots and virtual assistants. Some of the popular uses of Bard include content writing, creative writing, marketing material copy generation, and student writing, among others. Table 4.5 provides a comparison between the above-mentioned three GAI tools.

To conclude the overview of GAI, the following three vignettes present the evolution of GAI tools that are influencing many aspects of business and society.

- *Healthcare*: Developing new pharmaceutical products is time-intensive and costly. The entire process (from ideation to launch) could take several

Table 4.5 A comparison of the popular GAI models—ChatGPT, DALL-E, & Bard

	ChatGPT	DALL-E	Bard
What is it?	AI-powered chatbot that can engage in humanlike conversations with users	AI model that can create realistic images from text descriptions. It can create realistic images from text descriptions	Large language model chatbot developed by Google AI. It can engage in humanlike conversations with users
How does it work?	Uses natural language processing and machine learning to understand and respond to user queries	Trained on a massive dataset of text and images, it can generate images in a variety of styles—realistic photographs, paintings, and cartoons	Uses more recent data sources—includes information from the internet, scientific papers, mathematical expressions, and source code that other tools do not
Popular uses	Customer support, personal assistance, education, etc.	Art, design, education, and entertainment	Research, education, creative writing, customer service, etc.
Ideal for	Generating creative text formats (poems, codes, scripts)	Generating images of things that do not exist in the real world. It can generate realistic images that are difficult to distinguish from real photographs	Answering factual questions and providing up-to-date information to user queries

Source Authors' compilation

years with firms incurring an average investment of USD 1.5 billion.[18] With Generative AI, firms can automate time-intensive tasks such as drafting clinical trial communications, translating documents into different languages for different markets, and so on. For instance, Bayer has partnered with Google Cloud's Vertex AI and Med-PaLM 2 to enhance their clinical trial process. Moreover, the company is also using Google Cloud's Tensor Processing Units (TPUs) to perform high volumes of calculations that can deliver new insights into the drug discovery process.[19] Similarly, Microsoft is making a big push with GAI-based tools that can help healthcare organizations deliver better healthcare. For instance, Microsoft is developing the Azure AI Health Bot that can pull information from a health organization's internal data and integrate data from external sources to help treat specific diseases and identify internal protocols and processes. This bot can also be used by patients to ask clarifying questions about their symptoms and medical terms they encounter. The company has additional GAI-based initiatives that focus on all stakeholders in the healthcare system such as patients, doctors, nurses, administrators, clinicians, and medical specialists, among others.[20]

- *Fashion:* The partnership between designers and GAI deals with leveraging AI's capability to process datasets aligned to the designer's imagination.[21] The technology holds a lot of promise to be integrated across the industry (e.g., merchandising, product development, distribution, pricing), where GAI could enrich product ideation. Leveraging the technology's ability to mine through data, understand past product lines, and gain inspirational imagery and style could lead to augmenting the professionals' ideas.
- *Education:* A UNESCO global survey of over 450 schools and universities found that fewer than 10% have developed institutional policies and/or formal guidance concerning the use of generative AI applications. This is a telling finding considering the rapid gains made by GAI in many aspects of human lives. In this regard, the UNESCO report contends that education is a fundamentally human experience that relies on social interaction to be effective and impactful. Academic studies have also cautioned about the challenges that this tool throws to educators while identifying the opportunities that GAI can serve.[22,23] By promoting greater awareness of these applications, educators can effectively incorporate them into classroom instruction. Additionally, guiding students in discussing the benefits and drawbacks of AI can lead to a more comprehensive integration of this technology into education. Ultimately, this approach would enable educational institutions to develop a deeper understanding of GAI's capabilities

and limitations, which can help them navigate a future where GAI is likely to play an increasingly dominant role.

Generative AI in the Marketing 5.0 World

Marketing in the realm of GAI has revolutionized the way businesses promote their products and services. By harnessing the power of AI, marketers can create dynamic and engaging content that resonates with their target audience. This cutting-edge technology enables marketers to automate various aspects of their campaigns, from content creation to customer segmentation. By leveraging GAI, businesses can streamline their marketing efforts, saving time and resources while maximizing their reach. Furthermore, GAI algorithms can analyze vast amounts of data to identify patterns and trends, providing marketers with valuable insights into consumer behavior and preferences. Expanding on the Marketing 5.0 concept discussed in Chapter 2, this section presents how GAI operates in the Marketing 5.0 world. Particularly, this section discusses five examples of where GAI is applied through the lens of Marketing 5.0 and establishes how such actions can also bode well for humanity.

Data-Driven Marketing Using GAI

The emergence of GAI has made the marketing function a highly sought-after area due to its capacity to interact with customers, customize content, and decrease expenses and intricacies. Marketers are now adopting a data-driven approach to utilize this technology in customer service, with the aim of personalizing customer experience, increasing sales and retention, and providing support to frontline staff. Particularly, GAI enables companies to analyze user data, purchase history, browsing behavior, and demographic information to create customized messages that resonate with individuals. This approach allows for high levels of personalization, which can help build trust and rapport with customers over time. Furthermore, companies are leveraging generative AI to produce content that is well-structured and optimized for search engines, improving their online visibility and reach.[24]

Consider the case of Coca-Cola's GAI initiative. In March 2023, Coca-Cola launched a GAI initiative that provided fans with the opportunity to explore numerous branded elements. These elements included the iconic Coca-Cola contour bottle, the Spencerian script logo, and various symbols from Coke's advertising history, such as the Coca-Cola Santa Claus and Polar Bear. This initiative served as a platform for AI-powered experimentation and creative exploration, allowing fans to engage with these elements in new and innovative ways. The fan creations led to the designing of out-of-home digital art meant for billboards in New York and London. The company reported that the GAI campaign saw nearly 120,000 image creations within 11 days, all without utilizing paid media, with users spending an average of eight minutes on the platform. The success of this initiative has provided confidence to the company to roll out more such initiatives.[25] Through granting access to its proprietary data and brand assets, Coca-Cola facilitated an environment where participants could generate impactful results and establish a reference point for future generations of AI developers.

Predictive Marketing Using GAI

Predictive marketing using generative AI involves using algorithms to analyze data from a variety of sources, including social media, search engines, and customer behavior. This data is then used to create models that can predict future trends and consumer behavior. These models can be used to create targeted marketing campaigns that are more likely to be successful, as they are based on data-driven insights rather than guesswork. It can also help identify trends, forecast behavior, predict any impending challenges, and devise solutions for them.

Consider the case of Jet Blue. The US-based airline has collaborated with ASAPP, a technology vendor, to adopt a pre-packaged generative AI solution that enhances and automates its chat channel operations. This implementation has significantly benefited the airline's contact center, enabling them to save an average of 280 seconds per chat. Consequently, this translates to a remarkable 73,000 hours of agent time saved in just one quarter. With this newfound efficiency, agents now have more availability to assist customers with nuanced issues, ultimately improving the overall customer service experience.[26] In the future, this platform will possess the ability to learn from customer sentiment and the frequency of inquiries to provide decision-makers with practical recommendations concerning customer-facing actions and processes.

Contextual Marketing Using GAI

Contextual marketing is the activity of identifying and profiling as well as providing customers with personalized interactions by utilizing technology interfaces in the physical space. It is the backbone that allows marketers to perform one-to-one marketing in real-time, depending on the customer context. By understanding the context in which consumers engage with their brand, businesses can create highly personalized and timely marketing campaigns. Whether it is delivering targeted ads based on browsing history or sending personalized recommendations based on previous purchases, GAI empowers marketers to deliver seamless and tailored experience to each customer.

Consider the area of contextual advertising. Nowadays, advertising and media companies are developing context-driven marketing messages that speak directly to the consumer's currently exhibited tastes and preferences. For instance, Instreamatic, an audio marketing platform, has recently introduced a new product for connected TV.[27] This innovative offering generates various audio versions for a single creative while keeping the visuals unchanged. Leveraging the power of AI, Instreamatic replaces specific details in the voiceover, such as mentioning the viewer's current streaming service or TV show, as well as highlighting promotional codes, products, or deals available at specific store locations. This dynamic approach enhances the personalized experience for viewers and enables advertisers to tailor their messages more effectively. The aim is to swiftly produce numerous personalized versions of the same advertisement, potentially reaching hundreds or even thousands of variations within seconds.

In this regard, contextual AI is quickly gaining popularity among advertisers and is often seen as an answer to online privacy, intrusiveness, and irrelevant ads. Seedtag's contextual AI platform, Lin, empowers brands and agencies to develop customized creative content that aligns with the context of the surrounding page-level content.[28] This innovative solution enables advertisers to optimize their ads to seamlessly integrate with the online environment. By leveraging deep learning, computer vision, and NLP capabilities, Lin comprehends the desired contexts for the client's ad campaign and generates prompts to enhance the original creative, resulting in a more effective outcome. With the ability to create new creatives based on audience insights and campaign objectives, this AI generative platform offers endless possibilities while saving valuable time and resources.

Augmented Marketing Using GAI

Augmented Marketing, powered by GAI, has opened new possibilities for marketers to enhance their campaigns. With the ability to analyze vast amounts of data and consumer behavior patterns, generative AI algorithms can generate creative and compelling content that captures the attention of potential customers. This technology enables marketers to create personalized advertisements, product recommendations, and even interactive experiences that cater to individual preferences and interests. Moreover, with the availability of augmented reality (AR) and virtual reality (VR) devices, the integration of GAI with such devices is expected to bring unique personal experiences to users.

Consider the case of social anxiety. Many people experience awkwardness or even exhibit social anxiety when engaging in highly involved conversations such as in social events, public speaking engagements, or preparing for job interviews, among others. RizzGPT is an innovative augmented reality eyepiece developed by students at Stanford University to address this issue.[29] This eyewear device combines AI and augmented reality to assist individuals during difficult conversations. The eyepiece is equipped with a camera, a microphone, and an internal projector screen that displays words in front of the user's eye. During a conversation, RizzGPT uses its microphone to monitor the dialogue and transforms it into text. This text is then sent via GPT-4 and Whisper to generate appropriate responses based on the context of the questions asked. The response is displayed on the small monocle screen of the AR glasses after a short delay.[30]

This technology has the potential to revolutionize the way we communicate and interact with others. It can help individuals who struggle with social anxiety or have difficulty understanding others during conversations. The development of RizzGPT is a significant step forward in the field of augmented reality and AI, and it will be exciting to see how this technology evolves in the future. Bryan Chiang, the developer of RizzGPT, believes that advancements in technology and hardware can lead to more intelligent responses in a shorter amount of time. He cites examples of how the camera can be used to identify friends and provide relevant information or even help with ordering food at a restaurant by reading the menu and using GAI to suggest the best option. Chiang also mentions that there are many other possibilities for this technology and that the next generation will be even more impressive.[31]

Agile Marketing Using GAI

The rise of generative AI in marketing has led to an increase in GAI initiatives and budgets across various industries. However, as customer demands become more complex, companies must also possess organizational agility to adapt to changing market conditions. This requires the use of decentralized, cross-functional teams to quickly conceptualize, design, develop, and validate products and marketing campaigns. The integration of GAI into the agile marketing process can aid in achieving this goal.

For instance, Mitsui Chemicals, Inc. has successfully utilized GAI and IBM Watson to enhance its new application discovery process. By inputting over 5 million points of external big data, including patents, news, and SNS, into IBM Watson, Mitsui Chemicals has been able to efficiently analyze this data alongside a specific dictionary for their products. This has resulted in a significant increase in the volume of their unique dictionary, which has grown by approximately ten times.[32]

In addition to this, the efficiency of extracting new applications has also been improved by three times, allowing Mitsui Chemicals to discover new applications for their products that exceed human preconceptions and current knowledge. By utilizing the expertise of their specialists in the sales and business domain, Mitsui Chemicals has been able to analyze this big data in a way that is both agile and accurate, leading to the discovery of new applications that may have otherwise gone unnoticed.

One example of this is the discovery of a need for antifungal products in the local railway system, which was identified through SNS analysis. This led to sales activities for Mitsui Chemicals' antifungal products, demonstrating the real-world impact of their new application discovery process. Overall, Mitsui Chemicals' use of generative AI and IBM Watson has expanded the number of new applications discovered by approximately two times, highlighting the significant benefits of this innovative approach.[33]

Current Generative AI Applications in Marketing

Expanding the role of GAI beyond the marketing function, we can see that GAI is poised to transform roles and boost performance across business functions—sales and marketing, customer operations, and software development. In a worldwide survey by McKinsey, it was found that the top five professions that showed the most automation potential with and without GAI were educator and workforce training, business and legal professionals,

STEM professionals, community services, and creatives and arts management.[34] Table 4.6 provides the automation potential of GAI over non-GAI, by profession.

GAI aids marketers in various customer-related tasks and has the potential to be a part of the creative processes in marketing. For instance, in May 2023, WPP announced a partnership with Nvidia to transform the way brands create content. Through this partnership, they aim to integrate generative AI at a bigger and more tailored scale—enabling creative teams to produce high-quality content faster, with greater efficiency, and in full alignment with the client's brand.[35] Several studies have identified GAI as a promising technology that not only presents value-creating opportunities in marketing but also holds important implications for enhancing human lives. This section presents five specific application areas where GAI continues to help companies in developing marketing initiatives.

Table 4.6 Top 10 professions that show the most automation potential for GAI

Profession	Automation potential with Generative AI (%)	Automation potential without Generative AI (%)	Differential impact (%)
Educator and workforce training	54	15	39
Business and legal professionals	62	32	30
STEM professionals	57	28	29
Community services	65	39	26
Creatives and arts management	53	28	25
Office support	87	66	21
Managers	44	27	17
Health professionals	43	29	14
Customer service and sales	57	45	12
Property maintenance	38	29	9

Source McKinsey & Company. (June 14, 2023). Automation potential with and without generative artificial intelligence (AI) in the United States in 2023, by profession [Graph]. In *Statista*. Retrieved October 17, 2023, from https://www.statista.com/statistics/1411571/job-automation-potential-generative-ai/.

Understanding Customer Needs to Deploy GAI

Understanding customer needs using generative AI involves leveraging artificial intelligence techniques to extract valuable insights and information from customer data. Generative AI can play a significant role in this process by creating data, content, or responses that mimic humanlike creativity and understanding. Some of the customer-facing areas that can benefit from the use of GAI include the following:

- *Analyzing Customer Feedback*. Generative AI can be used to analyze customer feedback from surveys, social media, and other sources to identify common themes and trends. This information can then be used to understand customer needs and pain points. For instance, Amazon uses GAI to make it easy for customers to assess a product's review on Amazon's website. Using GAI, Amazon is testing an AI feature (limited to the US customers, as of this writing) to provide a short paragraph on the product detail page that highlights the product features and customer sentiment frequently mentioned across written reviews to help customers determine quickly whether a product is right for them. Figure 4.1 illustrates the concept currently being tested by Amazon. Such a feature will help customers better process the product feedback shared by other users, thereby ensuring the productive use of the customer review feature.

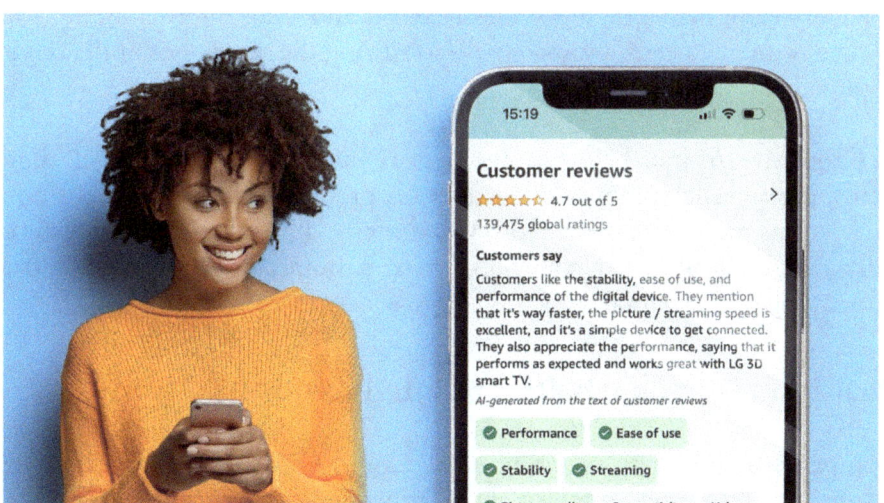

Fig. 4.1 Amazon's customer review highlights feature developed by GAI (*Source* Amazon.com, accessed from https://www.aboutamazon.com/news/amazon-ai/amazon-improves-customer-reviews-with-generative-ai)

- *Predicting Customer Behavior.* Generative AI can be used to predict customer behavior, such as which products they are likely to buy or when they are likely to churn. This information can be used to develop targeted marketing campaigns and improve customer retention. For instance, Stitch Fix is experimenting with GPT-3 and DALL-E 2 to help stylists quickly and accurately interpret reams of customer feedback and predict products that customers would be likelier to purchase. The GAI tool could analyze a customer's feedback, including email requests, product ratings, and online posts. Based on frequently used customer comments for a clothing item (for example, "good fit," "cool style," etc.) DALL-E could generate images of similar clothing items that the customer would likely want to purchase. The stylist could then find similar items in Stitch Fix's inventory and recommend them to that customer.[36]
- *Creating Personalized Experiences.* Generative AI can be used to create personalized experiences for customers, such as recommending products or services that they are likely to be interested in. This can help to improve customer satisfaction and loyalty. For instance, Morgan Stanley is developing a state-of-the-art AI-powered assistant that will revolutionize the way wealth managers navigate their extensive internal knowledge base. This next-generation assistant, built using the advanced GPT-4 technology, aims to provide quick and accurate responses to the complex queries of tens of thousands of wealth managers. By leveraging an innovative combination of search and content creation features, this GAI model will allow wealth managers to seamlessly access and tailor information for each client's unique needs, ultimately personalizing the experience of the service provided.[37]

Generative AI can help businesses gain valuable insights into customer needs. These insights can be used to tailor products, services, and customer interactions more effectively. However, it is crucial to use these insights ethically and responsibly, while also respecting customer privacy. Building trust in the process is essential.

Revisiting Firm Capabilities to Integrate GAI

Companies considering including GAI should revisit their capabilities that involve building the necessary skills, processes, and infrastructure within the organization. When integrating GAI into their capabilities, firms should consider the following aspects: (a) comprehending the potential applications of GAI for their business, (b) assembling a team with the necessary skills and expertise, (c) investing in the required infrastructure and tools, (d) collaborating with external experts, and (e) fostering a culture of experimentation and innovation.

When Levi Strauss embarked on integrating GAI into their business, they addressed the above five points. In 2021, the fashion clothing manufacturer took a step towards improving its employees' technological knowledge by launching a data science boot camp. The program aimed to train workers with limited technical know-how on how to use NATs in the company's design process. Upon completing the training, employees were equipped to create new AI tools that were relevant to their work. The company's objective with this program was to increase the diversity of employees with tech knowledge. This way, the company can uncover problems that employees from traditional technology backgrounds might otherwise miss. The program also helped different teams with different specializations, such as design and engineering teams, communicate effectively and find common ground. Additionally, Levi's also found that the program has improved employee retention.[38]

While GAI has the potential to be a disruptive technology, organizations need a clear strategy that enables them to move from experimentation to industrialization. To get the value organizations want from emerging technologies, they need a team to organize their responses to the emergence of GAI. Changing customer demands and market competition are among the largest factors influencing the need for GAI. When companies leverage the first-mover advantage, they can establish a competitive advantage and drive innovation at levels greater than ever seen.

Designing Marketing Mix Strategies with GAI

In a volatile environment where consumer preferences and demands change constantly, it can be challenging to determine a marketing strategy to execute. Today, AI allows businesses to examine these instant changes and adapt to the fast-paced environment. Breaking down AI's role in the marketing mix provides interesting insights into the extent to which it permeated through the organization.

Product: GAI can be a valuable tool for product development in various industries. It can help businesses create, improve, and innovate products more efficiently and effectively. It has brought a shift in the product development arena. The GAI models can be trained on a large dataset of customer reviews and product feedback to uncover common themes and potential areas of improvement. These insights could then be used to develop new products that are better at meeting customer needs. Some of how GAI can serve in the product development process include:

- To brainstorm and generate new product ideas or concepts. AI models can analyze market trends, consumer preferences, and existing products to suggest innovative concepts. Moreover, these models can be used to design product concepts and develop early prototypes.
- To analyze material properties and recommend the best materials and components for a product, considering factors like cost, durability, and sustainability.
- To help optimize the supply chain by predicting demand, managing inventory, and suggesting efficient distribution strategies.
- To implement quality control and testing. GAI can help identify defects or anomalies in products during the manufacturing process.
- To gather and analyze data from competitors, helping to identify gaps in the market and potential areas for product differentiation.
- To optimize product designs for energy efficiency and environmental sustainability, aligning with green initiatives.
- To facilitate collaboration among cross-functional teams working on product development, fostering idea sharing and innovation.

Several companies are including GAI in the product development process. For instance, Nike uses GAI to design new shoes that analyze data on millions of feet to create new shoe designs that are comfortable, stylish, and deliver the expected performance.[39] Similarly, Toyota uses GAI's text-to-image feature to design new electric vehicle models by using keywords such as "sleek", "SUV-like", and "modern" to arrive at an early prototype image of the car.[40] Also, Procter & Gamble uses GAI to manage their fragrance development process to have better control over digital scent creation, increasing speed to market and elevating processes across product development and design.[41]

Incorporating GAI into product development requires a thorough understanding of the specific industry and the needs of its customers. It is important to identify how GAI technologies can provide unique solutions. Collaboration between data scientists, engineers, and domain experts is essential to maximize the benefits of GAI in this context. To refine GAI models and improve product development processes over time, continuous monitoring and feedback loops are crucial.

Price: Generative AI can play a valuable role in making pricing decisions by providing data-driven insights, automating pricing strategies, and optimizing prices based on various factors. Additionally, this technology can allow firms to predict demand, set competitive prices, and develop personalized pricing strategies—thus leading to increased profits and improved customer experience offerings. Some of the key pricing decisions enabled by GAI include:

- Analyzing customer data, such as purchase history, browsing behavior, and feedback, to understand customer willingness to pay for different products and services. This information can then be used to set prices that are both profitable for the business and attractive to customers.
- Predicting customer demand for different products and services. This information can then be used to set prices that are aligned with expected demand.
- Optimizing prices in real-time based on factors such as customer demand, competitor pricing, and inventory levels. This can help businesses to maximize profits and minimize losses.

An example of using GAI for pricing decisions can be seen in the case of Uber Freight's GAI tool—Insights AI. Using LLMs, Insights AI can facilitate data discovery and data exploration and deliver intuitive insights from Uber Freight's vast store of transportation data. It can support transportation teams from very granular, tactical views to the most complex, strategic analyses. Shippers using this tool can realize insights on-demand using natural transportation language such as "What are my key service drivers?", "Why did this happen?", "What might happen in the future?", and "What should we do next?". Through this tool, the company is looking to significantly change the way logistics decisions are made across service, cost, routing guides, planning, and tracking.[42]

Place: Today's customers want everything, everywhere, and all the time. They desire a mix of traditional, remote, and self-service channels—with an increased preference for online ordering and reordering. Many players in today's markets are struggling to create value for their customers in a way that is strong enough to retain them. Some of how companies are considering the use of GAI are:

- To analyze data on factors such as population demographics, customer demand, and competition to identify potential locations for new businesses or facilities. This information can then be used to prioritize locations and to make more informed decisions about where to expand operations.
- To optimize the layout of existing businesses or facilities to improve efficiency and profitability. For example, generative AI can be used to identify

the best location for inventory storage, design a more efficient customer traffic flow, and optimize the placement of equipment.
- To analyze the impact of place decisions on customers and the community. For example, generative AI can be used to predict how customers will react to a new store location or to assess the impact of a new development on the local community.

Regarding the use of GAI to improve operational efficiency in business locations, many restaurants are considering the implementation of GAI tools to enhance their drive-thru business. Major chains such as McDonald's, Wendy's, Panera Bread, Carl's Jr., Hardee's, and Popeyes are already testing AI-powered ordering in their drive-thru formats.[43] Wendy's, for example, has recently launched FreshAI—a GAI tool that aims to improve the drive-thru ordering experience for customers. The tool uses an AI-powered voice experience and a digital menu board to make the interaction as natural as possible, much like speaking with a crew member. The system can provide quick answers to customer questions and take accurate food orders, even if the items are not phrased exactly as they appear on the menu. For instance, if a customer requests a large chocolate milkshake, the system understands that it should be a large chocolate Frosty®. Overall, the FreshAI tool enhances the drive-thru experience, ensuring that customers can place their orders with confidence, knowing that they will receive exactly what they asked for.[44]

Promotion: Perhaps the most "visible" part of GAI use in the marketing mix, GAI models are being trained on customer purchase history and interests to generate product recommendations, email campaigns, and social media posts. Some of the popular uses of GAI in this regard include:

- To analyze customer data, such as purchase history, browsing behavior, and feedback, to identify the customers who are most likely to be interested in specific promotions. This information can then be used to target promotions more effectively and to avoid wasting resources on customers who are unlikely to be interested.
- To personalize promotions for individual customers based on their interests, needs, and purchase history. This can help to make promotions more relevant and appealing to customers, which can lead to increased engagement and sales.
- To optimize promotion budgets by predicting the impact of different promotions on customer behavior. This information can then be used to allocate promotion budgets more effectively and to maximize the return on investment.

Beyond the typical recommendation engines and AI-curated suggestions, companies are coming up with interesting and novel uses of GAI. For instance, the Fashion Innovation Agency (FIA), a fashion company and platform, has been exploring the use of AI to design fashion shows and catwalks. Recently, FIA utilized AI prompt tools like Midjourney and Stable Diffusion. They trained the AI model to understand the looks of luxury brands that inspired them and applied the looks to one male model to create a photorealistic video. While they acknowledge the importance of human input in fashion experimentation, they believe that the new photorealistic opportunities will help to facilitate the mass adoption of digital fashion and promote fashion offerings.[45]

Driving Customer Engagement Through GAI

Customer engagement through GAI involves using artificial intelligence to create personalized, interactive, and meaningful interactions with your customers. It enhances customer experiences, fosters brand loyalty, and can lead to increased customer retention. Amazon, for instance, has been developing its GAI capabilities to make it easier for sellers on Amazon's website to create effective product titles, bullet points, and product descriptions. With this new feature, sellers only need to provide a brief description of their product, and Amazon will automatically generate high-quality content for them to review. This content can be refined further by the sellers or submitted directly to the Amazon catalog. The use of LLMs in this process will help sellers create listings that are more complete, consistent, and engaging for customers. Ultimately, this will lead to an improved shopping experience for customers.[46] Similarly, the Dubai Electricity and Water Authority (DEWA) has launched a GAI tool—Rammas—that provides 24/7 customer support and assists customers in finding answers to common questions and requests such as billing inquiries, outage information, and service requests. Touted as the first such implementation in the utility industry worldwide, Rammas has answered more than seven million inquiries as of April 2023.[47] Such uses of GAI are directed at improving and enhancing the quality of living and how people interact with brands. By creating personalized experiences, automating tasks, and improving customer satisfaction, GAI can help businesses to build stronger relationships with their customers and to increase customer loyalty.

Designing Digital Strategies with GAI

In today's digital landscape, having a strong online presence is crucial for businesses to succeed. With generative AI, companies can effectively design and implement digital strategies that improve various aspects of their online presence. This includes content creation, customer engagement, and other important elements that contribute to a successful online brand. By leveraging the power of AI, businesses can stay ahead of the competition and ensure their digital strategies are always up-to-date and effective. While companies are showing keen interest in GAI, it is still early days for using the technology in creating complete digital strategies. Some of the early initiatives employed by companies in designing digital strategies using GAI include:

- *Starting Small*. As companies explore the potential of GAI, they are taking a measured and careful approach. While eager to test the technology and its capabilities, they recognize the importance of avoiding a hasty shift toward full automation. Instead, they are cautiously implementing GAI to identify its strengths and limitations and to integrate it seamlessly into their existing operations. For example, the world-famous painting—The Milkmaid by Vermeer—has recently been in the news due to some new findings. Scientists have used X-ray technology to discover new objects hidden in the painting. Interestingly, Nestlé's famous yogurt, La Laitière, available in France, shares its name with the painting. Nestlé saw this as an opportunity to test their GAI capabilities. Nestlé's ad agency, Ogilvy Paris, used DALL-E 2 (outpainting tools) to reveal scenes beyond the borders of the painting's frame. With the help of prompts like "a kitchen wall with copper pans and tools painted by Vermeer," and through almost 1,000 iterations, Nestlé and the agency revealed an extended version of The Milkmaid, imagined by AI. This content generated a lot of national and global interest, despite having zero media budget. The video reached 15 million people and generated €700,000 of media value. France's major TV broadcasting network also covered the news segments about the extended version of The Milkmaid.[48] This is a successful example of how starting small can lead to impressive results.
- *Focusing on Personalized Campaigns*. Personalizing digital experiences for customers based on their interests and needs can be made easier with the help of Generative AI. This can lead to an improvement in customer engagement and loyalty, making it essential for businesses to implement GAI-driven personalization strategies. By tailoring content, recommendations, and user experiences based on individual preferences and behaviors,

businesses can effectively meet the needs of their customers. For instance, companies like Nestle, Unilever, and Mondelez are conducting early experiments regarding GAI's potential to generate advertisements that slash the time and money required for marketing campaigns. For example, WPP collaborated with Mondelez on a Cadbury campaign in India, featuring popular Bollywood actor Shah Rukh Khan. With the help of AI, they were able to generate more than 130,000 social media ads that were customized for specific local stores, without the need to produce any new ads. This was accomplished by using preexisting footage of Khan and AI-generated scripts. This resulted in 94 million video views while spending a fraction of a traditional ad budget.[49]

- *Using GAI to augment the ongoing efforts, not replace it.* As businesses continue to explore the potential of GAI, they are discovering that the technology can serve as a valuable addition to the team, enhancing human creativity and expertise. This approach not only allows employees to focus on more strategic initiatives but also enables them to leverage the unique strengths of GAI to achieve greater efficiency and productivity. By working in tandem with humans, GAI can help businesses unlock new opportunities and achieve their goals more effectively. For instance, Farfetch is an online marketplace that specializes in luxury fashion and beauty products. They utilized Phrasee, a GAI tool, to test various styles, tones, words, and phrases to determine the most effective language that resonates with their target audience. The goal was to use this information for email marketing campaigns. By using this tool, Farfetch was able to optimize subject lines for its broadcast and trigger campaigns, particularly those that included abandoned browse, basket, and wish list messaging.[50] Since implementing the tool, Farfetch has achieved impressive results.[51] As a result, Farfetch improved its brand by enhancing what makes it unique, rather than relying on GAI for a complete marketing overhaul.

Future of Generative AI in Marketing

Generative AI is becoming increasingly prevalent in our daily lives, and it is being used in various activities. The future of generative AI in marketing is expected to be transformative and full of opportunities. Technologies such as GPT-3 and advanced neural networks are already altering the marketing landscape, and their role is expected to expand significantly. Companies like Amazon (with its Amazon Bedrock) and Bloomberg (with BloombergGPT) are developing GAI models and platforms that have enormous potential to enhance human lives' quality and improve businesses' performance. GAI's technical capabilities, which include natural language processing, sensory perception, and social and emotional reasoning, are being developed at an accelerating rate. In the coming decades, generative AI is expected to reach human-level performance. The technology's ability to generate unique media, personalize content quickly, and take personalization to a new level is worth keeping an eye on. With that in mind, the following areas show significant promise for GAI's growth in marketing.

Ultra-Personalized Experiences

We are on the verge of a new era of marketing strategy, one in which ultra-personalized experiences reign supreme. Consider a marketing landscape in which personalized content strategies are not just a lofty ideal, but the norm. Marketers may soon find themselves crafting campaigns with razor-sharp precision, abandoning traditional audience segments in favor of campaigns that are uniquely tailored to individual users. This shift will be enabled by the introduction of generative AI, which meticulously customizes every campaign aspect by utilizing a user's specific behavioral patterns and profiles to generate bespoke graphics and content.[52]

This trend is expected to be accelerated by the integration of immersive and augmented reality (AR) experiences. Generative AI is on the verge of dynamically generating AR environments that incorporate not only a user's immediate surroundings but also their historical behavior and preferences. These adaptive AR experiences have the potential to forge a deep, resonant connection with the individual, resulting in AR campaigns that are not only visually stimulating but also personally meaningful.[53]

This paradigm shift also applies to seamless omnichannel engagement. Whether the touchpoint is a website, a social media platform, or a physical store, generative AI can ensure that a user's experience with a brand remains consistent through harmonized user interactions. Such integrated experiences form the foundation of a coherent omnichannel strategy, which is quickly becoming unavoidable in our interconnected world.

Personalized Marketing at Scale

In addition to ultra-personalization, the need for personalized marketing content for users at a large scale will be critical for the success of marketing campaigns.[54,55] Personalized marketing campaigns that cater to each customer's unique preferences and needs can be created using GAI. The campaigns can include personalized content such as social media posts, email campaigns, landing pages, and personalized experiences like chatbots and virtual assistants. Many global brands, such as Mondelez and PepsiCo, have rolled out personalized marketing communication strategies to promote their brand and engage with their customers.

For instance, PepsiCo and Synthesia worked together on their Messi Messages campaign, which featured personalized video messages from footballer Lionel Messi for their Lay's brand. PepsiCo was able to create 650 million tailored video versions in 8 languages using just 5 minutes of Messi footage to train an AI model. This proves how powerfully personalized AI can be. Additionally, Virgin Voyages used AI to design a customized cruise invitation tool that included their Chief Celebration Officer Jennifer Lopez. The platform enables prospective cruisers to produce AI-powered video invitations from Jennifer Lopez to invite family and friends to join their celebratory cruises.[56] Recognizing these advancements, startups like Typeface are emerging to provide dedicated GAI platforms for enterprises to create customized, on-brand content at scale. These platforms enable companies to leverage AI while maintaining data security, brand guidelines, and IP ownership. Looking ahead, more such startups and business platforms will emerge that will allow personalization on a large scale.

New Forms of Creative Content

Generative AI can be used to create new forms of creative content, such as images, videos, and text. This can help businesses create more engaging and effective marketing campaigns. The creation of unique types of creative content made possible by generative AI has transformed how we experience and interact with art, music, and literature. The limits of human creativity are pushed by this cutting-edge technology, which uses sophisticated algorithms to automatically develop creative and distinctive works.

In business, brands can venture into unexplored territory and create engaging works that defy accepted aesthetic rules by utilizing the potential of GAI. For instance, RTL Deutschland, Germany's largest privately held cross-media company, provides on-demand access to millions of videos, music albums, podcasts, audiobooks, and e-magazines through its streaming service—RTL+. The streaming platform largely relies on visuals to attract viewers. In this regard, the streaming service uses DALLE 2 to generate personalized images and artwork of the streaming content based on customers' interests. Additionally, the business is thinking about ways to leverage DALLE 2 to add images to content that does not already have any, including podcast episodes and audiobook scenes. Instead of repeatedly using the same generic podcast image, for instance, metadata from a podcast episode may be used to create a unique image to go with it. Similarly, for a person who is listening to an audiobook, DALLE 2 might also be used to create a special picture to go with each scene in each chapter.[57] Such initiatives have provided the company the ability to discover newer avenues of creativity on a previously unimaginable scale that is driven by the metadata about the kind of content a user has previously interacted with.

In the coming years, GAI can usher in a new era of creative content, offering brands access to a diverse set of marketing teams, creative teams, content creators, artists, musicians, and writers that can drive exploration and innovation. Using complex algorithms, this technology can enable the generation of visually stunning artworks, emotionally evocative music, and captivating narratives. As GAI continues to advance, it holds the potential to reshape the creative landscape, pushing the boundaries of human imagination and inspiring new forms of artistic expression.

Ethical Considerations for Developing Marketing Campaigns

Generative AI presents ethical considerations that warrant careful attention. A crucial aspect to consider is the impact of GAI on privacy. With increasing sophistication, this technology can produce remarkably realistic content (e.g., synthetic datasets, and computer-generated artwork). Consequently, concerns arise regarding the potential misuse of GAI for malicious purposes, such as disseminating misinformation or manipulating public opinion. Therefore, it is imperative to address the ethical implications of GAI concerning privacy and establish necessary safeguards to safeguard individuals from potential harm.

For instance, consider the development of GAI-generated content. The ownership and protection of GAI-generated works remain uncertain as companies across the globe continue to adopt this technology. For example, the US Copyright Office has issued guidance to clarify when artistic works created with the help of AI are copyright-eligible.[58] Accordingly, the agency contends that the majority of widely used AI systems, including Midjourney, ChatGPT, and DALL-E 2, are not capable of producing copyrightable work. This is because "…the generative AI technologies currently available, users do not exercise ultimate creative control over how such systems interpret *prompts* and generate material. Instead, these *prompts* function more like instructions to a commissioned artist—they identify what the prompter wishes to have depicted, but the machine determines how those instructions are implemented in its output" (p. 4).[59] However, the policy notes that this "does not mean that technological tools cannot be part of the creative process" (p. 4),[60] and requires copyright applicants to disclose the inclusion of AI-created material in their application. While India follows a similar approach to that of the United States in this regard,[61] specific laws for copyrighting AI-generated content are yet to be established in the European Union and are processed on a case-by-case basis.[62] Therefore, there is a lack of clarity across nations on how to address the copyright issue arising from GAI-inspired works.

Recognizing this, companies have started recognizing the need to account for the ethical aspects and are implementing appropriate measures. For instance, Mars, the pet food manufacturer, is using GAI to help them "…predict whether cats and dogs could develop chronic kidney disease; speeding up the sequencing of pet genomes to provide individualized nutrition and care; and unlocking efficiencies in our manufacturing operations through digital twin technology".[63] In doing so, the company has realized the ethical risks involved. To address the potential ethical risks, the organization has implemented a comprehensive approach by forming an enterprise working team. This team is dedicated to developing a robust framework of policies and governance about the utilization of GAI. Additionally, strategic alliances with partners such as Microsoft and reputable non-governmental organizations like the Responsible AI Institute help the company further enhance its efforts in ensuring responsible and ethical implementation of AI technologies.

Overall, ethical considerations surrounding GAI require a multi-stakeholder approach, involving developers, organizations, regulators, and the public. It is essential to balance innovation with ethical principles, ensuring that GAI technologies benefit society while minimizing potential risks and harms.

In addition to the above-mentioned specific examples, it is also possible that GAI could lead to the realization of entirely new aspects that we cannot even imagine today. As GAI continues to develop and become more sophisticated, it is likely to have a major impact on the way that marketing is done in the future.

Key Terms and Related Conceptualizations

Generative Adversarial Networks (GANs)	A framework that pits two neural networks against each other, one to generate data and the other to distinguish between generated and real data, resulting in highly realistic outputs
Generative AI (GAI)	A subset of deep learning, that uses supervised, unsupervised, and semi-supervised machine learning methods to generate new data instances based on the learned probability distribution of existing data
Text-to-3D GAI models	Refers to GAI models that create three-dimensional objects that correspond to a user's text description
Text-to-image GAI models	Refers to GAI models that are trained on a large set of images, where each image is captioned with a short text description
Text-to-task GAI models	Refers to GAI models that are trained to perform a specific task or action based on text input
Text-to-text GAI models	Refers to GAI models that take a natural language input and produce a text output
Text-to-video GAI models	Refers to GAI models that generate a video representation from a text input, where the input can range from a single sentence to a full script

Notes and References

1. Bloomberg. (June 1, 2023). Generative artificial intelligence (AI) revenue worldwide from 2020 with forecast until 2032 (in billion U.S. dollars) [Graph]. In *Statista*. Retrieved October 10, 2023, from https://www.statista.com/statistics/1417151/generative-ai-revenue-worldwide/.
2. A McKinsey survey reveals that 60% of respondent organizations with reported AI adoption are using GAI (Chui, M., L. Yee, B. Hall, A. Singla, & A. Sukharevsky [2023a], "The state of AI in 2023: Generative AI's breakout year," *McKinsey & Company*, August 1, accessed from https://www.mckinsey.com/capabilities/quantumblack/our-insights/the-state-of-ai-in-2023-generative-ais-breakout-year).

3. MarTech. (May 8, 2023). Marketing purposes for which professionals are using generative artificial intelligence (AI) in the United States as of March 2023 [Graph]. In *Statista*. Retrieved October 10, 2023, from https://www.statista.com/statistics/1386786/generative-ai-marketing-purposes-usa/.
4. Feuerriegel, S., J. Hartmann, C. Janiesch, & P. Zschech (2023). Generative AI. Retrieved From: https://www.researchgate.net/publication/370653602_Generative_AI.
5. Dwivedi, Y. K., N. Kshetri, L. Hughes, E. L. Slade, A. Jeyaraj, A. K. Kar, & R. Wright (2023a). So what if ChatGPT wrote it? Multidisciplinary perspectives on opportunities, challenges and implications of generative conversational AI for research, practice and policy. *International Journal of Information Management*, *71*, 102642; Dwivedi, Y. K., N. Pandey, W. Currie, & A. Micu (2023b). Leveraging ChatGPT and other generative artificial intelligence (AI)-based applications in the hospitality and tourism industry: Practices, challenges and research agenda. *International Journal of Contemporary Hospitality Management*. https://doi.org/10.1108/IJCHM-05-2023-0686; Kshetri, N. (2023). The economics of generative artificial intelligence in the academic industry. *IEEE Computer*, *56*(8), 77–83.
6. GAI exemplifies a distinct class of AI tools capable of creating seemingly novel content across a variety of mediums, including textual, visual, and others (Susarla, A., R. Gopal, J. B. Thatcher, & S. Sarker [2023], The Janus effect of generative AI: Charting the path for responsible conduct of scholarly activities in information systems. *Information Systems Research*, *34*(2), iii–vii. https://doi.org/10.1287/isre.2023.ed.v34.n2).
7. Dwivedi, Y. K., N. Pandey, W. Currie, & A. Micu (2023b). Leveraging ChatGPT and other generative artificial intelligence (AI)-based applications in the hospitality and tourism industry: Practices, challenges and research agenda. *International Journal of Contemporary Hospitality Management*. https://doi.org/10.1108/IJCHM-05-2023-0686.
8. Verhoef, P. C. (2020). Customer experience creation in today's digital world. *The Routledge companion to strategic marketing*, 107–122.
9. Grewal, D., A. L. Roggeveen, R. Sisodia, & J. Nordfält (2017), "Enhancing customer engagement through consciousness," *Journal of Retailing*, *93*(1), 55–64.
10. Anisin, A. (2023), Generative AI for content creation: How marketers can use it. *Forbes*. https://www.forbes.com/sites/theyec/2023/08/17/generative-ai-for-content-creation-how-marketers-can-use-it/?sh=7db8f8c7619e.
11. A survey conducted by the prestigious Conference Board reveals an overwhelming sentiment among marketers; 82% see GAI as a sign

of increased productivity, only 4% believe otherwise (The Conference Board [2023]. Survey: AI usage for marketers and communicators, August 3, https://www.conference-board.org/topics/AI-for-business/press/AI-in-marketing-and-communications).
12. Gartner (2023). "Generative AI," *Gartner*, accessed from https://www.gartner.com/en/information-technology/glossary/generative-ai.
13. Martineau, K. (2023), "What is generative AI?" *IBM*, April 20, accessed from https://research.ibm.com/blog/what-is-generative-AI.
14. Universal Marketing Dictionary Project (2023), "Generative AI," *The Universal Marketing Dictionary*, accessed from https://marketing-dictionary.org/g/generative-ai/.
15. Routley, N. (2023), "What is generative AI? An AI explains," *World Economic Forum*, February 6, accessed from https://www.weforum.org/agenda/2023/02/generative-ai-explain-algorithms-work/.
16. Open AI released GPT-1 in 2018 and had 117 million parameters. The model was trained on books to predict the next word in a sentence. In 2019, they developed GPT-2 with 1.5 billion parameters and the model could produce a coherent multi-paragraph text. GPT-3 developed in 2020 had 175 billion parameters and was able to write code, poetry, translate languages, and answer factual questions. By November 2022, they released GPT-3 and updated the fact-checking and mathematical abilities of the model for better accuracy and performance across more topics.
17. In September 2023, Open AI announced DALL-E 3, which is a significant leap forward in generating images that strictly align with the provided text. The model has several capabilities, including speed (the ability to generate images within a minute), customization, and accessibility (users do not require extensive training or programming skills to use it).
18. Wouters, O. J., M. McKee, & J. Luyten (2020), "Estimated research and development investment needed to bring a new medicine to market, 2009-2018," *Jama*, *323*(9), 844–853.
19. Balasubramanian, S. (2023), "Bayer is rapidly expanding its footprint with artificial intelligence," *Forbes*, September 4, accessed from https://www.forbes.com/sites/saibala/2023/09/04/bayer-is-rapidly-expanding-its-footprint-with-artificial-intelligence/?sh=5ea961724df8.
20. Capoot, A. (2023), "Microsoft announces new AI tools to help doctors deliver better care," *CNBC*, October 10, accessed from https://www.cnbc.com/2023/10/10/microsoft-announces-microsoft-fabric-and-azure-ai-tools-for-doctors.html.

21. McKinsey estimates that in the next three to five years, GAI could add up to $275 billion to the apparel, fashion, and luxury sectors' operating profits (Harries et al. 2023).
22. E.g. Stokel-Walker, C. (2022). AI bot ChatGPT writes smart essays—Should professors worry? *Nature*, accessed from https://doi.org/10.1038/d41586-022-04397-7; Eke, D. O. (2023). ChatGPT and the rise of generative AI: threat to academic integrity? *Journal of Responsible Technology, 13*, 100060.
23. Yu, H., & Y. Guo, (2023, June). Generative artificial intelligence empowers educational reform: current status, issues, and prospects. In *Frontiers in education* (Vol. 8, p. 1183162). Frontiers. Classify the applications of GenAI in education into the following four areas: (1) intelligent teaching systems (personalized course content and teaching plans based on student's learning process), (2) intelligent homework grading (analyzing students' homework, judging its correctness and errors, and providing corresponding scores and suggestions), (3) intelligent tutoring system (generation of tutoring content and strategies based on the analysis of students' learning situations and personalized needs), and (4) intelligent speech interaction system (achieving speech interaction with students to better understand their learning needs and questions).
24. According to a study conducted by Bain & Company, which involved around 600 companies across 11 industries, the rapid production of marketing materials has emerged as a leading use case for generative AI (Katzin, J., L. Beaudin, & M. Waldron [2023], "Ready for launch: How Gen AI is already transforming marketing," *Bain & Company*, May 23, accessed from https://www.bain.com/insights/ready-for-launch-how-gen-ai-is-already-transforming-marketing/). The study found that 47% of the participants either currently use or are considering implementing this technology for customer engagement and service applications, and 39% for creating marketing materials more efficiently.
25. Ostwal, T. (2023), "Coca-Cola's holiday campaign gets a generative AI-powered makeover," *AdWeek*, November 17, accessed from https://www.adweek.com/brand-marketing/coca-cola-holiday-campaign-create-real-magic-cards/#.
26. Bamberger, S., N. Clark, S. Ramachandran, & V. Sokolova (2023), "How generative AI is already transforming customer service," *BCG*, July 6, accessed from https://www.bcg.com/publications/2023/how-generative-ai-transforms-customer-service.

27. Boyle, A. (2023), "This audio startup is using AI to generate 'contextual CTV ads'," *AdExchanger*, August 10, accessed from https://www.adexchanger.com/digital-tv/this-audio-startup-is-using-ai-to-generate-contextual-ctv-ads/.
28. Seedtag (2023), "Seedtag launches industry first generative AI capability for contextual dynamic creatives," *PR Newswire*, May 17, accessed from https://www.prnewswire.com/news-releases/seedtag-launches-industry-first-generative-ai-capability-for-contextual-dynamic-creatives-301827150.html.
29. Frandino, N. (2023), "AI-powered monocle seeks to add sparkle to dull human chats," *Reuters*, May 25, accessed from https://www.reuters.com/technology/ai-powered-monocle-seeks-add-sparkle-dull-human-chats-2023-05-25/.
30. Verma, R. (2023), "Stanford students develop AR glasses that let you talk to ChatGPT in real time," *Business Insider India*, April 3, accessed from https://www.businessinsider.in/tech/news/stanford-students-develop-ar-glasses-that-let-you-talk-to-chatgpt-in-real-time/articleshow/99205100.cms.
31. Chitnis, S. (2023), "RizzGPT app inventor hoping to use generative AI to generate some charisma on demand," *CBS News*, July 6, accessed from https://www.cbsnews.com/sanfrancisco/news/rizzgpt-app-inventor-hoping-to-use-generative-ai-to-generate-some-charisma-on-demand/.
32. IBM (2023), "Combining generative AI with IBM Watson, Mitsui Chemicals starts verifying new application discovery for agility and accuracy," *IBM*, May 25, accessed from https://newsroom.ibm.com/2023-05-25-Combining-Generative-AI-with-IBM-Watson,-Mitsui-Chemicals-Starts-Verifying-New-Application-Discovery-for-Agility-and-Accuracy.
33. Mitsui (2023), "Double the number of new application discoveries by utilizing generative AI," *Mitsui Chemicals*, September 13, accessed from https://in.mitsuichemicals.com/release/2023/2023_0913.htm.
34. McKinsey & Company. (June 14, 2023). Automation potential with and without generative artificial intelligence (AI) in the United States in 2023, by profession [Graph]. In *Statista*. Retrieved October 17, 2023, from https://www.statista.com/statistics/1411571/job-automation-potential-generative-ai/.
35. Ziady, H. (2023), "The world's biggest ad agency is going all in on AI with Nvidia's help," *CNN*, May 29, accessed from https://edition.cnn.com/2023/05/29/tech/nvidia-wpp-ai-advertising/index.html.

36. Harreis, H., T. Koullias, K. Te, & R. Roberts (2023), "Generative AI: Unlocking the future of fashion," *McKinsey & Company*, March 8, accessed from https://www.mckinsey.com/industries/retail/our-insights/generative-ai-unlocking-the-future-of-fashion.
37. Chui, M., E. Hazan, R. Roberts, A. Singla, K. Smaje, A. Sukharevsky, L. Yee, & R. Zemmel (2023b), "The economic potential of generative AI: The next productivity frontier," *McKinsey & Company*, June 14, accessed from https://www.mckinsey.com/capabilities/mckinsey-digital/our-insights/the-economic-potential-of-generative-ai-the-next-productivity-frontier#introduction.
38. Harreis, H., T. Koullias, K. Te, & R. Roberts (2023), "Generative AI: Unlocking the future of fashion," *McKinsey & Company*, March 8, accessed from https://www.mckinsey.com/industries/retail/our-insights/generative-ai-unlocking-the-future-of-fashion.
39. Burgess, M. (2018), "How Nike used algorithms to help design its latest running shoe," *Wired*, January 25, accessed from https://www.wired.co.uk/article/nike-epic-react-flyknit-price-new-shoe.
40. Dreibelbis, E. (2023), "Toyota is using generative AI to design new EVs," *PC Magazine*, June 21, accessed from https://www.pcmag.com/news/toyota-is-using-generative-ai-to-design-new-evs.
41. Dominguez, L. (2023), "P&G Leans into intelligent fragrance development powered by AI," *Consumer Goods Technology*, October 3, accessed from https://consumergoods.com/pg-leans-intelligent-fragrance-development-powered-ai.
42. Uber Freight (2023), "Uber Freight Insights AI: Bringing the power of generative AI to enterprise shippers," *Uber Freight*, September 28, accessed from https://www.uberfreight.com/blog/uber-freight-insights-ai/.
43. Tyko, K. (2023), "Drive-thru mania pushes chains to rethink restaurants," *Axios*, August 11, accessed from https://www.axios.com/2023/08/11/fast-food-drive-thru-restaurants-future.
44. Spessard, M. (2023), "AI and beyond: Wendy's new innovative restaurant tech," *Wendy's*, June 2, accessed from https://www.wendys.com/blog/how-wendys-using-ai-restaurant-innovation.
45. Zwieglinska, Z. (2023), "How fashion brands are using generative AI," *Glossy*, March 28, accessed from https://www.glossy.co/fashion/how-generative-ai-will-impact-fashion/.
46. Westmoreland, M. B. (2023), "Amazon launches generative AI to help sellers write product descriptions," *Amazon*, September 13, accessed

from https://www.aboutamazon.com/news/small-business/amazon-sellers-generative-ai-tool.
47. Khaleej Times (2023), "Dubai: Dewa announces pilot use of ChatGPT to boost capabilities of its virtual employee," *Khaleej Times*, May 9, accessed from https://www.khaleejtimes.com/business/tech/dubai-dewa-announces-pilot-use-of-chatgpt-to-boost-capabilities-of-its-virtual-employee.
48. WPP (2022), "Ogilvy: Nestlé's The Milkmaid," *WPP*, accessed from https://www.wpp.com/en/featured/work/2022/12/ogilvy-nestles-the-milkmaid.
49. McKay, C. (2023), "Big brands experiment with generative AI for advertising," *Maginative*, August 18, accessed from https://www.maginative.com/article/big-brands-experiment-with-generative-ai-for-advertising/#:~:text=For%20example%2C%20WPP%20worked%20with,footage%20and%20AI%2Dgenerated%20scripts.
50. Phrasee (2023), "FARFETCH finds a perfect fit with AI content," *Phrasee*, accessed from https://phrasee.co/resources/farfetch-finds-a-perfect-fit-with-ai-content/.
51. An average click-rate uplift of 38% and an average open rate uplift of 31% for improving abandoned basket rates. In addition, sales and other campaign offers saw an average click rate uplift of 25% and an average open rate uplift of 7% (Phrasee 2023).
52. Pataranutaporn, P., V. Danry, J. Leong, P. Punpongsanon, D. Novy, P. Maes, & M. Sra (2021). AI-generated characters for supporting personalized learning and well-being. *Nature Machine Intelligence*, 3(12), 1013–1022.
53. KiwiTech. (2023). Applications of generative AI in augmented and virtual reality. Retrieved from: https://medium.com/@KiwiTech/applications-of-generative-ai-in-augmented-and-virtual-reality-20cecec50886.
54. A 2022 global survey found that 81% of consumers from Singapore were "definitely likely" or "somewhat likely" to stop using a brand if it did not personalize their customer experience. 80% from Brazil, 76% from Colombia, 75% from Mexico and 75% from Germany were the other top 4 countries where the respondents wanted greater levels of personalisation (Twilio [2022a]. Share of consumers who said they were likely to stop using a brand if it did not personalize their customer experience in selected countries worldwide as of January 2022 [Graph]. In *Statista*. March 28, Retrieved October 20, 2023,

from https://www.statista.com/statistics/1333314/marketing-personalization-consumer-loyalty-country/).
55. Another global survey revealed that 34% of business-to-consumer (B2C) marketers said that their organizations always personalized customer experiences, while only 11% of consumers agreed (Twilio [2022b]. Frequency of personalizing experiences according to B2C marketers and consumers worldwide as of January 2022 [Graph]. In *Statista*. April 7. Retrieved October 20, 2023, from https://www.statista.com/statistics/1333313/frequency-personalize-experiences/).
More importantly, while only 3% of B2C marketers said their organizations "rarely" or "never" personalize customer experiences, 13% of consumers disagreed. Such studies imply that consumers are constantly looking for personalized experiences from the brands they interact with.
56. McKay, C. (2023), "Big brands experiment with generative AI for advertising," *Maginative*, August 18, accessed from https://www.maginative.com/article/big-brands-experiment-with-generative-ai-for-advertising/#:~:text=For%20example%2C%20WPP%20worked%20with,footage%20and%20AI%2Dgenerated%20scripts.
57. Roach, J. (2023), "From Hot Wheels to handling content: How brands are using Microsoft AI to be more productive and imaginative," *Microsoft.com*, accessed from https://news.microsoft.com/source/features/innovation/from-hot-wheels-to-handling-content-how-brands-are-using-microsoft-ai-to-be-more-productive-and-imaginative/.
58. U. S. Copyright Office (2023), "Copyright registration guidance: Works containing material generated by artificial intelligence," *U. S. Copyright Office*, March 16, accessed from https://copyright.gov/ai/ai_policy_guidance.pdf.
59. U. S. Copyright Office (2023), "Copyright registration guidance: Works containing material generated by artificial intelligence," *U. S. Copyright Office*, March 16, accessed from https://copyright.gov/ai/ai_policy_guidance.pdf (p. 4).
60. U. S. Copyright Office (2023), "Copyright registration guidance: Works containing material generated by artificial intelligence," *U. S. Copyright Office*, March 16, accessed from https://copyright.gov/ai/ai_policy_guidance.pdf (p. 4).
61. Ojha, S. (2023), "Who owns AI-generated works? Here's what the laws say on copyright issue," *The Times of India*, September 22, accessed

from https://www.indiatoday.in/law/story/chatgpt-ai-generated-content-copyright-ownership-complexities-india-2439165-2023-09-22.
62. El Atillah, I. (2023), "Copyright challenges in the age of AI: Who owns AI-generated content?" *EuroNews*, July 10, accessed from https://www.euronews.com/next/2023/07/10/copyright-challenges-in-the-age-of-ai-who-owns-ai-generated-content.
63. Shein, E. (2023), "How Mars, Colgate-Palmolive, Nestle & Coca-Cola are exploring generative AI," *Consumer Goods Technology*, August 8, accessed from https://consumergoods.com/how-mars-colgate-palmolive-nestle-coca-cola-are-exploring-generative-ai.

5

Transformative Marketing with Machine Learning (ML)

Overview

Machine learning (ML) can be defined as computational methods that use experience to improve performance or to make accurate predictions.[1] By considering past information (i.e., referred to as experience), machines gain the ability to learn while they perform, thereby showing performance improvement. Past information can be in the form of collected data or information actively sourced through interaction with the environment. Learning quality depends on the volume and quality of data; the key outcome is predictions about key variables of interest. Simply put, ML deals with the process of training machines to learn over time.[2]

Machine learning is a technique that utilizes neural networks to identify and refine factors of importance to predict the probable outcomes of a given situation. This process requires manual programming upfront to adjust the factors of importance repeatedly until the desired outcome is achieved based on the data fed into the algorithm. However, once the algorithm has been trained using a training dataset, it can analyze new data inputs, recognize patterns, and produce increasingly accurate results without the need for human intervention. In essence, ML is a way to enhance the intelligence of machines by developing, comprehending, and evaluating learning algorithms.

This chapter is organized in the following manner. First, a brief history of the origin of ML is presented, followed by a definition of ML (from a marketing standpoint), along with three vignettes about ML usage and applications. Then, the role of ML in the Marketing 5.0 concept is explored. Next, some marketing applications of ML are discussed. Finally, the future of ML for the marketing industry is envisioned via emergent issues in this area.

Origin, Definition, and Components of ML

Machine learning finds its origin in neural networks. First proposed in 1943 by Warren McCulloch and Walter Pitts, they presented that the human thought process can be replicated through a combination of mathematics and algorithms.[3] Subsequently, in 1950, Alan Turing called for the development of computers that can "think."[4] Turing's seminal article was an important call for research in this area. This was followed by the design of the first artificial neural network (ANN) by Frank Rosenblatt in 1958 to detect shapes and patterns.

Early attempts in the 1950s and 1960s to advance the field of ML included teaching machines to play games like Checkers and making phone calls sound better to demonstrate that machines can deal with things that are understandable and complex. However, the interim years in the decades of the 1970s and the early part of the 1980s saw little impactful work in the field of ML. This lull was thought to be the outcome of research focusing on logical, knowledge-based approaches rather than algorithms.[5] In the late 1980s, the technique of backpropagation that was advanced by Geoffrey Hinton for use in shape recognition and word prediction rekindled interest in ML.[6] Soon after, successive ML advancements include the development of machine-readable text, advancements in text categorization and image classification, and improvements in short-term information storage and retrieval from machines' memory. In the early 2000s, the concept of deep learning was advanced which was a significant leap in terms of machines' processing ability regarding structured data and machines' ability to learn from knowledge with lesser human involvement. The deep learning concept has since driven (and continues to drive) ML developments with various business and end-user applications. The components of an ML algorithm can be broadly comprised of the following four elements—data, data mining, data augmentation, and ML models.

Data. Data always plays a crucial role in building any model. Typically, humans feed the data along with a set of explicit instructions and train the machine to repeatedly execute the command. However, with ML algorithms, as more data is made available, the machine makes self-corrections based on the accuracy of the output. In other words, it learns, over time, with more data becoming available. In this regard, the input data may be of two types—manually labeled and classified to be fed in,[7] or data classification rules can be learned by the machine through a semantic point of view.[8]

Additionally, the data being fed may be structured or unstructured. Whereas ML works remarkably well with large volumes of structured data (i.e., any data that resides in a database under specific fields with clearly defined values), it does even more so with unstructured data (UD). The rise of UD has changed markets and the management of marketing activities. UD is defined as a single data unit in which the information offers a relatively concurrent representation of its multifaceted nature without predefined organization or numeric values.[9] Further, the non-numeric, multifaceted, and concurrent representation of UD makes statistical methods difficult or inapplicable. However, because of such characteristics, UD can be highly beneficial toward deriving new marketing insights, especially along the following three aspects.

- First, UD does not have a predefined numeric form for the constructs of interest. Therefore, researchers must conduct pre-processing manually or automatically before the data is ready for analysis. Nonnumeric properties in UD offer greater flexibility for researchers to discover new theories. Highly unstructured data like video are only non-numeric, thereby requiring researchers to assign values to the data.
- Second, a single unit of highly unstructured data possesses multiple facets, each with potentially unique information that allows the researchers to select and analyze facets based on the research goals (especially voice and video data). Multiple facets in such types of data enable researchers to provide managers with richer and deeper marketing insights.
- Finally, concurrent representation is the simultaneous presence of multiple facets in a single data unit. Each facet can provide unique information that allows a UD unit to describe different phenomena at the same time. Therefore, researchers can examine different research questions with a single highly unstructured data unit by exploring the concurrent and dynamic flow of these unique facets.

Data Mining. Data mining refers to the process of discovering interesting patterns in databases that are useful in decision-making.[10] Data mining uses a broad family of computational methods that include statistical analysis, decision trees, neural networks, rule induction and refinement, and graphic visualization.[11] Companies have realized that information about their users (i.e., preferences, needs, wants, etc.) holds a lot of power in terms of overall decision-making. With specific reference to marketing, firms collect, store, and process vast amounts of highly detailed information about customers, markets, products, and processes through different programs. Data mining this information gives businesses the ability to make knowledge-driven strategic business decisions to help predict future trends and behaviors and create new opportunities. Further, data mining can assist in selecting the right target customers or in identifying (previously unknown) customer segments with similar behaviors and needs. A typical data mining process includes assessing and specifying the business objectives, data sourcing, transformation, creation of analytical variables, selecting relevant variables, training predictive models, selecting the best-suited model, and acting based on the findings.[12] Figure 5.1 illustrates a typical data mining process for marketing purposes.

Streamlining the laborious processes of data extraction, manipulation, quality monitoring, and enhancement is crucial. By automating these tasks, highly skilled quantitative data analysts can allocate their time towards more valuable tasks. This is where ML comes into play. Through data mining, companies can explore their data to uncover trends and patterns that can inform decision-making. On the other hand, ML can leverage existing data to continuously learn and improve its performance without human intervention. Unlike data mining, ML can detect relationships between different data points, making it a powerful tool for developing applications.

Data Augmentation for Better Business Insights. While ML can comb through data to deliver insights, the variety in data that ML can easily process will provide more layers of insights. In other words, extracting the data from various sources, transforming it for ML algorithms, and loading it

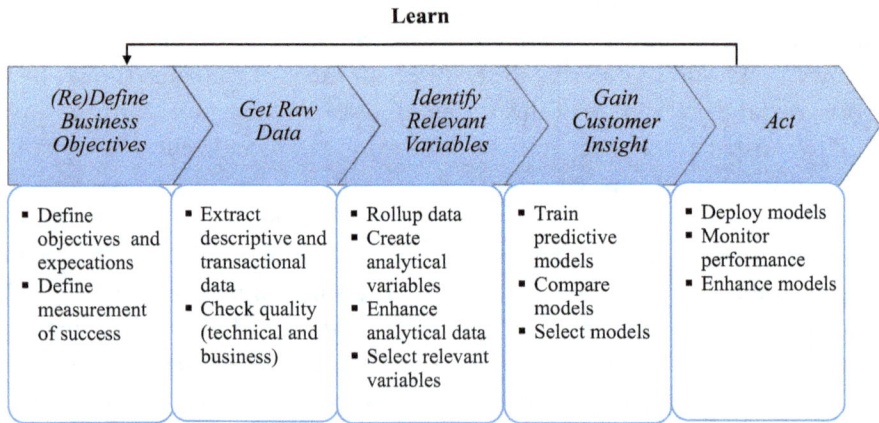

Fig. 5.1 Data mining process for marketing purposes
(*Source* Kumar, V., and W. J. Reinartz (2018). *Customer relationship management: Concept, Strategies, and Tools*. 3rd edition, Berlin, Germany: Springer-Verlag Berlin Heidelberg)

into a structured schema applicable to ML processes is referred to as an ETL (extract/transform/load) process. While such a process can add much value to an ML algorithm, it can also be challenging in terms of keeping track of where the data comes from, and how it is transformed, and loaded for further analysis. Additionally, given the wide range of data types (i.e., structured, and unstructured) and data sources (i.e., text, audio, video, location, etc.) that ML can handle, ensuring the sanity and relevance of the data can be a daunting task for many companies. This is because the ML process learns based on the data that is fed, and the quality of data matters a lot.

Types of ML Models. The models used by ML solutions largely fall into three types—supervised learning, unsupervised learning, and reinforcement learning. Supervised learning involves creating a concise model that represents the relationship between predictor features and class labels.[13] In this type of learning, the training data consists of pairs of input and output, where the output is typically known. For instance, let's consider a boutique fashion retailer who wants to categorize their customers as either local or national to determine shipping fees for deliveries. In this scenario, the input variable for a supervised learning algorithm would be the customer's state of residence, which can be obtained from the retailer's customer database. The output variables would be assigned a value of 1 if the customer resides in that state (indicating a local customer) and 0 if the customer resides outside of that state (indicating a national customer). Decision trees, neural networks, logistic regression, and k-nearest neighbors are a few examples of this learning type. Popular applications of the supervised learning model include spam filtering software and speech recognition software.

Unsupervised learning pertains to making the machine learn about performing a task without providing explicit instructions on how to do it. Here, the machine learns by exploiting the innate structures of the data, such as data variance, separability, and data distribution.[14] Dimension reduction methods and clustering procedures use this type of learning. Commercial applications of this type of learning can be found in fraudulent transaction detection software and image recognition software, among others.

Reinforcement learning, also known as semi-supervised learning, pertains to the learning of a mapping from situations to actions to maximize a scalar reward or reinforcement signal.[15] Here, the machine is not told which action(s) to take, rather it must discover which action(s) yield the highest reward by trying them. Feature selection integrates a small amount of labeled data into unlabeled data as additional information to improve the performance of an unsupervised feature selection. Commercial applications of this learning type include autonomous cars and news recommendation apps, among others. A more detailed discussion of these three types of ML models appears later in this chapter.

In recent years, ML has advanced significantly due to new computing technologies. ML originated from pattern recognition and the idea that computers can acquire knowledge without explicit programming. The iterative nature of ML allows models to adapt independently and make reliable decisions. Collaboration across disciplines has led to remarkable progress in ML, offering opportunities for users and businesses. The following three vignettes illustrate the potential of ML and its benefits for companies and individuals.

Analytics-Oriented Technology

Research reports and business trends indicate that ML is a rapidly growing business function within firms.[16] Yet, companies are also hesitant about the path forward. So, what is preventing businesses from taking the plunge into ML to achieve predictive analytics capabilities? Some of the critical factors that drive a successful ML adoption include developing perceptive managerial judgment, accumulating relevant domain knowledge, implementing a comprehensive technology-backed strategy, and a well-thought-out implementation approach,[17] Other organizational factors that could impede an organization's ML adoption include human talent management, not able or equipped to interpret results, and dealing with inadequate or irrelevant data.[18]

It is here that the distinction between statistical models (SM) and ML becomes pertinent. While SM (using quantitative techniques) has been identified as best suited for inference; ML works best for generating predictions. In this regard, the decision to use SM vs. ML potentially rests on the following five expectations from managers/researchers—(a) the number of variables to consider (fewer vs. more), (b) the type of relationships to be studied (simple interactions vs. higher-order interactions), (c) the type of use (used one time vs. repeatedly), (d) the nature of use (possibility for learning, or not), and (e) the timing of use (real-time needs, or not).[19] However, this does not have to be an either-or decision. Both SM and ML can be used collectively. That is, the convergence of boundaries between SM and ML can be the way forward.[20] As more organizations implement ML solutions, businesses are using ML in various capacities. Some business areas where ML is being used include:

- Marketing—ML is being extensively used in many marketing functions and e-commerce applications (see Image 5.1).[21] Additionally, ML provides companies with the capabilities to make quick decisions and implement digital transformation, in-house data management, and insights generation.
- Healthcare—ML is being increasingly used in the healthcare industry to enable healthcare providers to glean insights on patient diagnosis and identify/prevent health risks earlier. Since high-risk patients often require extra care, monitoring, and treatment, ML is well-equipped to handle the challenge by identifying high-risk patients to keep healthcare costs down. Here, ML models can comb through medical data to identify risk factors

Image 5.1 Shopify. Shopify facilitates businesses through its machine-learning capabilities
(*Source* Photo by *Roberto Cortese* on *Unsplash*)

and potential health issues.[22] Subsequently, medical care providers identify and design a care plan that includes appropriate intervention and care strategies.
- Food waste—Food waste is a major challenge faced by corporations across all industries, with potentially lasting implications on the climate and environment. Many companies are making efforts to reduce food waste. In this regard, Hitachi uses AI/ML solutions to monitor and combat food waste in hospitals. To track what and how much patients are eating, cameras are mounted on the food trays to take pictures to document what food is left over. This data is then fed to Hitachi's deep learning algorithms that analyze the data to find patterns in the waste that humans would not be able to as quickly. This would help with food service decisions and patient care, and the necessary changes that would be required.[23]

Organizations and technology companies are employing machine learning-based predictive analytics to gain an edge over the rest of the market. Machine learning advancements such as neural networks and deep learning algorithms can discover hidden patterns in unstructured data sets and uncover new information. In this regard, ML continues to drive analytics at organizations across various industries.

Link to Artificial Intelligence

While AI is the broad science of mimicking human abilities, machine learning is a specific subset of AI that trains a machine to learn. In this regard, AI and ML are conceptualized to be more aligned with an analytics orientation and related capabilities among new-age technologies.[24] As mentioned earlier, the varied types of data (i.e., text, image, video, etc.) that are captured, stored, and used for analytics purposes continue to drive the development of ML learning models and AI capabilities.

The rapid growth of ML and AI in delivering granular insights, thereby bringing us closer to the goal of transformative marketing, would have been nearly impossible for humans alone to accomplish. For instance, advancements in speech and voice recognition have spurred the growth of digital personal assistants such as Apple's Siri and Amazon's Alexa. Facial recognition continues to power Facebook's auto-tagging feature and iPhone X's facial recognition-based unlocking, and recommendation engines continue to drive Netflix, Spotify, and Pandora. Therefore, there is a natural link between ML and AI that is deeply rooted in the continued learning based on data analysis. This also makes them most conducive towards analytics purposes.[25]

Commercial applications involving a combination of AI and ML are plentiful and can be found across various industries. For instance, this combination can be seen in transportation through ride-sharing apps (e.g., Uber, Lyft), online maps (e.g., Google Maps incorporate user-reported traffic incidents like construction and accidents for suggesting the fastest route), and driverless cars (see Image 5.2).

Similarly, this combination can be found in communication tools such as emails (e.g., Gmail reads the emails to provide autofill options for email replies), online writing tools (e.g., Grammarly uses AI, ML, and NLP tools to suggest writing enhancements and identify potential plagiarism), and in education technology (e.g., ETS, the online testing service, uses automated scoring technologies developed using NLP to score the tests).

A prominent case of ML usage is PayPal. PayPal has access to data on more than 350 million customers and merchants in over 200 markets. A large part of PayPal's success is in helping their merchants detect and prevent fraud. Machine learning plays a role in detecting and mitigating fraud in a myriad of ways. The algorithms run thousands of queries in milliseconds and can assess individual customer behaviors in real time. This allows them to differentiate legitimate customers from fraudulent ones—aiding in approving authentic transactions and thus creating a seamless experience for trusted customers.[26] Additionally, PayPal's two-sided network is a rich source of

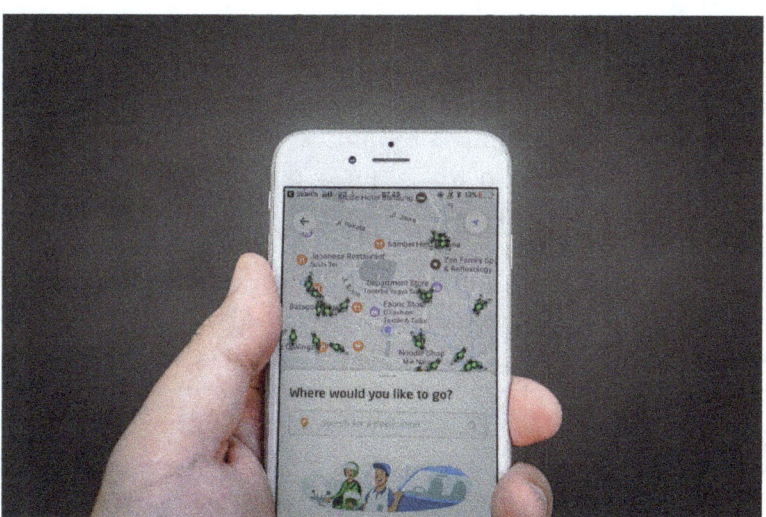

Image 5.2 Ride-sharing Applications. Ride-sharing apps such as Uber and Lyft use a combination of AI and ML to provide the most relevant route results
(*Source* Photo by *Fikri Rasyid* on *Unsplash*)

transaction and risk data from 432 million active global accounts that may help train algorithms and enhance fraud detection.

The most common frauds that PayPal encounters are of three types and the company uses ML tools to secure users from these frauds. First, in the case of signup frauds (i.e., when scammers create new bank or credit card accounts with stolen or synthetic identities), Paypal uses ML to analyze third-party data (email address, session data, enrolment data) to help spot and stop any fraudulent activity. Second, in the case of login frauds (i.e., taking over an existing customer account, or stealing logins), the fraud is mitigated by assessing customer behavior data, monitoring devices, IP addresses, and so on. Finally, regarding payment frauds (i.e., scammers using credit card details without the cardholder's knowledge), the company uses ML to analyze previous transactions to identify anomalies and indicate the occurrence of fraud.[27]

While PayPal and other transaction platforms are implementing machine learning to its full potential, scammers are also constantly testing filters, and designing new attacks to find a way around them. As e-commerce continues to grow, machine learning is pivotal for companies' e-commerce fraud strategy. In such a dynamic landscape, machine learning and other new-age technologies will play larger roles in payment fraud detection and mitigation.

Machine Learning Models

Machine learning is an application of AI that provides systems the ability to automatically learn and improve from experience without being explicitly programmed. Learning in ML assumes three forms—supervised, unsupervised, and reinforcement—and can be understood in terms of inputs, outputs, and outcomes.[28]

Supervised learning. This form is often used when the response variables are to be recorded; for instance, recognizing the hand-written text or identifying spam emails. Essentially, the learning system uses prior data as training information and accordingly presents related predictions for all future outcomes. This form of learning is often used for research problems in regression and classification.[29]

In some cases, the classification is useful when researchers want to identify the class and group in the response variable, and in some cases may even involve qualitative information. For instance, a bank may be interested in predicting whether an individual will default on their credit card payment, based on income and monthly credit card balance. Further, while some methods in supervised learning allow researchers to interpret the coefficient(s), others do not. Since the response variables are observed in supervised learning, methods such as leave-one-out cross-validation (LOOCV), K-fold cross-validation, or validation can be used by researchers to examine the prediction power of models.[30]

Unsupervised learning. This form is used when researchers only observe the input variables x, but not the response variables y. In such situations, researchers can explore to understand the relationships between the variables or between the observations. The methods used in unsupervised learning include association rule learning, principal component analysis, and clustering. Unsupervised learning is important for understanding the variation and grouping structure of a set of unlabeled data, such as sentiment analysis and topic modeling. For instance, from online customer reviews about products/services, researchers can mine information from text and emojis used by customers. A supervised analysis would be possible if researchers had information about these customers' usage patterns of the said products/services. In the absence of such information, researchers can use natural language processing (NLP) to classify the sentiment of each customer about products into a category scale: negative, neutral, and positive. The comments from customers can also be classified into some common topics (e.g., product features, product design, or the quality of service) and their purchase disposition towards such offerings can be ascertained accordingly.

Reinforcement learning. This form of learning is based on using rewards or incentives to motivate a given action within a given environment. In terms of distinction between the supervised and unsupervised forms of learning, the former focuses on learning from a training set of labeled examples; whereas the latter focuses on finding patterns hidden within unlabeled data. In contrast, this type of learning focuses on maximizing reward signals. However, to discover such actions, the machine has to try actions that it has not selected before. The machine has to not only exploit what it has already experienced to obtain a reward but also to explore new things to make better action selections in the future. The dilemma is that exploration and exploitation go through the process of trial and error.[31]

Reinforcement learning can improve customized offers of a product or services for customers based on their responses to each offer. Customers' responses such as comments, ratings, past preferences, competitors' actions, and current public sentiments work as a dynamic environment for the agent. The agent function can be assigned different goals by firms such as maximizing profits, sales, or customer engagements. Using reinforcement learning can help firms respond to customers' needs and competitors' marketing strategies faster and more efficiently than statistical models without knowing the specific functions of the surrounding environment.

Machine Learning in the Marketing 5.0 World

Machine learning has become an indispensable tool in the field of marketing. It allows businesses to optimize their marketing strategies by predicting customer behavior, segmenting audiences, and recommending personalized content. With ML algorithms, marketers can analyze customer data from various sources such as social media, website interactions, and purchase history to gain a deeper understanding of their target audience. This knowledge can then be used to tailor marketing messages and offers to specific customer segments, increasing the chances of conversion and customer satisfaction. Expanding on the Marketing 5.0 concept discussed in Chapter 2, this section presents how ML operates in the Marketing 5.0 world. Particularly, this section discusses five examples of where ML is applied through the lens of Marketing 5.0 and establishes how such actions can also bode well for humanity.

Data-Driven Marketing Using ML

One of the key benefits of data-driven marketing using ML is that it allows marketers to make more informed decisions. By analyzing data, marketers can gain insights into customer behavior and preferences, which can be used to develop more effective marketing strategies. Additionally, machine learning algorithms can be used to automate certain aspects of marketing, such as ad targeting and content creation, which can save time and resources.

For instance, Lenskart, an online eyewear platform, utilizes machine learning techniques to enhance the customer experience. By employing these advanced tools, Lenskart assists customers in selecting the perfect frame, minimizing uncertainties and the need for product returns or exchanges. Within the Lenskart application, users are presented with options such as "curated for you" or "view similar," which provide personalized recommendations to help them find the ideal product. Through the application of machine learning on diverse data points, Lenskart ensures that these recommendations are tailored to each customer, making the search process effortless and efficient.

Lenskart utilizes various methods to gather customer data and analyze their behavior. This includes monitoring the products customers view, added to wishlists, added to carts, and ultimately purchased. Additionally, Lenskart collects data on customers' browsing history, buying patterns, sub-brands purchased, and ratings. By assigning different weights to these interactions based on their significance (with purchasing being the highest and viewing being the lowest), Lenskart applies a series of ML algorithms to predict customers' future purchases. This data-driven approach allows Lenskart to personalize the shopping experience and offer tailored selections that align with individual preferences. As a result, Lenskart enhances customer satisfaction and drives conversions through the power of ML-driven predictive analytics.

Predictive marketing using ML

The integration of machine learning into predictive marketing has transformed the way businesses approach customer acquisition and retention. By harnessing the power of machine learning algorithms, marketers can now identify potential customers with a high likelihood of conversion and tailor their marketing efforts to effectively engage and convert these prospects. Additionally, machine learning can help businesses identify customers who are at risk of churn, allowing them to implement targeted retention strategies to keep these customers loyal.

For instance, ASOS, a prominent British fashion and cosmetics e-commerce company, boasts a vast customer base of more than 25 million active users across the globe. The company has implemented machine learning (ML) to enhance its personalization efforts, going beyond recommending similar items to suggest complementary pieces that can create a cohesive look. To achieve this, ASOS has integrated an ML tool that analyzes, and groups items based on their attributes, ensuring they match stylistically and can be worn together.[32]

The ML model is trained using a dataset called Buy the Look (BTL), which consists of nearly 600,000 outfits carefully curated by ASOS stylists. This dataset is derived from ASOS product description pages, ensuring that each product in the catalog appears at least once as a seed product. By sequentially adding items and re-scoring, new outfits can be generated. Each outfit comprises a seed product and a variable number of styling products, such as pairing a dress with a pair of shoes and a bag. ASOS has designed an outfit template, which consists of specific product types that should be included to complete the outfit. By harnessing the power of AI and ML, ASOS not only stays attuned to evolving consumer trends and preferences but also revolutionizes the way customers engage with their brands. The outcomes have been remarkable, as evidenced by a remarkable 329% surge in before-tax profits and a substantial 19% rise in global retail sales throughout the year 2020.

Contextual Marketing Using ML

Contextual marketing encompasses the process of identifying, profiling, and delivering customized interactions to customers in the physical space, by comprehending their engagements with the brand's digital touchpoints. Machine Learning assumes a critical role in this process, as it empowers the analysis of a multitude of data points to discern meaningful patterns and trends.

For instance, McDonald's Hong Kong implemented a system where customers could access coupons through their mobile app, which aimed to promote both new or seasonal items and their regular menu options, including value combos. However, initially, this process required a lot of manual effort and consumed a significant amount of time. To address this issue, the company decided to develop a more efficient and customer-focused approach by leveraging machine learning and data science techniques.[33] Particularly, McDonald's Hong Kong faced the challenge of effectively utilizing the vast amount of data collected from their 245 restaurants, which serve over a million customers daily. To make informed decisions regarding coupon promotions, they needed to centralize the data, analyze it to make predictions, and present it in a way that would provide actionable insights promptly.

The data collected from the central point-of-sale system is now consolidated into a data warehouse, which was created using Oracle. By utilizing an unsupervised machine learning technique, the ML tool can analyze the data and provide recommendations for relevant coupon types to individual customers based on their purchasing behavior, including recency, frequency, and monetary value. This has significantly improved the company's ability to plan targeted coupon campaigns with greater precision. Additionally, the data-driven approach and ML capabilities have enabled the company to make objective, analytical decisions that are more effective. As a result, the company has estimated that the implementation of this ML system has reduced the time required for planning and executing weekly coupon campaigns by half.

Augmented Marketing Using ML

The focus of many discussions has been on the advancement of computational capabilities, but there is also a growing emphasis on enhancing human intelligence with the help of technology. Intelligence Amplification (IA) is becoming increasingly important, as it involves utilizing powerful computational analysis to enhance human abilities. In the field of marketing, IA takes the form of augmented marketing, where computers act as support systems for tasks driven by humans. The goal of augmented marketing is to boost productivity by automating mundane tasks and aiding humans in making well-informed decisions.

In addition to its applications in business, machine learning is also utilized in various other fields, including sports. An example of this can be seen in the 2005 "freestyle" chess tournament hosted by Playchess.com. This unique competition allowed participants to form teams with either other players or computers. What made this tournament particularly intriguing was the involvement of multiple groups of grandmasters collaborating with computers. It was widely anticipated that a grandmaster paired with a supercomputer would dominate the tournament. However, contrary to expectations, the winning team consisted of amateur American chess players who effectively coordinated and coached their three computers. Their ability to work in harmony with their machines proved to be more successful than the combination of a skilled grandmaster and a high-powered PC. This remarkable outcome emphasizes a key takeaway: the efficiency of a partnership is determined by the way players and computers engage and collaborate. On this, the chess grandmaster Garry Kasparov opined, "Weak human + machine + better process was superior to a strong computer alone and, more remarkably, superior to a strong human + machine + inferior process."[34]

Agile Marketing Using ML

Agile marketing, when combined with machine learning, offers a dynamic and flexible approach to marketing that is highly responsive to customer needs. Machine learning algorithms can analyze vast amounts of data, including customer behavior, preferences, and market trends, to identify patterns and make predictions. This not only increases productivity but also allows marketers to experiment and iterate more quickly, testing different approaches and refining their campaigns based on real-time insights.

Consider the case of Amaggi, a Brazilian agribusiness multinational. With its vast expanse of over 400,000 hectares of productive planted area, the company displays the utmost dedication to sustainable practices. Their commitment is evident through their investment in precision agriculture, which aims to minimize environmental impacts. Moreover, Amaggi has a remarkable track record of embracing digital transformation and leveraging state-of-the-art technology. To gain a comprehensive understanding of crucial variables and weather-related effects, the Amaggi team recognized the necessity of acquiring additional information beyond what is collected by field workers and various sensors measuring factors such as humidity, temperature, and precipitation.[35]

Amaggi recognized that it was not feasible for humans to monitor the complex details of extensive farmlands daily, regardless of the number of people assigned to the task. To address this problem, they partnered with Planet, a web-geospatial platform that analyzes and shares Earth-related data, to utilize satellite imagery. By generating alerts, the company could quickly understand the issues affecting the crops, make informed decisions, and take prompt action. This approach proves particularly valuable for crops with longer growth cycles, such as soya and cotton, which typically span from 90 to 180 days. Failing to respond promptly to any anomalies can have a devastating impact on productivity. By utilizing a vast collection of more than 8.7 million images sourced from the Planet database, Amaggi successfully carried out trend analysis and adopted an agile strategy to tackle the diverse obstacles it encountered.

Current ML Applications in Marketing

Firms are always looking for ways to improve data literacy and provide tools to empower knowledge workers to transform data into insights.[36] In this regard, explorative data visualization tools introduced over a decade ago made it possible to better understand data, distributions and anomalies, outliers, and noise in the data. In this capacity, ML served to remove the dependency on a specialist to design and develop interactive dashboards. A similar trend continues to add augmented intelligence capabilities leveraging Auto-ML. For instance, NLP search-based interfaces add the ability to interact with data through text and voice. Just as smartphones have provided advanced features to users in a point-and-click format, ML too promises to deliver a similar ease of use. However, recent developments in ML have also generated significant interest among users who are feeling the need to go beyond the point-and-click results it provides. As a result, ML has become one of the most promising research methods in the marketing field, which also holds important implications for the development of marketing strategies. This section presents five specific application areas where ML continues to help companies in developing marketing initiatives.

Understanding Customer Needs to Deploy ML

The adoption of ML enables firms to refine their recommendations and promotions to consumers continuously, based on their behaviors over time. Recommendation engines are a popular application of ML, wherein users are matched with offerings that they liked in the past and/or may be interested in the future. Such curative actions by firms reduce the consumer cognitive load and take the responsibility of finding the best options for a consumer's choice context to the search platform or the brand.[37]

Several ML applications in marketing reflect the attention given by companies to addressing customer needs. For instance, Uber uses ML to estimate arrival times for rides, identify optimal pickup locations, estimate mealtimes on Uber Eats, and detect fraud. FICO uses ML to develop its credit rating (FICO scores) as well as to assess risks for individual customers. Amazon uses ML algorithms that can automatically learn to combine multiple relevant features and past search histories and generate individually customized search results for customers. Further, banks that provide text recognition on checks through their apps rely on ML tools.[38]

A significant part of understanding customers' needs is knowing the price they are willing to pay for products/services. Retailers can take advantage of the tremendous power of ML to build effective pricing automation solutions. For instance, the Nielsen Global Connected Commerce survey found that searching for product information, checking/comparing prices, and looking for deals/promotions/coupons are the most popular activities of internet shoppers.[39] As a result, price setting is a critical marketing function and one that is likely to resonate closely with consumers. For instance, Airbnb uses a dynamic price tool that recommends prices to its hosts, considering parameters such as seasonality, the day of the week, or special events, and more sophisticated factors such as photos of the property to be rented or the prices applied in the neighborhood. Other companies such as Amazon and Uber have adopted similar approaches.[40]

Revisiting Firm Capabilities to Integrate ML

The access to detailed and real-time information about various business functions presents important implications for firm capabilities. In this regard, the data maturity of organizations is undergoing significant changes. A well-developed, well-endowed, and well-connected data ecosystem is fundamental to deriving benefits from deep learning and ML capabilities. For instance, American Express relies on ML algorithms and data analytics to help fraud detection in near real-time. As a result, the firm is not only able to save millions in losses, but also reduce time-consuming manual reviews, costly chargebacks and fees, and denials of legitimate transactions.[41] This also implies that firms will have to invest in data scientists who can extract meaning from data and identify ways to develop actionable insights for firms.

Further, the adaptability and customization capabilities of ML applications have enabled marketers to establish personalized means of communication with their user base. Employees are now able to access all customer data and information on a point-and-click interface, connect and interact with other stakeholders involved in the marketing process, and deliver meaningful content and offerings. The network-wide interactions now made possible by the power of data are continuously evolving and are expected to bring in more changes in the business environment. For instance, Taco Bell uses ML technology in its app to show users the most relevant menu items, promotions, and content based on their individual preferences, past dining history, location, weather, and restaurant-specific menus and pricing.[42]

Additionally, for ML initiatives to succeed, ML must be aligned with firm goals. Essentially, ML must be an organization-wide initiative spanning hierarchies, functions, and stakeholders. In this regard, given the interdisciplinary nature of ML capabilities, firms may even want to consider an interdisciplinary format of operation, rather than a traditional hierarchy-based format (e.g., top-down). This would likely better prepare firms to counter the business shifts because of AI integration. For instance, Otto, the German online retailer uses ML capabilities for forecasting purposes that are 90% accurate in forecasting sales for the next 30 days. The retailer has integrated these capabilities into inventory management based on sales forecasts, thereby enabling them to plan order shipments and handle customer returns. Further, such integrated ML capabilities provide Otto the confidence to order over 200,000 items a month from vendors with no human intervention.[43] A distinguishing feature of Otto's ML implementation is that, unlike Amazon or eBay, Otto's efforts focus on non-customer-facing job functions such as demand forecasting, order management, merchandising, order fulfillment, and product returns rather than designing personalized content and offerings for consumers. Such efforts directly work towards valuable cost savings for Otto.

Designing Marketing Mix Strategies with ML

As mentioned earlier, ML is appropriately positioned to deliver impactful results to firms by way of personalization. In this regard, firms design marketing mix strategies that can deliver personalized content and offerings to users using ML solutions. Personalization occurs when the firm decides, usually based on previously collected customer data, what marketing mix is suitable for the individual.[44] Academic research has also discussed various lenses, in terms of personalization.[45] Further,[46] identify three levels of personalization adopted by firms—mass, segment-level, and individual-level. In mass personalization, firms personalize the same marketing mix offerings to customers based on customers' average preferences. While this may not be a "true" form of personalization, it does involve considering consumer tastes and preferences in developing offerings. An example of this type of personalization can be found in 3D printing. This technology is being used in a variety of industries such as medical training kits, automobile manufacturing, and footwear, among others. For instance, Ecco, a Danish footwear manufacturer, captures data in real-time, models the sole, and prints the 3D insole, all within 1 hour.[47]

In segment-level personalization, firms first create customer segments and then personalize marketing mix elements according to each segment. An example of segment-level personalization can be seen in education technology or edtech. Toppr is a cloud-based learning service in India where students learn in real-time through an app that not only provides live education content, but also tests, sample test questions, chats for answering student questions, and helpful preparation tips for appearing in exams. Other Indian companies operating in this market include Unacademy and Vedantu.[48]

Finally, in individual-level personalization, firms personalize the marketing mix to each customer's individual needs, tastes, and behaviors. An example of individual-level personalization is personalized nutrition. In a rapidly growing market, personalized nutrition aims to provide users with individual-specific health choices based on personal health metrics. Companies such as Apple (Apple Watch), Nestle, Amazon (Amazon Fresh), and Uber (Uber Eats) are looking to grow significantly in this market with relevant personalized offerings.[49]

A comprehensive implementation of ML for personalization can be seen at HelloFresh, the meal kit and food-delivery service company. To manage the competition, and make their offerings more customer-friendly, HelloFresh uses ML algorithms in a multitude of ways. Since they operate on a flexible subscription-based model, customers can pause their subscriptions indefinitely. This model, while it offers convenience to their customers, offers a bit of a challenge for the analysts at HelloFresh. As pauses violate the assumptions of traditional contractual CLV models that rely on simple parametric likelihood functions, they had come up with CCV (customer campaign value)—which measures the profit generated by a customer within each window between two conversion events.

By reframing customer profitability in this way, they introduced Morpheus—an algorithm that uses ML techniques to offer weekly customer-level predictions. Morpheus has 1360 different gradient boosting models, each trained on a specific customer segment that is defined by a market, time horizon, customer type, and so on. The algorithm uses hundreds of predictors from various data sources from HelloFresh's Enterprise Data Warehouse, Google Analytics, and third-party datasets that were custom-built for the company. These predictors provide essential information about customer engagement, incentives, pricing, ordering patterns, and user behaviors, among others. Through these features, Morpheus aids marketers in predicting future profitability from various perspectives such as customer segments, customer responses to recipe swaps, product experiences, and so on.

Morpheus has been integrated across functional departments within HelloFresh such as marketing, finance, product, and operations. The operations team uses the insights from Morpheus to answer questions in line with recent industry trends. The marketing team uses Morpheus to understand the impact of business decisions on consumer behavior and nudge customers—thus encouraging conversions. Through the individual predictions from Morpheus, HelloFresh can engage in customized and personalized communication with their customers. In the future, the company aims to democratize access to high-quality ML models for predictive analytics across the entire organization.

The impact of personalization initiatives by firms using ML solutions can be discerned by considering the four primary marketing mix elements—product, price, promotion, and place. Product personalization is seeing a steady increase in interest from firms, particularly driven by the proliferation of channels, especially new electronic channels, and an openness on the part of customers to interact through a multitude of channels. As a result, companies are now more equipped to test the omnichannel model, which focuses on the interplay between channels and brands.[50] In other words, the omnichannel extends beyond the typical channel management strategies to include a seamless transition between channels and superlative user experience.[51,52] Firms have gone beyond the "Recommendations for You" feature offered by Amazon and Netflix. For instance, Netflix personalizes the artwork of movie titles based on ML algorithms that can pick out which images may best resonate with the users. Additionally, they also have plans to create personalized movie trailers based on the streaming histories of individual viewers.[53]

Personalization via prices operates on the concept that customers derive varying levels of utility from firm offerings, and therefore vary in their willingness to pay.[54] In this regard, personalization of pricing can happen based on location, seasonality, and stated preferences of users, among others. ML continues to be used in such a form of personalization, owing to its rich data and analytic capabilities with information. For instance, the Munich-based Bavaria Boutique Hotel has implemented an AI/ML-driven pricing solution that considers the entire customer journey of potential guests, checks the prices and offers of relevant competitors (in Munich and the surrounding areas), accounts for important social events happening in the region, integrates additional costs of online travel platforms, and considers organizational key performance indicators (KPIs), among others, in generating appropriate price recommendation multiple times during the day in real-time. This approach is markedly different from the typical approach of setting room rates that were set manually based on experience. Such a pricing solution is expected to optimally determine room rates with the market, thereby improving turnover.[55] ML is also being used in traditional retail settings to determine the pricing strategy. For instance, Walmart has set up a cloud network driven by ML algorithms that constantly feeds data and analytics to store employees in real time. This has allowed them to stay competitive with Amazon on pricing, whereby they can adjust prices at its physical locations almost instantly across entire regions.[56]

Personalization activities in promotion have received a significant uptick in attention since the availability of individual-level data.[57] The individual-level data allows firms to perform a wide range of customer-related actions such as audience segmentation, dynamic online content creation, targeted promotional offers and discounts, and personalized campaigns, among others. Firms are increasingly using ML algorithms to drive such promotional activities. For instance, the Kansas City Chiefs are using ML algorithms to improve the fan experience. A decision cloud platform allows the team to connect multiple levels of fan data to many different offers, promotions, and solicitations. Additionally, the ML solution allows the team to ensure that the promotional content and offers are delivered only to those fans who would be most likely to purchase, and not cannibalize their retail sales.[58]

Personalization via the place element has changed significantly since the inception of e-commerce. What traditionally pertained to the physical locations of firms, now applies also to their online presence. For instance, Mystore-E, a Tel Aviv-based clothing store, has designed its stores to mimic the experience of a website within a store.[59] Using digital displays and augmented reality, customers can virtually try on products. With ML capabilities, employees then receive notifications that match customers' choices to provide highly personalized and curated offerings. Such initiatives provide customers and firms the ability to respond immediately to communication messages initiated by either party. Other instances of personalization that blur the distinction between physical and digital space include Macy's On Call (a mobile digital assistant that personalizes the customer's shopping experience and provides recommendations and directions to items around the store),[60] and Hilton's Connie (a robot concierge that uses NLP capabilities to provide personalized recommendations of places to visit and restaurants to try for the guests),[61] among others.

Driving customer engagement through ML

Traditional customer relationship management was based on the notion of differences in the cost of serving customers. With the increase in automation, the heterogeneity in the cost of serving customers decreases. This implies that the main difference in customer profitability on digital platforms is driven by customer retention and the gross margin provided by the consumers. In other words, in the new-age technology world, customer profitability must be viewed from a different viewpoint. The ML algorithms run on customer transaction data, among others, to improve their predictions. The algorithms also benefit from customer heterogeneity regarding customer preference, demographics, transaction frequency, and spending potential. Training of ML algorithms behind the curation engines, and the voice or image recognition software requires product preference inputs across a gamut of customers to better discriminate between products preferred by the highly profitable customers and low profitable customers. Further, the lower cost of serving customers implies that firms can make personalized product recommendations and serve customers across a range of profits. This implies that the knowledge value of customers (i.e., information voluntarily shared by customers to the firms towards the enhancement of future firm offerings) increases with the marginal improvement of the ML algorithms' predictive accuracy provided by the customers' transactions.[62] As a result, high knowledge value customers need not necessarily be higher profitable customers or customers with a high referral value.

Companies such as Google, Netflix, and Amazon that are geared towards building network effects (i.e., providing products for free or a nominal subscription), also focus on broadening their user base. The data collected from the portfolio of offerings (i.e., Google Search, Gmail, Amazon Prime) provides the basis for the development of recommendation algorithms that then provide autocomplete/recommendation results for search terms, emails, movies, music, related articles, and similar product bundles.

The success of an engagement strategy is dependent on customers developing an emotional attachment to the firm.[63] Even though customers may not prioritize direct engagement with firms, many firms such as Wendy's, Target, Patagonia, Chick-fil-A, and Whole Foods continue to trigger conversations about social topics and issues that are important to consumers to interact directly with customers, and thereby achieve a deeper level of engagement.[64] Firms are realizing that designing and delivering personalized experiences for multiple customer preferences and engagement segments constitute a valuable customer engagement strategy. In this regard, new-age technologies (and particularly ML) enable companies such as Disney, Amazon, Netflix, and Google to deliver such personalized experiences in physical and online environments.

Designing Digital Strategies with ML

The new-age technology landscape, including ML capabilities, places firms in an ecosystem that is characterized by smart objects that deliver intuitive digital services across an ever-expanding network of various stakeholders. The creation of such an ecosystem consisting of new-age technologies (including ML), essentially consolidates multiple functionalities on one digital platform thereby contributing towards increasing consumer convenience. Consumers benefit from the offers and rewards that the firm provides within this ecosystem. The machine-to-human interaction capabilities that the firm develops serve important roles in improving consumer welfare as they can provide convenience, peace of mind, and timely insights to consumers. Consumers can assign relatively straightforward tasks or queries to intelligent agents, thus minimizing their effort. By analyzing data on broader trends as well as individual behaviors, a firm can develop targeted and individually relevant offers and solutions for their customers.

Firms are cognizant of the potential of ML and new-age technologies in furthering their digital strategies. For instance, fashion retailer Burberry uses ML capabilities and big data to identify counterfeit products, improve sales, and build and enhance personal relationships with customers. To do so, Burberry uses data gathered from its reward and loyalty programs to develop personalized digital and in-store shopping experiences for individual customers. Other instances of digital strategies adopted by firms include Uber's use of ML capabilities to estimate arrival times for rides, identify optimal pickup locations, estimate mealtimes on UberEATS, and detect fraud; FICO's use of ML capabilities to develop its credit rating (FICO scores) as well as to assess risks for individual customers; and Amazon's use of ML algorithms that can automatically learn to combine multiple relevance features and past search histories, and to generate individually customized search results for customers.

Future of ML in Marketing

Given ML's proficiency and veracity in powering digital initiatives within firms, the future looks firmly entrenched in a digital, learning environment.[65] Such a development could raise questions on the relevance of customer relationship management (CRM) technologies currently adopted by many companies worldwide. In other words, will ML (and potentially other new-age technologies) replace CRM technologies? This is an important issue as companies have invested millions into setting up their current CRM infrastructure.

Research has posited that new-age technologies can potentially augment the capabilities of existing CRM technologies by enhancing the efficiency, effectiveness, responsiveness, and personalization of marketing strategies and activities.[66] For instance, ML can help CRM systems by automating routine tasks such as data input, forecast updating, determination of call lists, and other routine customer management tasks. By helping CRM systems identify behavioral patterns and preferences, they can automate and personalize customer responses, communication material, data collection, pricing quote generation, and other customer management actions. Over time, ML algorithms can expedite customer segmentation, lead customization, and marketing element customization. Employees can thus productively apply their time toward relationship-building and engagement activities. Similarly, other new-age technologies can complement CRM systems and capabilities firms have in place currently. Overall, the new-age technologies can work well with existing CRM technologies; and through such a combination firms would realize enhanced value creation. In this regard, the future of ML for marketing purposes appears to be promising and varied. While we can expect progress in ML capabilities in many organizational areas, three areas that stand out are discussed here.

ML and Customer Churn Analytics

Managing customer churn is a prickly issue impacting businesses across several industries such as telecommunications, financial services, retailing, and e-commerce, among others. When faced with customer churn, managers face several important questions such as: (a) How do we identify the customers who are likely to churn? (b) When are they likely to churn? (c) Should we intervene and, if so, when? and (d) What should the intervention offer(s) be to prevent churn? When left unaddressed, customer churn can prove very costly to a company, and could negatively impact the firm's performance in four ways. First, firms could lose out heavily on the revenue stream due to customer churn. Second, it becomes difficult for a firm to break even as it would have lost the opportunity to recover the acquisition cost from the churned customer. Third, a firm would also lose the opportunity to up-sell/cross-sell to customers who have defected, thereby causing a loss of potential revenue. Finally, potential negative word-of-mouth from the defected customers impacts future customer acquisition of a firm.

Before the advent of new-age technologies, research studies used extensive statistical modeling to address this issue. Using tests and control groups was a popular technique that could adequately demonstrate the impact of customer intervention strategies. For instance, using such intervention strategies, a telecom firm realized a net revenue gain of $345,000 (after accounting for the cost of intervention) and, an 860% increase in ROI.[67] However, in the current era of new-age technologies firms are increasingly looking toward ML-based algorithms to counter customer churn. The ML algorithms could work in tandem with existing customer management models that can effectively address customer churn.

Addressing churn can also be a challenge in an ML-enabled environment.[68] The challenge relates to how firms use machines (and ML algorithms) to interact with consumers. As machines become more conversant and interactive, firms must be careful in ensuring that machines accurately capture and transmit the firm's (or brand's) personality. Additionally, firms must also understand how to engender consumer trust through ML algorithms. This calls for firms to move away from the static imagery often involved in display advertising and media-related messages typically involved in intervention offers to a dynamic and interactive environment of voice-enabled virtual assistants and virtual reality.

In implementing human-machine combinations, research has identified the existence of an uncanny valley when balancing the deployment of virtual assistants to completely reflect humans versus maintaining some artificiality. The uncanny valley hypothesizes that a person's response to a humanlike robot would abruptly shift from empathy to revulsion (and even eeriness) as it approached, but failed to attain, a lifelike appearance.[69] In this regard, recent field implementations that involved human–machine interactive environments have demonstrated uneasiness in the humans involved.[70] Firms such as Poncho (from the Weather company), Slack, and Autodesk are trying to find the right balance for their AI bots between providing a human versus a machine interface.

However, recent advancements in ML have gained tremendous precision and the distinction between human-created and machine-created content is barely visible. This has led to a situation where people are slowly developing an appetite for such content and offerings. Examples of such solutions include Adobe's Adobe Cloak (a video editing tool) and Lyrebird (a voice imitation algorithm), among others.[71] (see Image 5.3). All these instances suggest that firms should design sophisticated multi-sensory solutions that provide personalized attention to users and must understand the human-machine interface to design effective customer intervention actions to successfully address churn.

Improvement to demand forecasting

Effective demand management allows firms to better plan and employ firm resources that can ultimately create more value for them and their customers. By leveraging the power of insights enabled by ML algorithms, firms can identify upcoming trends and craft responses in anticipation (e.g., design new offerings, update delivery mechanisms, etc.). The interconnectivity between business functions and the automation of analytical and business processes can help firms respond to these trends more efficiently and effectively. By anticipating customer needs, firms can surprise and delight customers with offerings that are aligned with their requirements.

Many firms gainfully employ ML algorithms for a wide range of actions that collectively help them manage demand and ensure users always have the best experience. For instance, the online streaming platform Netflix uses ML algorithms for making various predictions such as network quality to

Image 5.3 Video and Music Editing Software. Video and music editing software work in tandem with humans to create content that can be personalized and highly engaging
(*Source* Photo by *Jakob Owens* on *Unsplash*)

determine the quality of video to provide; drop in network connectivity; and predicting what a user will play next in his viewing list to cache the video in the device before the viewer hits play, enabling the video to start faster and/or at a higher quality, among others.[72] Such predictions allow Netflix to effectively plan its video lineup that satisfies user expectations. Other examples of ML use towards forecasting include the case of Domino's predicting when orders will be ready;[73] and Kraft Heinz towards demand forecasting during major events such as the Super Bowl, and for aiding in restocking decisions at retail outlets.[74]

As a result of more granular insights, increased automation, and greater interconnectivity of business functions, firms can improve their product development and enhancement processes and achieve process optimization.[75] In the future, we can expect this trend to only continue and bring plentiful gains to firms and consumers. Some areas that are already seeing impressive progress in this regard include applications such as smart warehousing and smart transportation enable intuitive demand fulfillment, warehouse automation, and route optimization for maximum efficiency (see Image 5.4). For instance, Volvo employs ML capabilities to predict failure and breakdown rates to determine the inventory volume of spare parts.[76] As firms continue to invest more resources into ML development, a prescient approach to demand forecasting can be developed that can drive more value for firms and users.

Image 5.4 Machine Learning-powered Warehousing Solutions. Machine learning solutions deployed at warehouses aid in demand fulfillment, warehouse automation, and route optimization for maximum efficiency
(*Source* Photo by *Nana Smirnova* on *Unsplash*)

Strategy Development for Customers and Products

The continuous developments made in ML algorithms ultimately get tested in business settings to see the real-world impact. Such developments lead to ML-based solutions that are instrumental in enabling firms to (a) manage customers, (b) develop new products/product concepts, (c) enhance promotion strategies, and (d) create effective brand-customer engagement. Among other activities, the insights from ML solutions can help firms manage their existing customers' needs and develop new products to cater to evolving consumer needs at an individual level.

An important area where ML continues to contribute towards strategy development in a firm-customer interface is the area of chatbots and intelligent agents (see Image 5.5). Using NLP, chatbots and intelligent agents can communicate like humans. Specifically, using technologies like deep learning, genetic algorithms, and natural language processing, machines can be trained to generate insights to accomplish specific tasks by processing large amounts of data and recognizing patterns in the data that are employed for personal and business uses. Popular solutions for personal uses that involve

ML include personal assistants (e.g., Alexa, Siri, Cortana), travel planning (e.g., Mezi), music (e.g., Pandora), financial planning (e.g., Olivia), language translation (e.g., Liv), and smart-home solutions (e.g., Nest), among others. Similarly, popular solutions for business uses that involve ML include plug-and-play solutions for business needs (e.g., Fluid AI), e-commerce and digital marketing (e.g., Sentient), process automation (e.g., Amazon MTurk), face recognition (e.g., Haystack), legal language assistant (e.g., Legal Robot), and credit scoring (e.g., Lenddo), among others. Such intelligent agents can respond to basic user queries and recognize and respond accordingly. Additionally, in a customer interface, such agents know when customers need to be transferred seamlessly to human representatives, leading to efficient customer service and lower costs.

Even the e-commerce domain is expected to be irreversibly impacted by ML capabilities that can positively impact strategy development. For instance, ML solutions such as shopping bots can monitor and compare prices, suggest repurchases, and even make purchases on behalf of humans via bot-to-bot interactions. Overall, ML can help firms master knowledge of consumer preferences, and deliver personalized products, pricing, and advertising content through relevant channels. Such actions, in the future, can help further

Image 5.5 Chatbots and intelligent agents. Chatbots and intelligent agents use ML capabilities to assist customers in making informed choices
(*Source* Photo by *Matthew Henry* from *Burst*)

strategy development for products and customers to extract more value for all.

Key Terms and Related Conceptualizations

Data mining	The process of discovering interesting patterns in databases that are useful in decision-making
ETL (extract/transform/load) process	Extracting the data from various sources, transforming it for ML algorithms, and loading it into a structured schema applicable to ML processes
Individual-level personalization	Firms personalize the marketing mix to each customer's individual needs, tastes, and behaviors
Intelligence amplification	Using powerful computational analysis to enhance human abilities
Machine learning	Deals with the process of training machines to learn over time.
Mass personalization	Firms personalize the same marketing mix offerings to customers based on customers' average preferences
Personalization	A strategy deployed by the firm, usually based on previously collected customer data, on what marketing mix is suitable for an individual
Reinforcement learning, or semi-supervised learning	Models where the machine is not told which action(s) to take, rather it must discover which action(s) yield the highest reward by trying them
Segment-level personalization	Firms first create customer segments and then personalize marketing mix elements according to each segment
Structured data	Any data that resides in a database under specific fields with clearly defined values
Supervised learning models	Models where the learning system uses prior data as training information and accordingly presents related predictions for all future outcomes.
Uncanny valley	The hypothesis that a person's response to a humanlike robot would abruptly shift from empathy to revulsion (and even eeriness) as it approached, but failed to attain, a lifelike appearance
Unstructured data	A single data unit in which the information offers a relatively concurrent representation of its multifaceted nature without predefined organization or numeric values.
Unsupervised learning models	Models that make the machine learn about performing a task without providing explicit instructions on how to do it

Notes and References

1. Mohri, M., A. Rostamizadeh, and A. Talwalkar (2018), *Foundations of machine learning*. Cambridge, MA: MIT Press.
2. Kumar, V. (2021). *Intelligent marketing: Employing new age technologies*. Sage Publications.
3. McCulloch, W. S., & W. Pitts (1943), "A logical calculus of the ideas immanent in nervous activity," *The Bulletin of Mathematical Biophysics*, 5(4), 115–133.
4. Turing, A. (1950), "Computing machinery and intelligence," *Mind*, 49(236), pp. 433–460.
5. Foote, K. D. (2019), "A brief history of machine learning," *Dataversity*, March 26, [accessed from https://www.dataversity.net/a-brief-history-of-machine-learning/].
6. Thomas, M. (2019), "History of deep learning: Formative moments that shaped the technology," *Built In*, April 2, [accessed from https://builtin.com/artificial-intelligence/deep-learning-history].
7. Chen, X., Y. Xia, P. Jin, & J. Carroll (2015), "Dataless text classification with descriptive LDA," In *Proceedings of the Twenty-Ninth AAAI Conference on Artificial Intelligence*, pp. 2224–2231.
8. Chang, M. W., L. A. Ratinov, D. Roth, & V. Srikumar (2008), "Importance of semantic representation: Dataless classification," In *Proceedings of the Twenty-Third AAAI Conference on Artificial Intelligence*, Vol. 2, pp. 830–835.
9. Balducci, B., & Marinova, D. (2018). Unstructured data in marketing. *Journal of the Academy of Marketing Science, 46*, 557–590.
10. Bose, I., and R. K. Mahapatra (2001), "Business data mining—a machine learning perspective," *Information & Management*, 39(3), 211–225.
11. Shaw, M. J., C. Subramaniam, G. W. Tan, and M. E. Welge (2001), "Knowledge management and data mining for marketing," *Decision Support Systems*, 31(1), 127–137.
12. Kumar, V., and W. J. Reinartz (2018). *Customer relationship management: Concept, Strategies, and Tools*. 3rd edition, Berlin, Germany: Springer-Verlag Berlin Heidelberg.
13. Kotsiantis, S. B. (2007), "Supervised machine learning: A review of classification techniques," In *Emerging artificial intelligence applications in computer engineering*, Maglogiannis, I., K. Karpouzis, M. Wallace, and J. Soldatos (Eds.), *160*, 3–24.

14. Chin, A. J., A. Mirzal, H. Haron, and H. N. A. Hamed (2015), "Supervised, unsupervised, and semi-supervised feature selection: a review on gene selection," *IEEE/ACM Transactions on Computational Biology and Bioinformatics*, *13*(5), 971–989.
15. Sutton, R. S. (1992), "Introduction: The challenge of reinforcement learning," In: Sutton R.S. (eds) *Reinforcement Learning*, The Springer International Series in Engineering and Computer Science (Knowledge Representation, Learning and Expert Systems), vol 173, Springer, Boston, MA.
16. For instance, the global market size for ML was estimated at around USD 59 billion in 2020. This is expected to grow to USD 250 billion by 2025, and USD 528 billion by 2030 (Statista Market Insights (2023), "Machine Learning—Worldwide." Retrieved October 06, 2023, from https://www.statista.com/outlook/tmo/artificial-intelligence/machine-learning/worldwide). The report also found that in 2022, the top five sectors employing ML capabilities are manufacturing (18.9%), finance (15.4%), healthcare (12.2%), transportation (10.6%), and security (10.1%). Further, the report identifies the USA, China, Germany, the United Kingdom, and Japan to be the biggest geographic regions for ML usage.
17. McCann, D. (2019), "Amid data deluge, judgment still makes the difference," *CFO.com*, June 6, [accessed from https://www.cfo.com/analytics/2019/06/amid-data-deluge-judgment-still-makes-the-difference/].
18. Falcon, W. (2018), "4 reasons why companies struggle to adopt deep learning," *Forbes*, July 5, [accessed from https://www.forbes.com/sites/williamfalcon/2018/07/05/4-reasons-why-companies-struggle-to-adopt-deep-learning/#46eb16874cda].
19. Kumar, V., and J. A. Petersen (2012), *Statistical methods in customer relationship management*. Chichester, West Sussex: John Wiley & Sons
20. Kumar, V., & Vannan, M. (2021). It takes two to tango: Statistical modeling and machine learning. *Journal of Global Scholars of Marketing Science*, *31*(3), 296–317.
21. Shopify uses ML solutions to determine the closest and most efficient fulfillment centers for businesses. This allows Shopify to predict demand and inventory allocation, and route orders to the closest fulfillment center based on inputs like locations of businesses, product details, shopping behaviors, etc.; Cannon, J. (2019), Shopify launches machine learning powered network for US merchants. *Shopify*, June

20, accessed from https://martech.org/shopify-launches-machine-learning-powered-network-for-us-merchants/.
22. Quotient Health uses ML to design electronic medical record systems that are optimized and standardized to lower medical costs; and PathAI uses ML to help medical care providers make quicker and more accurate diagnoses and identify new treatment options (Thomas, M. (2019a), "Ultra-modern medicine: Examples of machine learning in healthcare," *Built In*, July 4, [accessed from https://builtin.com/artificial-intelligence/machine-learning-healthcare]).
23. Marr, B. (2019), "The amazing ways hitachi uses artificial intelligence and machine learning," *Forbes*, June 14, [accessed from https://www.forbes.com/sites/bernardmarr/2019/06/14/the-amazing-ways-hitachi-uses-artificial-intelligence-and-machine-learning/#317568dc3705].
24. Kumar, V., D. Ramachandran, and B. Kumar (2020), "Influence of new-age technologies on marketing: A research agenda," *Journal of Business Research*, [accessed from https://www.sciencedirect.com/science/article/abs/pii/S0148296320300151].
25. (Kumar, V., D. Ramachandran, and B. Kumar (2020), "Influence of new-age technologies on marketing: A research agenda," *Journal of Business Research*, [accessed from https://www.sciencedirect.com/science/article/abs/pii/S0148296320300151]) contend that a firm that adopts ML and AI can enhance the analysis and interpretation of available data, to better understand its devices and customers.
26. PayPal (2023), "4 ways machine learning helps you detect payment fraud," *PayPal.com*, February 14, accessed from https://www.paypal.com/us/brc/article/payment-fraud-detection-machine-learning.
27. PayPal (2021), "The power of data: How PayPal leverages machine learning to tackle fraud," *PayPal.com*, December 22, accessed from https://www.paypal.com/us/brc/article/paypal-machine-learning-stop-fraud.
28. Kumar, V., & Vannan, M. (2021). It takes two to tango: Statistical modeling and machine learning. *Journal of Global Scholars of Marketing Science*, *31*(3), 296–317.
29. James, G., D. Witten, T. Hastie, and R. Tibshirani (2013), *An introduction to statistical learning*. New York, NY: Springer.
30. Please see (Cunningham, P., Cord, M., & Delany, S. J. (2008). Supervised learning. In *Machine learning techniques for multimedia: Case studies on organization and retrieval* (pp. 21–49). Berlin, Heidelberg: Springer Berlin Heidelberg) for more details on supervised learning models.

31. Sutton, R. S., and A. G. Barto (2018), *Reinforcement learning: An introduction* (2 ed.). Cambridge, MA: MIT Press.
32. Bettaney, E. (2020), "Automated outfit generation with deep learning," *Medium*, November 11, accessed from https://medium.com/asos-techblog/automated-outfit-generation-with-deep-learning-8f0eacc0ea86.
33. Preston, R. (2021), "McDonald's Hong Kong leverages machine learning to improve the customer experience," *Oracle*, November 30, accessed from https://www.oracle.com/apac/news/announcement/blog/mcdonald-leverages-machine-learning-2021-12-03/.
34. De Cremer, D., and G. Kasparov (2021), "AI should augment human intelligence, not replace it," *Harvard Business Review*, March 18, accessed from https://hbr.org/2021/03/ai-should-augment-human-intelligence-not-replace-it.
35. Torres, L. (2023), "How AMAGGI uses planet data to take sustainable agriculture to the next level," *Planet*, November 20, accessed from https://www.planet.com/pulse/how-amaggi-uses-planet-data-to-take-sustainable-agriculture-to-the-next-level/.
36. Kumar, V. (2021). *Intelligent marketing: Employing new age technologies*. Sage Publications
37. Kumar, V., B. Rajan, R. Venkatesan, and J. Lecinski (2019), "Understanding the role of artificial intelligence in personalized engagement marketing," *California Management Review*, 61(4), 135–55.
38. Narula, G. (2018), "Everyday Examples of artificial intelligence and machine learning," *Emerj.com*, October 29, [accessed from https://www.techemergence.com/everyday-examples-of-ai/].
39. Neilsen (2016), "Global connected commerce," *Nielsen Insights*, January 20, [accessed from https://www.nielsen.com/us/en/insights/report/2016/global-connected-commerce/#].
40. Shartsis, R. (2019), "Dynamic pricing: The secret weapon used by the world's most successful companies," *Forbes*, January 8, [accessed from https://www.forbes.com/sites/forbestechcouncil/2019/01/08/dynamic-pricing-the-secret-weapon-used-by-the-worlds-most-successful-companies/#755a8422168b].
41. Faden, M. (2019), "Machine learning helps payment services detect fraud," *American Express*, [accessed from https://www.americanexpress.com/us/foreign-exchange/articles/payment-services-fraud-detection-using-AI/].
42. Stine, L. (2020), "Taco bell deploys AI for in-app personalization," *Restaurant Dive*, January 14, [accessed from https://www.restaurantdive.com/news/taco-bell-deploys-ai-for-in-app-personalization/570361/].

43. Bughin, J., E. Hazan, S. Ramaswamy, M. Chui, T. Allas, P. Dahlström, N. Henke, and M. Trench (2017), "Artificial intelligence: The next digital frontier?" *McKinsey Global Institute*, [accessed from https://www.mckinsey.com/~/media/McKinsey/Industries/Advanced%20Electronics/Our%20Insights/How%20artificial%20intelligence%20can%20deliver%20real%20value%20to%20companies/MGI-Artificial-Intelligence-Discussion-paper.ashx].
44. Arora, N., X. Dreze, A. Ghose, J. D. Hess, R. Iyengar, B. Jing, Y. Joshi, V. Kumar, N. Lurie, S. Neslin, S. Sajeesh, M. Su, N. Syam, J. Thomas, and Z. J. Zhang (2008), "Putting one-to-one marketing to work: Personalization, customization, and choice," *Marketing Letters*, *19*(3), 305–321.
45. Research contends personalization to be a largely firm-controlled process that is powered using customer-level data (Murthi, B. P. S., and S. Sarkar (2003), "The role of the management sciences in research on personalization," *Management Science*, *49*(10), 1344–1362; Sundar, S. S., and S. S. Marathe (2010), "Personalization versus customization: The importance of agency, privacy, and power usage," *Human Communication Research*, *36*(3), 298–322; Vesanen, J., and M. Raulas (2006), "Building bridges for personalization—a process model for marketing," *Journal of Interactive Marketing*, *20*(1), 1–16). Additionally, research has conceptualized personalization as a process that interlinks customers and marketers (Murthi, B. P. S., and S. Sarkar (2003), "The role of the management sciences in research on personalization," *Management Science*, *49*(10), 1344–1362), and that interaction solidifies the relationship between customers and marketers (Simonson, 2005; Wind, J., and A. Rangaswamy (2001), "Customerization: The next revolution in mass customization," *Journal of Interactive Marketing*, *15*(1), 13–32).
46. Bleier, A., A. D. Keyser, and K. Verleye (2018), "Customer engagement through personalization and customization," in *Customer Engagement Marketing*, R. W. Palmatier, V. Kumar, and C. M. Harmeling (Eds.), pp. 75–94.
47. Vinoski, J. (2020), "New research shows consumers already expect mass personalization. time to get ready!" *Forbes*, January 20, [accessed from https://www.forbes.com/sites/jimvinoski/2020/01/20/new-research-shows-consumers-already-expect-mass-personalization-time-to-get-ready/#44fed95a223e].
48. Sriram, M. (2019), "Toppr launches live classes to boost growth," *LiveMint.com*, August 26, [accessed from https://www.livemint.com/market/mark-to-market/toppr-launches-live-classes-to-boost-growth-1566813568679.html].

49. Fitzgerald, M. (2020), "Personalized nutrition could be the next plant-based meat, worth $64 billion by 2040, says UBS," *CNBC*, January 19, [accessed from https://www.cnbc.com/2020/01/19/personalized-nutrition-could-be-the-next-plant-based-meat-worth-64-billion-by-2040-says-ubs.html].
50. Verhoef, P. C., P. K. Kannan, and J. J. Inman (2015), "From Multi-channel retailing to omni-channel retailing: introduction to the special issue on multi-channel retailing," *Journal of Retailing*, *91*(2), 174–81.
51. Further, a survey by the CMO Council and SAP Hybris found that 47 percent of consumers would abandon a brand that delivers poor, impersonal, or frustrating experiences.
52. Brynjolfsson, E., Y. J. Hu, and M. S. Rahman (2013), "Competing in the age of omnichannel retailing," *MIT Sloan Management Review*, *54*(4), 23–29.
53. Min, S. (2019), "Coming soon to Netflix: Movie trailers crafted by AI," *CBS News*, August 19, [accessed from https://www.cbsnews.com/news/netflix-trailers-made-by-ai-netflix-is-investing-in-automation-to-make-trailers/].
54. Esteves, R. B., and J. Resende (2016), "Competitive targeted advertising with price discrimination," *Marketing Science, 35*(4), 576–587.
55. Infor (2020), "Bavaria Boutique Hotel in Munich Is first to benefit from optimized pricing through Infor HPO," *PR Newswire*, February 10, [accessed from https://www.prnewswire.com/news-releases/bavaria-boutique-hotel-in-munich-is-first-to-benefit-from-optimized-pricing-through-infor-hpo-301001385.html].
56. Bose, N. (2018), "Walmart goes to the cloud to close gap with Amazon," *Reuters*, February 14, [accessed from https://www.reuters.com/article/us-walmart-cloud/walmart-goes-to-the-cloud-to-close-gap-with-amazon-idUSKCN1FY0K7].
57. Wedel, M., & P. K. Kannan (2016), "Marketing analytics for data-rich environments," *Journal of Marketing*, *80*(6), 97–121.
58. Vaccaro, A., S. Mager, N. Groff, and A. Bolante (2019), "Beyond marketing: Experience reimagined," *Deloitte Insights*, January 16, [accessed from https://www2.deloitte.com/us/en/insights/focus/tech-trends/2019/personalized-marketing-experience-reimagined.html#endnote-sup-3].
59. Windyka, K. (2018), "In-Store platform uses AI to digitally personalize shoppers' experience," *PSFK*, September 11, [available at https://www.psfk.com/2018/09/mystore-e-ai-personalized-shopping-experience.html].

60. White, D. (2016), "Artificial intelligence transforms the in-store shopping experience with the pilot of "Macy's On Call"," *IBM*, July 20, [accessed from https://www.ibm.com/blogs/watson/2016/07/artificial-intelligence-transforms-store-shopping-experience-pilot-macys-call/].
61. Trejos, N. (2016), "Introducing Connie, Hilton's new robot concierge," *USA Today*, March 9, [accessed from https://www.usatoday.com/story/travel/roadwarriorvoices/2016/03/09/introducing-connie-hiltons-new-robot-concierge/81525924/].
62. Kumar, V., B. Rajan, R. Venkatesan, and J. Lecinski (2019), "Understanding the role of artificial intelligence in personalized engagement marketing," *California Management Review*, 61(4), 135–55.
63. Pansari, A., & V. Kumar (2017), "Customer engagement: the construct, antecedents, and consequences," *Journal of the Academy of Marketing Science*, 45(3), 294–311.
64. Venkatesan, R. (2017), "Executing on a customer engagement strategy," *Journal of the Academy of Marketing Science*, 45, 289–293.
65. Kumar, V. (2021). *Intelligent marketing: Employing new age technologies*. Sage Publications.
66. Kumar, V., D. Ramachandran, and B. Kumar (2020), "Influence of new-age technologies on marketing: A research agenda," *Journal of Business Research*, [accessed from https://www.sciencedirect.com/science/article/abs/pii/S0148296320300151].
67. Kumar, V. (2008), *Managing Customers for Profits*, Upper Saddle River, NJ: Wharton School Publishing.
68. Kumar, V., B. Rajan, R. Venkatesan, and J. Lecinski (2019), "Understanding the role of artificial intelligence in personalized engagement marketing," *California Management Review*, 61(4), 135–55.
69. Mori, M., K. F. MacDorman, and N. Kageki (2012), "The uncanny valley," *IEEE Robotics & Automation Magazine*, 19(2), 98–100.
70. These instances include (a) consumers experiencing uneasiness when they first used a driverless car (Knight, W. (2016), "Novelty of driverless cars wears off quickly for first-timers," *MIT Technology Review*, October 18, [accessed from https://www.technologyreview.com/s/602689/novelty-of-driverless-cars-wears-off-quickly-for-first-timers/]), (b) users inclined to believe human forecasters more than machines, even when the machines are more accurate (Dietvorst, B. J., J. P. Simmons, and C. Massey (2016), "Overcoming algorithm aversion: People will use imperfect algorithms if they can (even slightly) modify them," *Management Science*, 64(3), 1155–1170), and (c) doctors exhibiting lack of trust with recommendations from IBM Watson about medical

diagnostics (Polonski, V. (2018), "People don't trust AI—here's how we can change that," *phys.org*, January 10, [accessed from https://phys.org/news/2018-01-people-dont-aihere.html]), among others.

71. Upson, S. (2017), "Artificial intelligence is killing the uncanny valley and our grasp on reality," *Wired*, December 16, [accessed from https://www.wired.com/story/future-of-artificial-intelligence-2018/].

72. Ekanadham, C. (2018), "Using machine learning to improve streaming quality at Netflix," *Netflix Tech Blog*, March 22, [accessed from https://netflixtechblog.com/using-machine-learning-to-improve-streaming-quality-at-netflix-9651263ef09f].

73. Whitehead, S. A. (2020), "What pizza operators can learn from Domino's use of AI," *Pizza marketplace.com*, January 15, [accessed from https://www.pizzamarketplace.com/articles/what-all-pizza-operators-can-learn-from-dominos-use-of-ai/].

74. Himes, M. (2020), "AI is coming to a grocery store near you," *BuiltIn.com*, January 29, [accessed from https://builtin.com/artificial-intelligence/kraft-heinz-machine-learning-ai].

75. Davenport, T. H., and R. Ronanki (2018), "Artificial Intelligence for the Real World," *Harvard Business Review, 96*(1), 108–116.

76. Marr, B. (2016), "Big data at Volvo: predictive, machine-learning-enabled analytics across petabyte-scale datasets," *Forbes*, July 18, [accessed from https://www.forbes.com/sites/bernardmarr/2016/07/18/how-the-connected-car-is-forcing-volvo-to-rethink-its-data-strategy/#3ea34de13e8d].

6

Transformative Marketing with Metaverse

Overview

Imagine a world in which the lines separating the real and virtual vanish, allowing people to travel through gorgeous landscapes, meet up with friends for a game on the other side of the globe, or create something entirely original and personalized. Welcome to the Metaverse!

The metaverse is a revolutionary frontier that is capturing people's attention globally as the digital world develops at an unprecedented rate. The concept of the metaverse encompasses a range of interconnected virtual realms that can be accessed through augmented and virtual reality technologies. Rather than being limited to a two-dimensional screen, it expands into a three-dimensional existence. Within these digital spaces, individuals have the freedom to assume any identity, engage in various activities, and establish connections that surpass the boundaries of the physical realm.

The metaverse is built upon a complex network of interconnected technologies such as virtual reality (VR), augmented reality (AR), blockchain, artificial intelligence (AI), and others. These technologies work together seamlessly to provide users with an immersive and unified digital experience. They are the foundation of a transformative era that is reshaping our interactions, collaborations, and the formation of communities within the digital world. Metaverse, which initially emerged from the gaming industry, has now extended its impact beyond that domain. It now encompasses virtual marketplaces, educational platforms, social gatherings, and professional conferences, forming a diverse ecosystem that is revolutionizing businesses and reshaping our online interactions.

The metaverse has become a focal point for the business world as it seeks to establish connections with its target audience. Major players such as Meta (formerly known as Facebook), Microsoft, and Nvidia Corporation are dedicating substantial financial resources to constructing a digital realm that aligns with the concept of the metaverse. Not only are retail giants like Gucci, Nike, and Gap venturing into the metaverse to explore customer engagement possibilities, but entertainment brands like Disney, fast-food chains like McDonald's and Chipotle, and professional sports brands like the Atlanta Braves are also joining the ranks of companies interested in leveraging the metaverse for interaction and involvement.

This chapter is organized in the following manner. First, a brief history of the origin of the metaverse is presented, followed by a definition of the metaverse (from a marketing standpoint), along with vignettes about the metaverse's usage and applications. Then, the role of the metaverse in the Marketing 5.0 concept is explored. Next, some marketing applications of the metaverse are discussed. Finally, the future of the metaverse for the marketing industry is envisioned via emergent issues in this area.

Origin, Definition, and Classifications of the Metaverse

Origin

Neal Stephenson is credited with coining the term "metaverse," which he introduced in his 1992 novel *Snow Crash*. In this literary work, Stephenson vividly portrays a virtual world that can be accessed by countless individuals through personalized avatars and creative tools.[1]

Relatedly, the late 1980s-early 1990s period saw the invention and introduction of the Internet, which brought about revolutionary changes that now shape our way of life. The notions of digital twins, bitcoins, the "fifth age" of virtual worlds,[2] etc., first appeared in the late 1990s and early 2000s. In the decade of the 2010s, there were decentralized virtual worlds, augmented reality (AR) games such as Fortnite (*See Image 6.1*) and Pokémon Go (*See Image 6.2*), and non-fungible tokens (NFTs). These are a few of the significant occasions that have shaped the development of the networked virtual and user-generated worlds, which are all reachable via the Metaverse user interface.[3]

Image 6.1 Fortnite. A person playing Fortnite on a mobile device (*Source* Photo by *Erik Mclean* on *Unsplash*)

Image 6.2 Pokémon Go. A person playing Pokémon Go on a mobile device (*Source* Photo by *Mika Baumeister* on *Unsplash*)

Definition

Considering its nascency, there is no consensus in academic research on the definition of metaverse. The metaverse was originally imagined as a virtual reality environment that was semi-physical and in which users interacted through avatars.[4] According to research conducted in the late 2000s, the metaverse is an immersive virtual environment that is three-dimensional and allows users to interact with both software agents and other users.[5] Consistent with the singular-world viewpoint, studies have recognized the scalable and social nature of the metaverse, characterizing it as a virtual environment that facilitates the simultaneous engagement of numerous individuals in social interactions.[6] According to articles in the popular press, the metaverse is the meeting point of the real world and the virtual world. Here, the convergence of web technologies, extended reality, and the internet has led to the conceptualization of the metaverse as a virtual environment that combines the physical and digital.[7]

The metaverse has evolved alongside technological advancements, expanding from a singular virtual world to a more comprehensive concept encompassing multiple interconnected virtual worlds. It has transitioned from a purely virtual representation to a blended reality perspective, incorporating various experiences along the extended reality spectrum, such as virtual reality, augmented reality, mixed reality, and the convergence of other technologies.[8] In essence, the metaverse is now perceived as a hyper-connected digital universe, seamlessly interlinking different virtual realities. Investing time and resources in the metaverse is becoming increasingly popular in today's society.[9] Moreover, it offers the opportunity to connect with others effortlessly, opens up new avenues for employment, and allows individuals to express themselves in unique ways.

Metaverse is being widely applied in the field of Information Technology (IT).[10] On the other hand, the education sector is also embracing technology to enhance learning engagement and effectiveness.[11] By incorporating the metaverse into the learning process, students are provided with a unique experience and a virtual space for socializing, fostering their creativity. Moreover, the metaverse enables learning materials to be tailored to individual students, promoting a student-centered approach to education.[12] The interconnectedness and immersive nature of the metaverse set it apart from other online experiences, making it even more appealing. Businesses can leverage this understanding to make informed investments in the right type of metaverse.

Classification

Metaverses can be categorized into two types: traditional and blockchain-based. Traditional metaverses are typically centralized and do not utilize blockchain technology. In a traditional metaverse, a single company owns and operates the entire virtual world, giving them complete control over all aspects of the metaverse. This centralized approach allows for real-life activities to be performed with a certain level of accuracy, remote collaboration to create new products, and enhanced customer experiences. The metaverse is governed by internal servers and rules, ensuring that one entity oversees the entire network.

On the other hand, blockchain-based metaverses are decentralized and owned by the community. In these metaverses, no single entity has control over the virtual world, and users have ownership and control over their data and assets. The virtual communities within these metaverses operate within the boundaries set by the community. With decentralization, users gain more power over the administration of the metaverse, allowing them to expand the universe and create immersive experiences for each other. In this model, the creators of the metaverse oversee the platform rather than a central authority, promoting a more democratic and inclusive environment.

Despite being in its early stages, the metaverse has already witnessed the initial steps towards a digital revolution. Prominent global corporations are dedicating substantial resources to the advancement of metaverse platforms and technologies. Simultaneously, independent creators are crafting mesmerizing virtual worlds and immersive encounters, challenging the boundaries of what can be accomplished. Table 6.1 provides the types of metaverses and exemplar offerings that represent opportunities and utilizations within the metaverse.

Metaverse in the Marketing 5.0 World

Online and virtual marketplaces have revolutionized customer loyalty and demand by harnessing cutting-edge technologies like AI, ML, and others. These advancements enable businesses to decipher shopping habits, comprehend customer order patterns, and tailor user experiences accordingly. The concept of the Metaverse, which has been extensively discussed in this chapter, represents a virtual realm that seamlessly merges the physical and digital worlds. This integration is made possible by the convergence of internet and web technologies with extended reality. Within this dynamic

Table 6.1 Types of metaverses

Type of metaverse	Meaning	Traditional example	Blockchain-based example
Gaming	Primarily focus on providing gaming and interactive entertainment experiences, centering around gaming mechanics that enable users to participate in gameplay, hunts, and explore virtual worlds.	Fortnite (https://www.fortnite.com), Roblox (https://www.roblox.com/)	The Sandbox (https://www.sandbox.game), Axie Infinity (https://axieinfinity.com/)
Social	Encompasses various aspects of social interaction, communication, and collaboration; fosters connections and facilitates the meeting of new individuals as well as the strengthening of existing relationships.	VRChat (https://hello.vrchat.com/), Second Life (https://secondlife.com)	Somnium Space (https://somniumspace.com/)
Commerce	Users engage in the buying and selling of virtual goods and services within a virtual environment that serves as a virtual marketplace, facilitating business transactions and e-commerce activities.	Shopify (https://www.shopify.com)	Decentraland (https://decentraland.org/)

Type of metaverse	Meaning	Traditional example	Blockchain-based example
Education	Enhances the educational journey and possibilities for its users by offering a virtual setting where students can attend classes, collaborate on group projects, and engage with fellow learners and instructors.	AltspaceVR	Engage (https://engage vr.io/)
Enterprise	An immersive digital environment that aims to optimize experiences and decision-making by replicating and connecting all aspects of an organization, through the development of digital twins.	Microsoft Mesh (http://www.microsoft.com/mesh), NVIDIA Omniverse (https://www.nvidia.com/en-us/omniverse/)	Cryptovoxels

Sources "Types of Metaverse Explained: A Comprehensive Overview," March 8, 2023, https://mudrex.com/blog/types-of-metaverse-explained/; "Enterprise Metaverse—The new way of business," https://www.leewayhertz.com/enterprise-metaverse

environment, data modeling tools play a crucial role in optimizing customer engagement behaviors and purchasing habits. Extensive research indicates that by utilizing customer engagement tools within immersive virtual spaces, businesses can create personalized digital shopping experiences that resonate with individual preferences and needs. Expanding on the Marketing 5.0 concept discussed in Chapter 2, this section presents how the metaverse operates in the Marketing 5.0 world. Particularly, this section discusses five examples of where the metaverse is applied through the lens of Marketing 5.0 and establishes how such actions can also bode well for humanity.

Data-Driven Marketing Using the Metaverse

The metaverse provides marketers with a unique platform to engage with consumers in a more immersive and interactive manner. By leveraging data-driven marketing techniques within the metaverse, marketers can create personalized experiences that captivate and engage users on a deeper level. This can include virtual product demonstrations, interactive advertisements, and even virtual events and experiences. By utilizing the metaverse for data-driven marketing, marketers can not only enhance their understanding of their target audience but also create more impactful and memorable marketing experiences that drive brand awareness and loyalty.

For instance, Decentraland is an Ethereum-based virtual reality platform where users can buy, create, and monetize virtual land using their cryptocurrency, MANA. It offers a decentralized environment for designing immersive experiences, customizing avatars, and interacting with others. The platform also has a digital real estate market and opportunities for content creators to earn revenue. Brands in Decentraland have reward programs that allow users to redeem digital assets for discounts in the physical world, helping to revitalize high streets post-pandemic. *The Voice* is one brand using this metaverse.

The Voice, an American singing competition series, made its debut on NBC in 2011. Contestants are selected through public auditions and receive training from four coaches who offer guidance and feedback. In November 2022, *The Voice* expanded its reach by launching a four-day virtual pop-up event in partnership with NBC at the Metaverse Music Festival in Decentraland. This immersive experience allowed the Decentraland community, music enthusiasts, and festival attendees to participate in the audition process, engage in themed games to collect notes, and have the opportunity to win branded merchandise. The fans' active involvement resulted in an average session duration of 49 minutes, which is 13 times higher than the engagement typically seen on social media platforms.[13] By embracing this virtual space, *The Voice* effectively develops marketing strategies that resonate with its audience.

Predictive Marketing Using the Metaverse

Brands are continuously searching for new and creative methods to connect with their target audience in the ever-changing marketing environment. Roblox, a popular online platform, has emerged as one such platform where users can create, share, and play games. This global platform has caught the attention of brands who are eager to leverage its potential for promotional and educational endeavors.

For instance, Walmart introduced two innovative virtual experiences, Walmart Land and Walmart's Universe of Play, on the popular metaverse platform Roblox in September 2022. These captivating spaces provide customers with interactive content and entertainment, showcasing the finest aspects of Walmart's aisles in a virtual realm. However, consumer advocacy groups expressed concerns about potential covert marketing to children in these games. Subsequently, Walmart pivoted in a new direction and launched Walmart Discovered in September 2023 in Roblox. This world is divided into different "departments," (e.g., sports, pets, etc.) wherein, players can shop for virtual items for their avatar, or enjoy gamified experiences.[14]

Predictive analytics plays a crucial role in analyzing user interactions within the virtual Walmart store and forecasting customer behavior. By utilizing data from the metaverse, it becomes possible to anticipate which products or sections within the virtual store users are more likely to explore, interact with, or make purchases. Through the implementation of predictive models, the virtual Walmart experience in Roblox can personalize recommendations for individual users based on their previous interactions, preferences, and in-game behavior. This customization may involve suggesting items or offers that align with a user's interests or past purchases. Furthermore, predictive analytics can assist Walmart in optimizing its in-game marketing strategies by accurately predicting the most effective methods to engage users, deploying promotions, or designing interactive elements within the virtual store.

Contextual Marketing Using the Metaverse

Metaverse-based contextual marketing is revolutionizing the way businesses connect with their target audience. By leveraging the immersive and interactive nature of the metaverse, companies can create personalized and engaging experiences for their customers. Unlike traditional marketing methods, which often rely on static advertisements, contextual marketing in the metaverse allows brands to seamlessly integrate their products or services into the virtual environment, making the marketing message more relevant and impactful. For example, a clothing brand can use data on a user's virtual wardrobe to suggest complementary items or offer exclusive discounts, creating a seamless shopping experience that feels tailored to the individual.

Consider the case of Africarare, the inaugural metaverse in Africa, which has constructed Ubuntuland to unearth Africa's latent talent, ingenuity, and inventiveness, while simultaneously forging connections between Africa and the global digital economy. Using the $UBUNTU Token or ETH, people can buy, sell, or rent land in Ubuntuland. Landowners can create various experiences like art exhibitions, retail stores, social interactions, gaming, virtual concerts, and more. Companies such as Nedbank, MTN, and Primedia are already part of Ubuntuland[15]

Now, Africarare has collaborated with Innovation Africa, a non-profit organization, to establish a unique Innovation Africa village in Ubuntuland. This village will serve as a platform to highlight the transformative efforts of the organization. The primary focus of this partnership is to uplift rural communities by granting them access to clean water and electricity through the utilization of Israeli solar, water, and agricultural technologies. By implementing this innovative approach, the lives of individuals within these communities will be positively impacted, bringing about significant change.

For instance, Africarare has recently introduced a distinctive collection of Water Drop NFTs named "Drops of Life."[16] This collection comprises five water drops, namely Diamond, Gold, Silver, Platinum, and Bronze. Each drop possesses unique attributes and variations based on the buyer's donation type. For instance, the Diamond Drop not only ensures a lifetime supply of water to a village but also grants the buyer an opportunity to visit the village and personally inaugurate the water supply. Additionally, it includes a virtual 3x3 village in Ubuntuland, where the buyer can explore comprehensive data regarding water production in a three-dimensional format. By creating such virtual spaces in the metaverse, Africarare empowers individuals to make a significant impact and improve the lives of people and society as a whole.

Augmented Marketing Using the Metaverse

Augmented marketing in the metaverse opens up a world of possibilities for brands and businesses. By leveraging AR and VR technologies, marketers can create interactive and immersive experiences that captivate consumers' attention and leave a lasting impression. Furthermore, by tracking user interactions within AR and VR experiences, marketers can gain a deeper understanding of consumer preferences, interests, and purchasing patterns. This data can then be used to refine marketing strategies, tailor product offerings, and deliver targeted advertisements, ultimately driving higher engagement and conversion rates.

For instance, Bon Viv Spiked Seltzer collaborated with immersive production firm Aircards to launch a marketing campaign that showed clients the potential of mixed reality experiences.[17] The project was centered on a cutting-edge out-of-home (OOH) approach in which consumers could scan a QR code found on many Bon Viv murals located in San Diego and Los Angeles. Using a code, patrons were able to gain entry to a virtual 3D vending machine where they could choose and obtain their desired flavor. The campaign also urged customers to choose digital delivery via Instacart integration or to visit nearby retail locations where Bon Viv was sold.

An average of two minutes were spent on the seamless experience, and 58% of consumers clicked through to purchase a can of Bon Viv. For the majority of traditional digital channels, these outcomes are orders of magnitude higher than industry averages. The combination of a well-known communication tool (QR codes) with augmented reality activities to "transport" customers to a location that appeals to their interests is what makes this campaign so successful. Customers benefited greatly since they were given a prompt call to action that they had chosen on their own. Overall, Bon Viv realized a significant return on investment and the ability to develop a quantifiable result-oriented marketing campaign.

Agile Marketing Using the Metaverse

Agile Marketing, a dynamic approach that emphasizes flexibility and adaptability, has found a new playground in the metaverse. This emerging technology allows marketers to transcend traditional boundaries and explore limitless possibilities. By harnessing the power of the metaverse, marketers can create interactive campaigns that blur the lines between the physical and digital worlds. This opens up a whole new realm of opportunities for brands to engage with their customers in innovative ways.

For a considerable period, 3D and 3D graphics have been present, but the metaverse takes it a step further by allowing organizations to quickly adapt it to specific situations through the use of elements like decentralized finance, tokenization, and commerce, resulting in an exceptional experience. For instance, NextMeet, an immersive platform based in India, offers a virtual conferencing and networking environment in real-time, where users can interact through avatars in a 3D setting. By prioritizing interactive collaboration, learning solutions, and efficient work practices, the platform strives to eliminate the sense of isolation and disconnection that can arise from remote and hybrid work setups.[18]

Following the COVID-19 pandemic, the company realized the industry needed to migrate to an online work mode at the earliest, while not compromising on the quality of workplace interactions. This platform allows employees to seamlessly navigate virtual offices and meeting rooms in real-time using digital avatars. They can easily approach a virtual help desk, deliver live presentations, socialize with colleagues in a networking lounge, or freely explore a conference center or exhibition using customizable avatars. By accessing the virtual environment through their desktop computer or mobile device, participants can effortlessly direct their avatars to move around the virtual office space. In terms of employee engagement, the platform offers a unique onboarding experience where new employees can explore the company by walking through a 3D hall or gallery with interactive stands, replacing the traditional method of reading an onboarding document.[19] Such a solution enabled companies to quickly migrate to virtual workplaces while ensuring employees stayed engaged with their colleagues and the workplace.

Current Metaverse Applications in Marketing

Metaverse has the potential to revolutionize customer experiences, customer engagement with the brand, and the concept of marketing. A virtually infinite number of users can experience the metaverse synchronously and persistently, with a massively scalable, interoperable[20] network of real-time rendered 3D virtual worlds that provide continuity of data, including identity, history, entitlement, objects, communications, and payments, and an individual sense of presence.[21] Businesses can use the metaverse to change their business methods, regardless of their size or target audience.[22] This section presents five specific application areas where the metaverse continues to help companies in developing marketing initiatives.

Understanding Customer Needs to Deploy in the Metaverse

During the 1990s, the internet faced criticism for being a passing trend, but it soon gained momentum. The growing number of consumers embracing the internet brought about a significant transformation. In a similar vein, the metaverse has captured the attention of consumers, signifying a notable shift in how technology is utilized.[23] Customers are drawn to novel experiences, and embracing new technologies such as the metaverse enables them to revolutionize customer experiences in a sustained manner.

Applications of the metaverse that go beyond gaming are becoming more and more apparent. They are incredibly influencing immersive experiences in sports, entertainment, retail, and education. High-end labels such as Gucci and Balenciaga have developed virtual showrooms that allow clients to peruse and engage with merchandise in an incredibly lifelike three-dimensional setting. Using their smartphones, users can virtually try on makeup with L'Oréal's Modiface app. Virtual employee training, teamwork with avatars, virtual prototyping in manufacturing and construction, virtual car showroom displays, and other less discussed enterprise applications and opportunities of the metaverse. It is interesting to note that governments are also experimenting with metaverse technology. For instance, Seoul announced the launch of Meta Seoul, a digital replica of South Korea's capital city Seoul where users can participate in a range of different activities. The virtual city will house all the tourist sites and attractions that people can visit from the comfort of their homes, among other key places of interest and even the Mayor's Office. Other global cities such as Sharjah, Dubai, and Hong Kong have also announced similar such initiatives.[24]

Gen Z is a powerful force when it comes to the demographic tailwinds influencing the metaverse's adoption in the corporate world. Compared to earlier generations, the income-earning population is more accustomed to virtual goods, virtual worlds, and virtual transactions.[25] Companies must determine their marketing objectives before deciding whether or not to implement the metaverse (in fact, doing so is not an option). This is dependent upon their brand positioning, the tastes of their current and prospective audiences, etc. After the objectives are established, the businesses must determine which platforms offer the best odds and brand alignment.

Revisiting Firm Capabilities to Integrate in the Metaverse

There are several platforms available for Metaverse implementation, including Roblox, Fortnite, Decentraland, Minecraft, and Meta's Horizon Worlds. Selecting the appropriate platform is crucial for a successful implementation. Roblox is widely recognized for its extensive and diverse user base, making it an ideal choice for those interested in user-generated content and younger audiences. Gucci, for instance, conducted numerous brand activations on Roblox and achieved remarkable success when it launched a metaverse version of its Gucci Garden, attracting 19.9 million visitors within two weeks.[26] On the other hand, Fortnite is particularly suitable for social gamers who enjoy competitive battle gameplay. Ralph Lauren capitalized on this platform by introducing a digital clothing and accessories collection in the Fortnite Item Shop, which was further complemented by a physical clothing line inspired by the digital collection. Notably, the collaboration also marked the first redesign of the iconic Ralph Lauren Polo Pony logo in 55 years.[27]

Despite the negative experiences encountered by Meta in the metaverse,[28] companies like Nvidia are forging ahead with this technology.[29] In a recent development, Nvidia introduced the NVIDIA Omniverse, a design and simulation platform, in September 2023, to further their progress in the metaverse. However, despite these advancements, there are still challenges to overcome. Intel, for example, argues that a significant increase in computing power, around 1,000 times greater than the current capacity, is necessary to sustain the vision of the metaverse.[30]

The firm's current computing capacity required to power the metaverse is expected to be addressed through the implementation of algorithms and software enhancements. Technologies such as ML-powered neural networks and AI-enhanced computational techniques have the potential to enhance computing capacity and ensure the development of a robust hardware roadmap. As businesses strive to bring their metaverse vision to fruition, it is crucial for them to also prioritize strategies that mitigate the heightened energy consumption resulting from these advancements. Once the potential of these capabilities is recognized and efforts are made to make them metaverse-ready, companies must shift their focus towards designing marketing mix strategies that align with the metaverse concept.

Designing Marketing Mix Strategies in the Metaverse

The metaverse offers immense marketing prospects for businesses of various scales and industries. It is poised to redefine how organizations engage with their target demographics, erasing the boundaries between the physical and virtual realms. As the virtual landscape expands, marketers are evolving their conventional strategies to cater to the distinct requirements of the metaverse. Consequently, the traditional marketing mix model is no longer effective and necessitates adaptation.

Product. In the realm of digital transformation, the shift from physical to virtual products has become increasingly prevalent. While companies have started to design products in metaverses (*See Image 6.3*), organizations are also leveraging immersive technologies to enhance their offerings. Consider the following cases:

- Nike offers virtual sneakers, clothing, and accessories within their virtual world, Nikeland. This innovative approach allows customers to not only get involved in the design of shoes but also make purchases and showcase their unique style and individuality.[31]
- Ikea has introduced a captivating AR game called "The Little Adventure" for families who visit their stores in Sweden. By accessing the game through Instagram, customers can immerse themselves in an interactive

Image 6.3 Product design using Metaverse. Product design and ergonomic features can be configured on the metaverse
(*Source* Photo by *XR Expo* on *Unsplash*)

experience that focuses on educating and engaging children about marine life. Through virtual swimming with different sea creatures, kids can learn about them and gain knowledge about the ocean. The game also addresses important themes such as littering and pollution prevention, showcasing Ikea's dedication to promoting plastic recycling, as evidenced by their Blåvingad collection featuring ocean-themed soft toys and children's accessories made from ocean-bound plastics.[32]

- Obsess has developed the AVA virtual platform, which draws inspiration from Shopify's traditional web grid interface model. This platform empowers brands to create and oversee their immersive 3D virtual storefronts, allowing them to adapt and modify merchandising, content, and styling dynamically throughout the year, thereby ensuring a next-generation shopping experience for their customers.[33]

These examples indicate that the field of product engagement and self-expression is changing, and virtual and physical experiences are starting to converge.

Price. The metaverse is increasingly being recognized as a platform where consumers can interact with brands and make purchases.[34] This perception among customers can potentially lead to a willingness to pay higher prices, as it sets the brand apart from its competitors. The use of AR and VR elements to enhance existing products also contributes to this differentiation. Conducting thorough market research is crucial in determining the added value of metaverse elements and the corresponding price premiums. Pricing activities in the metaverse include purchasing virtual land in platforms like Decentraland, buying and selling NFTs, and obtaining exclusive access to metaverse experiences. Cryptocurrencies have emerged as a popular method of conducting transactions within the virtual realm. Many companies have adopted Ethereum or their unique virtual currencies to facilitate purchases, providing a secure and decentralized payment system that promotes seamless transactions and builds trust between buyers and sellers.

The metaverse presents a distinct pricing landscape compared to traditional spaces, as evidenced by the significant price difference between Gucci's virtual sneakers, priced at $12.99, and their real-life counterparts, which can cost up to $1,000. To maintain appropriate pricing within the metaverse, companies have the opportunity to employ various strategies. One such strategy involves leveraging the capabilities of the metaverse to gather and analyze consumer data, enabling retailers to develop a comprehensive understanding of their customers' preferences and behaviors. This accurate segmentation of virtual consumers not only enhances retailers' understanding of their target audience but also strengthens customer loyalty. Additionally, companies can adopt competitive pricing approaches, closely monitoring competitors' prices and adjusting their own accordingly. Another viable option is algorithm-based pricing, where pricing algorithms utilize consumer data to determine the optimal price for a product. These are just a few examples of the pricing strategies that can be employed in the metaverse.

Place. The metaverse market is projected to experience significant growth,[35] indicating that retailers and brands will need to enhance their presence within this virtual realm. Alongside the ongoing debate regarding the metaverse's viability as a standalone sales channel, there is considerable discourse surrounding the overall concept of what a metaverse space might entail. Generally, the metaverse refers to a shared virtual environment that emerges from the fusion of physical and virtual realities. It is commonly perceived as a space where individuals can engage with computer-generated surroundings and interact with other users in real-time. Consequently, the metaverse offers a wide range of possibilities, spanning from imaginative realms to replicas of real-world locations (such as the ruins of Olympia, the Taj Mahal, or Niagara Falls) to hybrid spaces that blend elements of the real and virtual worlds (such as museums featuring art exhibits—*See Image 6.4*) to interactive playgrounds for gaming and even custom-made spaces (such as virtual replicas of workplaces, educational institutions, or hospitals). While the specific context may shape the nature of the metaverse, the place itself plays a pivotal role in fostering user engagement.

Promotion. In the metaverse, promotion goes beyond conventional marketing. For instance, Nike is developing NFTs—unique, blockchain-secured tokens—for digital goods to demonstrate ownership in its ".SWOOSH" platform.[36] Additionally, they are holding virtual races and product showcases for users to take part in. Another noteworthy trend is influencer marketing in the metaverse. People can communicate in immersive ways in the metaverse, giving public relations (PR) new opportunities to differentiate themselves from the competition. By combining metaverse elements into virtual events, PR firms can leverage the metaverse to foster brand engagement and create memorable customer experiences. The metaverse is also changing the social networking scene; when it is integrated into social media, marketers can make money, expand their user base, boost engagement, etc. The Horizon Worlds by Meta is an example of this, where users can hang out with friends, play games, and attend events.

In general, businesses prepared to invest have a lot of options in the metaverse. To provide customers with the most immersive experiencesv possible,

Image 6.4 Metaverse in public spaces. Metaverse can be used in public spaces such as museums to blend physical and virtual worlds
(*Source* Photo by *Sophia Sideri* on *Unsplash*)

every component of the marketing mix is being redesigned to accommodate the special qualities of the Metaverse.

Driving Customer Engagement Through the Metaverse

The metaverse can help put consumers in the driver's seat in three major ways, thus driving customer engagement.[37] First, the metaverse creates new ways to discover and explore products. For example, the Miami-based cruise line Celebrity Cruises has embraced the metaverse in full to reach out to new travelers. Celebrity Beyond is the first virtual cruise ship to be introduced in the metaverse.[38] Interested parties can take a thorough 360-degree tour of the ocean liner before setting sail on a real trip. Additionally, passengers can engage with the captain's AI-powered avatars to learn important details about the layout and amenities of the ship. Businesses can incorporate more excitement, customization, and interactivity into their customer interactions by utilizing the emerging metaverse.

Second, the metaverse facilitates the fusion of virtual and physical product experiences. In the metaverse, customers are presented with a combination of physical and virtual goods, in contrast to traditional commerce where customers typically order physical products online and consume them offline. For instance, in 2022, Coca-Cola commemorated its anniversary in the metaverse on International Friendship Day.[39] The collectible, which emphasized themes of unity and connection through a design modeled after the bubbles inside a Coke bottle, was airdropped into the digital wallets of current Coca-Cola collectible owners. By allowing the recipients to share collectibles with a friend, the open blockchain community of the brand's fans was expanded.

Lastly, brands are increasingly turning to the metaverse to create cohesive, realistic, and customized interactions. Digital humans, or AI-powered customer agents, are used for this. For example, Hanwa Life, a life insurance provider in South Korea, created Hannah, a virtual financial advisor, to represent the company's digital initiatives to bring the metaverse to life. This "virtual human" will assist not only clients (mainly millennials and Gen Z consumers) looking for a more customized experience but also insurer employees, whose workload will be reduced.[40]

All things considered, the metaverse shows promise as a potent tool for companies looking to interact and engage with clients in novel and creative ways. The metaverse empowers consumers to take charge of their journey by providing new avenues for product exploration, combining real and virtual experiences, and utilizing AI-powered digital humans. This, in turn, fosters consumer satisfaction and brand loyalty. We can anticipate even more creative methods from companies to firmly place the customer at the center of their operations as the metaverse develops.

Designing Digital Strategies Within the Metaverse

Using the special qualities of the metaverse to accomplish particular objectives is part of designing digital strategies within it. Businesses and individuals can experiment with different approaches to optimize their impact, engagement, and presence as the metaverse develops.

To develop a digital strategy, it is crucial to have a clear understanding of how the metaverse should be structured. This initial step involves three key actions. First, it is important to determine the level of centralization or decentralization that the metaverse will possess. This means recognizing that the metaverse will likely consist of a diverse landscape, with both centralized platforms like Meta's Horizon Worlds and decentralized networks such as The Sandbox. The chosen strategy must be flexible enough to navigate and adapt to these different environments. Second, careful consideration must be given to decisions regarding avatars and their interoperability. Avatars serve as digital representations of individuals in the metaverse, and it is essential to establish their identity and ensure seamless movement between platforms. Lastly, while the metaverse offers limitless possibilities for hyper-realistic experiences that blur the boundaries between the physical and virtual worlds, it is important to remain focused on creating meaningful engagement for users. It is easy to become overwhelmed by the vast potential of the platform, so efforts must be made to ensure that the immersive nature of the metaverse is purposeful and engaging.

After determining the structure, several other aspects require attention. First, it is important to understand the target audience of the metaverse relevant to the company or brand. This includes identifying whether the audience consists of gamers, professionals, or consumers seeking new experiences. Second, it is crucial to establish the value proposition of the metaverse. This can involve creating virtual products, hosting interactive events, or offering gamified experiences. Third, incorporating engaging and interactive content that goes beyond traditional formats is essential. This can include integrating augmented reality/virtual reality, as well as creating 3D environments. Additionally, building a community around the brand through interactive spaces and meaningful connections is vital. Lastly, finding ways to monetize the presence in the metaverse, such as through virtual goods or tokenization, is an important consideration. By combining these factors, businesses and individuals can develop digital strategies that align with the unique characteristics of the metaverse, enabling meaningful interactions and the achievement of objectives within this emerging virtual space.

Future of Metaverse in Marketing

Perhaps the biggest chance to completely rethink the customer experience is presented by the metaverse. Notwithstanding its existence, not everything about the metaverse is perfect. The current state of customer experiences and methods for creating them is called into question by the metaverse. A few challenges that businesses must overcome include choosing the best metaverse platform (one that aligns with the brand's target demographics, real estate costs, and growth prospects), coming up with novel ways to engage with customers and give them genuine experiences, and monitoring performance using metrics appropriate for the metaverse. As the metaverse continues to develop, several challenges and considerations arise, encompassing technical, social/ethical, and economic aspects. This section discusses these aspects as they relate to the future of the metaverse.

Technical Considerations

With the metaverse serving to blend the physical and virtual worlds, the technical considerations to mount a metaverse are significant. Among the considerations, the following three aspects will require attention in the future.

First, the metaverse's ambitious vision of vast and captivating virtual worlds is currently constrained by the limitations of existing technology. Advancements in areas like latency, data processing, and avatar realism are crucial for its development. Unlike the conventional Web, the metaverse inherently requires substantial computational resources to function smoothly. The rendering of virtual environments and the delivery of a seamless user experience demand significant computational power. While some platforms attempt to delegate these requirements to users, this approach restricts the potential user base to individuals with high-performance, expensive, and well-equipped computers, hindering widespread adoption.[41]

Second, the accessibility to hardware and infrastructure necessary for a seamless metaverse encounter is not equal for everyone. Take, for example, the availability of VR headsets. Although not every metaverse experience demands a VR headset, many do, and thus, consumers associate the concept of the metaverse with VR. However, the average prices of VR headsets are high and show no significant signs of decreasing.[42] Moreover, the global market for VR headsets is anticipated to experience a decline in revenue growth.[43] Similarly, the prerequisites for high-speed internet and powerful computers can create a barrier of exclusivity, particularly in emerging economies.

Finally, the rise of multiple metaverse platforms has brought about interoperability concerns. In other words, without the ability to seamlessly navigate between platforms, consumers may not find the metaverse appealing. However, achieving interoperability is not solely dependent on technical aspects of platform integration, but also on the content that is being shared. This presents a dilemma as content creators, such as brands and companies, are unlikely to invest in the metaverse without a substantial audience. Consequently, the issue of interoperability is closely intertwined with that of content. Thus, the challenge lies in ensuring smooth user migration and interaction across various virtual worlds, considering the specific content involved.

Social/Ethical Considerations

The development of the metaverse raises various social and ethical concerns that warrant careful consideration. As this virtual space becomes more integrated into our lives, it is important to address the following issues to ensure a positive and responsible evolution of the metaverse.

First, the act of extracting data from the metaverse presents significant challenges. Every action, preference, and interaction within the metaverse can be meticulously monitored and collected. While the metaverse holds the potential for immersive experiences, privacy concerns arise. Consequently, users may unknowingly become targets of potentially harmful advertisements or fall victim to their data being mishandled. This situation amplifies the issue of identity theft, particularly in a realm where customizable avatars and anonymity prevail. The boundaries between real and virtual identities become blurred, providing an opportunity for malicious individuals to exploit this for identity theft, financial fraud, or social manipulation. Furthermore, the risks associated with identity theft may extend beyond the virtual realm and infiltrate the real world through data breaches.[44]

Second, negative effects could be experienced on mental health and well-being. For example, the attraction of carefully designed virtual environments may result in addiction and escapism, endangering relationships, and obligations in the real world.[45] It is not implausible for users of such a platform to prioritize their virtual thrills over their career or physical health. Furthermore, in the metaverse, problems like cyberbullying and harassment that already exist in the real world can manifest themselves in even more dangerous ways. A user might, for example, become the object of stalking in the virtual world, which could be seen as an extension of the real world.

Fourth, the algorithms that are used to build these kinds of worlds in the metaverse can lead to bias and discrimination. That is, prejudice based on race, gender, or other characteristics may be sustained by the algorithms that create the metaverse experiences. Put another way, a user's perceived identity as represented by their digital avatar could result in them being refused access to particular virtual areas or opportunities, or even being treated differently. Furthermore, this would also include giving some users preferential treatment based on preconceived notions.

Finally, the metaverse presents issues with inclusivity and accessibility as well. Not everyone has equal access to engage in the metaverse due to the technical and technological requirements. This might make already-existing socioeconomic disparities worse and give rise to a brand-new group of marginalized people. This has the potential to create a risky precedent with real-world repercussions. Furthermore, although the metaverse can construct meaningfully interactive worlds for individuals, particularly those with physical disabilities, it must do so carefully. People with mobility issues would feel alienated if the virtual world was exclusively made for avatars on foot.

Economic Considerations

As the metaverse involves virtual economies, digital assets, and cross-platform interactions, the following economic and regulatory considerations become crucial.

First, the metaverse's monetization features need to be set up carefully. This necessitates a strategy that strikes a balance between monetization strategies and offering engaging experiences. That is, avatars who are constantly inundated with in-app purchases or advertisements might have a poor experience, which could be bad for the metaverse brands. This also necessitates careful management of content creators. That is to say, it is challenging to guarantee the appropriate content for the metaverse without guaranteeing just compensation for content creators, which impedes the richness and diversity of virtual experiences.

Second, it is important to give careful thought to the governance and regulatory frameworks. This implies that to appropriately handle concerns like intellectual property rights, data privacy, and criminal activity within the metaverse, the current legal frameworks may need to be modified. For instance, it is necessary to create explicit and straightforward legal redress for problems like online harassment and disputes over virtual land ownership. Furthermore, the decentralized structure of the metaverse makes it difficult to create consistent laws and enforce them on various platforms. To guarantee an exceptional virtual experience when several platforms are involved, smooth integration with uniform guidelines and standards needs to be established. This necessitates increased communication and understanding between nations to create a logical regulatory framework for the metaverse that safeguards users and promotes responsible development.

Ultimately, to prevent large corporations from controlling online spaces and resources and perpetuating injustice, fair competition must be maintained in the metaverse. Closer cooperation between international governments is also required in this situation to stop monopolies from forming and rent-seeking behavior from continuing. Governments and businesses can guarantee that everyone has an equal opportunity to engage with and profit from the metaverse by concentrating on bridging the global divide through programs to increase digital literacy and accessibility.

Looking ahead, these are just some of the considerations that arise with the metaverse. Addressing these challenges is crucial to ensure its development happens responsibly and ethically, benefiting all of humanity. Open dialogue, collaboration between stakeholders, and proactive development of regulations and processes are essential steps in navigating this complex landscape.

Key Terms and Related Conceptualizations

Blockchain-based metaverse	No single entity has control over the virtual world, and users have ownership and control over their data and assets
Interoperability	The ability to interact, exchange and make use of data and resulting information to enable movement, transactions and participation across systems, platforms, environments, and technologies
Metaverse	A range of interconnected virtual realms that can be accessed through augmented and virtual reality technologies
Traditional metaverse	An entire virtual world owned and operated by a single company that gives them complete control over all aspects of the metaverse

Notes and References

1. The immersive environment also features an interconnected virtual economy that seamlessly integrates with the global financial system (Au, W. J. (2023), "Neal Stephenson isn't giving up on the metaverse—or crypto," *Fast Company*, October 8, accessed from https://www.fastcompany.com/90935596/neal-stephenson-on-reclaiming-his-metaverse).
2. Richard A. Bartle advanced the concept of a virtual world which is "…an automated, shared, persistent environment with and through which people can interact in real time by means of a virtual self" (Bartle, R. A. (2010). From MUDs to MMORPGs: The history of virtual worlds. In Hunsinger, J., Klastrup, L, & Allen, M. (eds.), *International Handbook of Internet Research*, pp. 23-39. Springer). He further offered an evolution of a virtual world to comprise five ages of development (i.e., 1978–85, 1985–89, 1989–95, 1995–97, and 1997–Present). In the fifth age, graphics are introduced laying the foundation for modern multiuser video games and ultimately the marriage of video games and social interaction technology.

3. Dionisio, J. D. N., Iii, W. G. B., & Gilbert, R. (2013). 3D virtual worlds and the metaverse: Current status and future possibilities. *ACM Computing Surveys (CSUR), 45*(3), 1–38.
4. Perlin, K., & Goldberg, A. (1996). Improv: A system for scripting interactive actors in virtual worlds. In *Proceedings of the 23rd Annual Conference on Computer Graphics and Interactive Techniques* (pp. 205–216), August.
5. Davis, A., Murphy, J., Owens, D., Khazanchi, D., & Zigurs, I. (2009). Avatars, people, and virtual worlds: Foundations for research in metaverses. *Journal of the Association for Information Systems, 10*(2), 1.
6. Wright, M., Ekeus, H., Coyne, R., Stewart, J., Travlou, P., & Williams, R. (2008). Augmented duality: overlapping a metaverse with the real world. In *Proceedings of the 2008 International Conference on Advances in Computer Entertainment Technology* (pp. 263–266), December.
7. Lee, M. Y. H. (2021), "Seoul wants to build a metaverse. A virtual New Year's Eve ceremony will kick it off," *The Washington Post*, November 28, accessed from https://www.washingtonpost.com/world/asia_pacific/metaverse-seoul-virtual/2021/11/27/03928120-4248-11ec-9404-50a28a88b9cd_story.html.
8. Barrera, K. G., & Shah, D. (2023). Marketing in the Metaverse: Conceptual understanding, framework, and research agenda. *Journal of Business Research, 155*, 113420.
9. The metaverse's ability to be a platform for overcoming challenges, fostering creativity and imagination, and improving technological proficiency and abilities is boosting the investments in this new technology (Tidio. (2021). Leading benefits of the metaverse worldwide in 2021 [Graph]. *Statista*, December 1, accessed from https://www.statista.com/statistics/1285117/metaverse-benefits/). Moreover, it offers the opportunity to connect with others effortlessly, opens up new avenues for employment, and allows individuals to express themselves in unique ways.
10. Ramadhan, A., Pradono Suryodiningrat, S., & Mahendra, I. (2023). The fundamentals of metaverse: A review on types, components and opportunities. *Journal of Information and Organizational Sciences, 47*(1), 153–165.
11. Hu, P. J. H., & Hui, W. (2012). Examining the role of learning engagement in technology-mediated learning and its effects on learning effectiveness and satisfaction. *Decision Support Systems, 53*(4), 782–792.

12. Park, S., & Kim, S. (2022). Identifying world types to deliver gameful experiences for sustainable learning in the metaverse. *Sustainability*, *14*(3), 1361.
13. Spangler, T. (2023), "'The voice' free metaverse experience will let fans compete in virtual music battles, win prizes and more (EXCLUSIVE)," *The Variety*, May 10, accessed from https://variety.com/2023/digital/news/the-voice-studios-metaverse-free-virtual-launch-1235608477/.
14. Perez, S. (2023), "Walmart returns to Roblox after its first games were attacked by consumer advocacy groups," *TechCrunch*, September 27, accessed from https://techcrunch.com/2023/09/27/walmart-returns-to-roblox-after-its-first-games-were-attacked-by-consumer-advocacy-groups/.
15. Torrao, M. R. (2023), "Welcome To 'Ubuntuland'—Africa's First Ever Virtual Reality Metaverse [Video]," *2OceansVibe*, August 29, accessed from https://www.2oceansvibe.com/2023/08/29/welcome-to-ubuntuland-africas-first-ever-virtual-reality-metaverse-video/#ixzz8MKmBXRmI.
16. Africarare (2023), "Metaverse Helps Bring Water to Africa," *Africarare*, march 8, accessed from https://www.globenewswire.com/en/news-release/2023/03/08/2622834/0/en/Metaverse-Helps-Bring-Water-to-Africa.html.
17. Shlachter, A. (2023), "How AR and the 'real-world metaverse' can augment traditional media," *The Drum*, April 11, accessed from https://www.thedrum.com/opinion/2023/04/11/how-ar-and-the-real-world-metaverse-can-augment-traditional-media.
18. Bhura, S. (2022). "After Facebook's Meta, some Indian companies are rolling out 'native metaverses'," *The Week*, February 6, accessed https://www.theweek.in/theweek/leisure/2022/01/27/after-facebook-meta-some-indian-companies-are-rolling-out-native-metaverses.html.
19. Purdy, M. (2023). Building a great customer experience in the metaverse. *Harvard Business Review*, April 3, accessed from https://hbr.org/2023/04/building-a-great-customer-experience-in-the-metaverse.
20. The World Economic Forum defines interoperability as "The ability to interact, exchange and make use of data and resulting information to enable movement, transactions and participation across systems, platforms, environments and technologies" (World Economic Forum (2023), "Interoperability in the Metaverse," *World Economic Forum*, January, accessed from https://www3.weforum.org/docs/WEF_Interoperability_in_the_Metaverse.pdf).

21. Ball, M. (2022). *The metaverse: And how it will revolutionize everything*. Liveright Publishing.
22. By 2026, around 25% of people are expected to spend at least one hour daily in the metaverse, as per Gartner. The main benefit, cited by 39% of respondents, is the metaverse's power to help users overcome challenges like physical disabilities (Pratt, M. K. (2022), "10 real-world use cases of the metaverse, and examples," *TechTarget*, November 22, accessed from https://www.techtarget.com/searchcio/feature/Examples-of-the-metaverse-for-business-and-IT-leaders).
23. Hazan, E., Kelly, G., Khan, H., Spillecke, D., & Yee, L. (2022). Marketing in the metaverse: An opportunity for innovation and experimentation. *The McKinsey Quarterly*.
24. CNBC (2023). "Exploring Seoul's newly opened metaverse city and others like it," *CNBC-TV18*, January 18, accessed from https://www.cnbctv18.com/technology/exploring-seouls-newly-opened-metaverse-city-and-others-like-it-15707621.htm.
25. For instance, Snapchat's Gen Z survey found that 60% of the soon-to-be largest consumer base say AR experiences feel more personal (Snapchat (2022), "Gen-Z in 2022," *Snapchat*, accessed from https://downloads.ctfassets.net/inb32lme5009/1rPnekNZuxpa48Gd8tG9z4/77217b80f5b0ea535324b3437b9988ab/Gen_Z_in_2022_Culture__Commerce__and_Conversations.pdf).
26. Hazan, E., Kelly, G., Khan, H., Spillecke, D., & Yee, L. (2022). Marketing in the metaverse: An opportunity for innovation and experimentation. *The McKinsey Quarterly*.
27. Tsiaoussidis, A. (2023), "Every single Fortnite collab & crossover in battle royale's history," Dexerto, December 7, accessed from https://www.dexerto.com/fortnite/every-fortnite-collab-crossover-battle-royale-history-1645672/
28. Thorbecke, C. (2023), "What metaverse? Meta says its single largest investment is now in 'advancing AI'," *CNN*, March 15, accessed from https://edition.cnn.com/2023/03/15/tech/meta-ai-investment-priority/index.html.
29. NVIDIA (2021), "NVIDIA brings millions more into the metaverse with expanded omniverse platform," *NVIDIA*, August 10, accessed from https://nvidianews.nvidia.com/news/nvidia-brings-millions-more-into-the-metaverse-with-expanded-omniverse-platform.
30. Gartenberg, C. (2021), "Intel thinks the metaverse will need a thousand-fold increase in computing capability," *The Verge*, December

16, accessed from https://www.theverge.com/2021/12/15/22836401/intel-metaverse-computing-capability-cpu-gpu-algorithms.
31. Sutcliffe, C. (2022), "21m people have now visited Nike's Roblox store. Here's how to do metaverse commerce right," *The Drum*, September 22, accessed from https://www.thedrum.com/news/2022/09/22/21m-people-have-now-visited-nike-s-roblox-store-here-s-how-do-metaverse-commerce.
32. Mileva, G. (2023), "IKEA launches interactive AR game to teach children about marine life," *AR Post*, February 24, accessed from https://arpost.co/2023/02/24/ikea-ar-game-children-marine-life/.
33. Chan, A. (2023), "Obsess launches AVA, A dynamic self-serve, DIY tool that allows brands to quickly change and manage merchandising, visual display, and content for their virtual storefronts," *Forbes*, April 14, accessed from https://www.forbes.com/sites/angelachan/2023/04/14/obsess-launches-ava-a-dynamic-self-serve-diy-tool-that-allows-brands-to-quickly-change-and-manage-merchandising-visual-display-and-content-for-their-virtual-storefronts/?sh=42490e05388e.
34. According to a U.S. survey conducted in 2022, 87% of users who are already using the Metaverse or who wish to use it in the future said they thought it would have a big impact on how they shop and interact with brands (Sitecore (2022), "Consumer Perceptions about the Metaverse," *Sitecore*, August, accessed from https://www.sitecore.com/blog/metaverse/2022-research).
35. The global metaverse market was projected to be valued at USD 65.5 billion in 2022. This is anticipated to increase to USD 82 billion in 2023 and then soar to USD 936.6 billion by 2030 (Grand View Research (2023), "Metaverse market revenue worldwide from 2022 to 2030 (in billion U.S. dollars) [Graph]," *Statista*, February 27, accessed from https://www.statista.com/statistics/1295784/metaverse-market-size/).
36. Akolkar, B. (2023), "Nike soon to bring its popular. SWOOSH NFTs to EA Sports Games," *Coinspeaker*, June 2, accessed from https://www.coinspeaker.com/nike-swoosh-nfts-ea-sports-games/.
37. Purdy, M. (2023). Building a great customer experience in the metaverse. *Harvard Business Review*, April 3, accessed from https://hbr.org/2023/04/building-a-great-customer-experience-in-the-metaverse.
38. Dawes, J. (2022), "Celebrity cruises enters the metaverse with a virtual ship tour," *Skift*, December 14, accessed from https://skift.com/2022/12/14/celebrity-cruises-enters-the-metaverse-with-a-virtual-ship-tour/.

39. Wright, W. (2022), "Coca-Cola toasts one year in the metaverse with International Friendship Day NFT drop," *The Drum*, July 27, accessed from https://www.thedrum.com/news/2022/07/27/coca-cola-toasts-one-year-the-metaverse-with-international-friendship-day-nft-drop.
40. Si-young, C. (2022), "Hanwha Life Insurance unveils 'virtual human' in digital push," *The Korea Herald*, November 8, accessed from https://www.koreaherald.com/view.php?ud=20221108000593.
41. Rush, J. (2023), "It's time we had a frank discussion about the state of the metaverse," *Fast Company*, September 22, accessed from https://www.fastcompany.com/90955919/its-time-we-had-a-frank-discussion-about-the-state-of-the-metaverse.
42. In 2018, the average cost of a virtual reality headset was USD 385 worldwide. Since then, the price has risen to USD 422 in 2023 and is predicted to remain stable in 2028 at roughly USD 420 (Statista (2023), "Virtual reality (VR) headset average price worldwide from 2018 to 2028 (in U.S. dollars) [Graph]," *Statista*, September 14, accessed from https://www.statista.com/forecasts/1338351/vr-headset-average-price-worldwide).
43. The consumer electronics market's VR headset segment saw a 45.4 percentage point increase in global revenue between 2019 and 2021; however, between 2022 and 2028, it is expected to decline by 29.8 percentage points (Statista (2023a), "Revenue growth of the VR headsets market worldwide from 2019 to 2028 [Graph]," *Statista*, September 14, accessed from https://www.statista.com/forecasts/1331894/vr-headset-revenue-growth-worldwide).
44. Over 40% of participants in a 2021 global survey cited privacy concerns as one of the main threats posed by the metaverse (PC Magazine (2021), "Dangers of the metaverse according to internet users worldwide in 2021 [Graph]," *Statista*, December 1, accessed from https://www.statista.com/statistics/1288822/metaverse-dangers/). Similarly, in a 2021 study among Southeast Asian nations (Singapore, Malaysia, Indonesia, and the Philippines), worries about data security and privacy were the main reason more than 60% of respondents felt negatively about the metaverse (Techsauce (2022), "Leading reasons for feeling negative about the metaverse in Southeast Asia in 2021, by country [Graph]," *Statista*, January 13, accessed from https://www.statista.com/statistics/1292195/sea-top-concerns-about-the-metaverse-by-country/).

45. In a 2022 US survey, 60% of participants preferred metaverse activities to escape real-world challenges, mainly due to rising living expenses. Additionally, 46% used the metaverse as an escape from COVID-19 risks. It is worth noting that a mere 17% of the participants stated that they did not utilize the metaverse as a form of escapism (Sitecore (2022a), "Real-world issues that would make metaverse enthusiasts in the United States inclined to use the metaverse to escape the real world as of August 2022 [Graph]," *Statista*, October 19, accessed from https://www.statista.com/statistics/1346320/us-metaverse-real-world-issues-escape/).

7

Transformative Marketing with the Internet of Things (IoT)

Overview

In today's highly connected world, it is not only humans who establish connections, but devices do too. Through our daily lives, we see devices controlled through sensors and remotely located software such as connected streetlights, self-driving vehicles, smart home security systems, connected wearable devices, and much more. These devices collect, communicate, and process information in real-time through the internet to perform or aid in performing certain defined tasks. This elaborate and growing network of devices connected through the Internet is referred to as the Internet of Things (IoT). Simply put, any physical device can become an IoT device when connected to the internet.

Consider the case of digital screens installed in retail stores. When viewed from a distance, these screens look like big electronic billboards with ads. When a customer approaches these screens, the advertising images turn into digital representations of the products inside the cases, including any stockout information.[1] Using this, the brands can reach shoppers on smart screens that dynamically adjust to shopper behavior and data-driven context at the point of decision in-store. The privacy-safe IoT sensors and AI software can turn a screen (end caps, walls, banner aisles, windows, and coolers) into a smart screen, powering a dynamic and more relevant customer experience that adapts to the shopper based on their attention, distance, motion, and actions. More brands such as Anheuser-Busch InBev, Nestle, PepsiCo, Tyson,

© The Author(s), under exclusive license to Springer Nature Switzerland AG 2024
V. Kumar and P. Kotler, *Transformative Marketing*, Palgrave Executive Essentials,
https://doi.org/10.1007/978-3-031-59637-7_7

Unilever, and Red Bull use this for marketing their products. This technology was pioneered by Chicago-based Cooler Screens which partners with Walgreens, Kroger, and CVS for this initiative.

The digital screens are equipped with IoT sensors and other technology, enabling them to function as both merchandising and advertising platforms. These screens are also being used to collect data about shoppers (what products they are viewing and interacting with). This data can be used by retailers to improve their marketing approaches and tailor to customer requirements better. This technology is also used to display content including product information, promotion videos and images, social media feeds, weather, news, and so on. It benefits retailers by increasing sales (promoting products and engaging shoppers), improving merchandising (collecting data on user behavior and tailoring marketing strategy), and reducing energy costs (digital display instead of glass doors). It also benefits the customer through engaging shopping experience and building knowledge of product features.[2] As we witness around us, the number of connected things/devices is increasing at a rapid rate,[3] with cellular IoT being a significant driver for the proliferation.[4] Such a connected environment holds immense potential to continuously impact our daily lives, and significantly shape the world of business.

This chapter is organized in the following manner. First, a brief history of the origin of IoT is presented, followed by a definition of IoT (from a marketing standpoint). Then, a discussion on the various classifications of IoT is presented spanning individual to commercial uses such as wearables, smart homes, and industrial automation. Next, some marketing applications of IoT focusing on understanding customer needs, revisiting firm capabilities to integrate IoT, designing IoT-focused marketing mix strategies, driving customer engagement (CE) through IoT, and designing digital strategies with IoT are discussed. Finally, the future of IoT for the marketing industry is envisioned through specific business- and customer-facing tasks such as the role of IoT in shaping modern transportation, developing, and managing smart cities, and powering key business processes.

Origin, Definition, and Classifications of IoT

The IoT is a term generally applied to a network of connected devices communicating with each other and with human beings.[5] First proposed in 1999, the credit for coining this term goes to Kevin Ashton.[6] However, it wasn't until 2003 that IoT got noticed by way of its early application—Radio Frequency Identification (RFID). In 2003, Walmart required their major contractors and suppliers to mark their shipments with RFID tags for inventory control.[7] This was one of the earliest industry adoptions of RFID that subsequently made the case for the use of internet-connected devices to manage commercial processes. In this regard, the International Telecommunications Union (ITU) defines IoT as a "global infrastructure for the information society, enabling advanced services by interconnecting (physical and virtual) things based on existing and evolving interoperable information and communication technologies."[8] This definition recognizes the far-reaching and significant personal, commercial, and societal implications of IoT, and paves the way for considering IoT as a major game changer.[9] Currently, with the widespread implications and applications of IoT, the relevance of IoT is noticeable in five key areas—transportation and logistics, healthcare, smart environment, personal and social uses, and futuristic ideas.[10]

In terms of IoT classifications, research has proposed various classification structures. For instance, Gluhak et al.[11] classify IoT based on challenges encountered in IoT such as scale, heterogeneity, repeatability, mobility, and user involvement, among others. Similarly, Gubbi et al.[12] classify IoT based on application areas such as personal and home, enterprise, utilities, and mobile. Further, Sundmaeker et al.[13] propose a classification based on connectivity across time, place, device, person(s), content, path/network, and tasks/services. Given the marketing scope of this book, a classification based on IoT aggregation structures is presented here. Consequently, IoT can be aggregated along the following dimensions—individuals, organizations, industry, and national. A brief description of these four dimensions is discussed here.

Individuals

At the individual level, IoT devices work towards assisting in typical everyday activities through the detection and capturing of information. Information thus recorded is then shared in real-time with the computing infrastructure for subsequent analysis and interpretation of insights. Accordingly, user-friendly communication in the form of alerts and notifications is transmitted to the user, whereas further detection and analyses continue in the background which is not visible to the user. The resulting communication between users and devices, and within the various connected devices is streamlined and consistent. In this manner, IoT devices can be an inconspicuous part of daily human lives, while constantly enhancing the performance of regular functions, and eliminating the involvement of human intrusion.

Examples of individual IoT applications are plenty including wearables, automated driving, and home automation, among others. For instance, Evo is a popular health and wellness app that connects to customers' smartphones and wearable devices and captures data on customers' activities such as steps, exercise, sleep, and stress levels. The application analyzes this data to deliver customized wellness programs designed to achieve goals set by the customers themselves.[14]

Organization

At the organization level, IoT makes large-scale data capture possible—billions of devices and objects are connected on a network, each one being uniquely identifiable and constantly providing data that can be further utilized to influence the devices and objects in the physical world.[15] As a result, the benefits to organizations from IoT exceed beyond sensing and monitoring capabilities. Essentially, the data captured by the sensors involving billions of events represents the true value of IoT.[16] Such a scenario allows firms to develop strategies and respond in ways that deliver maximum value to the end user. For instance, the Hamburg Port Authority installed more than 300 roadway sensors to monitor traffic in the port area and to track the wear and tear on bridges. Sensors are also used on waterways with radar and automatic identification systems that enable coordination of ship traffic and offer an integrated solution to manage roadway traffic disruptions that may occur when ship traffic requires bridge closures around the port area.[17]

In this regard, Kumar et al.[18] propose that IoT can be viewed as a data-oriented technology that provides firms with access to greater and more granular data on their end customers or users. Accordingly, they contend that IoT is foundationally based on the sensing, recording, and exchange of real-time data about the state of devices and objects in the physical world. This enables streamlined communication among the connected devices that aid users in easing the performance of everyday actions. As a result, IoT-implementing firms stand to gain by the generation of insightful marketing actions, which is in turn made possible by the real-time collection and analysis of end-user information.

Industry

IoT has gained a firm place in several industries, wherein all major players in those industries employ IoT-driven solutions to deliver value-based offerings.

Prominent industries to adopt IoT on a large scale include manufacturing, transportation, healthcare, retail, and construction.[19] The insights generated from IoT data reveal patterns in consumer behaviors. Firms can utilize these insights to provide better customer experience by offering personalized recommendations, real-time alerts, and relevant promotional offers. By monitoring devices, controlling usage, and proactively initiating maintenance requests, firms can expect increased productivity, improved efficiency, and reduced operating costs. Prominent examples of IoT uses by a large number of firms in the respective industries include supply chain management, inventory management, and loss prevention in the retail industry; fleet management, asset protection, and operation efficiency in the manufacturing industry; and device monitoring, health monitoring, and facilities management in the healthcare industry.

National

With the rapid increase in IoT adoption among users and companies, governments are also getting actively involved in using IoT to conduct governmental operations and manage national resources. Research has suggested the need for national strategies for the promotion of IoT at a national level. For instance, New and Castro[20](p. 3) suggest that considering "market failures, the need for an innovation-friendly regulatory environment, and the need to promote equity, governments should develop comprehensive national strategies that remove obstacles and support the development and widespread adoption of the technology." As a result, governments around the world have begun promoting IoT solutions actively to manage national resources such as energy sources (e.g., solar, wind, biofuels, etc.), urban city planning, and governmental services to citizens.

Considering governmental initiatives in IoT, companies have responded positively with many companies investing heavily in developing IoT capabilities. For instance, the adoption rate of IoT in developed countries such as the USA, Germany, France, China, and Japan is more than 80%.[21] Additionally, developing countries such as Brazil and India are investing heavily in IoT solutions. For instance, the Brazilian government announced an IoT strategy in 2017 to accelerate its deployment to modernize private and public services through IoT innovations and to foster entrepreneurship and new business.[22]

Similarly, the IoT connections in India are expected to reach 1.9 billion in 2020 from 60 million in 2016. As a result, the Indian government is actively involved in the adoption of IoT through initiatives such as the Smart Cities mission that aims to "drive economic growth and improve the quality of life of people by enabling local area development and harnessing technology, especially technology that leads to Smart outcomes" by developing 100 smart cities (p. 6).[23] This includes developing smart solutions to suit India's needs in terms of utility management, city planning and administration, education, and citizen services, among others. Governments worldwide are realizing that the true potential of IoT may not be realized by relying only on market actions by companies, but also require active government participation and monitoring. This trend will likely continue in the coming years as this technology matures.

Overall, IoT is rapidly gaining momentum among users, firms, and governments in recent years as a result of advancements in computing technologies. IoT-enabled devices remotely monitor, control, and manage a network of connected devices. The key elements of IoT include (a) the involvement of sensors as the core of this technology that allows for the collection of device-level data, (b) the ability to capture information regarding physical actions, and transmit such information to elicit pre-defined reactions, (c) the presence of information infrastructure, which can generate insights in real-time, and can be instantly communicated to the connected devices, and (d) the opportunity to make information exchange easier and better for all the people and devices existing in a IoT-device connected network. To conclude the overview of IoT, the following three vignettes present the possibilities of IoT and how companies and users are deriving value from such offerings.

Wearables

Wearables is a popular application of IoT that is gaining immense traction among users. While IoT largely involves machine-to-machine (M2M) connectivity (e.g., sensors, RFID, etc.), the wearables operate on machine-to-human (M2H) connectivity. This presents important implications for marketers and product managers concerning satisfying user needs. Such M2H applications have made technology and consumer-level data inseparable. Consumers are now interacting with technology at several points in a typical day and sharing information about themselves and with firms. They expect products, services, and insights that are individually tailored to their needs and preferences. Technology now provides firms with the data to create marketing strategies, the tools to analyze and secure data, and eventually deliver on the strategies. The granularity of available data has the power to help firms create individually customized marketing strategies, that can encourage greater CE with firms. In such a consumer landscape, wearable technology is gaining a firm foothold in everyday life.

Wearables consist of devices such as fitness trackers (e.g., Fitbit, Apple Watch, and Samsung Galaxy Fit, etc.), health monitors (e.g., continuous glucose monitors, insulin pens, connected inhalers, etc.), and medical monitors (e.g., remote patient monitoring, ingestible sensors, heart rate monitors, etc.) (see Image 7.1). These wearables collect and process data related to various aspects of health and fitness routines that can be used by the user and in combination with medical practitioners to manage healthcare options. Wearables perform a range of activities from monitoring/preventive health functions to medical treatment functions. For instance, wearables can measure heart rate, detect muscle activity, monitor stress levels, track sleep patterns, and assess mental attention timelines, among others. These functions may be performed by wearable devices such as wristbands, rings, or even clothing.[24] Based on the data collected and analyzed, these devices can deliver personalized, task-specific recommendations for the users.

Further, since most wearables have open application programming interfaces (APIs), the involvement of third-party applications adds more value to users and product developers. For instance, Fitbit offers wearable devices to enable users to lead an active lifestyle. The Fitbit API enables third-party applications to access the activity data to create solutions for gaining health insights, making health changes, and managing health data, among others. As a result, the device manufacturers and API developers collectively offer

Image 7.1 Wearable. Personal wearables such as the Apple Watch can perform and monitor a wide range of actions
(*Source* Photo by *Luke Chesser* on *Unsplash*)

a wide range of solutions that keep users engaged in their healthcare needs. Therefore, it should come as no surprise that the wearables industry is rapidly growing.[25]

Smart Homes

With governments involved in establishing smart cities, the micro level consists of smart homes that are evolving at a fast pace. A smart home is a regular home, which has been augmented with various types of sensors and actuators.[26] Collectively, smart cities and smart homes aim to make better use of available resources and enhance the quality of the services, while reducing the operational costs involved in delivering the services.[27] Further, the creation of smart homes whereby activities are monitored and managed augurs well for the establishment of the well-being of the users (see Image 7.2).

Research has investigated consumer well-being and has conceptualized it as "a state of flourishing that involves health, happiness and prosperity;"[28] as reflective of the personal and societal aspects of human development;[29] or an alignment of individual and societal needs.[30] In a NAT environment, Kumar and Ramachandran[31] conceptualize consumer well-being as a multi-dimensional concept that describes a state of health and happiness for each stakeholder across physical, emotional, financial, societal, and environmental

Image 7.2 Smart Homes. Consumers can connect and control their devices via Google Home
(*Source* Photo by *Bence Boros* on *Unsplash*)

dimensions, as relevant to the stakeholder. The well-being concept of smart homes is reflected in the ambient assisted living (AAL) applications of IoT solutions that are directed at improving the lifestyle of the users.[32] In this regard,[33] provide AAL to encompass technical systems to support elderly people and people with special needs in their daily routines. Additionally, they contend that the main goal of AAL is to achieve benefits for the individual (increasing safety and well-being), the economy (higher effectiveness of limited resources), and society (better living standards). As a result, an AAL environment typically consists of services, products, and concepts that are connected, context-sensitive, personal, adaptive, and anticipative. Such an environment is made possible by IoT solutions that focus on user needs and preferences.

Within smart homes, smart appliances and IoT devices simplify consumers' lives by automating routine tasks and reducing the need for human intervention.[34] For example, June is an intelligent oven that can identify what is being cooked via a camera, provide suggestions on the cooking procedure, and allow remote tracking via connected devices. In combination with AI and ML analyzing IoT data continuously, consumers find themselves receiving personalized communication and relevant insights, and having better experiences with the devices. Evo is a popular and insightful health and wellness app that gathers biometric data from consumers' smartphones and wearables and applies data and behavioral science to deliver custom-made wellness programs.[35]

Industrial Automation

Perhaps the biggest impact of IoT can be observed in the area of industrial automation. Historically, through the various industrial revolutions, one of the focus areas has been the reduction or elimination of human intervention in industrial processes. In this pursuit, several technologies have served (and continue to serve) industries such as information and communication technologies, ethernet, and wireless networks, among others. Consequently, efforts to design and model processes that are independent of routine human interventions have typically involved a combination of sensors, devices, and actuators.[36]

The notion of interconnected production processes involving automation to form a cohesive ecosystem was first propounded via agent-based distributed manufacturing systems.[37] In the current NAT environment, IoT serves as the new technology platform through which industrial automation is planned and delivered. Further, the ecosystem is comprised of several mechanical machinery, sector-specific systems, and related software inputs. Specifically, the industrial automation ecosystem broadly comprises original equipment manufacturers (OEMs) and system integrators, component suppliers, and software/applications developers and providers.[38]

The development of the automation-driven ecosystem along with the increasing use of smart technologies for industrial production has led to the conceptualization of the term "Industry 4.0" that refers to a new-age industrial revolution wherein Internet technologies are used to create smart products, a smart production, and smart services.[39] This is also reflected in the following elaborate definition of IoT provided by the IEEE IoT Community:

> Internet of Things envisions a self-configuring, adaptive, complex network that interconnects 'things' to the Internet through the use of standard communication protocols. The interconnected things have physical or virtual representation in the digital world, sensing/actuation capability, and a programmability feature and are uniquely identifiable. The representation contains information including the thing's identity, status, location, or any other business, social, or privately relevant information. The things offer services, with or without human intervention, through the exploitation of unique identification, data capture and communication, and actuation capability. The service is exploited through the use of intelligent interfaces and is made available anywhere, anytime, and for anything taking security into consideration.[40]

The global industrial automation market shows vibrancy.[41] Additionally, companies are also looking specifically at Industrial IoT (IIoT) solutions to enhance revenue generation potential that focuses on user needs. The IIoT offers several organizational benefits such as increasing production efficiency, output management, and efficient resource deployment. Specifically, companies are beginning to realize benefits from industrial automation that include (a) the accurate identification of when machinery parts/components may need replacements, (b) the identification of potential failures in co-dependent processes that could lead to undesirable outcomes, (c) the cost savings from eliminating nonessential maintenance, (d) the advanced analytic insights on asset maintenance and overall productivity, and (e) the efficient (re)deployment of maintenance and design teams by preempting equipment failures, among others.[42]

IoT in the Marketing 5.0 World

IoT enables marketers to enhance customer engagement and loyalty through interactive experiences. Through these devices and their capabilities, marketers can (a) gain deeper customer insights to preempt/suggest solutions for customers (e.g., notify exactly when a customer needs a new ink cartridge for their printer), (b) tailor their messaging and offers to individual needs and preferences, (c) understand how customers interact with their products and identify areas for improvement, (d) analyze IoT data to predict future customer behavior (e.g., sending a maintenance reminder before a device breaks down), and (e) trigger contextually relevant marketing messages based on real-time data. Expanding on the Marketing 5.0 concept discussed in Chapter 2, this section presents how IoT operates in the Marketing 5.0 world. Particularly, this section discusses five examples of where IoT is applied through the lens of Marketing 5.0 and establishes how such actions can also bode well for humanity.

Data-Driven Marketing Using IoT

Data-driven marketing using IoT involves leveraging the vast amount of data generated by Internet of Things devices to make informed decisions, personalize marketing strategies, and optimize customer experiences. For example, smart fitting rooms equipped with IoT technology can provide personalized recommendations based on customers' body measurements and style preferences. This not only improves the shopping experience but also increases the likelihood of making a purchase. Similarly, IoT-enabled loyalty programs can reward customers for their engagement and purchases, fostering a sense of loyalty and encouraging repeat business.

For instance, consider the packaging industry that is undergoing a significant transformation due to the integration of smart and connected technologies. This convergence is not only adding value to packaging but also generating a wealth of data that can provide valuable insights to businesses, inform product design, and offer customers new experiences. One example of this is Wiliot, a provider of ambient IoT platforms. They have recently introduced the capability to sense and analyze humidity levels of individual products in real-time throughout the supply chain.[43] This is made possible through their battery-free, real-time locating visibility platform, which connects the digital and physical worlds using Wiliot Cloud and Wiliot IoT Pixels. These low-cost, self-powered devices are attached to products and packaging, continuously transmitting data to the Cloud via standard

Bluetooth devices. This innovative solution not only reduces operational costs and errors but also ensures the safety, integrity, freshness, and sustainability of moisture-sensitive products on a large scale.

With the addition of humidity sensing to Wiliot's visibility platform, companies can now enhance their ability to safeguard moisture-sensitive products. This feature complements the existing capabilities of temperature, location, and carbon emissions sensing. By leveraging this comprehensive set of data, businesses can ensure the end-to-end safety and integrity of their products at an unprecedented scale. This is particularly crucial for industries where moisture levels play a significant role in product quality and freshness. Wiliot's solution not only addresses these challenges but also offers a cost-effective alternative to traditional tracking methodologies. By reducing staffing requirements and operational costs, as well as minimizing error rates, waste, mis-shipments, mis-picks, and out-of-stocks, companies can streamline their operations and improve overall efficiency.

Predictive Marketing Using IoT

Predictive marketing takes data-driven marketing a step further, using the power of IoT to not only understand past and present customer behavior but also predict future actions and needs. This allows businesses to be proactive and anticipate customer wants before they even arise, leading to a more personalized and impactful marketing experience. Some of the areas in which IoT can be used for predictive marketing include (a) generating real-time data streams, (b) identifying patterns and predicting future behavior using AI and ML, (c) proactive problem-solving and value creation, and (d) adjusting prices dynamically based on usage patterns and inventory levels, among others.

For instance, IoT technology is utilized by Procter & Gamble to improve the manufacturing process of Pampers diapers, which are composed of fluff pulp, plastics, absorbent granules, and elastics.[44] The manufacturing process is highly automated and involves various techniques, including streaming hot glue and heat binding. However, if the temperature and pressure of the glue stream are inaccurate or if the valve becomes clogged and is not promptly addressed, the resulting diapers must be discarded. Therefore, measures must be taken to reduce the financial impact of discarding diapers during the manufacturing process.

The proprietary Hot Melt Optimization technique, utilized by the company, involves the use of exclusive sensors on the assembly line to collect data. This data, combined with Microsoft's predictive analytics and Azure cloud for manufacturing, allows the company to minimize diaper damage during the manufacturing process and achieve optimal results. To closely monitor and record glue stream temperature and pressure data, the company also employs programmable logic industrial controllers and other sensors on the assembly line. By feeding this data into analytics platforms and in-house developed code, the company can identify and correct errors or anomalies in real time without disrupting the manufacturing process. As a result, the company consistently surpasses its previous manufacturing output since the implementation of Hot Melt Optimization.

P&G's manufacturing process undergoes continuous testing against incoming data using Microsoft's edge analytics engine in a rules-based manner. This approach enables the company to identify necessary corrections hours before errors occur, thereby preventing any production or material loss. By predicting potential errors, P&G can take proactive measures to maintain and increase production capacity while reducing unplanned downtime and scrap generated during production. Since deploying the solution in 11 plants, P&G estimates it has eliminated 70% of the flawed diapers that have to be scrapped.

Contextual Marketing Using IoT

In a world where marketing messages are tailored to your current circumstances, seamlessly integrating into your everyday routine, the concept of contextual marketing powered by the IoT becomes a tangible reality. Gone are the days of generic advertisements; contextual marketing leverages real-time information from interconnected devices to provide highly pertinent and personalized messages precisely when they hold the most significance. This approach fosters a more captivating customer experience, resulting in improved conversion rates, heightened brand loyalty, and ultimately, a boost in revenue.

For instance, London-based knitwear company Sheep Inc. is taking big strides toward being the first carbon-negative fashion brand globally.[45] To achieve this, Sheep Inc. sources from the most environmentally friendly sources it can find, such as manufacturers that only use renewable energy sources or carbon-neutral farms, and then multiply the remaining carbon footprint of each of its components by ten. The outcome of this is the introduction of a crew neck sweater design that was made entirely of biodegradable, ZQ-certified Merino wool. An NFC tag with a distinct serial number is attached to the hem of every sweater. Full information about the garment's manufacturing process and carbon footprint can be accessed by scanning it with a smartphone. The tag is composed of ecological plastic, which is 100% carbon-neutral polyamide derived from renewable castor bean oil, even though it is not yet biodegradable. When it comes time to throw away the sweater, which will completely decompose in a year, the tag is easily removed and recycled.

To bring in context to the company's sustainability initiatives, Sheep Inc. uses IoT to engage and inform customers as they move toward carbon neutrality. The company gives users access to the identity of the sheep that provided the wool using an RFID tag embedded in each sheep's ear. In addition, the tag can transmit routine updates regarding the sheep's whereabouts, regular activities, health, significant life events, information about its offspring, and even when it gets a haircut. This gives customers a chance to interact with the business, learn about its manufacturing process, and get closer to the natural world.

Augmented Marketing Using IoT

The realm of augmented marketing with IoT involves the integration of digital encounters into the physical world, resulting in interactive and captivating brand experiences. As an example, imagine our coffee cup in the morning displaying tailored news updates as it brews, or our grocery shelf highlighting ingredients for a delectable meal based on our dietary preferences. Furthermore, our car windshield could project turn-by-turn navigation enhanced with nearby points of interest. Although these scenarios may appear imaginative, augmented marketing with IoT extends beyond mere visual appeal. Its purpose is to revolutionize our brand interactions, rendering them more pertinent, captivating, and ultimately, unforgettable.

For instance, consider the California-based mapping platform, Mapbox, which allows developers to create unique interactive maps and applications for businesses.[46] To improve key mapping and visualization features, the company has now teamed up with Qualcomm Technologies, a pioneer in the IoT and smartphone ecosystem. The Qualcomm Aware Platform's configurable API-first architecture was created for developers, allowing for interoperability with partner clouds. Mapbox believes that companies in supply chains and logistics will be able to build a complete hardware, connectivity, and service solution for the specific real-time location intelligence they require thanks to the customizable design and the ability to integrate tailored location features with Mapbox mapping and routing APIs.

The Qualcomm Aware Platform will assist Mapbox users with real-time asset visibility and control, whether it is determining how a winter storm will affect operations, monitoring the length of time a shipment is sitting at a specific location, or identifying potential hazards and finding alternate routes. Augmenting IoT capabilities with existing features is expected to enable users with accurate monitoring and strong connectivity even in situations where devices are submerged, indoors, or offline.

Agile Marketing Using IoT

Agile marketing is an iterative and flexible approach to marketing that emphasizes collaboration, adaptability, and customer feedback. When combined with the IoT, which involves connecting physical devices to the internet to collect and share data, marketers can leverage real-time insights and automation to enhance their strategies. For instance, IoT can be used in agile marketing campaigns in various ways such as using IoT sensors to track customer behavior in physical stores, using IoT devices to collect data about customer usage of products and services, using IoT data to trigger and measure the effectiveness of marketing campaigns, among others.

Consider Fasal, an Indian agritech startup, that has developed an innovative plug-and-play IoT solution specifically designed for farmers. This system incorporates remote sensors that are capable of collecting real-time data on various factors such as crop conditions, soil quality, rainfall, moisture levels, and other weather conditions.[47]

By utilizing AI and ML, the collected data is processed to generate customized insights and predictions that are delivered to farmers through the Fasal app in their local languages. These valuable insights enable farmers to effectively manage irrigation, control pests and diseases, apply fertilizers, fungicides, and pesticides, and make necessary adjustments to optimize crop growth conditions. Notably, advanced algorithms in the IoT system can even predict seasonal crop diseases up to a week in advance, empowering farmers to take proactive preventive measures. Additionally, this solution addresses the important issue of over-irrigation by encouraging water conservation through the "Water Credit" initiative. Under this initiative, farmers who maintain a specific water level for a certain number of hours in a month are eligible for a full refund of their monthly subscription fees. This initiative has successfully saved billions of liters of fresh water, even in the most arid regions of India.[48]

Overall, the implementation of this IoT solution has resulted in a significant increase in crop yields of 30-40%, a notable reduction in pests and diseases by 50-60%, and a substantial decrease in water usage by 30%. Consequently, farmers have experienced a remarkable 50% reduction in input costs, making their agricultural practices more agile, sustainable, and economically viable.

Current IoT Applications in Marketing

With the emergence of IoT, the ways consumers interact with firms are undergoing significant changes. In accommodating IoT, firms are now increasingly focusing on delivering superior experiences and engaging with consumers through IoT-driven offerings.[49] This has resulted in firms developing IoT solutions that offer various value propositions such as novelty, aesthetic design, convenience, low price, superior performance, and so on. As a result, IoT has become one of the most promising technologies that not only presents value-creating opportunities in marketing but also holds important implications for the development of marketing strategies. This section presents five specific application areas where IoT continues to help companies in developing marketing initiatives.

Understanding Customer Needs to Deploy IoT

IoT allows firms to improve their capabilities which results in increased convenience for users and ease in performing routine tasks. The connectivity of IoT devices allows customers the convenience and flexibility of being able to remotely monitor, control, and manage all of their connected devices at the click of a button. For instance, smart locks such as August, Friday, and Wyze allow remote access control reserved for authorized members of a household and always secure the home. Such smart locks also prominently feature guest-access controls and information logs regarding the device's usage. In addition to keeping homes safe, such smart devices address several consumer needs such as reducing the stress of losing keys, the ability to lock/unlock homes remotely, compatibility with traditional door lock systems, and pleasing aesthetics for homes, among others.

Incorporating customer needs into developing IoT solutions is perhaps most evident in the retail industry where retailers have implemented technologies such as geofencing for location-based marketing purposes. For instance, fashion retailer Sephora uses geofencing via a companion store app that uses customers' past purchase history to suggest product recommendations whenever a customer enters the store.[50] Similarly, Walgreens uses geofencing to improve participation in their rewards program by promoting coupons and deals when customers enter the geofenced location.[51] Further,

Burger King has established geofences around its competitors to woo customers to their stores.[52] Instances of other industries using IoT-driven data include the use of telematics data (i.e., data about a moving vehicle collected using an onboard device) in the insurance industry,[53] and the use of sensors in the real estate industry to help better manage energy usage, environmental comfort, and security.[54] A unifying theme in implementing such geofencing activities is the firms' attention to delivering personalized content and offerings that their customers would prefer.

Revisiting Firm Capabilities to Integrate IoT

To successfully integrate IoT, firms must assess or reassess their capabilities to determine the degree of firm adoption of IoT in the marketing aspect.[55] The implementation of IoT in firms provides them with the ability to sense, communicate, and respond to the needs of their environment. This creates opportunities for firms to understand customer usage patterns and builds on the firm's intellectual capital that can be sold or used as the basis for either internal innovation or external collaboration. Therefore, IoT helps firms develop dynamic capabilities that hold important implications on the business models of the implementing firms and help them on the path towards establishing competitive advantage. In this regard,[56] contends that strong dynamic capabilities enable the creation and implementation of effective business models. Using this perspective, Dunaway et al.[57] define IoT capabilities as "a unique type of IT capability that relies on the network of physical objects to sense new opportunities and threats, to move resources to address those new opportunities, and to reconfigure IT assets."

Alternatively, Day[58] offers that since dynamic capabilities are impacted by an inside-out orientation of the firm (i.e., a perspective that begins within the firm and looks outward to the market), from a marketing standpoint, it limits the firm's ability to detect and respond to immediate market changes. In this regard, adaptive marketing capabilities have been conceptualized to enable organizations to be sensitive to the emerging trends in the environment, to be agile in rapidly making necessary adjustments in implementation activities, and to be willing to learn through experimentation.

The differences in academic perspectives notwithstanding, firms continue to develop capabilities that can help them implement IoT in their enterprises. The development of such capabilities includes, among other things, (a) the creation of an enterprise-wide data strategy that can integrate and inform how data can power the IoT-driven initiatives, (b) the identification of IoT to further existing and new business functionalities, (c) the development/refinement of necessary talent pool to spearhead IoT initiatives, and (d) the constant monitoring of customer needs and preferences to develop appropriate IoT solutions. The benefits of developing capabilities can be seen in the case of companies such as DHL, GE, SAP, Google, and Oracle which have adopted continuous efforts in building firm capabilities to enable the deployment of IoT solutions.[59]

Designing Marketing Mix Strategies with IoT

As mentioned earlier, IoT operates in the domain of functionality, offering ease of use and convenience to users through the application of sensors.[60] This implies that the detection and capture of real-time data through various devices for subsequent analysis, interpretation, and implementation into marketing activities becomes the fundamental operating principle of IoT. As a result, reflecting the insights from the IoT devices becomes apparent when considering the marketing mix variables. Successful companies have realized impressive wins in each of the four key marketing mix variables—product, price, place, and promotion, as seen from the following examples.

Product. The traditional approach to developing products involves significant amounts of market research, customer feedback, and technical research, among others. In the NAT environment, companies are now able to integrate IoT at the product development stage so that the technology can continue to be one of the key drivers of growth and usage of the product. For instance, Diageo, the global alcohol producer, developed a "smart bottle" to enhance the consumer experience by using printed sensor tags.[61] These tags can detect both the sealed and opened state of each bottle. This approach scores over the conventional static quick response (QR) codes that may pose challenges in opening and reading content. The sensor tags in the bottle can dynamically detect if a bottle is sealed or open with the simple tap of an NFC smartphone. Further, the tags and the sensor information will allow Diageo to send personalized communications to consumers who read the tags with their smartphones. Additionally, it allows the company to send well-timed relevant marketing messages, along with promotional offers and exclusive content.

Price. When operating in price-sensitive markets, price is a heavily used marketing tool to ensure revenue growth and customer acquisition. In this regard, competitive pricing strategies can appeal to price-conscious shoppers that can make them stay with the company. The importance of pricing strategies can be seen in consumer-driven industries such as retail and fast-food restaurants. For instance, in 2018, Burger King established geofences around McDonald's locations in the U.S. and used that to promote their Whoppers for only one cent. For a limited time, using the Burger King app, customers were able to get the 1-cent deal when they were within 600 feet of a McDonald's. With this novel method of combining an IoT application (i.e., geofencing) with mobile capabilities, Burger King was able to attract customers from their main competitor using a low-priced promotion deal.[62]

Place. Location-driven marketing actions are usually effective when the intended reason is well-conceptualized. This is especially true in industries such as retail and media services where hyper-localized offerings can go a long way in engaging with customers. In such a scenario, IoT possesses the right capabilities to not only collect continuous data but also render smart, context-specific, highly personalized experiences, all in real time. For instance, the beacon technology (i.e., small radio transmitters that transmit data work over Bluetooth) is being used by many companies to provide hyper-specific, location-targeted content, directly to users. Organizations such as Walgreens, Major League Baseball, Kenneth Cole, and London's Heathrow Airport have used beacons to provide localized promotions, content, and personalized experiences that are meant to resonate well with their user base.[63]

Promotion. Marketing promotions also yield immense benefits to firms when done well at the local level and in the right context. Such a measure would augur well for the brand (in terms of establishing relevance to its users) and for the users (in terms of deriving value from the offerings). The power of such promotions is best observed in consumer-facing firm actions that create a lasting impact on the users. For instance, Nivea developed a promotional campaign for the Brazilian market aimed at increasing customer acquisition for their product, Nivea Sun Kids. The campaign focused on the theme of protection and was directed at parents. A magazine ad for Nivea Sun Kids was run that included a tear-out bracelet that could be placed on a child's wrist. This bracelet could be paired with the Nivea Protects app and be used to prevent the child from becoming lost on the beach. Accompanying adults could then identify the child on the app, and choose the distance the child could go on the beach before an alert would sound. The app would subsequently receive an alert when the distance was exceeded. Further, a radar feature allowed the adults to know if they were getting nearer or farther from children.[64] In addition to being an innovative use of the IoT, the Nivea campaign also generated impressive sales within its product segment in that region and had a high download rate for its app.

Driving Customer Engagement Through IoT

Customer engagement is receiving increasing attention among firms worldwide, given its positive impact on the firm's bottom line. Here, enjoyable customer experiences pave the way for a positive CE and better brand outcomes.[65] Such industry impacts continue to spur innovative offerings from firms, along with academic interest in improving CE.

Academic research has identified CE as a key success factor for firms.[66] In this regard, value contribution from customers to the firms extends beyond just purchase transactions to also include non-purchase-related customer behaviors.[67,68] Pansari and Kumar[69] identified the components of CE to be direct and indirect customer contributions, and the antecedents of CE to be satisfaction and emotion. Further, Kumar et al.[70] proposed a conceptual framework, especially for the service setting, that identifies an interaction orientation approach and an omnichannel model resulting in the creation of a positive service experience. They argue that the positive service experience ultimately impacts CE by ensuring customer satisfaction and creating emotional bonds with the firms. They also identify that customers' perceived variation in service experience moderates the influence of service experience on satisfaction and emotional attachment, which ultimately impacts CE.

In the NAT environment, IoT presents various opportunities for firms to ensure CE through their interactions and minimize variations in service experience that could potentially enhance CE. In this regard, IoT is being used in industrial and consumer settings to ensure CE. In industrial applications, IoT is used for various functions such as preventive maintenance (e.g., ABB and Hitachi use IoT solutions to monitor sensor health and optimize production), asset management (e.g., Capgemini and the Istanbul Airport have installed sensors to monitor building performance and ensure efficient internal ambiance), smart energy systems (e.g., Honeywell and Verizon are increasing their IoT capabilities by developing a platform that can host smart sensors, controllers, and other connected pieces of hardware on electric grids that can deliver energy savings and reduce outages), and fleet operations (e.g., fleet management companies such as Bransys use sensors to help fleet managers monitor the performance of their vehicular assets including temperature-controlled delivery systems, and Tesla uses over- the -air IoT connectivity to perform software updates remotely on almost all car operations, thereby saving trips to the service center), among others.

In consumer applications, IoT is being used for various functions such as home security (e.g., Ring and ADT provide IoT-driven home security by integrating features such as learning thermostats, smart plugs, home access

Image 7.3 Smart Thermostats. Smart home energy management systems such as Nest can automatically regulate room temperature based on learning energy usage patterns over time
(*Source* Photo by *Dan LeFebvre* on *Unsplash*)

control, and surveillance systems), healthcare (e.g., pharmaceutical companies such as GlaxoSmithKline and Boehringer Ingelheim develop sensors to be used in connected inhalers to provide better treatment care and insights), wearables (e.g., Apple Watch and Fitbit health monitoring functions through the devices, and companies such as Ambiotex and Under Armour offer athletic gear with built-in sensor chips for fitness tracking and monitoring), and senior care (e.g., the water-resistant Kanega watch meets the needs of seniors with functions such as medication reminders, GPS locator, an emergency call button, and so on; and Luna Lights offers senior-friendly lighting solutions for night time use such as illuminating pathways and emergency call buttons), among others. Overall, IoT is being used in a variety of consumer and industrial settings where the result seems to be improving CE (see Image 7.3).

Designing Digital Strategies with IoT

While many firms have already instituted technology components such as sensors, IoT, 3D printing, and so on in varying measures, the challenge of creating a unified system of network with symbiotic interdependencies remains critical to the success of firms. Few firms have been successful in creating such digital strategies that guide the effective implementation of NATs. For instance, through sensor-equipped products, Nike can know with great precision how individual customers use their shoes. This heightened awareness can allow Nike to orient itself to its customers with far greater accuracy than what was possible through conventional means. Furthermore, by strategically harnessing sensor data, Nike can also embrace its own emerging digital ecosystem. It can, for instance, tap into other connected products such as a Fitbit or an Apple watch, social networks such as Facebook or Twitter, or a large community of app developers to generate new mass-customized services.[71] Such a development of a cohesive strategy has been proposed to result in the creation of a competitive advantage.[72]

In this regard, Kopalle et al.[73] offer that digital ecosystems can be created, particularly by legacy firms, to create value through the establishment of a digital customer orientation, which refers to offering customized and enriched customer experiences by embracing digital ecosystems. They further offer that a digital customer orientation operates on three critical concepts viz., in-use information, digital customers, and digital experience. In the case of the Nike example discussed above, the in-use information is apparent with the involvement of sensors that continuously collect information regarding current use that can also be used for generating future insights. Digital platforms would refer to the firms' presentation of their offerings primarily through smartphone apps or the Internet. However, many firms continue to deliver their offerings in the traditional and digital routes. For instance, the same Nike consumer may use a sensor-equipped shoe for jogging but another shoe for walking. Finally, the digital experience refers to the sharing and amplifying of the value of the in-use information obtained from digital customers. Nike, for instance, can amplify the value of its in-use information generated from its sensor-equipped shoe by sharing it with other connected products and the app developer network for developing third-party apps that can generate even more value for the users.

Future of IoT in Marketing

IoT is emerging as a game changer for firms in the way they interact with the end users. The rise of platforms to nurture firm-customer engagement has led to the emergence of agents that operate between customers and providers. In the case of NATs, and IoT in particular, emerging business models aid in easing the processes, ushering in automation of insight generation, and improving an organization's capacity to track and respond to evolving user needs. IoT is quickly gaining traction as a technology that can operate in the background discretely while delivering functional benefits to the user in real-time.[74] This ability of IoT makes it important for organizations to include it in their technology portfolios. In this regard, the future of IoT for marketing purposes appears to be promising and varied. While we can expect progress in IoT capabilities in many organizational areas, three areas that stand out are discussed here.

IoT and Transportation

The transportation industry holds a pivotal place in the world economy with significant socioeconomic benefits. However, the industry also creates negative impacts on environmental systems that comprise air, water, and soil resources.[75] Given these significant negative impacts, governments and companies are developing solutions that can counter the negative effects. In this regard, IoT presents valuable opportunities for developing smart transportation solutions.

Traditional methods adopted in the transportation industry often worked in silos with limited interconnectivity. New advancements, particularly considering IoT, are giving rise to smart transportation systems that adopt a global view of all the components of the transportation system. The smart use of transportation enables passengers to select a more cost-saving option that is of a shorter distance and the fastest route, which saves a significant amount of time and energy. Specific examples of such smart transportation technology include sensors in vehicles for collision avoidance, anti-skidding, efficient tracking, predictive maintenance, and so on.[76]

Further, smartphone apps powered by IoT are increasingly being used to gain granular insights and offer solutions in real-time. A recent mobile-based IoT application will enable users to determine their arrival time and manage their schedule more efficiently across various transportation approaches. For instance, in the Phoenix metro area, Valley Metro is launching a new version of their smartphone app that will enable users to receive real-time travel information, purchase tickets for both public and private transportation modes, and utilize an optimized trip planning service that integrates taxis, ride-sharing, and bike-sharing services.[77] Such innovative offerings have the potential to shorten travel time, thereby saving time and energy for the users, and potentially extending resource utilization for the city governments. Additionally, this can remarkably reduce CO_2 emissions and other air-polluting gasses from transportation.

Similarly, research has proposed using data from the users' mobile devices to predict and manage traffic congestion.[78] As a practical application of this, the city of Mulhouse in France was able to use mobile data to measure the pedestrian movement in the city center and understand the visitor demographics. This meant it could revitalize the business conditions of the city by evaluating the impact of hosting events, planning business hours of the shops in the city center, and offering timely, and relevant citizen services, in addition to managing pedestrian flow and managing city congestion.[79] Further, research has also proposed the placement of sensor units in specified locations on the road for data collection and communication, with potential applications for monitoring vehicular traffic, coordinating with city utility vehicles, and administering weather advisories, among others.[80] As research continues in this area, we can expect more IoT solutions to develop smarter transportation options.

Smart Cities

Cities worldwide are increasingly facing pressure to manage their growth and the deployment of resources to meet their needs. The concept of smart cities evolved in the early 2000s with the earliest conceptualization of a smart city referring to a "…city that monitors and integrates conditions of all of its critical infrastructures…".[81] While several conceptualizations of smart cities have been advanced, a feature that stands out in most of the conceptualizations is the focus on computing and data technologies.[82]

Here, IoT can present valuable opportunities for creating smart cities by enabling various devices and software to communicate with each other through the Internet. Such a connection can create a network of things that interact in a smart way that would provide innovative city development solutions such as public transit solutions, public utilities and services, traffic monitoring and management, energy consumption, infrastructure maintenance, and citizen services, among others (see Image 7.4). Additionally, building managers and property developers worldwide are looking to incorporate IoT devices and solutions into their infrastructures to reduce costs and improve the quality of their buildings. In this regard, cities around the world such as Barcelona in Spain, Las Vegas in the U.S., Padova in Italy, and Kashiwa-no-ha in Japan have undertaken plans to develop smart cities using IoT.

- The city of Barcelona has created an integrated city-wide fiber optics network, providing free high-speed Wi-Fi that supports the IoT. Further, by integrating smart water, lighting, and parking management, Barcelona

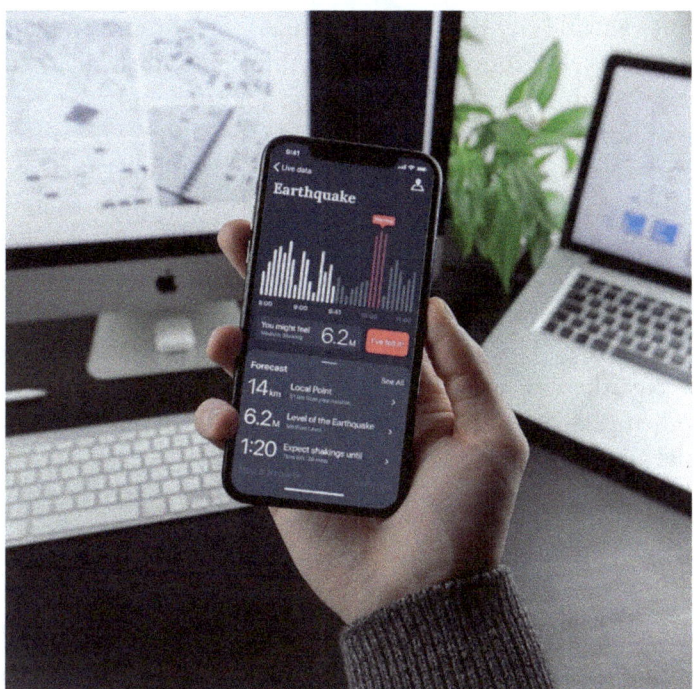

Image 7.4 IoT Warning Applications. IoT applications for smart cities such as this one, LOCUS, provide a direct connection between the citizens and the information system of the city in a visualized form
(*Source* Photo by *Balázs Kétyi* on *Unsplash*)

saved €75 million of city funds and created 47,000 new jobs in the smart technology sector.[83]
- The city of Las Vegas has installed IoT sensors to manage its traffic congestion and environmental issues. For instance, the sensors can detect carbon dioxide levels and nearby traffic conditions to determine the optimal traffic light duration by considering traffic wait times and the generation of exhaust.[84] Further, this smart city project is expected to use renewable energy sources such as solar, wind, and water, operate as an off-the-grid user, feature buildings with zero net energy consumption, and incorporate photovoltaic glass in buildings so that the building exterior can operate as solar panels.[85] These proposed features in Las Vegas are possible through IoT devices and the interconnectivity it provides.
- The city of Padova in Italy has implemented an urban IoT system, which is a communication infrastructure that provides unified, simple, and economical access to a plethora of public services that offer potential synergies and increase transparency to the citizens.[86] The IoT system

can collect valuable city data such as temperature, humidity, light patterns, and benzene levels (from traffic). Such information can help cities better plan energy production and consumption for efficient usage.
- The city of Kashiwa-no-ha in Japan has adopted an energy-conscious smart city project to promote resilience in the city. Using IoT, the city created a smart energy management system that reduces the area's energy usage by 26% through optimization of electricity distribution. In this connection, Japan has adopted a national initiative known as Society 5.0, which aims to realize a data-driven, human-centric, next-generation society that uses NATs such as IoT. This initiative is designed to apply to all citizens of the country, regardless of location, including the elderly population in rural areas, and emphasizes solving social issues while harmonizing sustainability and economic growth.[87]

Real-Time Buying Process and Purchasing

The adoption of NATs such as IoT allows firms to develop new business models that are platform-based and technology driven. While the benefits of IoT implementation are apparent on the customer-facing side of the business, the internal benefits of such implementations may always not be the case.[88]

Retailers are testing IoT solutions for customer-facing and non-customer-facing purchase instances. In terms of customer-facing purchase instances, the Amazon Go store combines machine vision, IoT sensors, and a mobile app swiped at the store entrance to create what it calls "just walk out technology" (see Image 7.5). The company has created a cashier-less retail setting where the customers can buy necessary products, charge them to their linked Amazon account, and simply walk out of the store when done, all without any interaction with the store employees. Such a setting not only creates an innovative business process but also secures the company several avenues for data collection and insights generation. In terms of non-customer-facing settings, beacons, and smart warehouses allow retailers to make merchandising and inventory management efficient. For instance, Kontakt is an IoT provider that makes beacons that can be used to track the movement of people and things in the commercial setting, in addition to monitoring ambient conditions such as light, heat, humidity, and so on.

Another area where IoT is making a positive impact is with the management of returnable transport packaging or returnable transport items (RTP/

Image 7.5 Amazon Go store. An Amazon Go store that uses a combination of machine vision, IoT sensors, and a mobile app to facilitate contactless retail customer transactions
(*Source* Photo by *Simon Bak* on *Unsplash*)

RTI) that include reusable pallets, racks, containers, trays, cylinders, crates, and so on. This alternative to disposable packaging assumes importance in the wake of sustainable supply chain practices expected by eco-conscious consumers and economical operations management adopted by various companies. In this regard, research has studied an RTI closed-loop supply chain where the receiver of the goods sends the RTI back to the sender which can be reused in subsequent shipments.[89,90]

Whereas RFID technology was used to track and monitor RTIs,[91] the solution was less than ideal given the shortcomings in the RFID technology such as heavy investment, significant coordination between manufacturer and channel partners, and RFID tag range considerations, among others. IoT circumvents most of these challenges due to its wireless, low-emission networks—such as the 0G network, which specializes in sending and receiving messages made up of small amounts of data across long distances. Such a solution allows organizations to track and manage RTIs with a considerably lesser investment of time and capital.[92] The logistics industry is responding positively to this technology with companies like An Post, an Irish logistics provider, implementing smart tracking devices that allow them to monitor the location of their assets, and using 0G network connectivity.[93] As IoT continues to spur advances in research and practice of developing efficient and effective connected devices, we can expect more value-generating innovations for firms and users.

Key Terms and Related Conceptualizations

Adaptive marketing capabilities	Capabilities that enable organizations to be sensitive to the emerging trends in the environment, to be agile in rapidly making necessary adjustments in implementation activities, and to be willing to learn through experimentation
Ambient assisted living	Technical systems to support elderly people and people with special needs in their daily routines. Typically consists of services, products, and concepts that are connected, context-sensitive, personal, adaptive, and anticipative
Consumer well-being	A multidimensional concept that describes a state of health and happiness for each stakeholder across physical, emotional, financial, societal, and environmental dimensions, as relevant to the stakeholder
Digital customer orientation	Offering customized and enriched customer experiences by embracing digital ecosystems
Industrial IoT (IIoT)	A network of connected devices that seeks to enhance revenue generation potential through a focus on user needs
Industry 4.0	A new-age industrial revolution wherein Internet technologies are used to create smart products, smart production, and smart services
Internet of Things (IoT)	An elaborate network of devices connected through the Internet
IoT capabilities	A unique type of IT capability that relies on the network of physical objects to sense new opportunities and threats, to move resources to address those new opportunities, and reconfigure IT assets
Smart city	A city that monitors and integrates conditions of all of its critical infrastructures
Smart home	A regular home that has been augmented with various types of sensors and actuators

(continued)

(continued)	
Wearables	Devices that can be worn (e.g., fitness trackers, health monitors, medical monitors) that collect, and process data related to various aspects of health and fitness routines. This data can be used by the user and in combination with medical practitioners to manage healthcare options

Notes and References

1. Muller, J. (2022), "Pop-up digital ads are taking over the freezer aisle," *Axios*, March 29, [accessed from https://www.axios.com/2022/03/29/pop-up-digital-ads-are-taking-over-the-freezer-aisle].
2. Dooley, J. (2019), "Chicago-based Cooler Screens, leverages smart screens powered by AI and IoT, to enhance the in-store customer shopping experience at Walgreens," *Clickz.com*, December 2019, [accessed from https://www.clickz.com/cooler-screens-is-bringing-the-digital-shopping-experience-to-brick-and-mortar-stores/?amp=1].
3. According to (Transforma Insights, & Exploding Topics (2023). Number of Internet of Things (IoT) connected devices worldwide from 2019 to 2023, with forecasts from 2022 to 2030 (in billions) [Graph]. In *Statista*. July 1. Retrieved October 09, 2023, from https://www.statista.com/statistics/1183457/iot-connected-devices-worldwide/), the number of IoT connections worldwide in 2020 was 9.75 billion devices, it is expected to reach 19 billion devices by 2025 and 29.4 billion deices by 2030. This growth is driven by cellular IoT.
4. Cellular IoT is expected to reach 5.4 billion by 2028, up from 2.7 billion in 2022. In terms of cellular IoT growth regions, Northeast Asia leads the global adoption, wherein the region is estimated to have more than 2 billion connections by 2023 (Ericsson. (February 23, 2023). Number of cellular IoT connections worldwide from 2022 to 2028, by connection technology (in millions) [Graph]. In *Statista*. Retrieved October 09, 2023, from https://www.statista.com/statistics/1388055/cellular-iot-connections-worldwide/).
5. Lee, G. M., N. Crespi, J. K. Choi, & M. Boussard (2013), "Internet of things," In *Evolution of Telecommunication Services* (pp. 257-282). Springer, Berlin, Heidelberg; Xia, F., L. T. Yang, L. Wang, & A. Vinel (2012), "Internet of things," *International Journal of Communication Systems*, 25(9), 1101–1102.

6. Ashton, K. (2009), "That 'internet of things' thing," *RFID Journal*, 22(7), 97–114.
7. Kaplan, D. A. (2018), "The rise, fall and return of RFID," *Supply Chain Dive*, August 21, [accessed from https://www.supplychaindive.com/news/RFID-rise-fall-and-return-retail/530608/].
8. ITU (2012), "Overview of the Internet of things," *International Telecommunication Union*, June, [accessed from http://handle.itu.int/11.1002/1000/11559].
9. IoT equips computers with data gathering, observational, analytical abilities without human dependence and intervention, in addition to containing a system of smart devices embedded in everyday objects that are connected via the internet (Kopetz, H. (2011), "Internet of things," In *Real-time systems* (pp. 307–323). Springer, Boston, MA).
10. Atzori, L., A. Iera, & G. Morabito (2010), "The internet of things: A survey," *Computer Networks*, 54(15), 2787–2805.
11. Gluhak, A., S. Krco, M. Nati, D. Pfisterer, N. Mitton, & T. Razafindralambo (2011), "A survey on facilities for experimental internet of things research," *IEEE Communications Magazine*, 49(11), 58–67.
12. Gubbi, J., R. Buyya, S. Marusic, & M. Palaniswami (2013), "Internet of Things (IoT): A vision, architectural elements, and future directions," *Future Generation Computer Systems*, 29(7), 1645–1660.
13. Sundmaeker, H., P. Guillemin, P. Friess, & S. Woelfflé, (2010), "Vision and challenges for realising the Internet of Things," *Cluster of European Research Projects on the Internet of Things, European Commision*, 3(3), 34–36.
14. Pennic, J. (2017), "Big cloud analytics rebrands as EVO health, launches wellness analytics app platform," *Hit Consultant*, October 9, [accessed from https://hitconsultant.net/2017/10/09/big-cloud-analytics-rebrands-evo-health/].
15. Coetzee, L., & J. Eksteen (2011), "The Internet of Things-promise for the future? An introduction," In *2011 IST-Africa Conference Proceedings* (pp. 1–9), May, IEEE.
16. Verhoef, P.C., A. T. Stephen, P. K. Kannan, X. Luo, V. Abhishek, M. Andrews, Y. Bart, H. Datta, N. Fong, D. L. Hoffman, & M. M. Hu (2017), "Consumer connectivity in a complex, technology-enabled, and mobile-oriented world with smart products," *Journal of Interactive Marketing*, 40, 1–8.
17. Macaulay, J., L. Buckalew & G. Chung (2015), "Internet of Things In Logistics," *DHL.com*.

18. Kumar, V., D. Ramachandran, and B. Kumar (2020), "Influence of new-age technologies on marketing: A research agenda," *Journal of Business Research*, [accessed from https://www.sciencedirect.com/science/article/abs/pii/S0148296320300151].
19. A Microsoft survey (from 2019) found that in industries such as manufacturing, retail, transportation, at least 85% of the decision-makers are actively incorporating IoT in their organization at high rates. Further, 88% of the adopters felt IoT to be critical for the overall success of their business. Additionally, the survey found IoT to be beneficial in streamlining processes and ensuring overall efficiency.
20. New, J. and D. Castro (2015), "Why countries need national strategies for the internet of things," *Center for Data Innovation*, December 16, [accessed from http://www2.datainnovation.org/2015-national-iot-strategies.pdf].
21. Microsoft (2019), "IoT Signals," *Microsoft*, July, [accessed from https://azure.microsoft.com/mediahandler/files/resourcefiles/iot-signals/IoT-Signals-Microsoft-072019.pdf].
22. Urban Hub (2018), "Brazil embraces the digital age with an ambitious Internet of Things strategy," *Urban Hub*, April 11, [accessed from http://www.urban-hub.com/technology/brazil-embraces-the-digital-age-with-an-ambitious-internet-of-things-strategy/].
23. Government of India (2015), "Smart cities—mission statement & guidelines," *Government of India*, June, [accessed from http://smartcities.gov.in/upload/uploadfiles/files/SmartCityGuidelines(1).pdf] (p. 6).
24. Piwek, L., D. A. Ellis, S. Andrews, & A. Joinson (2016), "The rise of consumer health wearables: promises and barriers," *PLoS Medicine*, *13*(2), e1001953, https://doi.org/10.1371/journal.pmed.1001953.
25. The wearables market is expected to reach USD54 billion worldwide, up from USD23 billion in 2018 (Barkho, G. (2019), "The wearable tech industry is expected to Hit $54 Billion by 2023," *Observer.com*, August 12, [accessed from https://observer.com/2019/08/wearable-tech-industry-hit-54-billion-by-2023/], and that more than 80% of consumers are willing to use fitness technology (Phaneuf, A. (2020), "Latest trends in medical monitoring devices and wearable health technology," *Business Insider*, January 31, [accessed from https://www.businessinsider.com/wearable-technology-healthcare-medical-devices].
26. Rashidi, P., & A. Mihailidis (2012), "A survey on ambient-assisted living tools for older adults," *IEEE Journal of Biomedical and Health Informatics*, 17(3), 579–590.

27. Ghayvat, H., J. Liu, A. Babu, E. E. Alahi, X. Gui, & S. C. Mukhopadhyay (2015), "Internet of Things for smart homes and buildings: Opportunities and Challenges," *Journal of Telecommunications and the Digital Economy*, 3(4), 33–47.
28. Mick, D., Pettigrew, S., Pechmann, C., & Ozanne, J. (2012), "Origins, Qualities, and Envisionments of Transformative Consumer Research," In *Transformative Consumer Research: For Personal and Collective Well-being* (pp. 3–25): Routledge.
29. Andreasen, A. R., M. E. Goldberg, & M. J. Sirgy (2012), "Foundational research on consumer welfare: Opportunities for a transformative consumer research agenda," In *Transformative consumer research for personal and collective well-being* (pp. 25–66): Routledge.
30. Burroughs, J. E., & A. Rindfleisch (2012). "What welfare? On the definition and domain of transformative consumer research and the foundational role of materialism," In *Transformative consumer research for personal and collective well-being*, (pp. 249–266): Routledge.
31. Kumar, V., & D. Ramachandran (2020), "Developing a firm's growth approaches in a new-age technology environment to enhance stakeholder wellbeing," working paper, Georgia State University, GA.
32. Ghayvat, H., J. Liu, A. Babu, E. E. Alahi, X. Gui, & S. C. Mukhopadhyay (2015), "Internet of Things for smart homes and buildings: Opportunities and Challenges," *Journal of Telecommunications and the Digital Economy*, 3(4), 33–47.
33. Dohr, A., Modre-Opsrian, R., Drobics, M., Hayn, D., & Schreier, G. (2010). The internet of things for ambient assisted living. In *2010 Seventh International Conference on Information Technology: New Generations*, Las Vegas, NV, USA, April, pp. 804–809.
34. In 2023, the top five nations that had the highest penetration rate of major smart appliances (e.g., refrigerators, washing machines) were India (36%), China (35%), South Africa (23%), South Korea (20%), and France (16%). In general, households are more likely to own a major smart appliance than a small smart appliance (e.g., coffee machines, microwaves) (Statista Consumer Insights. (2022). Ownership rate of small and big smart appliances in selected countries in 2023* [Graph]. In *Statista*. May 31. Retrieved October 09, 2023, from https://www.statista.com/statistics/1168812/smart-appliances-ownership-by-country/).
35. Pennic, J. (2017), "Big cloud analytics rebrands as evo health, launches wellness analytics app platform," *Hit Consultant*, October 9,

[accessed from https://hitconsultant.net/2017/10/09/big-cloud-analytics-rebrands-evo-health/].
36. Sauter, T., S. Soucek, W. Kastner, & D. Dietrich (2011), "The evolution of factory and building automation," *IEEE Industrial Electronics Magazine*, 5(3), 35–48.
37. Bratukhin, A., & T. Sauter (2011), "Functional analysis of manufacturing execution system distribution," *IEEE Transactions on Industrial Informatics*, 7(4), 740–749.
38. Bauer, H., M. Simon, M. Becker, M. Altmeier (2019), "Changing market dynamics—Capturing value in machinery and industrial automation," *McKinsey & Company*, July, [accessed from https://www.mckinsey.com/industries/advanced-electronics/our-insights/capturing-value-in-machinery-and-industrial-automation-as-market-dynamics-change].
39. Wollschlaeger, M., T. Sauter, & J. Jasperneite (2017), "The future of industrial communication: Automation networks in the era of the internet of things and industry 4.0," *IEEE Industrial Electronics Magazine*, 11(1), 17–27.
40. IEEE (2015), "Towards a definition of the Internet of Things (IoT)," *IEEE Internet Initiative*, May 27, [accessed from https://iot.ieee.org/images/files/pdf/IEEE_IoT_Towards_Definition_Internet_of_Things_Revision1_27MAY15.pdf].
41. The global industrial automation market was estimated at USD 157.04 billion in 2018 and is expected to reach USD 296.7 billion by 2026 (PR Newswire (2019), "Industrial Automation Market Will Rise at a CAGR of 8.4%; Increasing Demand for AI-Based Industrial Robots Will Aid Growth, Says Fortune Business Insights," *PR Newswire*, November 4, [accessed from https://www.prnewswire.com/in/news-releases/industrial-automation-market-will-rise-at-a-cagr-of-8-4-increasing-demand-for-ai-based-industrial-robots-will-aid-growth-says-fortune-business-insights-866899795.html]. Further, a recent survey found that nearly 57% of global companies have piloted automation in at least one function or business unit with an additional 18% indicating plans to automate within the next year (Edlich, A., F. Ip, R. Panikkar, & R. Whiteman (2018), "The automation imperative," *McKinsey & Company*, September, [accessed from https://www.mckinsey.com/business-functions/operations/our-insights/the-automation-imperative], indicating an overall global push towards incorporating automation in daily production operations.

42. Bolz, L., H. Freund, T. Kasah, & B. Koerber (2018), "IIoT platforms: The technology stack as value driver in industrial equipment and machinery," *McKinsey & Company*, September, [accessed from https://www.mckinsey.com/industries/advanced-electronics/our-insights/iiot-platforms-the-technology-stack-as-value-driver-in-industrial-equipment-and-machinery].
43. Packaging Europe (2023), "Congress Special: Wiliot adds humidity monitoring to its ambient IoT visibility platform," *Packaging Europe*, October 10, [accessed from https://packagingeurope.com/news/congress-special-wiliot-adds-humidity-monitoring-to-its-ambient-iot-visibility-platform/10439.article].
44. Rooney, P. (2023), "P&G enlists IoT, predictive analytics to perfect Pampers diapers," *CIO.com*, August 25, [accessed from https://www.cio.com/article/650197/pg-enlists-iot-predictive-analytics-to-perfect-pampers-diapers.html].
45. Street, C. (2019), "Sheep Inc.: the world's first carbon-negative fashion brand," *The Standard*, December 6, [accessed from https://www.standard.co.uk/lifestyle/fashion/sheep-inc-jumpers-carbon-negative-nfc-tag-a4303601.html].
46. Leidigh, R. (2023), "Mapbox joins partner ecosystem for Qualcomm Aware Platform," *Mapbox*, March 1,[accessed from https://www.mapbox.com/blog/mapbox-joins-partner-ecosystem-for-qualcomm-aware-platform].
47. Mitter, S. (2021), "Farming on autopilot: Agritech startup Fasal uses IoT to help horticulture farmers go remote," *Your Story*, January 7, [accessed from https://yourstory.com/2021/01/farming-agritech-startup-fasal-iot-horticulture-farmers].
48. Wangchuk, R. N. (2020), "Installing in 5 Mins, Bengaluru firm's tech helps save 3 Billion Litres of Water," *The Better India*, December 20, [accessed from https://www.thebetterindia.com/243842/bengaluru-agritech-startup-new-tech-innovation-fasal-kranti-water-saving-precision-farmer-irrigation-pest-management-india-nor41/].
49. Kumar, V. (2021). *Intelligent Marketing: Employing New Age Technologies*. Sage Publications.
50. Stewart, K. (2018), "5 ways Sephora creates a seamless customer experience," *National Retail Federation*, July 23, [accessed from https://nrf.com/blog/5-ways-sephora-creates-seamless-customer-experience].
51. eMarketer (2016), "Walgreens leverages customers' smartphone behavior to drive mobile purchases," *eMarketer*, June, [accessed from

https://www.emarketer.com/Article/Walgreens-Leverages-Customers-Smartphone-Behavior-Drive-Mobile-Purchases/1014030].
52. Lucas, A. (2018), "Burger King sells Whoppers for a penny at McDonald's locations to promote its app," *CNBC*, December 4, [accessed from https://www.cnbc.com/2018/12/04/burger-king-sells-whoppers-for-a-penny-at-mcdonalds-locations.html?__source=twitter%7Cmain].
53. Dickson, B. (2020), "3 ways AI is transforming the insurance industry," *TNW*, February 24, [accessed from https://thenextweb.com/growth-quarters/2020/02/24/3-ways-ai-is-transforming-the-insurance-industry/].
54. Moore, J. (2014), "Building automation systems: IoT meets facilities management," *TechTarget*, January 27, [accessed from https://internetofthingsagenda.techtarget.com/feature/Building-automation-systems-Internet-of-Things-meets-facilities-management].
55. Kumar, V. (2021). *Intelligent Marketing: Employing New Age Technologies*. Sage Publications.
56. Teece, D. J. (2018), "Business models and dynamic capabilities," *Long Range Planning*, 51(1), 40–49.
57. Dunaway M., Y. W. Sullivan, & S. F. Wamba (2019), "Building Dynamic Capabilities with the Internet of Things," In *Proceedings of the 52nd Hawaii International Conference on System Sciences*, January, pp. 5909–5918.
58. Day, G. S. (2011), "Closing the marketing capabilities gap," *Journal of Marketing*, 75(4), 183–95.
59. Computerworld (2019), "The most powerful internet of things (IoT) companies to watch," *Computerworld*, February 15, [accessed from https://www.computerworld.com/article/3412287/the-most-powerful-internet-of-things-iot-companies-to-watch.html#slide3].
60. Kumar, V., D. Ramachandran, & B. Kumar (2020), "Influence of new-age technologies on marketing: A research agenda," *Journal of Business Research*, [accessed from https://www.sciencedirect.com/science/article/abs/pii/S0148296320300151].
61. Diageo (2015), "Diageo and thinfilm unveil the connected 'smart bottle'," *Diageo.com*, February 25, [accessed from https://www.diageo.com/en/news-and-media/press-releases/diageo-and-thinfilm-unveil-the-connected-smart-bottle/?zd_source=mta&zd_campaign=12776&zd_term=chiradeepbasumallick].
62. Taylor, R. (2018), "BK Whoppers are only 1 cent when you order at McDonald's," *QSR Magazine*, December, [accessed from https://www.qsrmagazine.com/burgers/bk-whoppers-are-only-1-cent-when-you-order-mcdonalds].

63. Maycotte, H. O. (2018), "What data can a beacon actually collect?" *Multichannel Merchant*, April 9, [accessed from https://multichannelmerchant.com/marketing/data-can-beacon-actually-collect/].
64. Pathak, S. (2014), "Nivea Ad that turns into a Kid-Tracker wins mobile grand prix," *Ad Age*, June 17, [accessed from https://adage.com/article/special-report-cannes-lions/nivea-ad-turns-kid-tracker-wins-mobile-grand-prix/293745].
65. A global survey found that 73% of respondents identify customer experience as a key factor in determining their purchasing outcomes, only 49% of the consumers say companies provide a good customer experience today. The survey also found that 32% of global consumers will stay away from a brand, following a bad experience—this feature is higher in Latin America at 49% (Clark, D., & R. Kinghorn (2018), "Experience is everything: Here's how to get it right," *PwC*, [accessed from https://www.pwc.com/us/en/services/consulting/library/consumer-intelligence-series/future-of-customer-experience.html]).
66. Kumar, V., & W. J. Reinartz (2016), "Creating enduring customer value," *Journal of Marketing*, 80(6), 36–68; Verhoef, P. C., W. J. Reinartz, and M. Krafft (2010), "Customer engagement as a new perspective in customer management," *Journal of Service Research*, 13(3), 247–52.
67. Kumar, V., & A. Pansari (2016), "Competitive advantage through engagement," *Journal of Marketing Research*, 53(4), 497–514; Pansari, A., & V. Kumar (2017), "Customer engagement: the construct, antecedents, and consequences," *Journal of the Academy of Marketing Science*, 1–18.
68. For more detail on customer value contributions to the firms, and the conceptualizations of CE, please see (Kumar, V, L. Aksoy, B. Donkers, R. Venkatesan, T. Wiesel, & S. Tillmanns (2010), "Undervalued or overvalued customers: Capturing total customer engagement value," *Journal of Service Research*, 13(3), 297–310); (Van Doorn, J., K. N. Lemon, V. Mittal, S. Nass, D. Pick, P. Pirner, & P. C. Verhoef (2010), "Customer engagement behavior: Theoretical foundations and research directions," *Journal of Service Research*, 13(3), 253–66).
69. Pansari, A., & V. Kumar (2017), "Customer engagement: the construct, antecedents, and consequences," *Journal of the Academy of Marketing Science*, 1–18.
70. Kumar, V., B. Rajan, S. Gupta, S., & I. D. Pozza, (2019), "Customer engagement in service," *Journal of the Academy of Marketing Science*, 47(1), 138–160.

71. Ramaswamy, V., & K. Ozcan (2018), "Offerings as digitalized interactive platforms: A conceptual framework and implications," *Journal of Marketing*, 82(4): 19–21.
72. Govindarajan, V., & J. R. Immelt (2019), "Digital transformation is no longer optional for industrial companies. The problem is it's really, really hard," *MIT Sloan Management Review*, 60(3), 24–33.
73. Kopalle, P. K., V. Kumar, & M. Subramaniam (2020), "How legacy firms can embrace the digital ecosystem via digital customer orientation," *Journal of the Academy of Marketing Science*, 48(1), 114–131.
74. Kumar, V. (2021). *Intelligent Marketing: Employing New Age Technologies*. Sage Publications.
75. The U.S. Environmental Protection Agency (EPA) found that in 2018 the transportation sector generated the largest share of greenhouse gas emissions at 28%, with emissions primarily coming from burning fossil fuel for cars, trucks, ships, trains, and planes (EPA (2020), "*Draft* Inventory of U.S. Greenhouse Gas Emissions and Sinks: 1990–2018," *EPA*, March, [accessed from https://www.epa.gov/sites/production/files/2020-02/documents/us-ghg-inventory-2020-main-text.pdf).
76. Mohanty, S. P., U. Choppali, & E. Kougianos (2016), "Everything you wanted to know about smart cities: The internet of things is the backbone," *IEEE Consumer Electronics Magazine*, 5(3), 60–70.
77. KTAR (2018), "Valley Metro testing mobile ticket app for buses, light rail," *KTAR.com*, April 5, [accessed from https://ktar.com/story/2011520/valley-metro-testing-mobile-ticket-app-for-buses-light-rail/].
78. Martín, J., E. J. Khatib, P. Lázaro, & R. Barco (2019), "Traffic monitoring via mobile device location," *Sensors*, 19(20), 4505.
79. Orange (2018), "How mobile phone data could reduce traffic jams and train delays," *Orange*, December 27, [accessed from https://www.orange-business.com/en/magazine/how-mobile-phone-data-could-reduce-traffic-jams-and-train-delays].
80. Al-Dweik, A., R. Muresan, M. Mayhew, & M. Lieberman (2017), "IoT-based multifunctional scalable real-time enhanced roadside unit for intelligent transportation systems," In *2017 IEEE 30th Canadian Conference on Electrical and Computer Engineering (CCECE)*, April, pp. 1–6.
81. Hall, R. E. (2000), "The vision of a smart city," In *Proceedings of the 2nd International Life Extension Technology Workshop*, Paris, France, September 28, [accessed from http://www.osti.gov/bridge/servlets/purl/773961-oyxp82/webviewable/773961.pdf].

82. Please see (Washburn, D., U. Sindhu, S. Balaouras, R. A. Dines, N. Hayes, & L. E. Nelson (2009), "Helping CIOs understand "smart city" initiatives," *Growth*, 17(2), 1-17), (Caragliu, A., C. Del Bo, & P. Nijkamp (2011), "Smart cities in Europe," *Journal of Urban Technology*, 18(2), 65–82), (Zanella, A., N. Bui, A. Castellani, L. Vangelista, & M. Zorzi (2014), "Internet of things for smart cities," *IEEE Internet of Things journal*, 1(1), 22–32), and (Neirotti, P., A. De Marco, A. C. Cagliano, G. Mangano, & F. Scorrano (2014), "Current trends in Smart City initiatives: Some stylised facts," *Cities*, 38, 25–36) to learn about the various approaches in conceptualizing smart cities.
83. Ellsmoor, J. (2019), "Smart cities: The future of urban development," *Forbes*, May 19, [accessed from https://www.forbes.com/sites/jamesellsmoor/2019/05/19/smart-cities-the-future-of-urban-development/#1f14fb0f2f90].
84. Horwitz, L. (2017), "Can smart city infrastructure alleviate the strain of city growth?" *Cisco*, June, [accessed from https://www.cisco.com/c/en/us/solutions/internet-of-things/smart-city-infrastructure.html].
85. Blackman, J. (2019), "Cisco to 'make sci-fi real' as partner in $7.5bn Las Vegas smart city project," *Enterprise IoT Insights*, August 5, [accessed from https://enterpriseiotinsights.com/20190805/channels/news/cisco-to-make-sci-fi-real-in-las-vegas].
86. Zanella, A., N. Bui, A. Castellani, L. Vangelista, & M. Zorzi (2014), "Internet of things for smart cities," *IEEE Internet of Things journal*, 1(1), 22–32.
87. Buntz, B. (2020), "In Japan, Smart City Projects Have a Social Dimension," *IoT World Today*, February 26, [accessed from https://www.iotworldtoday.com/2020/02/26/in-japan-smart-city-projects-have-a-social-dimension/].
88. Research by (Stank, T. P., M. Crum, & M. Arango (1999), "Benefits of interfirm coordination in food industry supply chains," *Journal of Business Logistics*, 20(2), 21) and (Stank, T. P., S. B. Keller, & P. J. Daugherty (2001), "Supply chain collaboration and logistical service performance," *Journal of Business Logistics*, 22(1), 29–48) identified that firms with high levels of supply chain integration and that share collaborative channel partner relationships are more likely to adopt technologies that streamlines information exchange and enables faster inventory responses to changes in demand.

89. Glock, C. H. (2017), "Decision support models for managing returnable transport items in supply chains: A systematic literature review," *International Journal of Production Economics*, 183, 561–569.
90. Wang, M., & L. Zhao (2018), "Pricing decisions and environmental assessment in a two-echelon supply chain with returnable transport items," *Procedia Computer Science*, 126, 1792–1801.
91. Hellström, D. (2009), "The cost and process of implementing RFID technology to manage and control returnable transport items," *International Journal of Logistics: Research and Applications*, 12(1), 1–21.
92. Sainathan, P., and A. M. Giménez (2020), "Returnable packaging and IoT: Keys to a More Sustainable Supply Chain," *Supply Chain Brain*, January 13, [accessed from https://www.supplychainbrain.com/blogs/1-think-tank/post/30704-returnable-packaging-and-iot-keys-to-a-more-sustainable-supply-chain].
93. Business Wire (2020). "An post, the Irish leading mails, parcels and ecommerce logistics company, revolutionise their supply chain," *Business Wire*, February 28, [accessed from https://www.businesswire.com/news/home/20200228005183/en/].
94. Dooley, J. (2019), "Chicago-based Cooler Screens, leverages smart screens powered by AI and IoT, to enhance the in-store customer shopping experience at Walgreens," Clickz.com, December 2019, [accessed from https://www.clickz.com/cooler-screens-is-bringing-the-digital-shopping-experience-to-brick-and-mortar-stores/?amp=1].

8

Transformative Marketing with Robotics

Overview

Robots have continued to capture our imagination since their first introduction in the 1950s. While academic investigations and commercial developments in technology continue to shape the field of robotics, popular culture has also significantly enhanced the popularity of robots in real-world usage. Movies such as *The Terminator*, *WALL-E*, *The Matrix*, *RoboCop*, and *The Transformers* have etched robots in viewers' minds. While most of these movies were set in futuristic times, we are beginning to witness some elements of robots aiding human lives already.

We are assisted by robots that do specialized tasks while we refocus our attention on things and issues that we hold dear.[1] Specialized robots help us with everyday routine tasks such as cleaning (e.g., Roomba), smart-home video surveillance system (e.g., Lighthouse), virtual assistance (e.g., Alexa), mealtime assistance for senior care and differently-abled people (e.g., Bestic), personal transporter (e.g., Loomo), and so on. Robots are also involved in powering routine and advanced tasks such as assisting in banking transactions (e.g., Nao), serving as baristas (e.g., Café X), assisting around the home (e.g., Zenbo), dispensing medication (e.g., Pillo), assisting special-needs children (e.g., Leka), and so on.

It is noteworthy that some of these robots do not perform the tasks in a monotonous fashion, but rather learn and apply thinking as they continue to work. Eventually, they learn more about us and our needs through their interaction and get better at performing their tasks. In other words, they provide personalized service that uniquely matches the needs of every individual.

Such specialized robots are a representative faction of recent technological advancements, especially new-age technologies such as artificial intelligence (AI). They actively shape human lifestyles in almost every aspect of daily life, and the way they do it is through personalization.[2]

The prevalence and promise of robotics can be seen in its global growth.[3] Specifically, automation studies specific to the United States reveal that American companies could invest nearly $8 trillion in automation technologies by 2030, and that rapid automation of the US service sector could eliminate jobs two to three times more rapidly than in previous transformations.[4] Therefore, robotics presents valuable opportunities to firms and customers that could significantly reshape how value is created and transferred in industries worldwide.

This chapter is organized as follows. First, a brief history of the origin of robotics is presented, followed by a definition of robotics (from a marketing standpoint). Then, a discussion on the various classifications of robotics is presented. Then, the role of robotics in the Marketing 5.0 concept is discussed. Next, some marketing applications of robotics are discussed. Finally, the future of robotics for the marketing industry is discussed.

Origin, Definition, and Classifications of Robotics

Origin

Whereas modern-day robotics offer novel and interesting applications, the roots of robotics can be traced back several centuries to the various ancient mechanical devices that assisted in performing physical tasks. Over the centuries, many cultures have viewed self-operating devices, or automatons, with much curiosity. Notable among such devices include Chinese clock towers built around the tenth century BC and Greek hydraulics devised around the first century BC. Subsequent creations that included Arabian water clocks and figurines (first century AD), Leonardo da Vinci's mechanical inventions such as mechanical knight and rotor-powered flying machines (fourteenth century AD), Descartes' biological machines (seventeenth century AD), and Japanese mechanical toys (seventeenth century AD), continued to propel human inquisitiveness and the desire to create mechanical devices and life-like figurines that operated independently.

Early twentieth-century literary works contributed conceptualizations of mechanical devices and humanoids such as The Wonderful Wizard of Oz series (1900) by L. Frank Baum and the Foundation series (1951–1953) by

Isaac Asimov, among others. Most notably, the terms "robot" and "robotics" were first introduced in literary works. Specifically, the term "robot" was first used in the 1921 Czech play R.U.R. (Rossum's Universal Robots) which featured mechanical beings; and the term "robotics" was first introduced in Asimov's short stories collection written in the 1940s.[5] Largely fueled by human imagination, the first half of the twentieth century also saw the development of humanoid robots such as Japan's Gakutensoku in 1927 and Westinghouse Electric Corporation's Elektro in 1939. Such developments served as forebearers of future growth in biomechanical research and in aiding humans to perform various personal and industrial tasks.

The second half of the twentieth century began to see more targeted robotic developments that focused on specific applications centered around performing defined tasks. This phase was spurred by research and advancements in computing, programming, and machinery and government investments in building robotic capabilities. In this regard, the first industrial robot was developed in 1959 by Unimation and subsequently installed in General Motors in 1961 which was mainly used for moving objects. This was followed by developments of robotic arms such as The Rancho Arm (1963), the Orm (1965), the Tentacle Arm (1968), and the Stanford Arm (1969), which had the flexibility of a human arm. Further, the first mobile robot that could navigate its surroundings, Shakey, was developed in 1970 using artificial intelligence (AI) technology and fitted with audio and video capabilities. The 1970s and 1980s produced many "firsts" in robotics such as the first minicomputer-controlled industrial robot (1974), the first fully electric, microprocessor-controlled industrial robot (1974), the first motor-driven robot (1979), the first machine vision-enabled robot (1981), and the first flexible automated assembly lines (1983), to name a few.[6] The following decades saw the spread of robotics into various disciplines such as healthcare delivery, underwater vehicles, space exploration, human collaboration, and home cleaning systems, among others.

Definition

Robots confirm the formal area of study known as robotics. The term robotics has been defined as the science studying "the intelligent connection of perception to action" (p. 2).[7] Featured originally in his 1942 science fiction short story *Runaround*, Issac Asimov proposed the Three Laws of Robotics which lay down a set of rules for robots to follow. While the Three Laws of Robotics may have been advanced as a plot device in science fiction writing, public

Table 8.1 Select definition of robotics

Source	Definition
International Organization for Standardization	The science and practice of designing, manufacturing, and applying robots
Lynch and Park[9]	The creation of machines that can behave and think like humans
Siciliano and Khatib[10]	The science and technology of robots
Mentzer and Gandhi[11]	An automated manufacturing process

interest, and academic inquiry into robotics have since caught the imagination of many. Academic research in the field of robotics continues to be shaped by several established research streams such as mechanical engineering, mathematics, control systems, electrical engineering, and computer science.[8] However, there is no consensus on a single definition of robotics with many scholars and organizations presenting various definitions of robotics (see Table 8.1).

Classification of Robots

Academic research has conceptualized robots in various ways (see Table 8.2). Moreover, robots have been referred to as "actuated mechanisms programmable in two or more axes with a degree of autonomy, moving within its environment, to perform intended tasks" by the International Organization for Standardization. Table 8.3 provides seven distinct classifications of robots as identified by the International Organization for Standardization.[12]

Table 8.2 Select conceptualization of robots

Study	Conceptualization
Breazeal[13]	Being able to perceive the world, make independent decisions, and perform coordinated actions to carry out their tasks
Kaplan[14]	A *physical object* (i.e., perceives and acts in a physical environment), functioning in an *autonomous* (i.e., programmable, trainable, and mostly controllable), and *situated* manner (i.e., constantly reacting to their environment by constantly manipulating information and things)
Kurfess[15]	Machines or devices that operate automatically or by remote control
Wilson[16]	Advanced intelligent systems that can "...perform rule-based work and tend to be configurable with basic features like authentication, security, auditing, logging, and exception handling"

Table 8.3 Classification of robots

Type of robot	What does it do?	Some typical examples...
Industrial robot	An automatically controlled, reprogrammable, multipurpose manipulator, programmable in three or more axes, which can be either fixed in place or mobile for use in industrial automation applications	Robots for food packaging, material handling, biomedical applications, simulators, forging/welding, and coating applications
Service robot	A robot that performs useful tasks for humans or equipment excluding industrial automation applications	Robots for domestic tasks, entertainment, elderly assistance, home surveillance, and security, and personal transportation
Personal service robot	A service robot is used for a non-commercial task, usually by laypersons	Domestic help robots, an automated wheelchair, a personal mobility assist robot, and a pet exercising robot
Professional service robot	A service robot used for a commercial task is usually operated by a properly trained operator	Cleaning robots for public places, delivery robots in offices or hospitals, fire-fighting robots, rehabilitation robots, and surgery robots in hospitals
Mobile robot	Is a robot that can travel under its control	Unmanned vehicles for land, water, and space travel, robots for oil mining and rigging, and robots for surveillance and monitoring
Collaborative robot	A robot designed for direct interaction with a human	Picking and packing robots, robots for quality inspection, and robots for performing surgery
Intelligent robot	A robot that can perform tasks by sensing its environment and/or interacting with external sources and adapting its behavior	Robots for explorations in remote places such as space and deep sea; gesture and motion recognition; object detection; and environmental change detection

Source ISO (2012), "ISO 8373:2012—Robots and robotic devices—Vocabulary," *International Organization for Standardization*, March, [accessed from https://www.iso.org/obp/ui/#iso:std:iso:8373:ed-2:v1:en:term:2.6]

In terms of applications, the above-mentioned types of robots can be broadly applied in industrial and service settings. While industrial robots have demonstrated significant value over the decades in developing offerings through their critical roles in manufacturing and industrial operations, service robots are relatively newcomers. Popular service robots to date include robots in the retail industry (e.g., Lowe's "LoweBot") to answer customer queries and assist in-store navigation[17]; robots in healthcare such as surgical robots, medical transportation, and telepresence[18]; robots in the media and publishing industry[19]; and robots in the restaurant industry,[20] among others. The advent of service robots has removed the requirement of the mechanical component from the definition of a robot. The information revolution has substantially changed the scope of work. Much of today's work is knowledge-based, which can be completed with little or no physical labor. Therefore, robots continue to serve us in varied ways, with their repertoire only expected to increase in the future.

Overall, robotics is rapidly gaining momentum among the academic and practitioner communities because of various real-world application possibilities. In this regard, robotics is largely oriented towards executing tasks and activities as determined by managers. Any internal intelligence possessed by robotics is also powered by other new-age technologies (NATs) like artificial intelligence (AI) and the Internet of Things (IoT).[21] As a result, robotics is considered a function-oriented technology that serves to integrate with other existing technologies by performing last-mile tasks or activities as required. Kumar and Ramachandran[22] identify function-oriented technologies to allow firms to gain increased accessibility to areas and situations that humans cannot access safely. Further, the firm can achieve increased efficiency and accuracy in tasks requiring precision and attention to detail. Especially in the case of repetitive tasks, function-oriented technology can deliver consistently good results, quickly and without fatigue.[23] To conclude the overview of robotics, the following three vignettes present the possibilities of robotics in delivering valuable offerings.

Industrial and Business Applications

The robotics industry has experienced rapid growth since the first case of the adoption of robots in a Swedish metalworks plant in 1959.[24] The robotic process automation (RPA) market also saw a similar trend.[25] Such a trend indicates the dominance of robots in the industrial setting and their importance in developing products.

As listed in the definition mentioned earlier, industrial robots possess certain key distinguishing characteristics valued in production and operations settings (see Image 8.1). First, industrial robots are autonomous in that they can perform intended tasks based on information from sensors, without human intervention. Related to this is the robots' ability to be manipulated (i.e., controlled) by an operator or a programmable controller/device. For instance, Nguyen et al.[26] have developed a proximity sensor that can detect a human presence nearby and use that data to inform the robot of the person's distance and angle of approach. Developments such as these set up the stage for human–machine collaboration in a seamless manner. Second, industrial robots can be redesigned to accommodate changes in operations without physically altering the robot. For instance, industrial robots are being developed that can be reprogrammed within one minute using a touch-screen interface to perform other functions.[27] Third, industrial robots are also conducive to physical alterations to suit different applications. For instance, modifications in product lines or custom creations in manufacturing can be easily handled by industrial robots as they would be favorable to changes in their physical structure to handle different tasks.

In addition to their place in factories, robots hold a critical place in routine business applications. Popularly referred to as professional service robots, these robots are primarily used outside of factories, and in an assistive capacity to humans rather than replace them. In the marketing literature, service robots are defined as "…system-based autonomous and adaptable interfaces that interact, communicate and deliver service to an organization's customers".[28] Often fitted with some form of mobility (fully mobile or partly mobile), professional service robots can be found in many business settings such as retail, hospitality, healthcare, transportation and warehousing, construction, agriculture, space exploration, and many more. Business robots have been implemented in several commercial settings that drive value to corporations and users alike. The following uses provide a flavor of the various business applications of robots:

Image 8.1 Robots in manufacturing. Robots in an automobile manufacturing plant (*Source* Photo by *Lenny Kuhne* on *Unsplash*)

- *Robots in Education*—Personalization is a key ingredient in imparting quality education. By factoring in students' requirements and preferences, robots can provide individual care and attention to the student's learning needs. In this regard, robots are used in many education settings such as STEM classes (e.g., Root, Cubelets) and STEAM classes (e.g., Nao, Pepper), PreK-5 education (e.g., Dash & Dot, LEGO WeDo), and special-needs education (e.g., QTrobot, Leka).
- *Robots in General Hygiene*—Hospitals and public institutions regularly use robots for their hygiene needs via actions such as disinfecting places, dispensing sanitizers, trash removal, cleaning public spaces, and sterilization, among others. For instance, Danish company UVD Robotics has developed a UV light system-based robot that can disinfect and kill diseases, viruses, bacteria, and other types of harmful organic microorganisms in the environment by breaking down their DNA structure, thereby preventing and reducing the spread of infectious diseases, viruses, and bacteria. For hospital applications, this robot can clean and disinfect public spaces by moving autonomously from room to room, riding elevators, and opening doors automatically. Additionally, the robot pays special attention to infection-prone areas such as washbasins, patient beds, door handles, and so on.[29]
- *Robots in Healthcare*: Robots in healthcare have become more advanced in recent years, bringing in benefits for healthcare workers and patients alike. Reflecting the recent advancements, robots involved in healthcare fall into five broad types—(a) surgical robots (those working with the surgeons to perform minimally invasive procedures), (b) service robots (those performing non-patient-facing tasks to smoothen hospital operations), (c) exoskeleton robots (those that can be attached to humans that can facilitate specific actions), (d) rehabilitation robots (those that assist patient motion or perform actions for the patient), and (e) social robots (those that interact with patients and are capable of complex communication involving emotional responses).[30] Overall, robots have enhanced the quality of patient care, and efficiency of the clinical processes, while also bringing in a safe environment for the entities involved.
- *Robots in Agriculture*—Agriculture plays a critical role in the economic vibrancy of nations. As a result, agricultural productivity is an area that attracts attention from all members of the agricultural community such as farmers, agri-marketing companies, researchers, and policymakers. In this regard, research has established the vital role played by robots in improving agricultural output and productivity.[31] The key areas of agriculture where robots have been implemented include seeding, application of fertilizers/

pesticides, weeding, harvesting, autonomous farm vehicles, field mapping, environmental monitoring, and many more.
- *Robots for Customer Service*—An area where the use of robots is perhaps most felt is customer service, with retail and hospitality industries leading the way. Chui et al.[32] observed that the service sector is the most readily automatable in the US economy, with almost half of the existing service-related tasks being easily replaceable by robotics. In the restaurant industry, for instance, robots are increasingly being used for tasks such as food preparation, cooking, and serving food; cleaning food-preparation areas; preparing hot and cold beverages; and collecting dirty dishes (Image 8.2). Other robotic implementations include Aloft hotels' robot butlers to deliver toothbrushes, razors, and room service[33]; retail service robots in Lowe's[34]; and Walmart's Bossa Nova robots are used as floor cleaners, truck unloaders, in-store pickup towers, and shelf scanners,[35] among others.
- *Robots for Physical Therapy*—Robots are successfully used in physical therapy and rehabilitation for people with spinal cord injuries, neurological disorders, and strokes.[36] As mentioned earlier, wearable robots, also known as exoskeletons, support, replicate, or enhance the body's movements, thereby providing essential support for human motion.[37] Popular offerings in this category include ReWalk's Exo-Suit, Ekso Bionic's Ekso NR, and Cybderyne's Hybrid Assisted Limbs, among others.

Domestic-Oriented Technology

Domestic robots are those that are used to perform routine household tasks and assist in everyday living.[38] The tasks performed by these robots include vacuum cleaning (e.g., Roomba, Eufy), floor washing (e.g., iLife, iRobot), laundry and ironing (e.g., Effie, FoldiMate), cooking aids (e.g., Moley, Julia), home security systems (e.g., Xrana, JAMOR), swimming pool cleaning (e.g., Dolphin, Aquabot), window washing (e.g., HOBOT, Gladwell Gecko), lawncare (e.g., Husqvarna, Robomow), butlers (e.g., Ugo, Moro), social companionship (e.g., Pepper, Buddy), and more. Further, advancements in robotics are gradually making domestic robots more than just expensive gadgets.

The rapid growth in domestic applications of robotics can be attributed to improvements in performance speed, data storing, and processing capabilities.[39] Robotic assistants, like Google Home, Amazon Echo, and Apple's Siri, can help with information search, setting the calendar, timely reminders, connecting and controlling other home electronic devices, online shopping,

Image 8.2 Service robots. Robots serving drinks at a bar
(*Source* Photo by *David Levêque* on *Unsplash*)

scheduling car rides, ordering food, and many more jobs. In this regard, the category of social robots emerged.

Social robots were developed primarily to create humanlike interactions with robots.[40] Despite this simplistic purpose, conceptualizations of social robots are varied. Table 8.4 presents a flavor of the conceptualizations of social robots. Further, research has uncovered that the mere presence of social robots in the same room can have a motivating effect and lead to social facilitation effects compared to human counterparts.[41] Essentially, going beyond the typical functional uses, recent home robotic creations focus on the emotional side of the robots. For instance, Kiki is a home companion robot that develops a unique set of traits based on how the owner interacts with her. Further, the robot can understand emotions and feelings, learn over time, can be affectionate, learn from other Kikis, and create meaningful experiences as a

Table 8.4 Select conceptualization of social robots

Study	Conceptualization
Bartneck and Forlizzi[43]	"…an autonomous or semi-autonomous robot that interacts and communicates with humans by following the behavioral norms expected by the people with whom the robot is intended to interact."
Breazeal[44]	"…those that people apply a social model to interact with and to understand."
Fong et al.[45]	"… recognizing each other and engaging in social interactions, possessing histories, and explicitly communicating with and learning from each other."
Hegel et al.[46]	those robots that have a social interface, wherein a social interface encloses all the designed features by which a user judges the robot as having social qualities

companion.[42] Therefore, domestic robotic applications are expected to grow with more understanding of human relationships, robotic capabilities, and the nature of social interactions.

Humanoid Robots

As established thus far, robots are being used to perform boring, repetitive, or dangerous tasks for humans. A recent and high-profile example of a humanoid robot is Tesla's Optimus. On Tesla's AI Day in 2021, CEO Elon Musk unveiled the idea of a Tesla Bot that is friendly and can navigate through the human world. While this announcement was supported by a human walking around in a robot suit, Musk said that they would have a prototype released by the following year. On Tesla's AI Day 2022, Musk and engineers on the team introduced the humanoid robot: Optimus.[47] Tesla's vision with Optimus is to create a general-purpose, bi-pedal, autonomous humanoid robot that can perform unsafe, repetitive, and boring tasks. To achieve this end goal, software stacks that enable balance, navigation, perception, and interaction with the physical world need to be built. As of this writing, Tesla is involved in rolling out Optimus at high volumes, low costs, and high reliability.

Optimus has been designed to resemble the human body—with arms, hands, legs, and a head. The robot also has a brain which is the central computer located in the torso. The central computer possesses vision data from multiple sensors so it can perceive its surroundings. It also has a visual navigation system, managed by neural networks. The brain is also loaded with natural motion references. For this, engineers record human motions such as picking up boxes off a shelf, and map that motion data, which has been optimized to adapt to real-world motion to Optimus.

Optimus is also equipped with skills such as motor torque control (i.e., the ability to perform tasks like picking up delicate objects, following a specific trajectory, or exerting a precise force), and the ability to discover and memorize new environments. Tesla has long believed that they were in a strong position to develop a human bot by leveraging the hardware and software that was being used to create electric cars—which come with a degree of automated functionality. CEO Elon Musk stated "As full self-driving gets closer and closer to generalized real-world AI, that same software is transferable to a humanoid robot. My prediction is that the majority of Tesla's long-term value will be Optimus. And I am very confident in that prediction." Tesla predicts that the demand for Optimus could ultimately reach as many as 20 billion units soon, owing to Optimus' abilities to facilitate the fundamental transformation of civilization.[48]

Tesla's ambitious venture into humanoid robotics with Optimus is an example of the convergence of advanced technology and artificial intelligence. As Optimus slowly steps into the world, we are witnessing the potential for AI-driven robots to address mundane and risky tasks, alongside creating a path towards discussion about the transformative power of robotics in various industries. One such industry is marketing, where automation, personalization, and AI-driven insights are already reshaping how businesses connect with their audiences and streamline their operations. The integration of robotics into marketing strategies enhances customer engagement, optimizes product placement, and delivers innovative brand experiences. As we look ahead, the synergy between AI-powered robots and marketing presents exciting possibilities that could redefine how businesses interact with their customers and how products and services are promoted and delivered.

Robotics in the Marketing 5.0 World

The rate at which the modern world is progressing exceeds all expectations. Such progress has immensely benefitted from the confluence of NATs such as AI, ML, and others. One particularly intriguing combination of technologies that is gaining traction in business decision-making is intelligent automation, also referred to as cognitive automation.[49] By leveraging automation technologies such as AI, business process management, and robotic process automation, intelligent automation streamlines operations, allocates resources more effectively, and enhances overall efficiency. Expanding on the Marketing

5.0 concept discussed in Chapter 2, this section presents how robotics and intelligent automation operate in the Marketing 5.0 world. Particularly, this section discusses five examples of where robotic applications are applied through the lens of Marketing 5.0 and establishes how such actions can also bode well for humanity.

Data-Driven Marketing Using Robotics

The integration of robotics in data-driven marketing offers numerous benefits for businesses. Firstly, it allows for more efficient and accurate data analysis, eliminating the potential for human error and bias. Secondly, it enables marketers to personalize their marketing efforts by delivering targeted messages and offers to individual customers based on their preferences and behavior. Lastly, data-driven marketing robotics can help businesses optimize their marketing budgets by identifying the most effective channels and strategies for reaching their target audience.

For instance, AMP Robotics, a company based in the United States, utilizes artificial intelligence and robotics to create recycling infrastructure for the global supply chain. Through a data-driven approach, their AMP Cortex high-speed robotics system automates the sorting and identification of recyclables from mixed material streams.[50] Their unique technology employs computer vision and deep learning to guide high-speed robotics systems in recognizing, differentiating, and recovering recyclables based on various attributes such as color, size, shape, opacity, and more. The system also stores data about each item it detects, providing valuable insights. According to AMP Robotics, their sorting technology can pick up more than 80 items per minute, which is twice the speed of a human sorter. The company has achieved up to 150 picks per minute with their tandem units.

In addition to their sorting system, AMP Robotics offers another solution called AMP Clarity. This solution provides data and material characterization, allowing businesses and producers to optimize their recycling processes by identifying which recyclables are captured and missed. With their technology deployed worldwide, AMP Robotics recovers recyclables from various sources including municipal collection, electronic scrap, construction and demolition debris, and organic material, thereby contributing to the efficient utilization of valuable resources.

Predictive Marketing Using Robotics

The concept of predictive marketing using robotics combines the power of predictive analytics with the efficiency of robotic automation. This technology can help businesses identify the most promising leads, personalize marketing messages, and optimize marketing budgets for maximum ROI. By leveraging predictive marketing using robotics, businesses can also deliver personalized experiences to their customers, increase customer satisfaction, and drive revenue growth. Particularly, predictive analytics using robotics involves the use of sophisticated algorithms and artificial intelligence to analyze vast amounts of data and make accurate predictions about user needs.

For instance, the Advocate Aurora Research Institute, based in Milwaukee, USA, is utilizing predictive analytics to enhance the outcomes of surgical care throughout its operations.[51] Through a collaboration with KelaHealth, a predictive analytics company, the institute inputs clinical and robotics data into an intelligence platform, which employs AI to forecast patient risk based on historical data. The resultant risk scores, which are regularly updated, will be integrated with the electronic health record, enabling doctors to assess a patient's risk for a specific surgery and their recovery after the procedure. Additionally, the institute leverages robotics data obtained from robotic surgical systems to generate valuable insights that will enable surgeons to refine their surgical techniques, achieve better outcomes, and promote fiscal responsibility.

Contextual Marketing Using Robotics

Contextual marketing using robotics enables businesses to automate certain marketing processes, saving time and resources. Robots can analyze vast amounts of data quickly and accurately, allowing marketers to make data-driven decisions and optimize their campaigns in real-time. This automation also enables businesses to deliver personalized messages at scale, ensuring that each customer receives content that is relevant to their specific needs and interests. Contextual marketing using robotics revolutionizes the way businesses connect with their customers, providing a more personalized and efficient marketing approach.

Robots are becoming increasingly advanced, with the ability to perceive their surroundings and respond accordingly. Recent research has led to the development of an AI-based human–robot collaboration system that is suitable for use in factories.[52] This system provides robots with contextual information about their work environment and the people around them, allowing them to predict human behavior and work alongside humans on assembly lines more effectively than ever before.

Unlike traditional human–robot systems, which can only measure the distance between the robot and its human co-workers, the new system can identify individual workers and even their skeletal structure. This allows the robot to recognize each worker's posture and anticipate their next move. By utilizing AI, the system requires less computational power and smaller datasets than traditional machine learning methods. In experiments, the new system has demonstrated that such robots can operate more safely and efficiently, without slowing down production, thanks to their ability to understand context. As a result, context-aware robot systems are expected to improve efficiency and safety in the workplace.

Augmented Marketing Using Robotics

Augmented marketing using robotics opens new possibilities for interactive and immersive marketing experiences. Increasingly, robotics are being integrated with virtual reality or augmented reality technologies to create virtual shopping experiences or showcase products more engagingly and interactively. Moreover, robots can be designed to meet customer needs and preferences while working within the constraints of physical spaces, real-time performance, and personalized assistance. This creates a unique and memorable brand experience, leaving a lasting impression on customers.

Slice Factory, a pizza restaurant chain based in Chicago, has introduced a revolutionary addition to its kitchen—the Pizzaiola.[53] Developed by Nala Robotics, this robotic chef can prepare and serve a variety of pizzeria-style dishes, including pizzas, pasta, salads, burgers, and wings. The Pizzaiola is essentially a self-contained kitchen, equipped with food storage and preparation areas, ovens, and a 7-axis robotic arm that moves seamlessly throughout the cooking space.

When it comes to making pizzas, Pizzaiola offers an impressive range of options. It can choose from four types of dough, four sauces, 35 cheeses, and other toppings. The robot then proceeds to press the dough, add the sauce and toppings, and finally cook, slice, and box the pizza. With the ability to prepare up to 50 pizzas per hour, in various sizes ranging from 8 to 18 inches, the Pizzaiola is a game changer for Slice Factory. Thanks to ML technology, this robotic chef can replicate an infinite number of recipes across various cuisines with precise accuracy, making it a versatile and efficient addition to the kitchen.

Furthermore, Slice Factory has also embraced technology in its ordering process, allowing customers to place orders through multi-modal kiosks, virtual storefronts, or online platforms.[54] With plans to expand nationwide (beyond their current 12 outlets in Chicago), Slice Factory believes that the technology provided by Nala Robotics will play a crucial role in augmenting their growth and expanding their service.

Agile Marketing Using Robotics

Agile marketing is a modern approach that emphasizes flexibility, adaptability, and quick response to changing market dynamics. When combined with robotics, it opens a whole new realm of possibilities. Robotics can automate various marketing tasks, enabling businesses to streamline their processes, improve efficiency, and enhance customer experiences. Furthermore, agile marketing using robotics enhances personalization and customer engagement. To implement agile marketing with robotics successfully, organizations should start with a clear strategy and roadmap. They need to identify the marketing tasks that can be automated and prioritize their implementation. It is crucial to select the right robotics technology that aligns with the organization's goals and integrates seamlessly with existing marketing systems.

For instance, Volkswagen is strategically navigating the competitive Chinese market by focusing on intelligent driving technologies. Unlike the slower pace of transformation in Europe, the Chinese market demands constant innovation, pushing automotive companies and suppliers to stay ahead. Unable to meet consumer expectations satisfactorily, Volkswagen recently experienced a significant decline in market share in China. To address this setback, the Volkswagen Group has committed a substantial investment of USD 2.4 billion to accelerate innovation, promote technological localization, and enhance customer focus in China.[55]

To achieve these goals, Volkswagen has formed a new partnership between its software company CARIAD and Horizon Robotics, a leading provider of computing solutions for smart vehicles in China. This collaboration aims to improve the development of advanced driver assistance systems and autonomous driving systems specifically tailored for the Chinese market. Additionally, Volkswagen has increased its investments in e-mobility research and development, as well as design and production, to cater to the preferences of Chinese consumers.

One area of focus for Volkswagen in China is the production of new energy vehicles (NEVs), or battery-powered electric vehicles. In 2009, China launched the NEV program to promote the development and introduction of new energy vehicles.[56] Volkswagen plans to introduce more NEV models in the coming years while strengthening collaboration with Chinese partners in research and development, production, and supply chains. By doing so, Volkswagen aims to better respond to consumer demands and effectively implement its "In China, for China" strategy.[57]

Current Robotics Applications in Marketing

Robotic applications in marketing are increasing at a vigorous pace. With academic research[58] identifying robotics as a promising technology that not only presents value-creating opportunities in marketing but also holds important implications for the development of marketing strategies, the growth in marketing applications of robots is only obvious. This section presents five specific application areas where robotics continues to help companies in developing marketing initiatives.

Understanding Customer Needs to Deploy Robotics

Deploying robotics is a significant call that organizations need to make. With several business elements such as productivity, market share, technological expertise, and a steady customer base at stake, the decision to deploy robotics often places organizations at the crossroads of business transformation. A key decision variable in deploying robotics pertains to how well the organization understands its customers' needs. This applies to business-to-business (B2B) and business-to-customer (B2C) relationships. Since technology has the potential to deliver answers and solutions for firm expectations, a good understanding of a customer's needs can prepare firms well in terms of robotics deployment.

Often, marketers must contend with changes and trends in customer expectations. This is largely a result of changes in various factors that include demographic changes, prominence of NATs, changes in disposable income, need for authenticity, environmental consciousness, social connectedness, preference for experiences rather than products, technology-savvy, personalized content, and an openness to change, among others. This varied set of factors is very different from the traditional marketing approach. Such changes have materialized in changing customer needs that are exhibited to marketers at the consumers' point of usage. For instance, consider customer needs concerning fulfillment and delivery. With companies spending more resources to move offerings faster through the system, fulfillment and delivery systems are now more advanced to save time and costs. In a B2B setting, companies such as DHL are using autonomous mobile robots that can navigate semi-structured warehouse spaces and delivery processes.[59] Similarly, in a B2C setting, Amazon uses more than 100,000 wheeled, flat-topped robots called "drives" that can carry entire shelves of merchandise to workers filling orders.[60] Regardless of the business setting (i.e., B2B or B2C), improving speed and efficiency are the goals of deploying robotics. These goals reflect the consumer needs for immediate delivery of products and convenience of use. Here, evaluating customer readiness for robotic deployments is critical, and academic research continues to investigate this area.[61]

Revisiting Firm Capabilities to Integrate Robotics

From a resource management standpoint, Barney[62] argues that a firm's competitive advantage is derived from its unique bundle of resources that are difficult for competitors to duplicate. The resource-based view (RBV) classifies resources as (1) managerial resources, (2) input-based resources, (3) transformational resources, and (4) output resources.[63] The RBV was further extended to form dynamic capabilities that refer to companies' search for new resources and/or new ways of utilizing existing resources to build, integrate, and reconfigure internal and external competencies to achieve a competitive edge in a knowledge-based economy. The dynamic capabilities thus reflect a firm's processes to achieve new and innovative forms of competitive advantage given their resources, path dependencies, and market positions.[64] Further, Eisenhardt and Martin[65] emphasize the importance of dynamic capabilities to provide quick responses to mission-critical applications in information-intensive environments. In this regard, robotics play an important role as information resources that involve the nature and amount of information possessed by the firm about individual customers, competitors, and other stakeholders. By acquiring and analyzing customer and competitor information, robotics secures vital knowledge about key stakeholder groups in a real-world setting that can then be used to offer customized solutions and gain competitive advantage.

Further, the strategic flexibility of firms depends on resource identification, acquisition, and deployment capabilities.[66] While committed resources can reduce cost outlays when demand is predictable, flexible resource configuration provides the companies a buffer in meeting demand fluctuations.[67] As a result, optimal flexibility in firm resource configuration may impact firm costs and performance.[68] Successful companies such as Amazon, Walmart,

Google, and Tesla reap rich dividends from the excellence of their technological competence and their integration of marketing with backend support systems. Here, robotics can reinforce and augment these technical capabilities to optimize firm resource configuration. This can be done by better monitoring of resource usage based on an accurate assessment of changes occurring due to supply and demand fluctuations, product customizations, and changes in the marketing mix. As an outcome, Kumar, and Ramachandran[69] propose that the integration of robotics into firm functions is likely to infuse the firm with newer capabilities such as (a) increased automation of repetitive tasks without fatigue, (b) increased efficiency and accuracy in tasks that require extreme precision or consistent service quality, and (c) reduced need for human presence or intervention in unsafe, uncomfortable, or inaccessible situations.

Designing Marketing Mix Strategies with Robotics

As mentioned earlier, robotics operates as a function-oriented technology, offering ease of use, value, and convenience to users in an application setting.[70] Additionally, the coupling of AI and 5G network capabilities can provide robotics with the power to learn over time and process information more efficiently which can drive further value to users in a timely and relevant manner. As a result, showcasing robotics capabilities through marketing mix variables becomes apparent and critical to firms. Successful companies have realized impressive wins in each of the four key marketing mix variables—product, price, place, and promotion, as seen from the following examples.

Product. Organizations integrate robotics via three formats—(a) in designing physical products, (b) in designing service offerings for individual or commercial uses, and (c) meant for public consumption. In physical products, the focus is on delivering value as envisioned through the physical form, actions, and abilities of the robot. Examples of robotic products include Ugo butler, Google Home, Amazon's Echo, iRobot, Roomba, and Aibo robotic dog, among others. In designing service offerings for individual or commercial uses, the value is delivered through a blend of a tangible physical form and intangible functionality. The prominence of form over functionality (or vice versa) is often determined by the usage scenario. Examples of robotic services that can be used for individual or commercial uses include ElliQ the elder care assistant robot, and chef robots, among others. Examples of robotic services that are used in commercial settings include NPR's sportswriter robot, the autonomous medical robot Tug, Walmart's autonomous shopping cart Dash, and Wendy's chatbot, among others. Finally, robots are also used for delivering public services such as utility services, construction, and information kiosks. Examples of such robots include Volvo's robotic refuse collector ROAR, Volvo's autonomous load carrier HX2, and the FURO kiosk robot.

Price. Robots have been used to facilitate price comparison among shoppers. Popularly known as shopping robots, or simply shopbots, they have been used to lower search costs for users.[71] Further, Chen and Sudhir[72] and Diehl et al.[73] examined how shopbots affect price competition and sensitivity in an e-commerce setting. These robots are automated internet-based tools that let shoppers compare prices, offerings, deals/promotions, and availability across competing firms. Early examples of shopbots include BizRate, NexTag, and so on. More recently, the Nao humanoid robot has been developed as a social companion robot that can also be used for shopping trips. Specifically, the robot can compare the prices of each item and provide customers with the best advice.[74]

Research shows that though shopbots generally push prices downward, carefully applied robots can provide many opportunities to target micro-consumer segments based on their willingness to pay, maintain relationships, and leverage brand names.[75] According to Smith,[76] robots can help retailers find ways to maintain their price differentiation while improving the targeting of consumers with micro-segmentation. Retailers thus have greater opportunities to differentiate their products because of their careful understanding of their target market's preferences. The use of notification and recommendation agents also helps retailers up and cross-sell products, which results in higher sales volumes and market shares, as well as more satisfied and fulfilled customers. Furthermore, intelligent agents such as robots protect market share through careful competitor analysis and defense. They can increase ROI by reducing marketing costs because they support far more customers than a human salesperson or technical representative.[77]

Place. Robotics can significantly impact the final form of delivering firm offerings to the consumer, especially when their location-based preferences are satisfied. In this regard, robots deliver a high degree of value through their ability to move about (in the case of mobile robots), and through their ability to perform in the same manner and functionalities and the same level of performance, regardless of their installed/usage location. Further, robots are highly customizable to the usage environment and needs, and they almost seem to fit in perfectly in all instances. These features indicate that robots transcend place/geography restrictions and can deliver their full potential as designed by the developers. This implies that a companion robot for seniors can serve its full potential regardless of its use in Asia or the United States, with the right level of customized elements. As a result, robots serve a utilitarian purpose in serving the needs of the user/usage condition to their full potential. This aspect of robots has enabled its rapid growth and its almost contemporaneous use in various industries across the world.

Promotion. In addition to performing laborious and repetitive tasks, robots have also been implemented in creative promotional activities such as sales force assistance, advertising support, and online shopping. In the retail setting, robots have been used to free up sales associates' time by performing routine and tedious tasks such as physical inspection of stores, product placement locations, shelf stockouts, checking for special promotion tags, cleaning and maintenance, security/surveillance, and so on. Grocery retailers in the United States such as Giant Eagle, Schnucks Markets, Broad Branch Market, and Walmart have implemented robots and are beginning to see positive results.[78] Firms are also using robots in automated advertising/marketing communications efforts. Some of the current robotic applications include machines that can communicate/negotiate with other machines without human intervention, evaluate various types of audiences, generate, and distribute creative content, and so on.[79] Finally, robots are also helping consumers get the most out of online shopping by scouring for the best deals online. For instance, Honey is a coupon robot that exists as a web plug-in that works on web browsers. When users reach the checkout stage while shopping online, Honey meanwhile works in the background looking for the cheapest price and alerts the user to the location of the cheaper deal; thereby securing users valuable savings. Other such robots include eBay's ShopBot and Kelkoo and Pricerunner in the UK.

Robotics as a Service (RaaS). We are also witnessing the emergence of robotics as a service (RaaS), which is a pay-as-you-go, or subscription-based service model that allows users to benefit from robotic process automation (by leasing robotic devices and accessing a cloud-based subscription). Additional benefits from such a model include reduced hassles of purchasing expensive equipment and maintenance that comes along with it.[80] In recent years, RaaS has become popular due to its flexibility, scalability, and lower costs of entry (compared to traditional robotics programs) it poses. Many companies, ranging from warehouses, and security providers to healthcare facilities are integrating RaaS into their operations.

Typically, robots were seen as instruments to replace low-paying jobs done by humans at companies that come with expenses and take time to be realized as returns. But RaaS allows companies to scale up and down depending on the market conditions and client needs, while also offering predictable costs and less upfront capital to get started. As a result of this, and the familiarity with SaaS, many companies are warming up to the idea of implementing RaaS, regardless of the size of the firm. Big Tech companies like Amazon, Google, and Microsoft have developed tools to enable RaaS on a large scale and are used in many ways. Some prominent examples of RaaS use include:

- AWS Robomaker runs large-scale and parallel simulations, and cost-effectively scales and automates simulation workloads. It allows users to easily create refined, randomized 3D virtual environments.
- Google is developing the Google Cloud Robotics Platform, which combines AI, the cloud, and robotics into an open ecosystem of automation solutions that use cloud-connected collaborative robots.
- SavorEat, an Israel-based tech company, has developed a robotic system that cooks customizable plant-based burgers. These meatless products are created and cooked by a robot chef according to customer preferences and at the touch of a button.

While all of this sounds very encouraging, there are things to overcome to make the adoption of RaaS quicker. There is a lot of customization of the hardware that goes into the process of making the robots useful for individual organizations' specific needs. Once the companies find a way to reduce the time for customization, the popularity and adaptability of RaaS are expected to increase tremendously.

Driving Customer Engagement Through Robotics

Robotics plays a critical role in providing memorable customer experiences that in turn work towards enhancing customer engagement.[81] For instance, Elisa, a Finnish telecom company, deployed Pepper, the world's first personal robot that recognizes main emotions, to interact with and engage customers in a personalized way. The personalized actions include greeting customers, directing them to the right service member, and supporting the click-and-collect process of customers buying online and picking up the order in-store, all in a seamless manner to ensure meaningful engagement instances.[82] Further, robots being equipped with AI and 5G capabilities implies that programming the robots and the delivery of actions becomes instantaneous, thereby enhancing customer engagement. For instance, by integrating AI and 5G capabilities, companies can develop robots that are autonomous or be controlled remotely in real-time with the ability to make instant decisions that can be updated over time. Such features in robots in customer-facing roles such as in retail, hospitality, healthcare, and aviation can significantly enhance customer engagement.

In this regard, research has advanced the concept of Tactile Internet (TI), which refers to a communication infrastructure combining low latency, very short transit time, high availability, and high reliability with a high level of security.[83] Essentially, the TI will enhance human–machine interactions by reducing the time between initiating a data transfer and the beginning of data transfer (i.e., latency) such that real-time interactive systems can be developed that are instantaneous and impactful.[84] Such developments present important implications for industries such as education, telesurgery, construction, and so on that, in turn, can enhance customer engagement.

Research has also investigated the role of robotics in reducing variation in service experience delivered by firms. Specifically, Kumar et al.[85] propose that the perceived variation in service experience moderates the influence of service experience on satisfaction and emotional attachment, which ultimately impacts customer engagement. Since robots are controlled by computer programs, they can provide standardized service without variations and with a high degree of accuracy and precision, which is beyond human capabilities.[86] Given the same input, the output will always remain the same across robots, time, and context, thereby enhancing customer engagement.

Designing Digital Strategies with Robotics

Robotics adds to the technological capabilities of organizations. Technological capabilities refer to a firm's capacity to build and employ internal technological resources in sync with other internal resources of the firm to improvise the existing offerings or develop a new one responding to the shifting market conditions and consumer preferences.[87] The emergence of NATs (such as robotics) and consumer preferences to go digital compels firms to audit and develop their technological capabilities in the form of updated technological infrastructure such as hardware, software, and service integration. This compulsion on firms is expected to the development of competitive advantage, since the firm can respond to altered consumers' needs and demands more swiftly (Gupta et al. forthcoming).[88] In this regard, Saboo et al.[89] suggest that a firm's capability to absorb a new set of knowledge is mainly dependent on its existing processes and knowledge base. To become more open to new ideas, encourage customer feedback, and involve consumers in co-developing products, firms need to enhance customer-firm interactions via the use of appropriate technologies. A robust technological infrastructure will enrich the firm with comprehensive macro-level customer data in real-time, and robotics will play a crucial role in allowing firms to generate enhanced firm and customer value.

Firms primarily focus on personalization elements that are valued by consumers when developing their digital strategies. The use of robotics, such as NATs, allows for a high level of personalization, making them attractive for customer-firm interactions. These robotics solutions can be seamlessly integrated into various tasks, often without users even realizing they are interacting with technology. Examples of such interactions include robotic process automation software, robotics for senior care and assisted living, and robots used in physical rehabilitation and therapy. When technology can connect with users on a personal level, it fosters a strong bond. Marketers can leverage this bond to create significant customer value. However, the success of personalization initiatives is dependent on the availability and quality of customer information, the ability to derive insights from this data, and the effective implementation of these insights.[90] To overcome these constraints and enhance personalized offerings, companies are turning to robotics-powered solutions in a digital format. The scalability of robotic solutions, which can be achieved in a relatively short period with or without human intervention, makes them a favorable choice for companies.

Future of Robotics in Marketing

An era in which robots will feature in almost all aspects of human lives is fast approaching, the signs of which already exist. Rapidly developing robotic technologies that become smarter and cheaper will virtually transform all service sectors and bring opportunities for a wide range of industrial and service innovations that have the potential to dramatically improve customer experience, service quality, and productivity all at the same time.[91] Firms should refrain from apprehension of this trend and utilize the opportunities of this technological revolution. While firms would do well by paying careful attention to the oncoming robotic revolution, rushing into adopting robotics without thoughtful consideration of the implications would lead to significant losses. The role of NATs, and specifically robotics, in driving and facilitating technological advancements and their business uses requires nuanced examination, as they can automate vital business processes, accentuate insights and real-time decision-making, and enhance firms' abilities to engage with customers.[92] In this regard, Xiao and Kumar[93] offer a comprehensive view of when and how to adopt and integrate robotics into customer service operations, factors that would affect the degree of robotics adoption, and the likely consequences of such an adoption.

Further, the ever-expanding amounts of information (relating to customers, businesses, and markets) involved in everyday commercial operations, and the increasingly dynamic online business environment present a huge challenge for markets to extract value. Robotics occupies a vital place in such a transformed marketplace. In this regard, robotics will present important opportunities in two key areas that marketers will have to pay attention to.[94] First, robotics will present increased opportunities for increased learning and insights for companies. With further advancements in robotics, robots will acquire the capabilities to perform ever more complex tasks by collaborating, which in turn, will make marketing even more efficient and effective. They also may increase the intensity of competition and consumer power due to lower search costs. Further, the consumer adoption of robots may exert downward pressure on prices for undifferentiated products, but strong price/quality perceptions and branded variants ensure price variation in markets. Second, robotic implementations are likely to improve the decision-making capabilities of firms. As the plethora of robots for commercial and personal uses increases, robots' abilities and performance are expected to increase further. This will provide increased efficiencies in the areas of information handling and retrieval, inventory, and customer engagement, and offer consumer value in the form of more convenience, better information, and better selection. Therefore, the future of robotics for marketing purposes appears to be promising and varied. While we can expect progress in robotic capabilities in many organizational areas, three areas that stand out are discussed here.

Robotics and the Interactive Service Industry

Implementing robotics is a trend that companies cannot afford to ignore. This is especially so for customer service firms, due to the rising costs of human labor, enhanced robotic capabilities, and declining costs of robotics.[95] Technology-wise, robotics has the potential to replace human workers in many service functions, but when it comes to customer service that involves intensive interactions with customers, it is never a purely technical issue.[96] Instead, robots will act as a useful complement to the service force, and customers can expect to be served by a combination of a robotic and human workforce in most service encounters over the coming years.[97] So far, robots are superior only at simple, routine, repetitive, and algorithm-based tasks that require little creativity, expertise, and social skills, but are not appropriate for innovative and creative tasks that require high-order human mental processes, which are beyond algorithmic enunciation.[98] For instance, Chui et al.[99] found that less than 5% of jobs could be completely fulfilled by robots, which holds for both manufacturing and customer service.

With regards to the service industry, Xiao and Kumar[100] propose that employee acceptance of robots, customer acceptance of robots, and the level of human–robot interaction determine the degree of robotics adoption in a firm. Further, they contend that in addition to these factors, firms should consider the technical feasibility of firms, a cost-benefit analysis of robotic deployments, and legal/ethical considerations in determining when, where, and the extent to which robotics should be adopted in their customer service strategy.

In terms of industry applications, interactive robots are being increasingly implemented in industries such as education, healthcare, telepresence, construction, defense, and transportation, among others. Technological advancements, such as autonomous navigation, environmental sensors to detect obstacles in the vicinity, 5G network connectivity, and AI capabilities, have made robots more interactive, user-friendly, and endowed with operational features (see Image 8.3). Currently, a large part of the interactivity in robots is seen in concierge-type services developed for specific applications such as in airports (e.g., robots at Heathrow Airport can communicate with passengers in multiple languages) (see Image 8.4), retail outlets (e.g., Lowebots), online education (e.g., educational robots used in K-12 education for classroom instruction), and telepresence (e.g., robots fitted with audio/video features can place the viewer in a remote location via virtual presence). Looking ahead, technology companies are developing more task-agnostic robots that are not designed with a specific use-case, but instead with a set of specific capabilities that can be used in a wide range of real-world applications.[101] If this trend were to continue, we could see a boom in robotic deployments whereby many facets of everyday life could be filled with robots.

Interactive Marketing

As discussed earlier, robots are being successfully used in social settings (e.g., personal use, homes, etc.) in an interactive service format.[102, 103] Although service tasks are generally difficult to automate, it is theorized that with further advancements in AI towards higher intelligence tasks (i.e., from mechanical, analytical, intuitive, to empathetic), robots can gain the ability

Image 8.3 Interactive robots. Robots can be used in interactive settings in social spaces
(*Source* Photo by *Andy Kelly* on *Unsplash*)

to perform several service tasks typically performed by humans.[104] Interestingly, some types of chatbots and robots already exhibit empathy—the highest-order type of intelligence.

The collaborative nature of robots is most evident in interactive robots designed to work alongside humans in a specific workspace. These robots can integrate into various aspects of marketing. Not only can they drive essential processes that require integration, but they can also align marketing functions with company systems and objectives. These robots can synchronize and update information across different management and marketing functions, as well as across multiple companies. In terms of marketing applications, these robots can provide transparency in customer relationships and sales initiatives, incorporating reward systems into the process. Additionally, they can gather and synthesize information for proactive marketing and future planning. This information can be utilized to design future strategies and enhance existing models to improve decision-making. Collaborative robots are currently being utilized in pick and place operations, packaging processes, quality inspections, and industrial cleaning (see Image 8.5). However, there are also potential novel applications for collaborative robots in areas such as farming, healthcare, aviation, and restaurants. The future holds the promise of further innovations and improvements in collaborative robots, allowing them to work in harmony with humans and bring value creation, efficiency, and convenience to both business and personal uses.

Image 8.4 Robots in airports. A robot assisting passengers at Incheon airport, South Korea
(*Source* Photo by *Author*)

Creative Content Curation

Curation as a strategy, has been conceptualized towards future-oriented activities, more specifically the set of practices that select, maintain, and manage information in ways that are intended to promote future consumption of that information.[105] Curation[106] of product, price, place, and promotion to individual customers assume more significance for companies in this digital age where customers are exposed to information explosion.[107]

Within the robotics environment, the process of curation would still involve selecting, maintaining, and managing information. However, such efforts may or may not involve human interference. In this regard, we are beginning to see early applications where robots are used to curate and deliver personalized content. Here are three cases of robots aiding in curating content.

Image 8.5 Collaborative robots in manufacturing. Collaborative robots are used alongside humans in an industrial setting
(*Source* Photo by *Amin Khorsand* on *Unsplash*)

- Ria 2.0, a bot developed by Healthifyme, a health and fitness app from India, is capable of tracking and managing daily calorie needs and workout regimens, as well as providing suggestions on healthy lifestyle habits.[108] The bot can analyze user-uploaded photos of food plates and menu card options to identify healthy and unhealthy foods and can also consider medical conditions to offer personalized food suggestions, diet plans, and general information on healthy lifestyles. With the bot handling a significant portion of messages (about 20%), it demonstrates the potential of bots in efficiently handling large volumes of data to deliver personalized content to users with minimal human interaction.
- Mystore-E, a Tel Aviv-based clothing store, has designed its stores to mimic the experience of a website within a store[109]. Using extensive digital displays and augmented reality, the store has enabled customers to virtually try on products. Further, the addition of AI capabilities allowed employees to receive notifications that match customers' choices to provide highly personalized and curated offerings.
- McCormick Foods is using IBM Watson to help their research and development teams in developing new spice combinations based on insights about customer consumption and social listening.[110]

Such curative actions by firms reduce consumer cognitive load and take the responsibility of finding the best options for a consumer's choice context to the search platform or the brand.[111] These are but only early cases of robotic implementations. We can expect future developments in this area to develop more value-creating offerings and services.

Key Terms and Related Conceptualizations

Collaborative robot	A robot designed for direct interaction with a human
Curation strategy	The set of practices that select, maintain, and manage information in ways that are intended to promote future consumption of that information
Domestic robot	A robot that is used to perform routine household tasks and assist in everyday living
Dynamic capabilities	A firm's processes to achieve new and innovative forms of competitive advantage given their resources, path dependencies, and market positions
Industrial robot	An automatically controlled, reprogrammable, multipurpose manipulator, programmable in three or more axes, which can be either fixed in place or mobile for use in industrial automation applications
Intelligent robot	A robot that can perform tasks by sensing its environment and/or interacting with external sources and adapting its behavior
Mobile robot	Is a robot that can travel under its control
Personal service robot	A service robot is used for a non-commercial task, usually by laypersons
Professional service robot	A service robot used for a commercial task is usually operated by a properly trained operator
Robotics	The science of studying the intelligent connection of perception to action
Robotics as a service (RaaS)	A subscription-based service model that allows users to benefit from robotic process automation (by leasing robotic devices and accessing a cloud-based subscription)
Robots	Actuated mechanisms programmable in two or more axes with a degree of autonomy, moving within its environment, to perform intended tasks
Service robot	A robot that performs useful tasks for humans or equipment excluding industrial automation applications

(continued)

(continued)

Tactile Internet (TI)	A communication infrastructure combining low latency, very short transit time, high availability, and high reliability with a high level of security
Technological capabilities	A firm's capacity to build and employ internal technological resources in sync with other internal resources of the firm to improvise the existing offerings or develop a new one responding to the shifting market conditions and consumer preferences

Notes and References

1. Kumar, V. (2021). *Intelligent marketing: Employing new age technologies*. Sage Publications.
2. Kumar, V., B. Rajan, R. Venkatesan, & J. Lecinski (2019a), "Understanding the role of artificial intelligence in personalized engagement marketing," *California Management Review*, 61(4), 135–155.
3. In 2021, the global market for industrial robots was estimated at USD 81 billion. This market is expected to grow to around USD 129 billion by 2025 and reach around USD 165 billion by 2028 (Inkwood Research. (October 25, 2021). Size of the market for industrial robots worldwide from 2018 to 2020, with a forecast through 2028 (in billion U.S. dollars) [Graph]. In *Statista*. Retrieved October 05, 2023, from https://www.statista.com/statistics/728530/industrial-robot-market-size-worldwide/). Further, as of 2022, the sales value of the industrial robotics market worldwide was estimated at USD 15 billion, with China, the United States, Japan, South Korea, and Germany representing the top five regions (Statista. (2021). Sales value of the industrial robotics market worldwide from 2018 to 2022, by main country (in million U.S. dollars) [Graph]. In *Statista*. February 24, Retrieved October 05, 2023, from https://www.statista.com/statistics/1018634/industrial-robotics-sales-value-by-country/).
4. Harris, K., A. Kimson & A. Schwedel (2018), "Labor 2030: The collision of demographics, automation and inequality," *Bain & Company*, February 7, [accessed from https://www.bain.com/insights/labor-2030-the-collision-of-demographics-automation-and-inequality/].
5. Hegel, F., C. Muhl, B. Wrede, M. Hielscher-Fastabend, & G. Sagerer (2009), "Understanding social robots," In *2009 Second international*

conferences on advances in computer-human interactions, pp. 169–174, IEEE.
6. IFR (2020), "Robot history," *International Federation of Robotics*, [accessed from https://ifr.org/robot-history].
7. Sciavicco, L., & B. Siciliano (2012), *Modelling and control of robot manipulators*, Springer Science & Business Media (p. 2).
8. Craig, J. J. (2009), *Introduction to robotics: mechanics and control*, 3/E. Pearson Education India.
9. Lynch, K. M., & F. C. Park (2017), *Modern robotics*, Cambridge University Press: Cambridge, UK.
10. Siciliano, B., & O. Khatib (2016), *Springer handbook of robotics*, Springer.
11. Mentzer, J. T., & N. Gandhi (1993), "Expert systems in industrial marketing," *Industrial Marketing Management*, 22(2), 109–116.
12. ISO (2012), "ISO 8373:2012—Robots and robotic devices—Vocabulary," *International Organization for Standardization*, March, [accessed from https://www.iso.org/obp/ui/#iso:std:iso:8373:ed-2:v1:en:term:2.6].
13. Breazeal, C. (2003), "Toward sociable robots," *Robotics and Autonomous Systems*, 42(3–4), 167–175.
14. Kaplan, F. (2005), "Everyday robotics: robots as everyday objects," In *Proceedings of the 2005 joint conference on Smart objects and ambient intelligence: Innovative context-aware services: usages and technologies*, October, pp. 59–64.
15. Kurfess, T. R. (2018), *Robotics and automation handbook*, (Ed.), CRC Press: Boca Raton, FL.
16. Wilson, H. James (2015), "What is a robot, anyway?" *Harvard Business Review*, April 15, [accessed from https://hbr.org/2015/04/what-is-a-robot-anyway].
17. Taylor, H. (2016), "Lowe's introduces LoweBot, a new autonomous in-store robot," *CNBC*, August 30, [accessed from https://www.cnbc.com/2016/08/30/lowes-introduces-lowebot-a-new-autonomous-in-store-robot.html].
18. Crawford, M. (2016), "Top 6 robotic applications in medicine," *The American Society of Mechanical Engineers (ASME)*, September 14, [accessed from https://www.asme.org/topics-resources/content/top-6-robotic-applications-in-medicine].
19. Radcliffe, D. (2019), "Seven ways robots are being used by publishers and newsrooms," *What's New in Publishing*, May

28, [accessed from https://whatsnewinpublishing.com/seven-ways-robots-are-being-used-by-publishers-and-newsrooms/].
20. Papadopoulos, L. (2020), "Flippy the robot is your new burger chef," *Industrial Engineering*, February 29, [accessed from https://interestingengineering.com/flippy-the-robot-is-your-new-burger-chef].
21. Swearingen, J. (2019), "A.I. is flying drones (very, very slowly)," *The New York Times*, March 26, [accessed from https://www.nytimes.com/2019/03/26/technology/alphapilot-ai-drone-racing.html].
22. Kumar, V., & D. Ramachandran (2020), "Developing a firm's growth approaches in a new-age technology environment to enhance stakeholder wellbeing," working paper, Georgia State University, GA.
23. Tilley, J. (2017), "Automation, robotics, and the factory of the future," *McKinsey & Company*, September, [accessed from https://www.mckinsey.com/business-functions/operations/our-insights/automation-robotics-and-the-factory-of-the-future]; Huang, M. H., & Rust, R. T. (2018), "Artificial Intelligence in Service," *Journal of Service Research*, 21(2), 155–172. https://doi.org/10.1177/1094670517752459.
24. As of 2015, the global spending on robotics was estimated at USD 27 billion. The spending witnessed a steep increase to USD 43 billion by 2020, and an estimated USD 67 billion by 2025 (Nasdaq OMX. (May 21, 2018). Global spending on robotics from 2000 to 2025 (in billion U.S. dollars), by category [Graph]. In *Statista*. Retrieved October 05, 2023, from https://www.statista.com/statistics/943113/spending-on-robotics-worldwide-by-category/).
25. The RPA market was estimated at USD 2.65 billion in 2021. This market is forecast to grow with a CAGR of 27.7 percent from 2021 to 2030, with an estimated market size of USD 23.9 billion by 2030 (GlobeNewswire. (January 6, 2022). Spending on robotic process automation (RPA) software worldwide from 2020 to 2030 (in billion U.S. dollars) [Graph]. In *Statista*. Retrieved October 05, 2023, from https://www.statista.com/statistics/1309384/worldwide-rpa-software-market-size/).
26. Nguyen, T. D., T. S. Kim, J. Noh, H. Phung, H. R. Choi, & G. Kang (2020), "Skin-type proximity sensor by using the change of electromagnetic field," *IEEE Transactions on Industrial Electronics*, [accessed from https://ieeexplore.ieee.org/stamp/stamp.jsp?tp=&arnumber=9014491].

27. Simonite, T. (2020), "These Industrial Robots Get More Adept With Every Task," *Wired*, March 10, [accessed from https://www.wired.com/story/these-industrial-robots-adept-every-task/].
28. Wirtz, J., P.G. Patterson, W. H. Kunz, T. Gruber, V. N. Lu, S. Paluch, & A. Martins (2018), "Brave new world: Service robots in the frontline," *Journal of Service Management*, 29(5), pp. 907–931.
29. European Commission (2020), "Danish disinfection robots save lives in the fight against the Corona virus," *European Commission*, March 16, [accessed from https://ec.europa.eu/digital-single-market/en/news/danish-disinfection-robots-save-lives-fight-against-corona-virus].
30. Urwin, M. (2023), "Medical Robots Transforming Healthcare: 11 Examples," *BuiltIn*, April 26, accessed from https://builtin.com/robotics/surgical-medical-healthcare-robotics-companies.
31. Pedersen, S. M., S. Fountas, H. Have, & B. S. Blackmore (2006), "Agricultural robots—System analysis and economic feasibility," *Precision Agriculture*, 7(4), 295–308; Bechar, A., & C. Vigneault (2016), "Agricultural robots for field operations: Concepts and components," *Biosystems Engineering*, 149, 94–111.
32. Chui, M., J. Manyika, & M. Miremadi (2016), "Where machines could replace humans—and where they can't (yet)," *McKinsey Quarterly*, July, [accessed from https://www.mckinsey.com/business-functions/digital-mckinsey/our-insights/where-machines-could-replace-humans-and-where-they-cant-yet].
33. Mest, E. (2017), "Aloft Dallas Love Field opens with Savioke's robot butler," *Hotel Management*, March 10, [accessed from https://www.hotelmanagement.net/tech/aloft-dallas-love-field-opens-savioke-s-robot-butler].
34. Taylor, H. (2016), "Lowe's introduces LoweBot, a new autonomous in-store robot," *CNBC*, August 30, [accessed from https://www.cnbc.com/2016/08/30/lowes-introduces-lowebot-a-new-autonomous-in-store-robot.html].
35. Ciment, S. (2020), "Walmart is bringing robots to 650 more stores as the retailer ramps up automation in stores nationwide," *Business Insider*, January 13, [accessed from https://www.businessinsider.com/walmart-adding-robots-help-stock-shelves-to-650-more-stores-2020-1].
36. Burgar, C. G., P. S. Lum, P. C. Shor, & H. M. Van der Loos (2000), "Development of robots for rehabilitation therapy: The Palo Alto VA/

Stanford experience," *Journal of Rehabilitation Research and Development*, 37(6), 663–674; Volpe, B. T., H. I. Krebs, N. Hogan, L. Edelstein, C. Diels, & M. Aisen (2000), "A novel approach to stroke rehabilitation: robot-aided sensorimotor stimulation," *Neurology*, 54(10), 1938–1944.

37. The global exoskeleton market size stood at around USD 1.5 million in 2022 and is expected to reach nearly USD 11.5 million by 2027 (Statista. (2022). Global exoskeleton market size from 2019 to 2027 (in million U.S. dollars) [Graph]. In *Statista*. January 19, Retrieved October 06, 2023, from https://www.statista.com/statistics/888936/global-exoskeleton-market/).

38. The value of domestic consumer robotics globally in 2020 was estimated at USD 3.4 billion and is expected to reach USD 6.8 billion by 2025 (Loup Ventures. [2019a]. Value of the domestic consumer robotics market worldwide from 2015 to 2025 [in billion U.S. dollars]* [Graph]. In *Statista*. May 10, Retrieved October 06, 2023, from https://www.statista.com/statistics/730885/global-domestic-robotics-market-value/.). In the same period, 13.2 million domestic robots were shipped worldwide in 2020 and are expected to reach nearly 30 million units by 2025 (Loup Ventures. (2019b). Unit shipments of domestic consumer robots worldwide from 2015 to 2025 (in millions)* [Graph]. In *Statista*. May 10, Retrieved October 06, 2023, from https://www.statista.com/statistics/730884/domestic-service-robots-shipments-worldwide/).

39. Xiao, L., & V. Kumar (2021). "Robotics for customer service: A useful complement or an ultimate substitute?" *Journal of Service Research*, 24(1), 9–29.

40. Hegel, F., C. Muhl, B. Wrede, M. Hielscher-Fastabend, & G. Sagerer (2009), "Understanding social robots," In *2009 Second international conferences on advances in computer-human interactions*, pp. 169–174, IEEE.

41. Riether, N., F. Hegel, B. Wrede, & G. Horstmann (2012), "Social facilitation with social robots?" In *2012 7th ACM/IEEE international conference on Human-Robot Interaction (HRI)*, March, pp. 41–47.

42. Ackerman, E. (2019), "This "useless" social robot wants to succeed where others failed," *IEEE Spectrum*, September 19, [accessed from https://spectrum.ieee.org/automaton/robotics/home-robots/kiki-social-home-robot].

43. Bartneck, C., & Forlizzi, J. (2004). A design-centred framework for social human-robot interaction. In *RO-MAN 2004. 13th IEEE international workshop on robot and human interactive communication*, September, 591–594.
44. Breazeal, C. (2003), "Toward sociable robots," *Robotics and Autonomous Systems*, 42(3–4), 167–175.
45. Fong, T., I. Nourbakhsh, & K. Dautenhahn (2002), "A survey of socially interactive robots: Concepts, design and applications," *Robotics and Autonomous Systems*, 42(3–4), 142–166.
46. Hegel, F., C. Muhl, B. Wrede, M. Hielscher-Fastabend, & G. Sagerer (2009), "Understanding social robots," In *2009 second international conferences on advances in computer-human interactions*, pp. 169–174, IEEE.
47. Biba, J. (2023), "The Tesla robot: Here's what we know," *BuiltIn*, May 31, accessed from https://builtin.com/robotics/tesla-robot.
48. McCallum, S. (2022), "Tesla boss Elon Musk presents humanoid robot Optimus," *BBC.com*, October 1, accessed from https://www.bbc.com/news/technology-63100636.
49. IBM (2023), "What is intelligent automation?" *IBM*, accessed from https://www.ibm.com/topics/intelligent-automation.
50. Kenyon, T. (2022), "How AMP Robotics is applying AI and robotics to recycling," *Technology*, May 30, accessed from https://technologymagazine.com/ai-and-machine-learning/how-amp-robotics-is-applying-ai-and-robotics-to-recycling.
51. Gliadkovskaya, A. (2023), "Advocate health's research arm pilots KelaHealth's predictive software to assess surgical risk, improve outcomes," *Fierce Healthcare*, April 10, accessed from https://www.fiercehealthcare.com/health-tech/advocate-aurora-health-pilots-kelahealths-predictive-software-improve-or-outcomes.
52. Liu, H., & Wang, L. (2021). "Collision-free human-robot collaboration based on context awareness." *Robotics and Computer-Integrated Manufacturing*, 67, 101997.
53. Coxworth, B. (2022), "Pizzaiola aims to robotize the humble pizzeria," *New Atlas*, June 7, accessed from https://newatlas.com/robotics/pizzaiola-robotic-pizzeria/.
54. Verdict Food Service (2022), "Slice Factory to install Nala Robotics' automated chef," *Verdict Food Service*, June 30, accessed from https://www.verdictfoodservice.com/news/slice-factory-nala-robotics/?cf-view&cf-closed.

55. Volkswagen, (2022), "Volkswagen to strengthen regional development competence for autonomous driving in China through joint venture between CARIAD and Horizon Robotics," *Volkswagen.com*, October 13, accessed from https://www.volkswagen-newsroom.com/en/press-releases/volkswagen-to-strengthen-regional-development-competence-for-autonomous-driving-in-china-through-joint-venture-between-cariad-and-horizon-robotics-15248.

56. World Bank (2011), "The China new energy vehicles program—Challenges and opportunities," *World Bank*, April, accessed from https://documents1.worldbank.org/curated/en/333531468216944327/pdf/612590WP0PRTM01BOX358342B01PUBLIC11.pdf.

57. Linwan, Z. (2023), "Volkswagen ramping up profile in Chinese market," *ChinaDaily.com*, August 28, accessed from https://www.chinadaily.com.cn/a/202308/28/WS64ebfc2ea31035260b81e8a4.html.

58. For more information, please see studies on robotics related to the service sector (e.g., Achrol, R. S., & P. Kotler (2012), "Frontiers of the marketing paradigm in the third millennium," *Journal of the Academy of Marketing Science*, 40(1), 35–52; Bitner, M. J. (2017), "Service research: Rigor, relevance, and community," *Journal of Service Research*, 20(2), 103–104; Huang and Rust 2017; Wirtz and Zeithaml 2018); customer–robot interactions (e.g., Holzwarth, M., C. Janiszewski, & M. M. Neumann (2006), "The influence of avatars on online consumer shopping behavior," *Journal of Marketing*, 70(4), 19–36; Toure-Tillery, M., & A. L. McGill (2015), "Who or what to believe: Trust and the differential persuasiveness of human and anthropomorphized messengers," *Journal of Marketing*, 79(4), 94–110; Kim, S., R. P. Chen, & K. Zhang (2016), "Anthropomorphized helpers undermine autonomy and enjoyment in computer games," *Journal of Consumer Research*, 43(2), 282–302); performance (e.g., Herrmann, P. N., D. O. Kundisch, & M. S. Rahman (2015), "Beating irrationality: Does delegating to IT alleviate the sunk cost effect?" *Management Science*, 61(4), 831–850); impact of robots (e.g., Smith 2002; Huang and Rust 2018; Shankar, V. (2018), "How Artificial Intelligence (AI) is reshaping retailing," *Journal of Retailing*, 94 (4), vi–xi); impact of robot laws (e.g., Olazabal, A. M., A. Cava, & R. Sacasas (2001), "Marketing and the Law," *Journal of the Academy of Marketing Science*, 33(4), 116–118); and the antecedents and consequences of robotics in customer service (e.g., Xiao, L., & V. Kumar (2021). "Robotics for customer service: A useful complement or an

ultimate substitute?" *Journal of Service Research*, https://doi.org/10.1177/1094670519878881). This is only a representative list and not an exhaustive list.

59. Nichols, G. (2020a), "DHL expands robotic footprint with 1000 autonomous robots," *ZD Net*, March 12, [accessed from https://www.zdnet.com/article/dhl-expands-robotic-footprint-with-1000-autonomous-robots/]; Nichols, G. (2020b), "CES 2020: Is this robot concierge the future of service robots?," *ZD Net*, January 10, [accessed from https://www.zdnet.com/article/ces-2020-is-this-robot-concierge-the-future-of-service-robots/].
60. Rolfsen, B. (2019), "Amazon's growing robot army keeps warehouses humming," *Bloomberg Law*, May 1, [accessed from https://news.bloombergenvironment.com/safety/amazons-growing-robot-army-keeps-warehouses-humming].
61. Evaluating customer readiness for robotic deployments continues to be studied (Mims, Christopher (2010), "Why Japanese love robots (And Americans fear them)," *MIT Technology Review*, October 12, [accessed from https://www.technologyreview.com/s/421187/why-japanese-love-robots-and-americans-fear-them]; Forlizzi, Jodi (2014), "How robots will work with us isn't only a technological question," *Harvard Business Review*, March 20, [accessed from https://hbr.org/2014/03/how-robots-will-work-with-us-isnt-only-a-technological-question]). Meuter et al. (Meuter, M. L., M. J. Bitner, A. L. Ostrom, & S. W. Brown (2005), "Choosing among alternative service delivery modes: An investigation of customer trial of self-service technologies," *Journal of Marketing*, 69(2), 61–83) refer to the consumer readiness concept as a condition or state in which a consumer is prepared and likely to use an innovation for the first time. Customer readiness is conceptualized to consist of role clarity, motivation, and self-efficacy, and to have a substantial influence on customers' decision to adopt, attitude towards, and the actual usage of the technology (Venkatesh, V., M. G. Morris, G. B. Davis, & F. D. Davis (2003), "User acceptance of information technology: Toward a unified view", *MIS Quarterly*, 27(3), 425–478.; Meuter et al., 2005; Venkatesh, V., & H. Bala (2008), "Technology acceptance model 3 and a research agenda on interventions," *Decision Sciences*, 39(2), 273–315; Kohler, C. F., A. J. Rohm, K. de Ruyter, & M. Wetzels (2011), "Return on interactivity: The impact of online agents on newcomer adjustment," *Journal of Marketing*, 75(2), 93–108; Xiao and Kumar 2021).

62. Barney, J. B. (2001), "Is the resource-based view a useful perspective for strategic management research? Yes," *Academy of Management Review*, 26(1), 41–56.
63. Menguc, B., & S. Auh (2006), "Creating a firm-level dynamic capability through capitalizing on market orientation and innovativeness," *Journal of the Academy of Marketing Science*, 34(1), 63–73.
64. Teece, D. J., G. Pisano, & A. Shuen (1997), "Dynamic capabilities and strategic management," *Strategic Management Journal*, 18(7), 509–533.
65. Eisenhardt, K. M. and J. A. Martin (2000), "Dynamic capabilities: What are they?" *Strategic Management Journal*, 21(10–11), 1105–1121.
66. Johnson, J. L., R. P. Lee, A. Saini, & B. Grohmann (2003), "Market-focused strategic flexibility: Conceptual advances and an integrative model," *Journal of the Academy of Marketing Science*, 31(1), 74–89.
67. Hansen, D. R., & M. M. Mowen (2011), *Cornerstones of cost accounting*, South-Western Cengage Learning, Mason, OH.
68. Kumar, V., A. Dixit, R. R. G. Javalgi, & M. Dass (2016), "Research framework, strategies, and applications of intelligent agent technologies (IATs) in marketing," *Journal of the Academy of Marketing Science*, 44(1), 24–45.
69. Kumar, V., & D. Ramachandran (2020), "Developing a firm's growth approaches in a new-age technology environment to enhance stakeholder wellbeing," working paper, Georgia State University, GA.
70. Kumar, V., & D. Ramachandran (2020), "Developing a firm's growth approaches in a new-age technology environment to enhance stakeholder wellbeing," working paper, Georgia State University, GA.
71. Smith, M. D. (2002), "The impact of shopbots on electronic markets," *Journal of the Academy of Marketing Science*, 30(4), 446–454.
72. Chen, Y., & Sudhir, K. (2004). When shopbots meet emails: Implications for price competition on the Internet. *Quantitative Marketing and Economics*, 2, 233–255.
73. Diehl, K., Kornish, L. J., & Lynch Jr, J. G. (2003). Smart agents: When lower search costs for quality information increase price sensitivity. *Journal of Consumer Research*, 30(1), 56–71.
74. Bertacchini, F., E. Bilotta, & P. Pantano (2017). "Shopping with a robotic companion." *Computers in Human Behavior*, 77, 382–395.
75. Iyer, G. and A. Pazgal (2003), "Internet shopping agents: Virtual co-location and competition," *Marketing Science*, 22(1), 85–106.

76. Smith, M. D. (2002), "The impact of shopbots on electronic markets," *Journal of the Academy of Marketing Science*, 30(4), 446–454.
74. Kumar, V., A. Dixit, R. R. G. Javalgi, & M. Dass (2016), "Research framework, strategies, and applications of intelligent agent technologies (IATs) in marketing," *Journal of the Academy of Marketing Science*, 44(1), 24–45.
78. Bandoim, L. (2020), "How robots are helping grocery stores during the coronavirus outbreak," *Forbes*, March 30, [accessed from https://www.forbes.com/sites/lanabandoim/2020/03/30/how-robots-are-helping-grocery-stores-during-the-coronavirus-outbreak/#2436a74b242a]; Meyersohn, N. (2020), "Grocery stores turn to robots during the coronavirus," *CNN*, April 7, [accessed from https://www.cnn.com/2020/04/07/business/grocery-stores-robots-automation/index.html].
79. Schultz, D. (2016), "The future of advertising or whatever we're going to call it," *Journal of Advertising*, 45(3), 276–285.
80. Biba, J. (2022), "What is robotics as a service (RaaS)?," *BuiltIn*, October 25, accessed from https://builtin.com/robotics/robotics-as-a-service-raas.
81. Kumar, V. (2021). *Intelligent marketing: Employing new age technologies*, Sage Publications.
82. Qmatic (2016), "Qmatic's customer journey platform integrates humanoid robot to serve customers and improve the customer experience in New Elisa Flagship Store," *Qmatic*, June 15, [accessed from https://www.qmatic.com/meet-qmatic/news/2016/june/qmatics-customer-journey-platform-integrates-humanoid-robot-to-serve-customers-and-improve-the-customer-experience-in-new-elisa-flagship-store/?zd_source=mta&zd_campaign=13760&zd_term=vanditagrover].
83. ITU (2014), "The tactile internet—ITU-T technology watch report," *International Telecommunications Union*, August, [accessed from https://www.itu.int/dms_pub/itu-t/oth/23/01/T23010000230001PDFE.pdf].
84. Simsek, M., A. Aijaz, M. Dohler, J. Sachs, & G. Fettweis (2016), "5G-enabled tactile internet," *IEEE Journal on Selected Areas in Communications*, 34(3), 460–473.
85. Kumar, V., B. Rajan, S. Gupta, & I. Dalla Pozza (2019b), "Customer engagement in service," *Journal of the Academy of Marketing Science*, 47(1), 138–160.

86. Aron, R., S. Dutta, R. Janakiraman, & P. A. Pathak (2011), "The impact of automation of systems on medical errors: Evidence from field research," *Information System Research*, 22(3), 429–446.
87. Moorman, C., & R. J. Slotegraaf (1999), "The contingency value of complementary capabilities in product development," *Journal of Marketing Research*, 36(2), 239–257.
88. Gupta, S., A. Leszkiewicz, V. Kumar, T. Bijmolt, D. Potapov, "Digital analytics: Modeling for insights and new methods," forthcoming, *Journal of Interactive Marketing*.
89. Saboo, A. R., A. Sharma, A. Chakravarty, & V. Kumar (2017), "Influencing acquisition performance in high-technology industries: The role of innovation and relational overlap," *Journal of Marketing Research*, 54(2), 219–238.
90. Arora, N., X. Dreze, A. Ghose, J. D. Hess, R. Iyengar, B. Jing, Y. Joshi, V. Kumar, N. Lurie, S. Neslin, S. Sajeesh, M. Su, N. Syam, J. Thomas, & Z. J. Zhang (2008), "Putting one-to-one marketing to work: Personalization, customization, and choice," *Marketing Letters*, 19(3), 305–321.
91. Wirtz, J., & V. Zeithaml (2018), "Cost-effective service excellence," *Journal of the Academy of Marketing Science*, 46(1), 59–80.
92. Kumar, V. (2021). *Intelligent marketing: Employing new age technologies*. Sage Publications.
93. Xiao, L., & V. Kumar (2021). "Robotics for customer service: A useful complement or an ultimate substitute?" *Journal of Service Research*, https://doi.org/10.1177/1094670519878881.
94. Kumar, V., A. Dixit, R. R. G. Javalgi, & M. Dass (2016), "Research framework, strategies, and applications of intelligent agent technologies (IATs) in marketing," *Journal of the Academy of Marketing Science*, 44(1), 24–45.
95. Frick, W. (2014), "Experts have no idea if robots will steal your job," *Harvard Business Review*, August 8, [accessed from https://hbr.org/2014/08/experts-have-no-idea-if-robots-will-steal-your-job]; Miremadi, M., S. Narayanan, R. Sellschop, & J. Tilley (2015), "The age of smart, safe, cheap robots is already here," *Harvard Business Review*, June 15, [accessed from https://hbr.org/2015/06/the-age-of-smart-safe-cheap-robots-is-already-here].
96. Xiao, L., & V. Kumar (2019). "Robotics for customer service: A useful complement or an ultimate substitute?" *Journal of Service Research*, https://doi.org/10.1177/1094670519878881.

97. Miremadi, M., S. Narayanan, R. Sellschop, & J. Tilley (2015), "The age of smart, safe, cheap robots is already here," *Harvard Business Review*, June 15, [accessed from https://hbr.org/2015/06/the-age-of-smart-safe-cheap-robots-is-already-here]; Shah, J. (2016), "Robots are learning complex tasks just by watching humans do them", *Harvard Business Review*, June 21, [accessed from https://hbr.org/2016/06/robots-are-learning-complex-tasks-just-by-watching-humans-do-them].

98. Miremadi, M., S. Narayanan, R. Sellschop, & J. Tilley (2015), "The age of smart, safe, cheap robots is already here," *Harvard Business Review*, June 15, [accessed from https://hbr.org/2015/06/the-age-of-smart-safe-cheap-robots-is-already-here]; Nedelescu, L. (2015), "We should want robots to take some jobs," *Harvard Business Review*, June 5, [available at https://hbr.org/2015/06/we-should-want-robots-to-take-some-jobs]; Torres, N. (2015), "Research: Technology is only making social skills more important," *Harvard Business Review*, August 26, [accessed from https://hbr.org/2015/08/research-technology-is-only-making-social-skills-more-important].

99. Chui, M., J. Manyika, & M. Miremadi (2016), "Where machines could replace humans—And where they can't (yet)," *McKinsey Quarterly*, July, [accessed from https://www.mckinsey.com/business-functions/digital-mckinsey/our-insights/where-machines-could-replace-humans-and-where-they-cant-yet].

100. Xiao, L., & V. Kumar (2021). "Robotics for customer service: A useful complement or an ultimate substitute?" *Journal of Service Research*, 24(1), 9–29.

101. Nichols, G. (2020b), "CES 2020: Is this robot concierge the future of service robots?," *ZD Net*, January 10, [accessed from https://www.zdnet.com/article/ces-2020-is-this-robot-concierge-the-future-of-service-robots/]

102. Various studies have been conducted on the impact of robotics in human-centric settings. For example, Čaić, M., Mahr, D., & Oderkerken-Schröder, G. (2019). Value of social robots in services: social cognition perspective. *Journal of Services Marketing*, 33(4), 463–478, examine if social robots can evoke a similar social response as human agents and find evidence that the elderly humanize the robots, exhibit warmth and competence judgements in their interactions with them.

103. A study by Mende, M., Scott, M. L., Van Doorn, J., Grewal, D., & Shanks, I. (2019). Service robots rising: How humanoid robots influence service experiences and elicit compensatory consumer responses.

Journal of Marketing Research, 56(4), 535–556, investigate customers' response to humanoid service robots versus human service providers, giving empirical evidence of the uncanny valley—a phenomenon that that interacting with humanoid robots makes people uncomfortable. The insights from a series of experiments shows that customer interacting with humanoid robots engage in compensatory behavior (for example, status signaling, social belonging, or increased food consumption) to reduce the threat to self-identity.

104. Huang, M. H., & R. T. Rust (2017), "Technology-driven service strategy," *Journal of the Academy of Marketing Science*, 45(6), 906–924.

105. Whittaker, S. (2011), "Personal information management: From information consumption to curation," *Annual Review of Information Science and Technology*, 45(1), 1–62.

106. A recent survey by Accenture found that 48 percent of consumers moved their purchase to a different provider (online or in-store) because the offerings were poorly curated. It is established that customer engagement improves with better curation (Karp, P. D. (2016), "Can we replace curation with information extraction software?" *Database*, December, [accessed from https://doi.org/10.1093/database/baw150]).

107. Beath, C., I. Becerra-Fernandez, J. Ross, & J. Short (2012), "Finding value in the information explosion," *MIT Sloan Management Review*, 53(4), 18.

108. Sushma, U. N. (2018), "An Indian startup has created an AI-driven nutritionist for fitness freaks," *Quartz India*, May 28, [accessed from https://qz.com/india/1279254/healthifyme-has-an-artificial-intelligence-led-nutritionist-for-fitness-freaks/]; Dhapola, S. (2019), "Healthifyme wants to improve your diet with its Ria2.0 AI assistant: Here's how," *Indian Express*, January 21, [accessed from https://indianexpress.com/article/technology/social/healthifyme-wants-to-improve-your-diet-with-its-ria2-0-ai-assistant-here-is-how-5544698/].

109. Windyka K. (2018). In-store platform uses AI to digitally personalize shoppers' experience. PSFK, September 11, available at https://www.psfk.com/2018/09/mystore-e-ai-personalized-shopping-experience.html

110. Holt, K. (2019), "McCormick hands over its spice R&D to IBM's AI," *Engadget.com*, February 4, [accessed from https://www.engadget.com/2019/02/04/ibm-ai-food-seasonings-mccormick/].

111. Kumar, V., B. Rajan, R. Venkatesan, & J. Lecinski (2019a), "Understanding the role of artificial intelligence in personalized engagement marketing," *California Management Review*, 61(4), 135–155.

9

Transformative Marketing Using Drones

Overview

Drones have been receiving increasing attention among companies, largely due to their varied applications in real-world uses. Formally known as unmanned aerial vehicles (UAVs), enterprise drones (i.e., drones used by commercial enterprises in their regular operations) have captivated businesses and users alike for their multipurpose civilian uses. However, drones were first developed for use in specialized military operations. Since their initial development, the commercial applications of drones have been muted, until recently.[1]

From a business standpoint, the developer community continues to serve as a major source of growth drivers by developing various commercial uses and applications for drones. Some of the popular uses of drones currently include asset tracking and management, preventive maintenance, environmental management, security and surveillance, media, and photography, and so on. Further, drones have emerged as a valuable NAT in several industries such as agriculture, construction, transportation and warehousing, mining, insurance, and civil services such as law and order, emergency operations, and disaster management, in addition to becoming a popular hobby.[2]

Further, many companies have expressed optimism about the growth and adoption of drones in the coming years. On the consumer side, nearly 65% of Americans expect that in the next 20 years, most deliveries in major cities will be made by robots or drones rather than humans.[3] As seen in the case of other NATs, drone applications are also expected to increase even further as they develop advanced capabilities, receive regulatory support, enjoy consumer acceptance, and witness advancements in public infrastructure.[4] In this regard, the marketing applications of drones appear to be particularly appealing as businesses strive to demonstrate and deliver value-enriching offerings.

This chapter is organized as follows: A brief history of the origin of drones is presented, followed by a definition of drones (from a marketing standpoint). Then, a discussion on the various classifications of drones is presented spanning military, consumer, and business applications, with a special focus on disaster response applications. Next, marketing applications of drones focusing on understanding customer needs, revisiting firm capabilities to integrate drones, designing drone-focused marketing mix strategies, driving customer engagement (CE) through drones, and designing digital strategies with drones are discussed. Finally, the future of drones for the marketing industry is discussed through specific business and customer-facing tasks such as businesses' enhanced ability to establish CE, and ways of advancing customer contact solutions.

Origin, Definition, and Classification of Drones

Origin

The UAVs have their origins in military actions with the earliest instance being unmanned balloons loaded with explosives used when Austria attacked Venice in 1849. While these balloons did not involve technology, the first technological creation of UAVs occurred in 1916 during World War I. The United States developed the Kettering Bug, an aerial torpedo that was capable of striking ground targets. However, the war ended before the Bug could be deployed. Subsequent advancements of the Bug led to the development of the first remote-controlled aircraft called the Radioplane OQ-2 in 1941.[5]

Drones borrow their name from the male bees that have limited and focused use in the bee community—i.e., to mate with a fertile queen bee. They were first introduced to the public as remotely controlled aircraft for a battleship weapon's target practice. Examples of such drones include the Fairy Queen and the De Havilland Queen Bee seaplane introduced during World War I.[6] The following decades witnessed the development of drones for various military purposes such as battlefield operations, surveillance and reconnaissance, communications, delivery, and relief measures, among others. More recent sophistication in drones relates to capabilities on performance, flying at higher altitudes, better fuel efficiency, covering longer distances, solar-based models, and so on. Now, drones are not restricted only for military purposes but are being successfully used in commercial applications such as environmental assessment, goods transportation, security, media and photography, agriculture, rescue operations, and many more.

Definition

While the concept of a drone may seem straightforward, the definition of a drone is far from it. The definition of a drone varies based on terminologies used, applications/markets served, and physical/technical characteristics. A drone can, therefore, be "defined" based on these three aspects. The following discussion provides a brief overview of these three aspects that can be illustrative in demonstrating the difficulty in identifying a widely accepted definition of drones.

Regarding the terminologies used, several terms such as unmanned aerial vehicle (UAV), unmanned aircraft system (UAS), remotely piloted vehicle (RPV), remotely piloted aircraft (RPA), remotely piloted aircraft systems (RPAS), and drones have appeared in the literature. Table 9.1 explains these terms. While all these terms refer to the basic concept of driverless flight onboard, the level of overlap between these terms indicates the complex nature of drones. Going forward, in this chapter, we will use the term "drone" to refer to unmanned aircraft that fly as per human-assisted commands and are capable of flying autonomously.

Regarding the applications/markets served, drones continue to be used in a wide range of settings. The Association for Unmanned Vehicle Systems International (AUVSI) identifies the following five markets for drones—academic market (i.e., for scientific research purposes), civil market (i.e., for government non-military purposes such as the first responders), commercial market (i.e., uses developed by for-profit businesses), consumer market (i.e., for individual consumers and hobbyists), and military market (i.e., for military purposes).[14,15]

Classification of Drones

Drones are also understood based on their physical/technical characteristics. Drone characteristics such as wing systems, autonomy, size, energy source, payload, and sensors have been identified as particularly prominent in understanding and classifying drones.[16] These drone characteristics are discussed briefly here.

Table 9.1 Similar terms relating to drones

Term	General description	Reference
Unmanned aerial vehicle (UAV)	Aerial vehicles that provide wireless connectivity by transmitting data remotely, and typically without an onboard pilot	Zeng et al.[7]
Unmanned aircraft system (UAS)	An aerial system is made up of many sub-systems that include the aircraft, its payloads, and the control station(s). Essentially, it's an aircraft with its crew removed and replaced by a computer system and a radio link	Austin[8]; Watts et al.[9]
Remotely piloted vehicle (RPV)	Class of UAVs designed to have some degree of interaction with a human controller via a data link but may possess autonomous flight control capability	Larm[10]
Remotely piloted aircraft (RPA)	A sub-category of an unmanned aircraft where the flying pilot is not on board the aircraft	ICAO[11]
Remotely piloted aircraft systems (RPAS)	A set of configurable elements consisting of an RPA, its associated remote pilot station(s), the required command and control links, and any other system elements as may be required, at any point during flight operation	ICAO[12]
Drone	An unmanned aircraft that can fly autonomously	Villasenor[13]

Wing systems. This relates to the wing system of the drone. Three broad types of wing systems have been identified.

- *Fixed-Wing Systems.* Refers to fixed, static wings in combination with forward airspeed to generate lift. Therefore, these drones are built to cover long distances. Such drones can be seen in military operations and delivering relief measures (see Image 9.1).
- *Multirotor Drones.* Such drones are equipped with multiple small rotors, at least four. Known for their ability to hover in the air, be noiseless, and be lightweight, these drones are ideally suited for aerial photography and carrying small loads. However, they can remain airborne only for a short duration (see Image 9.2).
- *Hybrid Systems.* Possess characteristics of fixed-wing systems and multirotor drones. Ongoing research on these drones has developed models that can stay airborne for a longer duration, be powered by batteries and electric motors, and fly longer without having to refuel. Such drones can be useful in conducting research and performing search and rescue operations, especially in hazardous conditions.

Image 9.1 Fixed-wing drone
(*Source* Image by *US Air Force Photo / Lt. Col. Leslie Pratt*)

Image 9.2 Multirotor drone
(*Source* Image by *Inmortal Producciones* from *StockSnap*)

Autonomy. Drones have some degree of autonomy, owing to the absence of an in-flight operator. Here, the distinction between autonomous systems and automatic systems provided by the US Department of Defense (US DoD) is critical.[17]

- *Automatic Systems*. Fully preprogrammed systems that act repeatedly and independently of an external influence or control. While automatic systems can be self-steering or self-regulating and can follow an externally given

path while compensating for small deviations caused by external disturbances; they are unable to define the path according to some given goal or to choose the goal dictating its path.
- *Autonomous Systems.* Self-directed systems perform towards a goal in that they do not require outside control, but rather are governed by laws and strategies that direct their behavior. In this sense, an autonomous system is self-directed by choosing the behavior it follows to reach a human-directed goal. Most notably, they cannot exercise a "freedom of choice".
- The US DoD identifies the following four levels of autonomy—(a) *human-operated* (a human operator makes all decisions), (b) *human-delegated* (the vehicle can perform many functions independently of human control when delegated to do so), (c) *human supervised* (the system can perform a wide variety of activities when given top-level permissions or direction by a human), and (d) *fully autonomous* (the system receives goals from humans and translates them into tasks to be performed without human interaction)

Size. The size of drones is a key character to understand and classify drones. Clarke[18] contends the size of drones is the most important factor in recognizing the distinct categories of drones, and classifies drones as (a) large drones (100 kg–150 kg), (b) mini-drones (20–30 kg), (c) micro-drones (0.1kg–7 kg), and (d) nano-drones ("smart dust" or "smart particles"). As a result of the varying sizes, these drones would likely serve different markets and applications. For instance, while large drones could be used in commercial applications such as transportation and rescue operations; micro-drones could be used in applications such as reconnaissance and environmental monitoring.

Energy Source. Drones are typically powered by one of the following energy sources such as (a) traditional airplane fuel (e.g., kerosene) that is primarily used in fixed-wing drones, (b) battery cells (e.g., rechargeable battery cells) that are used in multirotor drones, (c) fuel cells meant for use in fixed-wing drones, and (d) solar cells meant for use in fixed-wing drones.

Payload. This refers to the weight a drone can carry. While it does not include the weight of the drone itself, it does include anything placed or fitted in the drone such as sensors, task-related equipment (e.g., camera, weapon, etc.), and items for delivery/transportation. Therefore, smaller-sized drones typically used for hobby purposes are expected to have a lower payload (less than 2 kg (i.e., 4.4 lbs)), while drones used for military or professional purposes are expected to have a higher payload (even up to 200 kg). Further, the payload handling range is jointly determined by the flying time and flying range of the drone. Therefore, while hobby drones are designed to maximize flight time and flight range, the payload capacity is often not too high. Similarly, for drones involved in rescue and relief missions, payload capacity could be prioritized over flight time and flight range.

Sensors. Sensors are an important category of payload included in drones. Examples of sensors include cameras, microphones, and scientific sensors used for various purposes such as testing, measurement, security, and many more. Drones being developed now often include cameras and microphones. The popular audio/video uses of sensors include security monitoring, surveillance, access control, intelligence gathering, cartography, geo-mapping, land surveys, archeological surveys, wildlife photography, and media and entertainment, among others. The popular types of scientific sensors include biological/chemical/meteorological sensors for various measurement and testing purposes, sensors for testing environmental emissions, surveying landfills, estimating environmental degradation and pollution, scientific studies involving data collection, agricultural crop spraying, and monitoring, combating natural disasters, assessing the impact of natural disasters, estimating populations, conducting atmospheric studies, and wildlife conservation and management, among others.

As seen from the above discussion and Table 9.1, the closeness of the related concepts involving drones indicates the evolving nature of this technology, and therefore the absence of a precise definition. Broadly, drones have been referred to as any type of vehicle, including aircraft, characterized by the absence of an onboard pilot and either autonomous or piloted from the ground.[19] It is important to note that many military forces do not prefer the term "drone", instead preferring the use of terms such as UAV (e.g., in the United States and Australia) and RPA (e.g., in Europe and Australia).[20] However, the popular usage of the term drones now refers to any unmanned aircraft that is flown by an operator on the ground or is capable of fully autonomous flight with no direct human intervention.[21]

Overall, whereas drones present important strategic implications to governments and militaries worldwide, they represent a fast-growing area that is of keen interest to corporations and application developers. The ever-expanding capabilities of drones provide corporations with more access to users, more opportunities for customer interaction touchpoints, more avenues for operational efficiencies, and richer sources of information, among others. In this regard, Kumar and Ramachandran[22] propose that drones qualify as a function-oriented technology that can allow companies to develop capabilities to gain increased accessibility to areas and situations that humans cannot access safely. Additionally, the firm can achieve increased efficiency and accuracy in tasks requiring precision and attention to detail, in addition to consistently obtaining positive results.[23] To conclude the overview of drones, the following vignettes present the possibilities of drones and how companies and users are deriving value from such offerings.

Military-Oriented Technology

Drone applications are perhaps the most visible in military operations.[24] In addition to birthing this technology, the military remains the most advanced user of this technology that hinges on significant goals and outcomes. Specifically, the ability to make offensive strikes on adversaries away from immediate danger presents critical strategic advantages to the user. Further, the operational efficiencies provided by drone usage have not only prevented loss of lives but also continued to aid in vital military rescue missions, thereby significantly impacting countries' foreign policies.[25] The vitality of drones in the military can be seen in the development of drone electronics (i.e., the sensors).[26] In this regard, world military organizations (e.g., the UK Ministry of Defence) have also recognized the importance of civilian drone popularity and commercial expertise in advancing drone technology that can help the military in significantly driving drone adoption and use.[27]

While the validity of drones in a military setting is increasingly justified by their continued usage around the world, the critical strengths, and weaknesses of drones from tactical and strategic perspectives warrant attention. Specifically, drones strengthen militaries from various aspects such as (a) doing the dull, dirty, and dangerous work deemed for humans, (b) ensuring vital presence where manned forces are not feasible, (c) are economical to use and operate, (d) safeguarding human military personnel, (e) facilitating limited physical presence in dangerous territories, (f) securing more intelligence to gain a good understanding of the local situation, especially in hostile areas, (g) allowing to be used clandestinely, (h) effectively countering time-sensitive targets, and (i) augmenting military capabilities through ongoing technological improvements (e.g., satellite capabilities, advanced sensors, etc.).

In contrast, drones also present critical weaknesses for the military such as (a) exposure to information and communications hacking, (b) performance subjective to inclement weather (e.g., snow, wind, etc.), especially in lower-end drone models, (c) lower drone speeds could increase risk exposure, (d) high development costs, especially in updating with advanced drone electronics, (e) inability to distinguish between friendly and hostile human populations, (f) lesser than ideal load carrying capacities, especially weaponry,

(g) easy availability to adversaries, (h) challenges in securing radio frequency spectrum, and (i) lack of clarity in proportion and suitability of manned vs. unmanned drone operations.

In addition to combat-related functions, drones also render vital support in non-combat military projects.[28] Such projects are often in the areas of nation-building, peacekeeping missions, infrastructure support, and sensitive civilian-focused projects. Military organizations around the world use drones for vital functions such as mapping, identifying geohazards, construction, and maintenance of critical country infrastructure (e.g., highways, bridges, military bases, etc.), assistance in civil engineering projects (e.g., dams, refineries, energy projects, etc.).[29] Further, through its research and development initiatives, the military often develops applications using NATs that subsequently became available for civilian use.[30] Popular historical examples include the development of duct tape, the microwave oven, GPS, the Internet, and virtual reality which were first created by the US military for their internal operations.[31] Therefore, drones are a fast-emerging technology that continues to power the military in war and non-war projects.

Consumer Applications

Consumer use of drones has increased due to the inclusion of exciting drone features.[32] While military drones are equipped with highly functional and essential features that are used in strategic and tactical operations, consumer drones focus on hobbyists expecting fun and recreation-related features. In the United States, the Federal Aviation Administration (FAA) considers recreational or hobby UAS or drones as those used for enjoyment and not for work, business purposes, or compensation or hire. The FAA deems such aircraft as "model aircrafts" and defines them as "an unmanned aircraft that is (1) capable of sustained flight in the atmosphere; (2) flown within visual line of sight of the person operating the aircraft; and (3) flown for hobby or recreational purposes".[33] In this regard, popular consumer drone applications largely focus on recreation aspects such as photography and sporting activities, among others.

Perhaps the biggest attraction of drones for personal use lies in the features of photography. While using drones for commercial photography may be classified as a business application, individuals and photography enthusiasts increasingly use drones for taking visually stunning photographs. With high-quality cameras and recording devices becoming a standard feature in newer drone models, aerial photography has become a fun and creative pastime (see Image 9.3). Further, wildlife enthusiasts also use drones to capture dramatic images. When handled well, drone photography can be useful in educational pastimes such as bird watching, identification of flora/fauna, and independent scientific research explorations.[34] However, experts caution how using drones for capturing images of birds, for example, can be disruptive for the birds when not sensitively conducted.[35] This can especially be so in the case of beginner or amateur drone photographers. Another interesting area of aerial photography for personal use is event photography (e.g., weddings, social gatherings, graduation parties) and social media participation (e.g., photos by social media influencers, high-quality images for sharing).

Drone racing is another area of personal drone use that is making rapid progress. This sport requires the drone operator to wear a first-person view (FPV) headset device that is connected to a camera mounted on the drone. This allows only the racer to see the path of the drone, and the goal of the race is to complete the set course as quickly as possible (see Image 9.4). Such drones typically carry features such as agility to make sharp turns, lightweight, and the ability to make acrobatic turns. This sport, which originally began in

Image 9.3 Drones used in Aerial Photography
(*Source* Image by *Bobby Stevenson* from *Unsplash*)

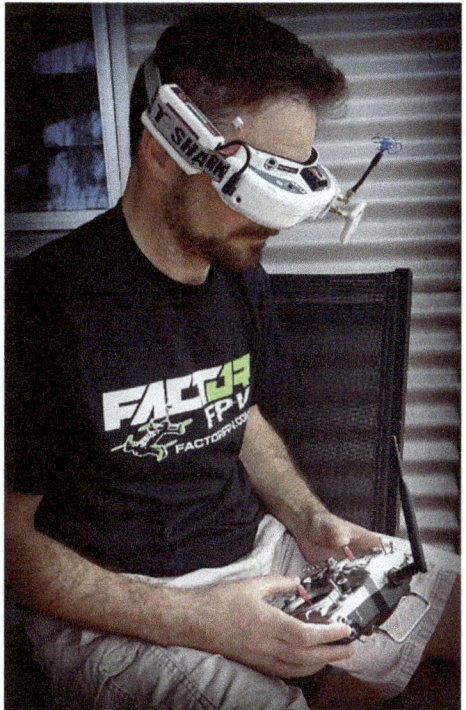

Image 9.4 Drone Racing. First-person view drone racing
(*Source* Image by *Siggy Nowak* from *Pixabay*)

Australia in 2014, has now attracted worldwide participation and viewership involving several professional organizations.[36]

Business Applications

The extent and impact of drones on business applications are expanding at a vigorous pace. Advancements in various commercial operations are being developed to create more value for businesses and customers.[37] Research from the Boston Consulting Group estimates that by 2050, the industrial drone fleet in Europe and the United States will comprise more than 1 million units and generate $50 billion per year in product and service revenues,[38] and analysts at Barclays contend that the use of drones will result in cost savings of some $100bn.[39] Overall, companies are identifying opportunities to infuse more value into their offerings with the expectation of deriving more value from customers. The following uses provide a flavor of such business applications using drones:

- *Drones in Agriculture.* Many developing countries' economies are heavily dependent on agricultural produce for sustenance and exports. Despite its importance, the sector is prone to crop failure due to adverse weather conditions, uncontrolled pests, etc. In India, the farmers are dependent on monsoon rains for irrigation and implement age-old farming methods. The quality and quantity of the produce are compromised despite the efforts of the farmers. Through the integration of technological advancements in farming practices, the sector could mitigate failure and disasters. Drone-based agricultural practices are picking up momentum in India, with key roles to play in precision agriculture, improvement in crop yield, and locust control. For instance, farmers in India using drones for spraying herbicides and pesticides have realized significant time and labor savings. Instead of around three to four hours to spray over an acre, a drone can finish the work in just 10–12 minutes. This translates to significant cost savings incurred due to hiring farm labor.[40]

  The use of drone technology in agriculture aids in reducing time and increasing the efficiencies of the farmers. With infrared mapping, drones can gather information about the health of the soil and the crop—thereby ensuring crop health. They detect minute signs of pest attacks and provide accurate data about the degree and range of the attack. Since agriculture is prone to be impacted by extreme weather conditions, drones can be useful in detecting upcoming weather conditions and can prepare farmers for adversities in advance. Agri drones are sturdy, low-cost, and require minimum maintenance. However, these drones are heavily reliant on internet connectivity, weather-dependent, and require the right sets of skills and knowledge to operate them.

  In 2019 survey by the California Farm Bureau Federation (CFBF) found that 56% of participating farmers were unable to hire all the employees they needed at some point during the past five years.[41] A similar situation can be seen across the United States. For example, between 2002 and 2014, the number of field and crop workers in America fell by 146,000, and the wages of field and crop workers during this period increased by 12%.[42] The above two facts indicate that rising wages and a decline in the number of farm laborers have accentuated the challenges faced by the agriculture industry.

  In this regard, drones are viewed as a labor-saving technology with many farmers actively using drones for a range of farm-related activities.[43] Drones are used in farming activities such as crop estimation, yield assessment, irrigation leak detection and management, pest control, seeding, spraying of fertilizers/pesticides, crop/livestock health assessment, soil, and

Image 9.5 Drones used in spraying farms
(*Source* Image by *DJI-Agras* from *Pixabay*)

field analysis, and so on (see Image 9.5). However, the adoption has not been as widespread as expected due to operational challenges such as drone safety, privacy issues, and insurance coverage.[44]

- *Drones in Construction.* Drones have been demonstrating significant value in the construction industry, primarily with their varied applications in construction sites. Some of their key implementations include (a) aerial surveys of work sites, (b) progress tracking, (c) construction planning and management (especially at the preconstruction stage), (d) quality control, (e) work site safety, (f) risk mitigation and management, (g) work site security and surveillance, (h) stockpile management, (i) marketing communications of real estate, (j) equipment storage and installation, and so on.[45] Further drone advancements such as thermal sensors, GPS units, and high-quality cameras, in addition to augmenting drones with artificial intelligence (AI) and machine learning (ML),[46] are expected to make the drone a valued capability for the construction industry (see Image 9.6).
- *Drones in Transportation.* Drones are expected to provide critical first-mile and last-mile delivery solutions for companies and consumers. Companies such as DHL, UPS, Amazon, and Google have already started developing and testing drone deliveries and are seeing impressive results. For instance, UPS Flight Forward, a dedicated drone delivery unit, is the first organization to be certified by the US FAA to be operated as a drone airline.[47] Further Flight Forward is working with the WakeMed hospital system in North Carolina to transport medical samples to speed up diagnosis and is exploring drone delivery options for prescriptions and retail

Image 9.6 Drones used in construction
(*Source* Image by *Shane McLendon* from *Unsplash*)

products for CVS.[48] As with other industries, the ability to capture data efficiently is serving businesses well in terms of customer management. Further, when coupled with real-time communications and information-sharing capabilities, drones improve operational efficiencies and accentuate value creation.

Disaster Response

Mass disaster events always attract widespread public interest and require immediate attention from first responders and disaster management teams. While the timely mobilization of rescue and relief efforts is critical, the method of execution and operational details are vital in ensuring the success of the mission. In this regard, the Emergency Events Database (EM-DAT) containing global mass disasters that are compiled by The Center for Research on the Epidemiology of Disasters (CRED) can be used to improve decision-making for disaster preparedness.[49] While mega-disasters are not a common occurrence, it does bring to light the importance of timely and coordinated recovery/rescue efforts that can potentially minimize loss of lives and economic damages. Here, technological advancements such as drones are proving to be highly beneficial in assisting with disaster management efforts.

In the event of a major disaster, research has identified that drones can help secure better situational information for relief workers, locate and rescue survivors, perform inspection and analysis of critical infrastructure, and deliver vital supplies.[50] Further, drones can be used to install temporary communications infrastructure, generate maps of affected areas, and identify specific spots where rescue teams must prioritize efforts.[51,52]

Companies and relief organizations have also been actively using drones to coordinate relief efforts and develop better drone systems that can deliver the maximum results. This has been implemented in dealing with chemical spills, infrastructure damages (e.g., bridges, tunnels), fighting wildfires, and distributing relief items. For instance, in the fight to contain the COVID-19 pandemic, US companies such as UPS Flight Forward, DroneUp, and Workhorse Group are testing to see how drones can be used in the coronavirus response by speeding up testing and increasing social distancing.[53,54]

Drones in the Marketing 5.0 World

In the era of marketing 5.0, drones have emerged as a game changer, transforming the way businesses approach their promotional strategies. These cutting-edge aerial devices have paved the way for innovative marketing techniques that were previously unimaginable. By harnessing the power of drones, marketers can now capture data (through images and videos) and deliver personalized messages to their target audience. The versatility of drones allows marketers to showcase their products and services in a way that is both visually appealing and engaging, leaving a lasting impression on consumers.

Data-Driven Marketing Using Drones

Data-driven marketing using drones involves the use of UAVs to collect and analyze data for marketing purposes. Drones can capture various types of data, including imagery, video, and sensor-based information, to provide marketers with valuable insights. Some ways through which drones collect data that can be used for marketing campaigns include (a) delivering targeted advertisements to individuals in populated spaces (e.g., beaches, crowded parks), (b) displaying real-time data, product demos, or interactive content, engaging audiences in a dynamic and personalized way, (c) collecting user-response information (e.g., foot traffic patterns, crowd density, and even individual reactions to advertisements), and (d) gathering visual data on competitors' activities (e.g., store layouts, promotional events, product displays).

Aerodyne, a Malaysian drone solutions company, has partnered with Amazon Web Services (AWS) to use its DRONOS software to help drone operators around the world.[55] DRONOS is a cutting-edge platform that provides a broad variety of drone services, allowing users to quickly manage and analyze drone data to improve operations, increase productivity, and conduct aerial inspections while protecting the safety of ground workers.

Aerodyne's expertise has found a significant application in agriculture, where it helps to address global food security issues by using precision farming techniques using drones. The company has successfully developed solutions such as the Agrimor platform, which is powered by DRONOS and enables farmers and agriculture service providers to use drones for various tasks including planting, spraying, plant analysis, and mapping. This platform has been developed in collaboration with AWS and has resulted in a significant increase in crop yields, with some cases reporting up to a 67% rise. Independent farmers and large palm oil plantation corporations in Malaysia and Indonesia have adopted the Agrimor platform, using it to quickly identify crop issues such as under-irrigation or disease and then deploy fertilizers or pesticides more effectively. This not only optimizes resource allocation but also contributes to the overall food security and profitability of farmland.

Predictive Marketing Using Drones

Predictive marketing using drones involves leveraging data collected by drones to make informed predictions about consumer behavior, market trends, and other factors that can influence marketing strategies. This is an exciting new frontier, offering businesses unprecedented opportunities to reach the right audience at the right time with the right message. Drones equipped with sensors and cameras can gather a wealth of information, including demographics, location, behavior, and environmental data, among others, that can be used to predict individual behaviors and interests and suggest appropriate marketing actions.

For instance, Sustainable Skylines, an American drone aerial advertising company, has obtained official approval from the Federal Aviation Administration (FAA) to operate in Miami Beach.[56] This achievement signifies a significant milestone as it is the first time a drone banner-towing operation has been granted FAA approval for commercial purposes in the United States. Unlike conventional crewed aircraft, these drones have the advantage of vertical takeoff and landing, eliminating the need for a runway or airport and reducing fuel consumption. Once in the air, the company plans to utilize camera footage from the drones as well as third-party mobile data to evaluate the effectiveness of their advertising campaigns. By employing predictive analytics, Sustainable Skylines aims to offer dynamic pricing, adjusting their rates based on the anticipated visibility of the aerial ads. This pricing strategy mirrors the approach taken by Facebook and Google ads, which rely on actual data to support their pricing decisions.

Contextual Marketing Using Drones

Contextual marketing using drones involves decision-making, structuring activities, and delivering content based on the specific context or environment of a user. In addition to several business and marketing uses, drones can be used for coordinating emergency response and public safety messaging. In the case of emergencies or public safety announcements, drones can be deployed to deliver important messages to specific areas, ensuring that relevant information reaches the right audience promptly.

For instance, Belgium-based Citymesh is revolutionizing emergency response with its latest innovation, SENSE.[57] This groundbreaking system consists of a network of 70 Safety Drones that are strategically deployed to support police and fire services. What sets SENSE apart is its use of Drone-in-a-Box (DiaB) solutions, which are automated docking stations for drones. Within just 15 minutes of an emergency call, these DiaB stations are deployed, providing essential support to emergency centers. Not only do they serve as hubs for drone deployment, recharging, and data transmission, but they also house the drones when not in use. Designed specifically for combating fires, these drones capture high-definition 4K and thermal images, enhanced with AI technology. This valuable information greatly enhances the speed and effectiveness of emergency interventions.

To ensure comprehensive coverage, SENSE will be deployed across all 35 emergency zones in Belgium. Each zone will have two DiaB units, resulting in a total of 70 Safety Drones. This extensive network of drones aims to create a drone grid that enables emergency services to respond in a more targeted and efficient manner. Remote Operations Centres (ROCs) play a crucial role in this system, as they are equipped with skilled pilots who are available 24/7 to conduct flights and coordinate the activities of the drones. Additionally, a UTM platform ensures the safety of the flights and logs all activity. UTM, or Urchin Tracking Module, is a code that generates Google Analytics data for digital campaigns. In the context of SENSE, UTM helps track the progress of the drones' activities on various online platforms, further enhancing their effectiveness.

The capabilities of the Safety Drones are truly impressive. They capture live HD video feeds and high-resolution images, which are transmitted in real-time to ROCs, police forces, fire brigades, and other emergency services. This real-time information allows these entities to anticipate risks and select the most suitable equipment for successful rescue missions. Moreover, the remote operators of the drones can fulfill specific requests from dispatch and local first-response teams. By focusing the drone's cameras on specific areas of interest, they provide valuable insights and support to on-ground personnel. To ensure flight safety and coordination with other aircraft, the drone operators work closely with air traffic services. This collaborative approach guarantees the safe and efficient operation of the Safety Drones in emergencies.

Augmented Marketing Using Drones

Augmented marketing using drones involves combining drone technology with existing technologies and practices to enhance marketing experiences. Additionally, the fusion of drones with related new-age technologies creates interactive and immersive campaigns that can engage consumers in novel ways. Drones can capture 360-degree views of products or environments that can be used to enhance existing capabilities and functionalities by providing additional information, features, or interactive elements. This is particularly useful for showcasing real estate, travel destinations, or complex products. Increasingly, drones are also used in niche work environments such as equipment maintenance and defense purposes.

For instance, Boeing is currently assessing how routine maintenance on its aircraft can be expedited and improved through the assistance of drones. The company has introduced the Autonomous Aircraft Inspection (AAI) program, which utilizes drones to aid in maintenance tasks and has presented its potential benefits to the US Air Force.[58] With the AAI program, an airman selects the specific area of the aircraft that requires inspection, and the drone captures photographs that are then transmitted back to the airman on the ground. These images, obtained by Air Force-owned drones, are stored in a cloud-based environment, and analyzed, allowing for data accessibility from any location. This proves advantageous in the event of identifying a defect, as technicians in different locations can collaborate and devise a plan to address the issue.

While Boeing acknowledges that the AAI program is not flawless, it asserts that it has demonstrated greater accuracy compared to relying solely on human operators, with an estimated precision level of approximately 78%. Additionally, the utilization of drones significantly reduces the time required for inspections, reducing pre-flight checks from four hours to a mere 30 minutes. The company emphasizes that the technician ultimately determines which data is stored in the cloud, highlighting that the system is not intended to entirely replace human operators. Rather, Boeing aims to enhance the expertise of human inspectors, ensuring that they possess the necessary knowledge when commencing a maintenance task, rather than relying on guesswork. By implementing this system, maintenance workers are expected to speed up getting the aircraft out of the hangar, back to the crews, and swiftly back into operation.

Agile Marketing Using Drones

Agile marketing using drones involves applying agile methodologies to existing firm practices that leverage drone technology. The agile approach emphasizes adaptability, collaboration, and the ability to respond quickly to changing circumstances. Moreover, the ability of drones to provide rapid data and insights allows marketers to respond quickly to market changes. Agile marketing principles support the flexibility needed to adjust strategies in response to emerging trends or shifts in consumer behavior.

Consider Tevel, an Israeli startup, that has developed groundbreaking robots that are specifically tailored for fruit picking (see Image 9.7). These autonomous flying drones utilize advanced AI and computer algorithms to harvest fruit efficiently and optimize the entire harvesting process.[59] Although the idea of using drones for apple picking is not entirely new, more and more companies are recognizing the potential benefits of agricultural drones and exploring how automation can contribute to efficient harvesting solutions. For instance, these agile drones can operate continuously, providing cost-effective solutions for farmers and real-time monitoring of the orchard's harvesting progress. The information collected by these drones provides valuable insights into the unique characteristics and contents of each bin before it is transported to the packing house. This data empowers growers to eliminate uncertainties related to market value, quality, and output while also enhancing on-site efficiencies.

Farmers can benefit from the use of drones, as they provide access to a plethora of information about the harvested fruit, such as its quantity, weight,

Image 9.7 Drones used in apple-picking
(*Source* Tevel technology, https://www.tevel-tech.com/)

color grading, ripeness, diameter, timestamp, geolocation, and other essential data. These drones are equipped with sensors and 3D cameras, which enable them to accurately identify ripe fruit, measure sugar content, and detect diseases. The drones are autonomous and have decision-making capabilities, some even utilizing electrostatic charges that mimic bee movements for pollination. Technology companies are leading the way in designing fruit-picking drones and tree-pollinating "paddles," to improve farm efficiency and agility in the face of labor shortages and climate change challenges.

Current Drone Applications in Marketing

Drones are quickly assuming an important role in the marketing function through their varied roles. They enable firms to integrate the power of scalable computing resources with enduring, affordable sensors that can function in most work environments.[60] When paired with other technological advancements such as virtual reality, AI, and ML, they also help in the creation of an environment in which businesses can make quick, accurate decisions based on rich information directly from the source. Since drones can substitute for conventional fuel-powered vehicles, they not only provide valuable assistance in transportation but also work in reducing congestion from the roads and containing harmful emissions. As a result, drones are becoming a valuable addition to organizations in many industries that not only present value-creating opportunities in marketing but also hold important implications for the development of marketing strategies. This section presents five specific application areas where drones continue to help companies in developing marketing initiatives.

Understanding Customer Needs to Deploy Drones

Companies often look to automation to infuse operational efficiencies, establish competitive advantage, and provide exceptional service to customers. Consumers now demand innovative and technology-enabled devices and solutions to meet their needs. With the emergence of NATs, technology and consumer-level data have become inseparable. Companies can now gather rich and varied information from customer interactions that can be used to drive more value through the exchange. In this regard, drones can capture a wide range of information depending on the task it was designed for.

While a significant portion of drone data may be in the form of images of geospatial information, it provides an enormous scope for companies to do a lot more with such images. For instance, such images can be (a) processed into a sequentially/logically organized dataset to convey a visual message, (b) appended with other forms of data (e.g., thermal, chemical, physical, etc.) to learn more about a specific location, (c) illustrative in informing about the local conditions, (d) tracked over time to better understand a particular occurrence, (e) compared against similar or diverse forms of data to reveal further insights, and (f) easily delivered and consumed through smartphone apps. This vivid information can be indicative of customer needs and expectations that companies can focus on. As a result, drone data can subsequently aid companies in the development and implementation of marketing strategies.[61]

In consumer applications of drones, the deployment of drones is perhaps most impactful in delivery solutions. Especially in e-commerce, delivery options and perceived quality of delivery service are critical for consumers to shop online.[62] In a survey conducted by the European Union Aviation Safety Agency, respondents were asked how likely they were to try out delivery drones, assuming that drone delivery would cost about double today's standard shipping fees and would be guaranteed within 2 hours of placing the order. The results showed that 72% of respondents from Milan were receptive to trying out delivery drones, followed by residents of Barcelona (68%) and Budapest (67%). The more northern cities of Hamburg in Germany (59%) and the Nordics' Öresund (57%) were slightly less open to the idea.[63]

While consumers are more open to trying out delivery drones, they are also expressing more frustration in any instance of bad service. Specifically, a survey found that 84% of customers are more likely to spend more money to shop from a brand that provides great customer service. In contrast, 51% of consumers indicated switching to competition after 1–2 poor customer experiences.[64] The implication of such findings indicates that companies may not get a second chance to undo the effect of bad service experience and that they must be vigilant in all service experiences. In this current NAT environment, this implication is very pertinent to drone delivery and its effect on service experience.

Such survey findings are also in line with academic research that has highlighted the importance of minimizing service experience variance in establishing satisfaction and emotional attachment with consumers. Specifically, Kumar et al.[65] conceptualize that (a) the positive relationship between service experience and satisfaction is enhanced when the perceived variation in service experience is low and (b) the positive relationship between service experience and emotional attachment is enhanced when the perceived variation in service experience is low. Additionally, studies have shown that (a) technology has a global appeal and applicability concerning its relevance to real-time information,[66] (b) technology can render the time and place irrelevant for delivery of products and services (e.g., e-commerce, online banking),[67] and (c) technology can strengthen branding efforts that can result in a competitive advantage for firms.[68] Therefore, understanding customer needs vis-à-vis drone usage will enable brands to improve customer interactions and provide superior service experiences.

Revisiting Firm Capabilities to Integrate Drones

While drones can perform a wide range of tasks, firms can realize the full potential of drones only when the firm's capabilities and drone potential are aligned.[69] Given that drones have just emerged into the technology space, their utility to businesses remains to be seen. Therefore, companies investing in drones today will only see the results in the future. The implication is that firms must remain committed, able, and willing to reevaluate their business models and operations to include any new technological advancement to realize valuable gains. This is a crucial aspect of all NATs, especially drones. This is because, drone technology has significant commercial benefits as seen by (a) its conduciveness towards miniaturization, (b) lower costs of electronic components, and (c) a good testing ground for integrating other NATs such as AI, ML, and virtual reality.[70] Research has identified that firms that are future-focused have been recognized as being more focused on adopting technologies that build their capabilities to manage future needs.[71] Regarding drones, firms must develop/update technological capabilities that can bring out the best results from a drone implementation. In this regard, academic research has studied the development of technological capabilities of drones extensively.[72]

With the emergence of drone technology, the development of technological capabilities may involve firms to be (a) open to newer technologies, changing dynamics, and business practices, (b) perceptive in managing risks, (c) led by strong and decisive senior management, (d) agile and in keen anticipation of market-related changes, and (e) innovative with newer technologies.[73] This involves firms having a deep understanding of their immediate and long-term firm requirements, goals, and challenges that make a real impact on the bottom line. Further, firms will also have to gain a clear assessment of the implications of adopting drones. In this regard, Kumar and Banda[74] propose that a firm's technological capabilities influence its propensity to adopt drones, in addition to other factors such as the readiness of its managers and customers, drone suitability for the business, and a regulatory framework.

Designing Marketing Mix Strategies With Drones

Like robotics, drones operate as a function-oriented technology, offering ease of use, value, and convenience to users in an application setting.[75] Given the newness of drone technology in business, a concerted effort at integrating drones into marketing strategy is noticeably absent. Current drone implementations in businesses appear to be ad-hoc in nature where drones as used in specific marketing tasks and not featured as part of a broader marketing mix strategy. However, this is likely to change in the future with drones demonstrating their impact on customer experience, operating costs, and bottom lines.

The evolving customer preferences and needs become apparent in a technology-focused environment. As customers and firms interact closely, learning occurs continuously. Specifically, the increased access to information about firms and offerings allows customers to evaluate the alignment of the proposed offerings with that of their values. Likewise, customers share their data with firms in the course of using products and services in a NAT environment. This creates a space for firms to know and observe more about their customers. Further, with the compiled customer data, firms can provide customers with personalized experiences and offerings, thereby validating/updating their knowledge of the customers. In this cycle of firms and customers constantly evaluating and informing each other, information and knowledge are exchanged. This exchange powers the creation of value from and to firms and customers. Additionally, over time, such an exchange allows for the evolution and refinement of marketing strategies from firms that are aimed at creating value for both firms and customers.

A hallmark of the NAT environment is the presence of a business atmosphere that focuses on personalization, delivering positive experiences, productivity enhancements, and value growth (for firms and customers). This implies that firms direct their attention to understanding individual customer preferences to determine marketing mix variables. Further, this calls for firms to ascertain the various offering combinations of marketing mix variables that deliver the expected level of personalization, which is typically delivered through newer technologies.

With the increasing emphasis of firms on NATs such as drones to deliver positive experiences, firms also focus on monitoring and maintaining their devices/platforms, to increase productivity, improve efficiency, and reduce operating costs. For instance, drones are increasingly used to survey damage from natural disasters such as hurricanes, wildfires, and earthquakes. In such times of loss, consumers often depend on insurance to help them rebuild their lives. With drones being used in surveying damages, consumers can expect faster processing of insurance claims, thereby making a meaningful difference to consumers. Another area where drones can make a positive service experience is in delivery, as witnessed by the developments made by major companies such as Amazon, Google, DHL, and UPS.

Similarly, in-store navigation assistance is a key area that can result in positive experiences, as seen in the case of Walmart's proposed in-store drones for customer assistance[76] and in-store package pickup.[77] Given the assistance of drones with generating data-driven insights and delivering positive customer experiences, firms can potentially not only change the way they communicate with consumers in real time but also accurately measure the effectiveness of their marketing efforts, thereby increasing the opportunities for firm and customer value growth.

Driving Customer Engagement Through Drones

The topic of customer engagement has attracted significant practitioner and academic attention.[78] Practitioners worldwide continue to focus on developing valuable offerings while engaging with customers. Some of the marketing functions in which customer engagement continues to be most visible include marketing communications, customer co-creation, loyalty programs, and social media marketing, among others. As with other NATs, drone technology continues to demonstrate its utility and value in many business settings (industrial and consumer), thereby steadily entrenching itself as a valuable tool in firms' customer engagement efforts. In doing so, two key drone capabilities are emerging as well-primed for more drone-related customer engagement efforts.

Interactivity. Drones were originally developed to perform automated tasks that were either difficult, dangerous, or dirty for humans. This implies that interactivity was not an intended feature of drones. While this automation may be well-suited for many industrial situations, consumer applications may require drones to have interactivity as a capability. This is because the customer-focused market structure dictates that it is vital for firms to establish a long-term value-driven relationship with their customers to enjoy continued patronage and financial robustness. With the increasing popularity of drones and the high number of consumer applications, interactivity is now a feature that drone developers are focusing on. An example of drone interactivity can be seen in the case of the Hyderabad, India-based Biryani By Kilo. The fast-food seller specializing in biryanis decided to launch an initiative to deliver biryanis by drone. Along with the initiative, the company paired it with a social media campaign by engaging with social media influencers based in Hyderabad. The initiative and the social media campaign were a success with nearly 815 thousand views, around 85 thousand engagements, and a 44% increase in sales after the campaign.[79] This shows that drones can be made interactive when integrated within a company's marketing campaigns.

With advances made in speech recognition technologies, it is possible to equip drones with audio response capabilities (e.g., such as Alexa) that can interact with consumers in an exchange setting.[80] Such a feature will be most useful in situations like customer deliveries, in-store assistance, and navigation, customer assistance in public attractions (e.g., malls, museums, and amusement parks), and event management venues (e.g., queue management), among others. These applications are likely to enhance customer engagement as the drones will have the ability to instantly respond to customer queries.

Delivery. Drones are poised well to disrupt the delivery business, especially in fulfilling orders in highly populated areas. Many companies across countries have initiated delivery programs using drones. Some of the prominent ones include DoorDash launching a drone pilot program in the Southeast Queensland region in Australia, Walmart partnering with four drone delivery companies to establish drone delivery hubs in seven US states, Tesco launching its drone delivery service in Galway, Ireland, and Chinese food delivery platform, Meituan, starting drone delivery operations in 2021.[81] Consider Amazon, for instance. Most products sold by Amazon weigh five pounds or less.[82] Many drones are equipped to handle this weight. Therefore, this is an area that online retailers are looking at with great interest and one that can enhance customer engagement in a significant way.

However, given the limited air space, it is likely that firms will face challenges in drone delivery, with several instances of collision and property damage. Here, a traffic management system (TMS would help firms and users to have efficient usage of air space and serve as a way to enhance customer engagement. For instance, NASA is working on creating a platform known as the UAS Traffic Management (UTM) to create a system that can integrate drones safely and efficiently into air traffic that is already flying in low-altitude airspace.[83] Such a system is expected to monitor and regulate package delivery and hobby drones from intruding into the air space of regular air transport (e.g., airplanes, helicopters) and first responder drones.

Designing Digital Strategies With Drones

In the fast-evolving NAT environment, media and consumers are increasingly going digital. For marketers, this change presents important implications in two key areas—solutions-focused offerings and changing user demographics.

Solutions-focused offerings refer to those types of offerings that directly relate to customer requirements by leading them to the solution they seek rather than going through a long search process. When faced with choices, consumers typically look for more information to help them make decisions. While new information (e.g., competing offerings, alternative solutions) may be acquired through traditional and/or digital means, it also assists in avoiding decision regret,[84] and thereby helps consumers feel confident about their choices. Further, when consumers face a non-routine (or less frequent) decision, they would likely seek more information to assuage their concerns. Seeking and processing large amounts of information may lead to "information fatigue" and potentially an unsatisfactory decision-making process. In this regard, digital strategies can facilitate faster decision-making by shortening customers' purchase journeys and making them more efficient and convenient. When companies use drones in their marketing programs, the level and depth of information that is communicated is very rich and informative to the viewers. For instance, using drone footage/images in commercials provides dramatic aerial views that convey much more than traditional ground-based footage/images. Often captivating, drone images

Table 9.2 Changing nature of user demographics in the United States

User age group	Percentage of adults who								
	Own a smartphone in...			Use social media in...			Own a tablet computer in...		
	2012	2018	2021	2012	2018	2021	2012	2018	2021
18–29	66	94	96	81	88	84	20	63	61
30–49	59	89	95	64	78	81	12	56	53
50–64	34	73	83	39	64	73	10	50	46
65 and above	13	46	61	16	37	45	6	38	44

Source Faverio, M. (2022), "Share of those 65 and older who are tech users has grown in the past decade," *Pew Research Center*, January 13, accessed from https://www.pewresearch.org/short-reads/2022/01/13/share-of-those-65-and-older-who-are-tech-users-has-grown-in-the-past-decade/

add dimension and movement to the marketing content, thereby nudging them towards a decision.

The changing nature of user demographics has moved towards digital avenues. While younger users are known to be early adopters of technology compared to older users, the rate of adoption of newer technologies by the oldest age group has increased significantly in recent years. Particularly, a recent survey has found the gap between the oldest and youngest adults has narrowed. The results of the survey are presented in Table 9.2.

As shown in Table 9.2, among Americans 65 and older between 2012 and 2021, there was a nearly five-fold increase in the ownership of smartphones, a three-fold increase in the usage of social media, and a seven-fold increase in the ownership of a tablet computer. While other age groups also showed increases, it was not as significant as the 65 and older group.[85] The implication of such generational shifts is, that firms that can take advantage of ongoing developments in drone capabilities, drone electronics, and sensors; creatively use drone data and insights; plan drone deployment in a precise manner; and implement digital strategies that involve drones in the right measure can reap impressive rewards while delivering the most value to consumers.

Future of Drones in Marketing

With the rapid progress made in technological innovations, the future looks loaded with gadgets, algorithms, and platforms. As with all NATs, drones too will become a regular feature in our daily lives. As we move towards a data-rich and innovation-focused environment, the presence and usage of consumer data by firms, the quality of insights generated, and the way technology is used to implement solutions based on the insights will inform the usefulness and relevance of marketing strategies.[86] While a technology-intensive future is inevitable, firms must adopt a customer-focused approach while designing marketing strategies that create value for firms and consumers. Drones will undoubtedly continue to impact marketing strategies and marketing practices. In doing so, the lessons learned from drone implementations and the marketplace changes will continue to drive future drone implementations. While we can expect progress in drone capabilities in many organizational areas, three areas that stand out are discussed here.

The "Good," "Bad," and "Ugly" of Drones

It is apparent that personalization has increased tremendously, and data is being generated in more ways than one can expect. While there have been a few concerns over the role of these technologies, drones require specific attention. Here, three perspectives about drones are presented—the "good" (why we must embrace drone use), the "bad" (that which must be worked on), and the "ugly" (that which must be re-evaluated) to facilitate decision-making for customers and organizations.

The "Good." As discussed earlier, drones have many uses that benefit society such as for inspection in law enforcement, construction, and safety and disaster management, among others. Drones are also being used in ecosystem management for identifying poaching or illegal deforestation—they were used in Kenya in fighting poachers. Drone photography and videography also have a transformative effect on humans. In business contexts, drones are used by firms to offer better customer experiences. In 2016, Domino's Pizza flew the peri-peri chicken, chicken, and cranberry pizzas to a couple in Whangaparaoa, New Zealand—the first people in the world to get pizzas delivered by drones.[87] Around the same time, Amazon delivered their goods using drones, following the Amazon Prime Air business model.

The "Bad." It is to nobody's surprise that drones have infiltrated our daily lives with ease, but the long-term consequences of this action are relatively underexplored. Drones are a safety threat. When operated by inexperienced fliers, when poorly made, or when flying in unfavorable conditions—they may fall out of the sky unexpectedly (susceptible to engine malfunctions). Additionally, there are rising concerns over drones' invasion of privacy. The idea of a drone flying above people's homes and capturing images to store as data is very unsettling to many. These are being mitigated by drone manufacturers and developers—they are developing new technologies; cameras that automatically blur or pixelate faces. Customers are using privacy screens to block the view of their homes, some apps detect drone presence around set premises.

The "Ugly." Flying drones over crowds is becoming common nowadays—this is a serious hazard as drones could collide with other people or objects in the crowd. They are also very noisy, contributing significantly to noise pollution. Drones are being equipped with weapons and are being used to carry out other criminal offenses. Drones flying in restricted airspaces are also picking pace—in 2014, a helicopter-style drone nearly collided with an Airbus 320 taking off from Heathrow Airport in London. Such acts pose a serious threat to humanity, only regulations and awareness can reduce the possibilities.

Enhanced Customer Experience

Drones are continuing to prove their worth in improving customer experience. As evidenced by the above discussion, while drone technology is a game changer in improving customer experience in end-user-focused interactions, drones also work just as effectively "behind the scenes" in delivering a superlative experience. In the future, this ability of drones is only expected to increase as more firms see value in such implementations. A few such drone implementations are discussed here.

Consider the insurance industry. This industry was one of the first to begin using drones for claims inspections. Companies such as Allstate, Travelers, USAA, and Liberty Mutual are using drones for damage inspection and processing claims, with more companies planning to adopt drones.[88] Whereas claims inspection is but one function for insurers, drone deployment is being evaluated or used in many more functions. Specifically, drones are being considered for assessing the loss before and after a negative event occurs. Regarding the determination of loss before a negative event occurs, drone data and inputs are used in calculating premiums, including risk mitigation clauses in the insured property, and collecting information relating to potential threats from natural disasters. Once a loss-creating event has occurred, drones can be considered for assisting in several tasks such as inspecting damages to property and lives, assessing risks to avoid future losses, processing claims, and validating damages to prevent insurance fraud, among others. While all these actions may not occur in direct interaction with customers, their involvement in the background ultimately impacts how insurers manage customer expectations and provide superior experience.

Consider the public utilities industry. Drones serve a vital use in assisting with aerial surveys for maintenance purposes. For instance, critical infrastructure such as power lines, communications towers, roads, rivers, bridges, etc., needs routine maintenance and monitoring, to avoid any service failures. While trucks, helicopters, and boats are typically used for such maintenance purposes, it is often expensive and could place members of the maintenance team in hazardous conditions. Here are three examples of drone usage by public utility companies.

- An early user of drones, Dominion Energy in Virginia has been using drones for routine power line inspections since 2014.[89] Recently, the company also won approval from the FAA for expanded beyond visual line of sight (BVLOS) drone flights. The company expects such advancements in drone usage to serve its customers better by providing a superior service experience.
- In 2017, the New York Power Authority (NYPA) tested the use of drones to inspect the Niagara ice boom for any damages and preventive maintenance. While it can cost $3,500 for a helicopter or $3,300 to send a crew of four for a full-day inspection by boat, a drone could cost only $300 per trip, thereby leading to valuable cost savings.[90]
- In 2017, Oklahoma Gas and Electric (OG&E) recently deployed inspection drones to speed up storm assessment and restoration times during winter storm Jupiter. By continuing the use of drones to undertake advance inspections of power lines, wind farm turbines, and plat equipment, the company estimates the outage duration to have been reduced by 50%.[91]

Essentially, by reducing the number of breakdowns and/or providing more accurate information on service restoration, such implementations are expected to ultimately provide a better customer experience for users of public utility companies.

Customer Contact Solutions

Drones have the potential to demonstrate improvements in product development and enhancement, process optimization, and derive deeper insights for decision-making when well-integrated into marketing strategies. Further, they can help firms master the knowledge of consumer preferences, and deliver personalized products, pricing, and advertising content through relevant channels. Several companies continue to use drones for display advertising that can be eye-catching while being economical. For instance, Moscow-based Wokker Noodles used drones to carry small promotional fliers past the windows of Moscow office buildings, informing the lunch specials just as people were getting ready for lunch. The success of this innovative campaign was immediately observed with lunch deliveries in the campaign areas increasing by 40%.[92] Other major brands such as Red Bull, Coca-Cola, GE, and Intel have used drones for advertising and promotional marketing campaigns.[93] Such initiatives have significantly helped the brands stay closer to their consumers.

Another area where drones can serve as effective customer contact vehicles is event marketing. Visitors to an event serve as a committed audience to which firms can pitch their offerings. Given that the attention of the audience is at a high level, an innovative way of communicating the marketing message will likely have a high impact. For instance, when events are covered via a live stream using drones, in addition to the regular mode of coverage, consumers get an immersive experience of the event. Examples of such experiences include recreational adventure sports (e.g., hang gliding, paragliding, parasailing, etc.), indoor sporting events (e.g., drone cameras for capturing close-ups and replays), drone racing, behind-the-scene footage of live events, and so on. When brands make their presence felt during such events, consumers may associate those brands with positive experiences thereby boosting the brand image and recall. The Intel Drone Show at the *Pepsi Super Bowl LIII Halftime Show* is an example of how brands can elevate the memorability of an event while making its presence felt .[94] Further, the company has performed more than 600 light shows in over 20 countries, signifying the value of drones as a prized, innovative event management tool that can benefit brands and consumers.

Drones can also make a significant positive impact on customer satisfaction by enhancing the quality of customer interactions during a purchase event. Drone delivery is a good example of this. With many companies like Amazon, Google, DHL, Flirtey, and UPS rapidly increasing the technological capabilities of drones, regulatory bodies are now beginning to facilitate and simplify the regulatory policies governing the use of drones in business.[95] Such actions are further expected to lower the barriers to entry for other drone adopters, drone developers, and drone service providers, thereby creating a vibrant drone ecosystem.

Key Terms and Related Conceptualizations

Drone	An unmanned aircraft that can fly autonomously
Drone racing	A sport that requires the drone operator to wear a first-person view (FPV) headset device that is connected to a camera mounted on the drone
Fixed-wing systems	Fixed, static wings in a drone that can aid with forward airspeed to generate lift
Hybrid systems	Drones that possess characteristics of fixed-wing systems and multirotor drones
Multirotor drones	Drones that are equipped with multiple small rotors, at least four, to allow them to hover in the air, be noiseless, and be lightweight
Payload	The weight a drone can carry
Remotely piloted aircraft (RPA)	A sub-category of an unmanned aircraft where the flying pilot is not on board the aircraft
Remotely piloted aircraft systems (RPAS)	A set of configurable elements consisting of an RPA, its associated remote pilot station(s), the required command and control links, and any other system elements as may be required, at any point during flight operation
Remotely piloted vehicle (RPV)	Class of UAVs designed to have some degree of interaction with a human controller via a data link but may possess autonomous flight control capability
Unmanned aerial vehicle (UAV)	Aerial vehicles that provide wireless connectivity by transmitting data remotely, and typically without an onboard pilot
Unmanned aircraft system (UAS)	An aerial system is made up of many sub-systems that include the aircraft, its payloads, and the control station(s). Essentially, it's an aircraft with its crew removed and replaced by a computer system and a radio link

Notes and References

1. The global drone services market has expanded significantly and is expected to grow from USD 4.4 billion in 2018 to USD 63.6 billion by 2025 (Markets Insider (2019), "Global Drone Service Market Report 2019: Market is Expected to Grow from USD 4.4 Billion in 2018 to USD 63.6 Billion by 2025, at a CAGR of 55.9%," *Markets Insider*, April 29, [accessed from https://markets.businessinsider.com/news/stocks/global-drone-service-market-report-2019-market-is-exp ected-to-grow-from-usd-4-4-billion-in-2018-to-usd-63-6-billion-by-2025-at-a-cagr-of-55-9-1028147695]).
2. Research by Verizon has found that more than 90% of surveyed businesses reported increased efficiencies, time-saving, and better information capture as a result of drone adoption with nearly 50% reporting potential losses in the bottom line if they had not adopted drones (Skyward (2018), "State of Drones in Big Business," *Skyward*, [accessed from http://go.skyward.io/rs/902-SIU-382/images/2018%20State%20of%20Drones.pdf]).
3. Smith, A., & M. Anderson (2017), "Automation in everyday life" *Pew Research Center*, October 4, [accessed from https://www.pewres earch.org/internet/2017/10/04/americans-attitudes-toward-a-future-in-which-robots-and-computers-can-do-many-human-jobs/].
4. Cohn, P., A. Green, M. Langstaff, and M. Roller (2017), "Commercial drones are here: The future of unmanned aerial systems," *McKinsey & Company*, December, [accessed from https://www.mckinsey.com/ind ustries/capital-projects-and-infrastructure/our-insights/commercial-drones-are-here-the-future-of-unmanned-aerial-systems].
5. Keane, J. F., & S. S. Carr (2013), "A brief history of early unmanned aircraft," *Johns Hopkins APL Technical Digest*, 32(3), 558–571; O'Donnell, S. (2019), "A Short History of Unmanned Aerial Vehicles," *Consortiq*, June 16, [accessed from https://consortiq.com/media-centre/blog/short-history-unmanned-aerial-vehicles-uavs].
6. Dekoulis, G. (2018), *Drones: Applications*, (Ed.) IntechOpen Limited.
7. Zeng, Y., R. Zhang, & T. J. Lim (2016), "Wireless communications with unmanned aerial vehicles: Opportunities and challenges," *IEEE Communications Magazine*, 54(5), 36–42.
8. Austin, R. (2011), *Unmanned aircraft systems: UAVS design, development and deployment* (Vol. 54), John Wiley & Sons.

9. Watts, A. C., V. G. Ambrosia, & E. A. Hinkley (2012), "Unmanned aircraft systems in remote sensing and scientific research: Classification and considerations of use," *Remote Sensing*, 4(6), 1671–1692.
10. Larm, D. (1996), *Expendable remotely piloted vehicles for strategic offensive airpower roles*, Air University Press, AL., USA.
11. ICAO (2011), "Unmanned Aircraft Systems (UAS) Circular," *International Civil Aviation Organization (ICAO)*, CIR 328, AN/190, Montreal, Quebec, CA.
12. ICAO (2011), "Unmanned Aircraft Systems (UAS) Circular," *International Civil Aviation Organization (ICAO)*, CIR 328, AN/190, Montreal, Quebec, CA.
13. Villasenor, J. (2012), "What is a drone, anyway?" *Scientific American*, April 12, [accessed from https://blogs.scientificamerican.com/guest-blog/what-is-a-drone-anyway/].
14. AUVSI (2019), "Global trends of unmanned aerial systems," *Association for Unmanned Vehicle Systems International*, [accessed from https://02f09e7.netsolhost.com/AUVSIDocs/Global%20Trends%20for%20UAS.pdf].
15. AUVSI reports the top six common applications for drones as imaging (86%), followed by reconnaissance, surveillance, and intelligence (69%), patrol and security (69%), disaster response (66%), survey/mapping (64%), and environmental monitoring (64%) (AUVSI 2019).
16. Vergouw, B., H. Nagel, G. Bondt, & B. Custers (2016), "Drone technology: Types, payloads, applications, frequency spectrum issues and future developments," in *The future of drone use: Opportunities and threats from ethical and legal perspectives*, B. Custers (Ed.), Springer.
17. US DoD (2011), "Unmanned Systems Integrated Roadmap FY2011-2036," *US Department of Defense*, October, [accessed from http://info.publicintelligence.net/DoD-UAS-2011-2036.pdf].
18. Clarke, R. (2014), "Understanding the drone epidemic," *Computer Law & Security Review*, 30(3), 230–246.
19. Gregory, D. (2011), "From a view to a kill: Drones and late modern war," *Theory, culture & society*, 28(7–8), 188–215; Klauser, F., & S. Pedrozo (2015), "Power and space in the drone age: A literature review and politico-geographical research agenda," *Geographica Helvetica*, 70(4), 285.
20. Clarke, R. (2014), "Understanding the drone epidemic," *Computer Law & Security Review*, 30(3), 230–246.

21. Goldberg, D., M. Corcoran, & R. G. Picard (2013), "Remotely piloted aircraft systems and journalism: Opportunities and challenges of drones in news gathering," *Reuters Institute for the Study of Journalism*, June, [accessed from https://ora.ox.ac.uk/objects/uuid:a86 8f952-814d-4bf3-8cfa-9d58da904ee3]; Floreano, D., & R. J. Wood (2015), "Science, technology and the future of small autonomous drones," *Nature*, 521(7553), 460–466.
22. Kumar, V., and D. Ramachandran (2020), "Developing a firm's growth approaches in a new-age technology environment to enhance stakeholder wellbeing," working paper, Indian School of Business, India.
23. Huang, M. H., & R. T. Rust (2018), "Artificial intelligence in service," *Journal of Service Research*, 21(2), 155–172.
24. Boucher, P. (2015), "Domesticating the drone: the demilitarisation of unmanned aircraft for civil markets," *Science and Engineering Ethics*, 21(6), 1393–1412.
25. Sparrow, R. (2009), "Predators or plowshares? Arms control of robotic weapons," *IEEE Technology and Society Magazine*, 28(1), 25–29.
26. Clouet, L. M. (2012), "Drones as future air power assets: The dawn of aviation 2.0?" In *Power in the 21st Century*, pp. 177–192.
27. Ministry of Defence (2017), "Joint Concept Note 1/17: future force concept," *UK Ministry of Defence*, September 7, [accessed from https://www.gov.uk/government/publications/future-force-concept-jcn-117].
28. Apgar, M., & J. M. Keane (2004), "New business with the new military," *Harvard Business Review*, 82(9), 45–56.
29. The U.S. Army Corps of Engineers is constantly involved in nation-building efforts, responding to natural disasters, and setting up large-scale civilian infrastructure that typically involves the use of current technological advancements (Gilsinan, K. (2020), "The race to build new hospitals," *The Atlantic*, April 18, [accessed from https://www.theatlantic.com/politics/archive/2020/04/army-corp-engineers-hospitals-coronavirus/610195/]; Kramnik, I. (2020), "To sequestrate, or not to sequestrate: The impact of Covid-19 on military budgets," *Modern Diplomacy*, April 12, [accessed from https://moderndiplomacy.eu/2020/04/12/to-sequestrate-or-not-to-sequestrate-the-impact-of-covid-19-on-military-budgets/]).
30. Matthews, K. (2020), "Military robotics market shows strength for new applications," *Robotics Business Review*, January 31, [accessed from https://www.roboticsbusinessreview.com/news/military-robotics-market-shows-strength-new-applications/].

31. Frolich, T., E. Comen, & G. Suneson (2019), "15 commercial products invented by the military include GPS, duct tape and Silly Putty," *USA Today*, May 16, [accessed from https://www.usatoday.com/story/money/2019/05/16/15-commercial-products-invented-by-the-military/39465501/].
32. The global consumer drone market size was expected to grow from USD 4.85 billion in 2022 to USD 8.74 billion by 2027 (Statista, & BRC. (January 15, 2023). Consumer drone market size worldwide in selected years from 2020 to 2027 (in billion U.S. dollars) [Graph]. In *Statista*. Retrieved October 08, 2023, from https://www.statista.com/statistics/1234655/worldwide-consumer-drone-market-size/). Also, the consumer drone market was the first to develop outside the military (Goldman Sachs (2016), "Drones: Reporting for Work," *Goldman Sachs*, October 24, [accessed from https://www.goldmansachs.com/insights/technology-driving-innovation/drones/index.html]).
33. FAA (2012), "FAA modernization and reform Act of 2012," *Pub. L. No. 112-95*, [accessed from https://www.congress.gov/112/plaws/publ95/PLAW-112publ95.pdf].
34. Mayntz, M. (2019), "The impact of drones on birds," *The Spruce*, June 9, [accessed from https://www.thespruce.com/birds-and-drones-3571688].
35. Verhagen, J. (2019), "Drones and bird photography: Why it's just not worth it," *National Audubon Society*, October 1, [accessed from https://www.audubon.org/news/drones-and-bird-photography-why-its-just-not-worth-it].
36. Organizations such as Fédération Aéronautique Internationale (FAI), Canadian Federation for Drone Racing, and Drone Racing Chile serve as governing bodies of such sporting events. Racing leagues such as MultiGP, Drone Racing League, RotorMatch League, and X Class Drone Racing host and coordinate drone racing events regularly.
37. In 2020, 5.1 million units of drones were sold globally garnering USD 2.9 billion in revenue. The revenue is estimated to increase to USD 4.3 billion (in 8.2 million units sold) by 2024, and USD 4.7 billion (in 9.3 million units sold) by 2028. The top five geographic markets for drones are China, the United States, France, Germany, and the United Kingdom (Statista (2023). Drones - Worldwide. (n.d.). In Statista. Retrieved October 08, 2023, from https://www.statista.com/outlook/cmo/consumer-electronics/drones/worldwide*).

38. Amoukteh, A., J. Janda, & J. Vincent (2017), "Drones go to work," *Boston Consulting Group*, April 10, [accessed from https://www.bcg.com/en-us/publications/2017/engineered-products-infrastructure-machinery-components-drones-go-work.aspx].
39. McGee, P. (2019), "How the commercial drone market became big business," *Financial Times*, November 26, [accessed from https://www.ft.com/content/cbd0d81a-0d40-11ea-bb52-34c8d9dc6d84].
40. Biswas, P. (2023), "Maharashtra's agri-entrepreneurs take to the skies: How drone are being used tackle farm labour shortage," *The Indian Express*, September 3, accessed from https://indianexpress.com/article/cities/pune/drones-the-new-tool-for-farmers-in-maharashtra-8921730/.
41. CFBF (2019), "Still searching for solutions: Adapting to farm worker scarcity survey 2019," *California Farm Bureau Federation*, April 30, [accessed from https://www.cfbf.com/news/survey-california-farms-face-continuing-employee-shortages/].
42. New American Economy (2020), "Agriculture," *New American Economy*, [accessed from https://www.newamericaneconomy.org/issues/agriculture/].
43. The 2019, CFBF survey found that 74% of the respondents adopted technology because of rising workforce costs, and 56% said because of a labor shortage (CFBF 2019).
44. Mazur, M. (2016), "Six ways drones are revolutionizing agriculture," July 20, *MIT Technology Review*, [accessed from https://www.technologyreview.com/2016/07/20/158748/six-ways-drones-are-revolutionizing-agriculture/].
45. Burger, R. (2019), "6 Ways drones are affecting the construction industry," *The Balance*, August 15, [accessed from https://www.thebalancesmb.com/drones-affecting-construction-industry-845293]; Goodman, J. (2020), "Tech 101: Construction drones," *Construction Dive*, January 8, [accessed from https://www.constructiondive.com/news/tech-101-construction-drones/569796/].
46. Winick, E. (2018), "AI and drones are being used to control construction projects," MIT Technology Review, March 15, [accessed from https://www.technologyreview.com/2018/03/15/144645/ai-and-drones-are-being-used-to-control-construction-projects/].*
47. UPS (2019a), "UPS flight forward attains FAA's first full approval for drone airline," *UPS*, October 1, [accessed from https://pressroom.ups.com/pressroom/ContentDetailsViewer.page?ConceptType=PressReleases&id=1569933965476-404].

48. UPS (2019b), "UPS flight forward, CVS pharmacy to develop drone delivery applications," *UPS*, October 21, [accessed from https://pressroom.ups.com/pressroom/ContentDetailsViewer.page?ConceptType=PressReleases&id=1571676331520-698].
49. CRED reports that in the decade of 2008–2017, an annual average of 348 global disaster events occurred that resulted in an annual average of 67,572 deaths, affected an annual average of 198.8 million people and caused economic losses of an annual average of USD 166.7 billion. In comparison, 2018 saw 315 global natural disaster events that resulted in 11,804 deaths, affected over 68 million people, and caused economic losses of around USD 131.7 billion (CRED 2018). The reason for the higher annual averages for the decade of 2008–2017 could be attributed to the occurrence of mega-disasters such as the 2010 Haiti earthquake, the 2011 Japan earthquake and tsunami, and the 2015–16 drought in India that claimed several thousands of lives, affected millions of people, and created several billions in economic losses.
50. Measure-Red Cross (2015), "Drones for disaster response and relief operations," *Measure* and *American Red Cross*, April, [accessed from http://www.issuelab.org/resources/21683/21683.pdf].
51. Al-Tahir, R., M. Arthur, & D. Davis (2011), "Low cost aerial mapping alternatives for natural disasters in the Caribbean," *International Federation of Surveyors*, May, [accessed from https://www.fig.net/resources/proceedings/fig_proceedings/fig2011/papers/ts06b/ts06b_altahir_arthur_et_al_5153.pdf].
52. Research has investigated the use of drones in logistics operations (Gupta, L., R. Jain, & G. Vaszkun (2015), "Survey of important issues in UAV communication networks," *IEEE Communications Surveys & Tutorials*, 18(2), 1123–1152; Erdelj, M., & E. Natalizio (2016), "UAV-assisted disaster management: Applications and open issues," In *2016 international conference on computing, networking and communications (ICNC)*, IEEE, February, pp. 1–5), to deliver supplies (Hayat, S., E. Yanmaz, & R. Muzaffar (2016), "Survey on unmanned aerial vehicle networks for civil applications: A communications viewpoint," *IEEE Communications Surveys & Tutorials*, 18(4), 2624–2661), and to recover hazardous materials (Pauner, C., I. Kamara, & J. Viguri (2015)., "Drones. Current challenges and standardisation solutions in the field of privacy and data protection," In *2015 ITU Kaleidoscope: Trust in the Information Society (K-2015)*, IEEE, December, pp. 1–7), among others, and developed frameworks to economically deploy

drones to serve a disaster-affected region (Chowdhury, S., A. Emelogu, M. Marufuzzaman, S. G. Nurre, & L. Bian (2017), "Drones for disaster response and relief operations: A continuous approximation model," *International Journal of Production Economics*, 188, 167–184).
53. Fisher, J. (2020), "UPS and workhorse test drones to help COVID-19 response," *FleetOwner*, April 21, [accessed from https://www.fleetowner.com/covid-19-coverage/article/21129382/ups-and-workhorse-test-drones-to-help-covid19-response].
54. Zipline assisted the Ghanaian government in containing the spread of the coronavirus by delivering test samples in rural areas to medical laboratories in two major cities in long-distance drones (Muller, J. (2020), "A coronavirus first: Zipline drones deliver test samples in Africa," *Axios*, April 20, [accessed from https://www.axios.com/coronavirus-zipline-drone-delivery-africa-1d4d2680-ce4f-4efe-b3b4-b91714c4a254.html]). Similarly, India deployed drones for surveillance purposes in the fight against COVID-19 to track large gatherings, minimize physical contact, monitor narrow lanes that cannot be easily accessed by police vehicles, and spray disinfectants (Srivastava, A. (2020), "Coronavirus lockdown: Drones deployed for surveillance across Bihar," *India Today*, April 20, [accessed from https://www.indiatoday.in/coronavirus-outbreak/story/coronavirus-lockdown-drones-deployed-for-surveillance-across-bihar-1669110-2020-04-20]; Shekhar, G. C. (2020), "Chennai's drone army joins city's fight against coronavirus; plays crucial role in red zones," *Outlook*, April 22, [accessed from https://www.outlookindia.com/website/story/india-news-chennais-drone-army-joins-citys-fight-against-coronavirus-plays-crucial-role-in-red-zones/351249]).
55. Economic Times (2023), "Aerodyne teams up With AWS to solve complex industrial issues with drone data," *Economic Times—CIO Southeast Asia*, December 4, accessed from https://ciosea.economictimes.indiatimes.com/news/corporate/aerodyne-teams-up-with-aws-to-solve-complex-industrial-issues-with-drone-data/105712904.
56. Sheena, J. (2023), "Drone aerial advertising startup gets green light from aviation authorities," *Marketing Brew*, August 29, accessed from https://www.marketingbrew.com/stories/2023/08/29/drone-aerial-advertising-startup-gets-green-light-from-aviation-authorities.
57. Ghosh, B. (2023), "World's first: Citymesh to deploy 70 drone-in-a-box systems across Belgium for emergency response," *flytbase*, March 16, accessed from https://www.flytbase.com/blog/citymesh-to-deploy-70-drone-in-a-box-systems-across-belgium-for-emergency-response.

58. Gill, J. (2023), "Boeing sees 5G, drone inspectors and augmented reality training key to future aircraft maintenance," *Breaking Defense*, June 29, accessed from https://breakingdefense.com/2023/06/boeing-sees-5g-drone-inspectors-and-augmented-reality-training-key-to-future-aircraft-maintenance/.
59. Jackson, A. (2023), "Agribots: The possible future development of food harvesting," *Food Digital*, July 17, accessed from https://fooddigital.com/articles/agribots-the-possible-future-development-of-food-harvesting.
60. Kumar, V. (2021). *Intelligent Marketing: Employing New Age Technologies*. Sage Publications.
61. Companies are considering delivery through drones to improve their last-mile connectivity performance. Between 2021 and 2022, trends indicate that the number of packages delivered by drone increased by more than 80%, reaching almost 875,000 deliveries worldwide. Further, by 2023, commercial drone deliveries are projected to exceed 1 million (Cornell et al. 2023).
62. By 2025, it is likely that same-day and instant delivery will reach a combined share of 20 to 25% of the market, thereby highlighting the importance of drones in fulfilling last-mile delivery needs; and that 60% of consumers are in favor of, or at least indifferent to, drone delivery (Joerss, M., F. Neuhaus, & J. Schröder (2016), "How customer demands are reshaping last-mile delivery," *McKinsey*, October, [accessed from https://www.mckinsey.com/industries/travel-transport-and-logistics/our-insights/how-customer-demands-are-reshaping-last-mile-delivery]).
63. Fleck, A. (2023). European city dwellers would try delivery drones. In *Statista*. January 13, Retrieved October 08, 2023, from https://www.statista.com/chart/29109/share-of-people-that-would-try-delivery-drones/.
64. Islam, Z. (2020), "Great service drives revenue in Gladly's 2020 customer expectations report," *Gladly*, [accessed from https://www.gladly.com/latest/great-service-drives-revenue-in-gladlys-customer-expectations-report/].
65. Kumar, V., B. Rajan, S. Gupta, & I. D. Pozza (2019), "Customer engagement in service," *Journal of the Academy of Marketing Science*, 47(1), 138–160.
66. McLaughlin, C. P., and J. A. Fitzsimmons (1996), "Strategies for globalizing service operations," *International Journal of Service Industry Management*, 7(4), 43–57.

67. Jayawardhena, C., and P. Foley (2000), "Changes in the banking sector–the case of Internet banking in the UK," *Internet Research*, 10(1), 19–31.
68. Wright, A. (2002), "Technology as an enabler of the global branding of retail financial services," *Journal of International Marketing*, 10(2), 83–98.
69. Kumar, V. (2021). *Intelligent marketing: Employing new age technologies.* Sage Publications.
70. Gupta, S., Leszkiewicz, A., Kumar, V., Bijmolt, T., & Potapov, D. (2020). Digital analytics: Modeling for insights and new methods. *Journal of Interactive Marketing*, 51(1), 26–43.
71. Srinivasan, R., G. L. Lilien, & A. Rangaswamy (2002), "Technological opportunism and radical technology adoption: An application to e-business," *Journal of Marketing*, 66(3), 47–60.
72. Technological capabilities have been identified as those abilities that competitively distinguish the firm and allow it to create a sustained competitive advantage based on the technology in a changing context (Leonard-Barton, D. (1992), "Core capabilities and core rigidities: A paradox in managing new product development," *Strategic Management Journal*, 13(S1), 111–125; Prahalad, C. K., & G. Hamel (1990), "The Core Competence of the Corporation," *Harvard Business Review*, 68(3), 79–91). This becomes even more relevant in the NAT environment where firms have to contend with emerging technologies, competitive pressures, and evolving regulatory policy environment. Lall (Lall, S. (1992), "Technological capabilities and industrialization," *World Development*, 20(2), 165–186) refers to the development of a firm's technological capabilities as the outcome of investments undertaken by the firm in response to external and internal stimuli, and interaction with other economic agents, both private and public, local, and foreign. The implication is that several micro-level and macro-level factors jointly determine the level of technological capabilities of firms.
73. Kumar, V., and D. Ramachandran (2020), "Developing a firm's growth approaches in a new-age technology environment to enhance stakeholder wellbeing," working paper, Indian School of Business, India.
74. Kumar, V., & S. Banda (2020), "CX in a drone world," working paper, Indian School of Business, India.
75. Kumar, V., and D. Ramachandran (2020), "Developing a firm's growth approaches in a new-age technology environment to enhance stakeholder wellbeing," working paper, Indian School of Business, India.

76. Martin, C. (2018), "Walmart Files Patent For Drone Customer Service In Stores," *MediaPost*, March 26, [accessed from https://www.mediapost.com/publications/article/316641/walmart-files-patent-for-drone-customer-service-in.html].
77. Leonard, M. (2019), "Patent pending: Walmart plans for drone delivery, others tackle faster picking and the end of lost inventory," *Supply Chain Dive*, October 4, [accessed from https://www.supplychaindive.com/news/patent-pending-walmarts-plans-for-drone-delivery/564359/].
78. Academic research has covered several engagement concepts such as customer engagement (Kumar, V., L. Aksoy, B. Donkers, R. Venkatesan, T. Wiesel, & S. Tillmanns (2010), "Undervalued or overvalued customers: Capturing total customer engagement value," *Journal of Service Research*, 13(3), 297–310; Pansari, A., and V. Kumar (2017), "Customer engagement: The construct, antecedents, and consequences," *Journal of the Academy of Marketing Science*, 1–18; Verhoef, P. C., W. J. Reinartz, & M. Krafft (2010), "Customer engagement as a new perspective in customer management," *Journal of Service Research*, 13 (3), 247–252), customer engagement behaviors (Van Doorn, J., K. N. Lemon, V. Mittal, S. Nass, D. Pick, P. Pirner, & P. C. Verhoef (2010), "Customer engagement behavior: Theoretical foundations and research directions," *Journal of Service Research*, 13(3), 253–266), consumer brand engagement (Hollebeek, L. D., M. S. Glynn, & R. J. Brodie (2014), "Consumer brand engagement in social media: Conceptualization, scale development and validation," *Journal of Interactive Marketing*, 28(2), 149–165), and customer engagement marketing (Harmeling, C. M., J. W. Moffett, M. J. Arnold, & B. D. Carlson (2017), "Toward a theory of customer engagement marketing," *Journal of the Academy of Marketing Science*, 45(3), 312–335), among others. Kumar et al. (2019) investigate customer engagement in a service setting wherein, service experience is defined as "…the overall customer experience that is borne out of all forms of customer interactions, communications, and transactions regarding the service offerings, over time" (p. 139).
79. Social Samosa (2022), "Case study: How biryani by kilo created buzz around their drone delivery campaign," *SocialSamosa.com*, accessed from https://www.socialsamosa.com/2022/10/case-study-biryani-by-kilo-buzz-drone-delivery-campaign/.

80. Fuhrman, T., D. Schneider, F. Altenberg, T. Nguyen, S. Blasen, S. Constantin, & A. Waibel (2019), "An interactive indoor drone assistant," *arXiv preprint*, arXiv:1912.04235; Padhy, R. P., S. Verma, S. Ahmad, S. K. Choudhury, & P. K. Sa (2018), "Deep neural network for autonomous UAV navigation in indoor corridor environments," Procedia Computer Science, 133, 643-650.*
81. Cornell, A., Mahan, S., & Riedel, R. (2023), "Commercial drone deliveries are demonstrating continued momentum in 2023," *McKinsey*, October 6, accessed from https://www.mckinsey.com/industries/aerospace-and-defense/our-insights/future-air-mobility-blog/commercial-drone-deliveries-are-demonstrating-continued-momentum-in-2023.
82. Guglielmo, C. (2013), "Turns out Amazon, touting drone delivery, does sell lots of products that weigh less than 5 pounds," *Forbes*, December 2, [accessed from https://www.forbes.com/sites/conniegug lielmo/2013/12/02/turns-out-amazon-touting-drone-delivery-does-sell-lots-of-products-that-weigh-less-than-5-pounds/#1372924455ed].
83. Blake, T. (2020), "What is unmanned aircraft systems traffic management?" *NASA*, January 30, [accessed from https://www.nasa.gov/ames/utm/].
84. Tsiros M., & V. Mittal (2000), "Regret: A model of its antecedents and consequences in consumer decision making," *Journal of Consumer Research*, 26(4), 401–417.
85. Faverio, M. (2022), "Share of those 65 and older who are tech users has grown in the past decade," *Pew Research Center*, January 13, accessed from https://www.pewresearch.org/short-reads/2022/01/13/share-of-those-65-and-older-who-are-tech-users-has-grown-in-the-past-decade/.
86. Kumar, V. (2021). *Intelligent marketing: Employing new age technologies*. Sage Publications.
87. Reid, D. (2016), "Domino's delivers world's first ever pizza by drone," *CNBC*, November 16, accessed from https://www.cnbc.com/2016/11/16/dominos-has-delivered-the-worlds-first-ever-pizza-by-drone-to-a-new-zealand-couple.html.
88. Marquand, B. (2017), "Meet your new claims inspector: A drone," *NerdWallet*, June 9, [accessed from https://www.nerdwallet.com/blog/insurance/drones-home-insurance-claims-inspectors/].
89. Lillian, B. (2019), "Dominion energy brings BVLOS experience to small UAV coalition," *Unmanned Aerial*, August 1, [accessed

from https://unmanned-aerial.com/dominion-energy-brings-bvlos-experience-to-small-uav-coalition].
90. NYPA (2017), "First ever drone inspection of Niagara Ice Boom," *NY Power Authority*, January 27, [accessed from https://www.nypa.gov/news/press-releases/2017/20170127-drone-inspection].
91. OG&E (2017), "Move over Amazon; OG&E using drones for storm recovery," *Oklahoma Gas and Electric*, March 15, [accessed from https://ogeenergy.gcs-web.com/news-releases/news-release-details/move-over-amazon-oge-using-drones-storm-recovery].
92. Feloni, R., & A. Taube (2014), "These drone-based advertisements were super cool and only a little creepy," *Business Insider*, September 29, [accessed from https://www.businessinsider.com/drones-in-advertising-2014-9].
93. Walgrove, A. (2016), "How 3 major brands are using drone marketing to reach new heights," *Sprinklr*, June 2, [accessed from https://blog.sprinklr.com/brands-using-drones-marketing/]; Agrawal, A. J. (2017), "5 Ways marketers can take advantage of drone technology," Forbes, June 10, [accessed from https://www.forbes.com/sites/ajagrawal/2017/06/10/5-ways-marketers-can-take-advantage-of-drone-technology/#489af0de58cc]*.
94. Intel (2020), "Why an Intel® drone light show?" *Intel.com*, [accessed from https://www.intel.com/content/www/us/en/technology-innovation/aerial-technology-light-show.html].
95. Nearly 88% of respondents cited a change in the regulatory environment as a key growth driver for the subsequent use of drones (Comptia (2019), "The drone market: Insights from customers and providers," *Comptia*, June, [accessed from https://www.comptia.org/content/research/drone-industry-trends-analysis]).

10

Transformative Marketing Using Blockchain

Overview

In the NAT environment, blockchain technology is rapidly gaining attention among firms and users. Blockchain operates on a peer-to-peer (P2P) network and is characterized as a distributed ledger technology wherein data can be stored on servers anywhere in the world. Such a system allows for the creation of a permanent record of actions while providing the participants of the system the ability to verify each action ever performed. Essentially, this technology works based on creating a distributed consensus in the digital online world, thereby firmly establishing trust in actions even when operating in the online world.

The promise of this technology can be seen in its global growth. According to the IDC, the market for blockchain solutions is expected to reach $6.6 billion by 2024, growing at a five-year compound annual growth rate (CAGR) of 48% between 2019 and 2024.[1] Additionally, the IDC study makes 3 bold predictions for the future of blockchain into the year 2028. First, the market for crypto loans will grow to $5 trillion by 2026 as more people use them as a standard platform for both lenders and borrowers. Second, as a technology channel for private and public stocks, debt, and derivatives, by 2027, 50% of new securities issued globally will be NFTs (or Blockchain-based tokens). Finally, assuming trade ecosystems become interoperable, standardized, technology-neutral, and widely available to clients by 2028, digital trade finance transactions will account for 30% of all trade finance transactions. Key factors like cybersecurity and risk, digital business, economic instability, ecosystem-based innovation, embracing the metaverse, global supply shock, and storms of disruption are what are driving these forecasts.

Bolstered by several salient features such as economic considerations, being Internet-savvy, and enhanced privacy settings, this technology is gaining acceptance and usage in various commercial and industrial settings. For instance, a global Deloitte survey found that in the next 24 months, digital assets will be "very/somewhat important" to their respective businesses, according to roughly 80% of all respondents.[2]

This chapter is organized as follows. First, a brief history of the origin of blockchain is presented, followed by a definition of blockchain (from a marketing standpoint). Then, a discussion on the various classifications of blockchain is presented spanning individual to commercial uses such as security applications, interfacing technology between other NATs, and end-user applications. Next, some marketing applications of blockchain focusing on understanding customer needs, revisiting firm capabilities to integrate blockchain, designing blockchain-focused marketing mix strategies, driving CE through blockchain, and designing digital strategies with blockchain are discussed. Finally, the future of blockchain for the marketing industry is envisioned through specific business- and customer-facing tasks such as the role of blockchain in shaping data and transaction security, ensuring advertising transparency, and powering online marketing campaigns.

Origin, Definition, and Classification of Blockchain

Origin

The development of blockchain technology is the most recent among the NATs considered in this book. Its origins can be traced back to 2008 when Satoshi Nakamoto first proposed the introduction of the first cryptocurrency—Bitcoin, a blockchain-based digital currency application.[3] The Bitcoin application is based on cryptographic proof instead of the traditional third-party mediation for two willing parties to execute an online transaction over the Internet.[4] For instance, when two parties (say A and B) want to transact over the Internet using blockchain, the general operational procedure of the transaction would be as follows. When A wishes to send money to B, a "block" denoting the transaction is created online. Then, the network participants are notified of the transaction's intent and initiation. The network participants then approve the transaction as legitimate.

The block can then be appended to the chain indicating its authenticity and permanence in history. Following this, the money gets transferred to B. The two critical aspects that are verified before recording any transaction are (a) A maintains and owns the cryptocurrency that they would like to send and (b) A holds enough cryptocurrency balance in their account for the proposed transaction, after checking their transaction details with other members in the network. The entire transaction is protected with the presence of public keys and private keys (see Image 10.1). Studies such as Crosby et al.,[5] de Kruijff and Weigand,[6] Lin and Liao,[7] Zheng et al.,[8] and Zīle and Strazdiņa[9] offer a detailed exposition of the working details and structure of blockchain.

As the origins of blockchain started with Bitcoin, the two have been mistaken for each other, with many instances of interchangeable usage.[10] Whereas Bitcoin is the first successful cryptocurrency created to address the need for a secure online digital currency, prior attempts at creating a cryptocurrency faced several challenges. These attempts include the creation

Image 10.1 Bitcoin. Bitcoins are used widely as a reliable means of digital currency (*Source* Photo by David Shares on Unsplash)

of ecash, HashCash, Digicash, and e-gold, among others.[11] After Bitcoin's success, several cryptocurrencies have been developed such as Ethereum, Ripple, Litecoin, Cardano, and Solana to name a few. While Bitcoin ushered in a new way of transacting online safely and securely, the underlying blockchain technology has found subsequent uses in several real-world applications such as distribution, finance, healthcare, and supply chain, among others.

Definition

Blockchain refers to a distributed ledger and immutable database for securely transferring data. The name is a combination of two words—the "block" that contains batched transactions and a "chain" that represents cryptographically linked blocks.[12,13,14] It is important to note that there is no consensus on a globally accepted definition of blockchain, and there are several conceptualizations of blockchain.[15] Table 10.1 provides a flavor of the various conceptualizations of blockchain.

Blockchain technology is better understood by considering the underlying elements driving it. A brief discussion of the main elements is provided here.

Decentralized. Traditional online transaction systems require the involvement of a central agency (such as a central bank) that is trusted with monitoring and regulating the smooth functioning of the system. Such a setup invariably adds procedures and protocols to the operational aspects of the transactions thereby imposing monetary and non-monetary costs on the transacting parties. In a blockchain network, no centralized authority monitors, oversees, or approves the transactions. Instead, many validating network participants (known as nodes) confirm the transactions' authenticity. In this regard, Nakamoto[16] offers the proof-of-work consensus as an approach that

Table 10.1 Select conceptualizations of Blockchain

Study	Conceptualization of blockchain
Hileman and Rauchs[130]	"…type of distributed ledger that is composed of a chain of cryptographically linked 'blocks' containing batched transactions; generally, broadcasts all data to all participants in the network."
Tama et al.[131]	"…a part of the implementation layer of a distributed software system."
Zheng et al.[132]	"…is distributed and can avoid the single point of failure situation."
Yli-Huumo et al.[133]	"…to create a decentralized environment where no third party is in control of the transactions and data."

can replace the central agency, while providing incentives that would keep the network participants honest.

Secure and Immutable. Blockchain is a replicated ledger format where records may not be altered or removed. Such a setup creates a unique record of the transaction history that is immutable unless most of the nodes decide to do so. This feature establishes trust in the system and creates confidence among users.

Instantaneous. Given that blockchains do not involve intermediaries, are final, and are irreversible, the speed at which transactions can materialize is enormous. Additionally, the instantaneous nature of transactions makes the exchange cheaper as no intervening procedures or oversight are necessary.

Transparent. Each node in a blockchain has access to all the data, and all records can be reviewed and checked publicly. This feature of the blockchain makes it secure and trustworthy to use. Additionally, blockchain allows the creation of third-party applications, as permitted by its open-source architecture. This provides several value offerings to users and creates numerous commercial opportunities for developers.

Hash Functions. A mathematical process known as a cryptographic hash function accepts an input (or "message") and outputs a fixed-length string, which is often a series of digits and letters. The result, also known as the hash value or digest, should be distinct for each input or at the very least exceedingly unlikely to be duplicated. This implies that even the slightest alteration in the input will result in a significantly altered hash.[17]

Tokens and Tokenization. On many blockchains, especially those that support smart contracts, tokens act as a representation of resources or utility. They can serve as a mechanism of commerce inside the blockchain ecosystem or reflect ownership or value supported by an asset. Tokens have the fungibility property, which can categorize them as either fungible or non-fungible. In contrast to traditional currencies, which are interchangeable and of equal value, non-fungible tokens are valued independently and are frequently used to represent digital assets like artwork or collectibles. Utility Tokens give users access to platform services or features. Security tokens represent ownership and are linked to physical assets, much like stock shares in a firm. Asset-backed Tokens are tied to tangible or intangible assets, such as gold. Governance tokens allow token holders to vote on decisions regarding their host blockchain. Tokens are essentially flexible tools in the blockchain, enabling everything from straightforward transactions to intricate platform interactions.[18]

Autonomous. Blockchain ensures that parties around the world can conduct activities online automatically without the need for any human intervention.

Using private/public key algorithms, ensuring trust, verifying transactions or reconciliation efforts can be performed automatically through the software. Essentially, the software ensures that conflicting or double records cannot be permanently written in the ledger. In this regard, algorithms can self-execute, self-enforce, self-verify, and self-constrain the performance of the transactions.[19]

Classification of Blockchain

Research has identified that blockchains can be classified based on the level of access and openness into public, private, and hybrid (see Table 10.2).

As mentioned earlier, while blockchain was developed primarily to develop a secure way of transaction online, later applications of blockchain have identified process economies for firms by expediting and securing the processes and data records underlying interactions and transactions.[20] Such applications of blockchains can be seen in a wide range of industries worldwide. Commercial applications of blockchain usage include data management (e.g., managing contracts, planning network infrastructure, and organizational data management), data authentication (e.g., document verification, quality inspection, and notary services), financial services (e.g., online payments, insurance services and currency exchange), and business processes (e.g., supply chain management, content management services, and media management).

To improve operations, promote transparency, and provide new services, many businesses across numerous industries have implemented blockchain technology. Here are a few noteworthy instances:

- BMW: Traces and verifies the provenance of the minerals used in the construction of their cars using blockchain to ensure ethical sourcing.[21]
- JPMorgan Chase: Launched the "JPM Coin," a digital token used to instantly settle transactions between institutional accounts.[22]
- MediLedger: Blockchain technology is being used by a group of pharmaceutical businesses to track and validate prescription drugs. Its members include the major U.S. wholesalers and top manufacturers including Genentech, Pfizer, Bayer, Gilead, and Amgen.[23]
- Microsoft: Offers blockchain as a service (BaaS) via its Azure cloud computing platform.
- Propy: A global real estate marketplace that uses blockchain to record property deeds and conduct international transactions.[24]

Table 10.2 Classification of Blockchain

Type of blockchain	Meaning	Key features/benefits	Select examples
Public blockchain	• Also known as permissionless blockchain, all participants in the network have access to all the ledgers • No central agency/body manages the network, including approving or banning transactions	• Secured by the combination of economic incentives and cryptographic verification using mechanisms such as proof of work or proof of stake • Adhere to a general principle that the degree to which someone can influence the consensus process is proportional to the number of economic resources that they can bring in[134]	Bitcoin, Ethereum
Private blockchain	• Also known as permission blockchain, authority regarding read and write operations in the blockchain is reserved for limited members • An invitation-only network governed by a central authority that decides the level and extent of read/write access participants get in the operations of the blockchain	• In some cases, readers and writers could be part of blockchains that exist contemporaneously and are interconnected[135] • Allows firms to adopt distributed ledger technology without making data public	Hyperledger, Ripple

(continued)

Table 10.2 (continued)

Type of blockchain	Meaning	Key features/benefits	Select examples
Hybrid blockchain	• Also known as consortium blockchain, the determination of what blocks get added to the chain and what the current state is, is controlled by a select group of participants[136] • Constitutes a hybrid between the public blockchains and the single highly trusted authority model (i.e., private blockchains)	• Here, a group of 10 legal service firms (for instance) may run a blockchain, with at least seven members signing off every block for the block to be valid • The rights to read (i.e., public vs. restricted) the data may be decided by the group and could also vary by each participant	XinFin, Kadena

- Spotify: To aid in tracking credit and royalty payments, Spotify purchased blockchain firm Mediachain.[25]
- Starbucks: Focuses on fair trade principles while using blockchain to track the path of its coffee beans from farmers to shops.[26]
- Walmart: To secure the safety of its food supply, it uses blockchain to track the origin of agricultural items.[27]

These are but a few instances of blockchain implementations. Businesses are quickly adopting blockchain as they become aware of its potential advantages, which range from efficiency and cost savings to transparency and security.[28] To conclude the overview of blockchain, the following three vignettes present the possibilities of blockchain and how companies and users are deriving value from such offerings.

Security-Oriented Technology

As with many NATs, blockchain is a practitioner-driven technology. While proponents of blockchain consider it to be one of the best ways to secure transactions, it is not without concern. Academic research has identified concerns in the privacy and security settings of blockchain, and scripting language design, among others.[29]

Recent academic research efforts have codified security features and attributes of blockchain that can be used to assess, (re)design, and improve newly developed solutions. Specifically, the following six security concepts have been proposed that have gained wide consensus.[30]

- *Accountability*. Also referred to as non-repudiation, this concept states that undeniable proof will exist to verify the truthfulness of any claim of a participant. In the non-profit industry, this could mean tracking the movement of donations (in the form of cryptocurrency) from wallet to wallet, thereby making auditing and accounting easier for the firm.
- *Authenticity*. This concept refers to the identification or verification of the source of origin of data in the network. In the media industry, this could mean using blockchains to verify the source of a news item and tracking the circulation of fake news.
- *Availability*. This concept ensures that network services are available and will survive possible attacks or failures that could occur. This also includes protection against any incident that threatens the network's availability. In an online transaction system, this could mean ensuring the payment system can always serve transaction requests as created by authorized users and complete the requests when the service is active.
- *Confidentiality*. This concept refers to the assurance that data will be disclosed only to authorized individuals or systems. In the case of smart homes fitted with metering devices for measuring utility consumption, this could mean that no entity (other than the customer and the utility company) will have access to the appliance(s) and their usage patterns. Such levels of confidentiality would also include customer preferences regarding how much detail the utility can have access to and what details cannot be accessed.
- *Fairness*. Whereas the concept of fairness can be best understood only in the usage context since the application of fairness could vary accordingly, a general understanding of this concept relates to a protocol that does not discriminate against the honest and correctly participating members. Additionally, transparency could also be related to this concept—one that talks about fair and just usage practices in the network. In the food industry, this could mean companies using blockchains to allow consumers to get detailed information about the origin of ingredients, food preparation, food inspection reports, food recalls, and so on.
- *Integrity*. This concept refers to the assurance that the accuracy of the information is always maintained. This involves not allowing tampering (i.e., changed, modified, or altered) of information by participants not authorized to do so. Additionally, this also involves the detection of unauthorized modifications and the prompt notification of such occurrences

to the network participants. In the manufacturing industry, blockchain integrity could mean verifying 3D printers to deliver finished parts that are in adherence to industry standards and practices. Thus, for integrity purposes, maintaining the consistency, accuracy, and trustworthiness of data over its entire lifecycle becomes crucial.

From the practitioner world, the security aspects of blockchain continue to receive attention. For instance, governance agencies such as ISACA, non-profit organizations such as Open Web Application Security Project (OWASP), and technical associations such as the Institute of Electrical and Electronics Engineers (IEEE) closely monitor and advance the ideal security protocol for blockchains. These organizations regularly develop security standards, conduct ongoing industry discussions, and monitor security risk areas that could impact commercial enterprises.

Link to AI and ML

As mentioned earlier in this book, AI and ML offer significant benefits to the implementing firms and the end users, thereby delivering value to firms and customers. While these two NATs' usefulness has been adequately demonstrated, they are not without concerns or challenges. Specifically, AI operates in the field of automation and continuous learning, acting as the intelligence that drives data-focused analytics and decision-making.[31] ML, on the contrary, deals with the process of training machines to learn over time with the key outcome being predictions about key variables of interest wherein, the quality of learning is dependent on the volume and quality of data. To perform at the peak potential, both AI and ML rely on key conditions. Specifically, while AI relies on data or information to learn, infer, and make final decisions, ML performs better when data is reliable, secure, trusted, and credible.[32]

The challenge for firms arises when the reliance on the above-mentioned key conditions of the two NATs is not ensured. Separately, blockchain focuses on storing data with high integrity and resiliency and cannot be tampered with. Put simply, the key conditions for AI and ML to perform well happen to be one of blockchain's defining characteristics. Such a situation naturally gives rise to complementarities that can well serve both AI/ML and blockchain (for example, the supply chain industry uses blockchain to verify food origins and AI to analyze crop patterns, growing cycles, and price fluctuations). As a result, the consolidation of AI/ML and blockchain can create secure, tamper-free, decentralized systems conducive to high-quality inference, decision-making, and learning. In this regard, both AI/ML and blockchain can improve each technology's efficiency and effectiveness.

AI/ML Improving Blockchain's Effectiveness

Ensuring decentralization, autonomy, immediacy, security, and transparency in a blockchain transaction involves various levels of parameter considerations and nuanced coding, not to mention decision steps resulting in adjustments. AI can ease the decision steps and automate and optimize blockchain for higher performance and better governance.[33]

A key area where AI/ML can make a difference in blockchain effectiveness is security. While blockchains per se are highly secure, the applications developed on top of the blockchain platform are not always so. This makes the platform and all the users vulnerable to hacking.[34] In this regard, AI/ML algorithms can help in detecting attacks on a blockchain and initiating appropriate recourse options. Further, it is possible for AI/ML algorithms to detect and potentially isolate the hacked component so that the rest of the blockchain remains safe. Other areas where AI/ML continues to make a difference in blockchain's effectiveness include predictive analytics, smart contracts, and privacy controls, among others.

Another crucial area where blockchain can aid AI/ML's effectiveness is knowledge management. From a firm standpoint, knowledge has been identified as an asset of the company to be managed,[35] and a key issue of knowledge management is observed to be the organization, distribution, and refinement of knowledge.[36] Additionally, knowledge management has been positively linked to organizational learning,[37] adaptive organizations,[38] and competitive advantage,[39] among other strategic firm outcomes. Given the high level of importance accorded to knowledge, the successful management of knowledge depends on how knowledge is organized and managed. Research has identified the ability, the motivation, and the opportunity to act on the knowledge as important elements in this regard.[40]

Further, establishing the boundary conditions under which knowledge can be utilized is essential. For instance, the presence of an interdisciplinary team that reflects a broad continuum of knowledge levels, the closeness of ties between actors using the knowledge, and the newness of tasks in which the knowledge is being used can help leverage the power of knowledge.[41] Additionally, research has distinguished between information and knowledge and the process of transferring information versus the transfer of knowledge.[42] Here, carefully selecting, interpreting, and integrating knowledge is known to add value to organizations over a mere addition of newer technology tools. In this regard, blockchain can provide a safe and reliable environment wherein firms can use blockchain capabilities to collect, compartmentalize, and provide access to data and information gathered that can subsequently be used in developing AI/ML solutions. In addition, blockchain can encourage data sharing because it provides transparency and accountability regarding which users' data is accessed, when, and by whom.[43] Other areas where blockchain can improve the effectiveness of AI/ML include personalization efforts, data security, data provenance and integrity, collective decision-making, model transparency and traceability, enhanced security, monetization and micropayments, management of hardware networks, crowdsourced model training, ensuring ethical standards, automation and transparency with smart contracts, and decentralized operations leading to firm efficiency, among others.

Blockchain in the Marketing 5.0 World

Blockchain is displaying a lot of potential in revolutionizing marketing by building trust and transparency, enhancing customer engagement, protecting intellectual property, streamlining data management, and enabling new forms of marketing. Additionally, blockchain is also indicating potential applications relating to combating fraud and counterfeiting by creating a tamper-proof record of all transactions, improving supply chain efficiency by creating a single, shared source of truth for supply chain data, and enabling new forms of payment such as cryptocurrency, among others. Expanding on the Marketing 5.0 concept discussed in Chapter 2, this section presents how robotics and intelligent automation operate in the Marketing 5.0 world. Particularly, this section discusses five examples of where robotic applications are applied through the lens of Marketing 5.0 and establishes how such actions can also bode well for humanity.

Data-Driven Marketing Using Blockchain

The combination of data-driven marketing and blockchain technology has opened new possibilities for businesses to enhance their marketing strategies. With blockchain, marketers can track and verify every step of the customer journey, from the initial interaction to the final purchase. This level of transparency not only builds trust with customers but also allows marketers to optimize their operations by identifying the most effective channels, messages, and offers.

Consider the case of ride-sharing apps. Despite their popularity, the business model of ride-sharing companies faces serious challenges such as labor regulations (e.g., wage levels, classification of drivers, etc.), competitive threats (e.g., self-driving vehicles, increase in food delivery services, etc.), pricing structure (e.g., surge pricing, free promotional rides, etc.), and regulatory compliance (e.g., federal lawsuits, city ordinances, etc.), among others. A distinguishing feature of the current ride-sharing services business model is the centralization of demand and supply of rides. This implies that a request for a ride is not always satisfied immediately, and drivers often lack a steady line of rides. The ideal scenario, however, should be different. Specifically, the need for a ride for a rider must be met immediately with little to no wait time and the supply of drivers must be consistent so that they have a steady stream of rides with little to no downtime. This is where blockchain can make a difference.

Blockchain-based apps such as Drife and Arcade City are changing the way ridesharing is done by focusing on decentralizing operations.[44] For instance, Drife uses blockchain to offer non-commission rides and incentivize services; instead, they charge drivers an annual fee for access to the app. Similarly, Arcade City enables riders and drivers to connect directly with each other; wherein, drivers determine their charges, and work hours and establish their base of repeat customers. Another ride-sharing service, TADA, operating in South Korea aims to bring riders, drivers, and car parts manufacturers into one ecosystem. Apart from being a zero-commission service and instituting a rewards system for drivers, this blockchain service records the entire vehicle history such as maintenance, repairs, previous rides, and rating of the driver to improve services to customers.[45] Therefore, blockchain can provide significant benefits to users by way of changing the way ride-sharing works.

Predictive Marketing Using Blockchain

The incorporation of blockchain technology in predictive marketing has presented businesses with fresh opportunities to acquire valuable knowledge about their intended customer base. With blockchain, marketers can access a vast network of data that is securely stored and verified by multiple participants. This eliminates the need for intermediaries and ensures the authenticity and integrity of the data. By analyzing this data, businesses can identify patterns, trends, and correlations that can help them make informed decisions about their marketing campaigns.

Consider the case of Volvo. The automobile company has implemented an innovative approach to enhance its supply chain network by harnessing real-time data and creating a digital twin. This enables the company to effectively calculate and analyze the CO_2 emissions associated with its supply chain operations.[46] By closely examining the sourcing procedures for nickel, a crucial component in batteries, Volvo discovered a significant disparity in prices depending on the location and extraction methods. It became evident that the CO_2 impact of one ton of nickel can vary considerably based on its source.

To address this issue, Volvo has turned to blockchain technology to trace the materials used in batteries, including nickel, cobalt, and lithium. In a strategic move, Volvo Cars made an undisclosed investment in Circulor, a blockchain technology provider, in 2020. This partnership has allowed Volvo to gain transparency into its battery supply chain, utilizing Circulor's blockchain application throughout the process. Furthermore, Volvo has extended the use of blockchain technology to monitor the CO_2 impact of these minerals, encompassing both mining and processing stages, as well as their transportation to the battery cell production site. By implementing these measures, Volvo can precisely track the shipment of parts and materials, thereby comprehending the environmental footprint of the transportation process.

Contextual Marketing Using Blockchain

The integration of blockchain into contextual marketing has brought significant advancements in how brands connect with their target audience. With blockchain, marketers can now track and verify the authenticity of user data, ensuring that the information used for targeting is reliable and up to date. This not only enhances the effectiveness of contextual marketing but also fosters trust between brands and consumers, as users have more control over their transactions and can trust their engagement with brands.

Consider the act of counterfeiting. While brands cannot easily prevent counterfeiters from creating versions of the original products, they can introduce processes that evaluate the authenticity of the products. In 2021, to tackle the problem of counterfeiting, major global luxury brands joined together in investing in blockchain and associated technologies, which led to the creation of the Aura Blockchain Consortium. It was founded by LVMH, Prada Group, and Cartier (part of Richemont). Mercedes-Benz joined as a founding member in 2022, and the group together aims to develop applications of blockchain technology and raise the standards of luxury. Accordingly, the products of the Aura Blockchain Consortium's members are fitted with a QR code as they leave the warehouse and to the store. Along with the QR Code, any type of authentication technology (like an NFC chip) could be used. When customers buy the product, they can scan the QR code on the item, claim ownership, and certify its authenticity with access to the product information. This generates a certificate of authenticity which will be made available digitally. As the brand becomes known for authenticating its products on the blockchain, people will get familiar with using QR Codes, NFC, and other AI solutions—thus creating demand in primary and secondary markets for genuine luxury products.[47]

In addition to authenticating luxury goods, Blockchain also opens new channels of engagement, builds customer loyalty, and creates the means to build brand-centric communities. For instance, consider the Italian clothing retailer—Diesel. The brand is exploring the possibilities of using NFTs through its D:verse platform, which offers wearables alongside a limited-edition physical collection. D:verse community also offers exclusive benefits (invitations to real-world fashion shows, pre-sales access, etc.) to its customers. Thus, Diesel can identify loyal customers who value being a part of the online community and engage with such customers in innovative ways.[48]

In another implementation of blockchain, establishing provenance, in wines, for example, remained a big challenge to the industry players until the use of blockchain. Crurated, a member- and blockchain-based membership wine community, is leveraging the blockchain and NFTs with every bottle of wine that enters their warehouse. Moreover, the company allows its members to participate in the bidding for fractional barrel offerings wherein members can bid for the liters that they want of the wine from the finest wine producers.[49] Additionally, members can also pick the size of the bottles they would like and personalize the labeling. By using blockchain technology, Crurated has not only addressed the problem of wine origin but also made the process more democratic. In this regard, the company has been able to attract a younger audience due to the accessible nature of blockchain. Since the platform's debut in 2021, 70 percent of members are younger than 45 years old, and 35 percent are under 35 years old.[50] For a product that has been largely consumed by people over 60 years, this opens a new market segment for the company to cater to.

Augmented Marketing Using Blockchain

Augmented marketing using blockchain aims to enhance marketing experiences, increase transparency, and improve user engagement. Instances of how these manifests include tokenizing content using blockchain that allows content creators to be rewarded with tokens when users interact with or view their content, integrating gaming into marketing campaigns for a superlative marketing experience, allowing users to unlock special experiences or discounts as part of the loyalty programs; and validating the effectiveness of advertising efforts, among others.

While the applications of blockchain in augmenting marketing activities are being actively documented, its use in non-business applications is also being increasingly identified. Consider the case of voter management. Regardless of the geographic location, voter turnout receives significant media and research attention, given its long-lasting implications on governance and policymaking.[51] Additionally, a blockchain-based system has been identified as helpful in combating voter fraud.[52] Further, start-ups such as Voatz, Follow My Vote, and BitCongress have created secure voting systems that aim to create secure voting options. Such voting systems ensure that a vote is recorded only one time to a candidate of the voter's choice that cannot be changed. Further, such applications have additional features such as sharing opinions on civic and citizen issues, thereby increasing the usefulness of such applications.[53] In 2020, the state of West Virginia in the United States discontinued its usage of the Voatz platform indefinitely, citing industry experts' security worries.[54] Although these pilots are still in the early stages and have difficulties, they demonstrate how blockchain technology can completely change how we think about and trust digital voting systems.

Agile Marketing Using Blockchain

Agile marketing is a marketing approach that emphasizes flexibility, iteration, and rapid response to change. It focuses on short sprints, continuous feedback, and adaptation to changing requirements. Such usage of blockchain allows companies to deliver value to end users.

Consider the use of blockchain in food safety systems. The salmon industry in Norway is currently encountering difficulties in implementing effective tracking methods for its salmon. A recent study conducted in 2019 examined the supply chains and sourcing practices of various salmon products sold in European supermarkets such as Sainsbury's, Aldi, and Tesco. The study revealed that many of these products, despite having environmental certifications like Responsible Supply, were likely produced using fishmeal and fish oil obtained through highly unsustainable fishing practices in countries like India, Vietnam, and the Gambia.[55] In response to this issue, Atea, a Norwegian technology firm, has partnered with IBM's blockchain-based platform Food Trust and the Norwegian Seafood Association to establish the Norwegian Seafood Trust. This network, built on blockchain technology, collaborates with major fish farming companies worldwide. By gathering extensive data on fish welfare, water quality, genetics, feed, processing, and distribution, the industry is experiencing unprecedented levels of transparency and accessibility to valuable information.[56]

Moreover, by allowing firms to be transparent about tracking the food origins, blockchain in food safety systems can benefit in a variety of ways such as (a) improving sustainability by reducing waste, (b) lowering costs by eliminating food system efficiencies, (c) tracking foodborne outbreaks, (d) counterfeit foods, (e) enhanced food data resulting in efficient food flows, among others.[57] Essentially, if the entire production and supply chain system is logged onto the blockchain, consumers can easily trace their food from its origin to their plates (see Image 10.2). This makes it easy for regulators to identify and control the source of any food-based illnesses. Companies such as Alibaba, Carrefour, Greenfence, and Walmart are using blockchain to bring efficiency to food chains such that users can be aware of the food journey from farm to table.[58]

Image 10.2 Tracking food origin using blockchain. Nestlé allows users to trace the coffee origins of their Zoégas coffee brand through blockchain-recorded data (*Source* Photo by *Katya Austin* on *Unsplash*)

Current Blockchain Applications in Marketing

Aside from the critical data management capabilities for firms, blockchain presents several marketing applications valued by firms. Particularly, what makes blockchain appealing to firms is its ability to automate the process of drawing and managing structured and UD from diverse sources, and provide instant access in a discernible manner, while maintaining the integrity and sanctity of data.[59] Additionally, blockchain can help avoid data duplication and unify data entries to present an accurate and holistic perspective on customers. This section presents five specific application areas where blockchain continues to help companies in developing marketing actions.

Understanding Customer Needs to Deploy Blockchain

A recent development in consumer expectations is the need to know the source of firm offerings they consume (e.g., food, medicines, donations, etc.). For instance, in the case of the agri-food industry, research has found that rational decision-making, utility maximization, systematic interpretation of information, and optimal choice are hampered because information is often imperfect, incomplete, inaccessible, asymmetrically distributed, non-standardized, or costly to collect.[60] Such a situation gives rise to information asymmetry among consumers, which leads them to make choices that are not in line with their preferences.[61] Further, when faced with information uncertainties, research has found that users do not behave as if they were maximizing expected utility.[62] In this regard, research has identified that if asymmetric information is at the core of market failures and sub-optimal choices, it can reasonably be assumed that better information and more transparency will be at the core of any solution.[63] Blockchain presents one such solution that offers consumers access to information on request safely and transparently.

Using blockchain, consumers can trace the journey of the products and components to verify their authenticity. Additionally, under blockchain's transparency, users can also evaluate the alignment of a firm's values with their values. Specifically, they can follow the journey of firms' offerings through the supply chain, verify smart contracts and ownership transfers, and so on, giving them greater insight into the firms' offerings.[64] The following list provides a few recent applications of blockchain that focus on providing information and transparency to consumers.

- Alibaba is considering blockchain solutions for coordinating cross-border supply chain activities.[65]
- Everledger uses NATs like IoT, AI, and blockchain to track the movement of goods from raw materials source to sales, to provide greater clarity and confidence in marketplaces.[66] To ensure ethical EV battery recycling, Everledger and Ford announced the beginning of a world-first battery passport pilot in October 2022.[67]
- In Europe, Carrefour uses blockchain technology to ensure the traceability of 24 products, including chicken. Using a mobile device, customers can scan a QR code on a packet of chicken to get details regarding the bird's birth, daily feed, bird's origin (farm/farmer), the type of slaughter and processing, and its arrival in store.[68] With its announcement that it would begin using blockchain technology with its products in April 2022, Carrefour Bio is blazing new ground. The project is motivated by customers' increased demand for transparency regarding the origins of organic products and the manufacturing processes utilized to create them.[69]
- Volkswagen and Renault have developed telematics systems that capture a vehicle's data on mileage, maintenance, and repair; and the engine usage history via the blockchain that can then be used by manufacturers, buyers, insurance companies, and dealers to know about a vehicle.[70] In July 2021, Renault Group implemented in numerous Renault plants around Europe, a new blockchain system for the certification of vehicle compliance, called XCEED. This is the first industrial-scale blockchain project in the automotive industry.[71]

Revisiting Firm Capabilities to Integrate Blockchain

While firm capabilities may refer to a wide range of functional areas, with regard to blockchain, four specific firm capabilities come to the fore—data management, nature of exchanges, organizational excellence arising from internal processes, and managing supply chain partners. Implementing blockchain in an organization calls for reviewing how firms can improve on these four firm capabilities to ensure that the firm is equipped and well-prepared to handle the new marketplace demands.

Companies have started to make considerable progress in improving these capabilities when introducing blockchain solutions.[72] For instance, regarding data management, LogSentinel and ReCheck in Bulgaria have developed blockchain solutions that will allow Bulgarian businesses to expand their activities outside of the country while ensuring the security of communication and data sharing. Additionally, services such as digitizing documents, authenticating documents, and maintaining secure digital identities are also possible with the new blockchain platform.[73] With regard to the nature of exchanges, De Beers and other diamond manufacturers have developed a blockchain platform called Tracr that can successfully track a diamond through the value chain, providing asset-traceability assurance.[74, 75]

Regarding managing supply chain partners, Vodafone aims to integrate blockchain into its internal processes to advance its supply chain by promoting and verifying suppliers through a digital identity platform. Further, this platform can influence procurement decisions alongside other standard criteria, such as safety, value, delivery, and technology when Vodafone invites suppliers to work with them.[76] Utilizing the Internet of Things (IoT), the Digital Asset Broker (DAB) division of Vodafone has partnered with the Aventus blockchain network to track cargo pods. Using a special SIM card embedded with a DAB IoT identification passport, DAB logs data on the blockchain while cargo pods travel. To resolve the expensive problem of missing cargo pods, also known as Unit Load Devices, Aventus has previously worked with Heathrow Airport to track luggage, mail, and freight.[77]

A successful integration of blockchain in firms would therefore imply (a) greater traceability of assets, titles, and currencies, (b) direct firm–customer transactions, without the involvement of intermediaries, (c) greater data security, and (d) quicker processing of contracts, transactions, and title transfers.[78]

Designing Marketing Mix Strategies with Blockchain

As mentioned earlier, blockchain offers process economies by expediting and securing the processes and data records' underlying interactions and transactions.[79] This implies that blockchain's security and automatic execution of transactions help hasten processes that would otherwise be dependent on the approval of intermediaries or transacting parties. By specifying the conditions under which a transaction may be executed, a blockchain allows two or more parties to complete their transactions efficiently and more quickly, with greater security of data and assets. Such critical implications on data, assets, and processes ultimately reflect on the marketing mix variables of the implementing firms. Specifically, companies that have been successful in implementing blockchain have realized impressive gains in each of the four key marketing mix variables—product, price, place, and promotion, as seen from the following examples.

Product. Blockchain is being effectively used to secure firm offerings. This can be seen in various industry applications such as retail, pharmaceuticals, transportation, automobiles, healthcare, and real estate, among others. For instance, Indonesia has announced plans to implement blockchain solutions to enhance the efficiency and security of global trade and support information sharing and transparency between all supply chain members.[80] Through actions such as container tracking, monitoring of shipment transit time, and shipment movement information, blockchain can improve shipment visibility and increase trust among the transacting members. Similarly, the Indian state of Andhra Pradesh has adopted blockchain solutions to facilitate land registration. This solution, apart from digitizing the purchase and sale of land, works towards avoiding potential land ownership disputes, as the ownership details are secure, transparent, and indisputable.[81] Other countries that have initiated the adoption of blockchain for land registry purposes include the United States, Sweden, Switzerland, France, Japan, and Brazil.[82] The whole route of diamonds, from extraction to retail, is tracked by De Beers using blockchain technology. This guarantees and confirms that diamonds are obtained ethically and without passing through conflict areas. This increases the product's authenticity and ethical assurance for consumers. By providing adequate protection in safeguarding a firm's assets, blockchain can be efficiently integrated to manage products and services in a wide range of industries.

Price. While blockchain may not be directly used in pricing strategies of firm offerings, it does have an indirect effect on prices, through cost savings. For instance, Data Gumbo's blockchain technology designed specifically for oil and gas companies to automate payments is expected to generate about $3.7 billion annually in cost savings for the implementing companies.[83] Such cost savings can then be used to create value by capturing lost revenues and generating new revenue sources. In this regard, the biggest impact area of blockchain in an organization is in cost savings by enhancing operational efficiencies. A recent study found that approximately 70 percent of the value at stake in the short term for firms implementing blockchain is in cost reduction.[84] In this regard, over time, blockchain could guide firms beyond just realizing cost savings to generating value, thereby moving away from a price-conscious mode of operation. This would likely manifest through new business models and enhanced revenue streams that focus on process efficiencies. Blockchain technology can also be used to guarantee transparent pricing. Examples include blockchain initiatives like Ocean Protocol that seek to democratize the value of data and establish transparent pricing for data services.[85]

Place. Blockchain delivers significant advantages to firms in terms of location. Specifically, firms have started using location intelligence technologies such as GIS to ensure transparency in operations. This has given rise to geo-spatially enabled blockchains, or simply geo-blockchains, that use a crypto-spatial coordinate system to add an immutable spatial context that regular blockchains lack.[86] A key distinguishing feature of a geo-blockchain is the inclusion of proof of location that allows for accurate locating of physical world events. Specifically, geo-blockchain records transactions that are agreed on by all coordinating parties and recorded in one distributed ledger, providing proof of location and other details. Accordingly, geo-blockchain records not just what goods changed hands, but where that happened, and under what conditions (Chiappinelli, 2019). Such a system removes the instances of firms having to reconcile contradicting versions of an object's journey details, as captured by the coordinating parties. Many firms across various industries such as retail, healthcare, manufacturing, and logistics have implemented geo-blockchains to mainly track the origin/journey of goods, in addition to documenting transaction details. For instance, companies such as Walmart, Porsche, DeBeers, Nespresso, and FOAM have adopted geo-blockchain technology to obtain data that all transacting members agree on efficiently (Bolger, 2019).[87]

Promotion. Since blockchain is technology-oriented around the security needs of users,[88] its crucial benefits are seen during interactions between parties. With specific regard to marketing promotions, blockchain can be used effectively in marketing communications and media management. Several firms that have started implementing blockchain for their promotional activities are seeing early gains. For instance, Cathay Pacific has implemented blockchain in managing its loyalty program so that customers, airline partners, and the airline itself can manage member rewards in real time.[89] In terms of media management, Unilever has implemented blockchain to improve online advertising efficiency. Through this implementation, Unilever was able to improve ad reconciliation efficiency wherein advertisers ensure contracted agreements are delivered.[90] Similarly, Toyota implemented a blockchain solution for managing its digital ad strategy. The implemented solution involved directing ad spending in an efficient manner that subsequently reduced ad fraud and increased web traffic by 21 percent.[91]

Additionally, blockchain might offer a remedy for more transparent advertising. In one such instance, the Basic Attention Token (BAT) of the Brave Browser is used to change how consumer ads are delivered. Users receive BAT in return for watching commercials, ensuring a more open and cooperative advertising paradigm. Influencer marketing authenticity certification may be another instance of blockchain-assisted promotion. Blockchain can be used to confirm the legitimacy of influencers' following and engagements, as fraudulent followers and engagement are a major concern in influencer marketing. Platforms like SocialBook give businesses the tools enabled by blockchain they need to ensure authentic influencer collaborations.[92] Finally, content authenticity may be achieved using blockchain. Blockchain technology can be used to validate promotional information in the age of fake news. For instance, The New York Times has been experimenting with using blockchain to verify news images and other information.[93]

Driving Customer Engagement Through Blockchain

Blockchain has enormous potential in allowing firms to engage with their customers which can result in enhanced levels of direct contribution (i.e., purchases) and indirect contribution (i.e., referrals, influence, and feedback) to the firm.[94] Companies that have implemented blockchain to improve CE have started seeing early success. For instance, counterfeiting in the wine industry is estimated to cost the industry around $70 billion annually.[95] To stave off such losses and improve revenues, blockchain is being used to remedy the situation.

For instance, Cellr is a blockchain solution that embeds RFID tags in bottle caps that allow wine buyers to verify the product's origin and that the wine has not been tampered with. Further, through a mobile phone app the RFID tags are designed to deliver product information, conduct promotions/content, offer usage tips, and provide product discounts that can improve customer engagement. Additionally, in the event of the cap being tampered with, a message regarding the breach can be sent to the prospective buyer and/or the company officials. Therefore, blockchain is being used to not only protect the firm's offering but also drive CE which can ensure customers continue to stay with the firm. Miller Lite uses blockchain to engage with its customers. The company has designed and deployed a mobile game about beers and has geo-targeted customers in over 230,000 bars and restaurants across the US Consumers answering all the trivia questions correctly get to win a $5 prize that can be used to purchase a Miller Lite. This game is built on blockchain and uses non-fungible tokens to provide the quiz, social badges, and rewards for social media sharing and to ensure that the $5 prize token cannot be counterfeited.[96]

Research has identified that strengthening loyalty can help stimulate CE.[97] In this regard, aside from promoting one-time uses, blockchain is also being used to promote CE by building/strengthening customer loyalty. For instance, online beauty brand Cult Beauty implemented blockchain to provide information to enable decision-making, ensure transparency regarding product information, and communicate the sustainable impact of their products (i.e., vegan, cruelty-free, recyclable, etc.) to their shoppers directly and consistently. This system is expected to improve engagement and loyalty for both the brands and the retailer.[98] Similarly, blockchain is also being used to manage reward points. For instance, Singapore Airlines' digital wallet, KrisPay, allows members to transfer KrisFlyer points to partner retail merchants in real time. The redeemed points can be applied across a variety of retailers in several product categories. Further, rewards can be used for either full or partial payment and accumulate in the same way as traditional miles.[99] NBA Top Shot, a platform developed by Dapper Labs on the Flow blockchain, enables fans to purchase, sell, and exchange legally licensed NBA collectible highlights. Both basketball fans and cryptocurrency enthusiasts have been highly engaged because of these digital "moments".[100] Therefore, blockchain is being increasingly used to drive CE, with more companies expressing interest and commitment to do so.

Designing Digital Strategies with Blockchain

Blockchains have two key characteristics—they are distributed, and they are in digital form.[101] Therefore, they have much to contribute in terms of aiding firms in designing digital strategies. To understand blockchain's contribution in designing digital strategies, firms need to ascertain two critical components—the capabilities they have, and the value they intend to generate.[102]

The journeys that companies undergo in developing their said capabilities are largely unique. In this regard, research has investigated the differences between legacy firms and digital natives in developing certain capabilities.[103] Developing successful digital strategies requires substantial upfront and sustained investment in firm capabilities in three key areas—technology, marketing, and human resources.

The existing technological capabilities (i.e., software, applications, systems, and technical know-how) of firms will inform them of their preparedness to embrace the digital ecosystem and identify gaps to be filled to achieve digital maturity. While digital natives are expected to be well-prepared in technological expertise and know-how, legacy firms will have to adopt a more thoughtful approach to making them technologically adept.

A legacy firm that has successfully used blockchain to revamp itself is Kodak. The company has been having a difficult time since the introduction of smartphones and advanced digital photography formats. In 2018, Kodak used blockchain technology to launch KodakOne, a digital management platform for the creation of an encrypted digital ledger of copyright ownership. Accordingly, photographers can add new images as well as archive images to the system. The blockchain system stores the images in a public ledger format, thereby providing protection to the rightful owners of the image and preventing any ownership dispute.[104] Further, Kodak subsequently announced the launch of their token named KodakCoin, designed to work on the KodakOne platform to provide a completely secure method of digital rights management for photographers. Accordingly, token holders will be able to upload new images, archive older work, and manage rights for their images on the platform.[105]

With periodic changes in customer needs, constant updating of marketing capabilities is essential for firms to develop successful digital strategies. Given recent consumer preferences to know about a product's origin and journey before they make a purchase, luxury brand manufacturer LVMH is implementing blockchain for proving the authenticity of high-priced goods and tracing the origins from raw materials to the point of sale and beyond to the used-goods markets.[106]

The development of successful digital strategies depends on skillful human talent and technology management. In addition to relevant talent acquisition and management, technological capabilities also include continuous learning management, especially regarding NATs and organizational vision in incorporating all relevant NATs in all value-creating functions. Since technology is constantly evolving, employees also need to be able to don multiple hats, work across departmental silos, and constantly update and upgrade their skills regarding NATs. Newer firms in traditional industries such as human resource management, legal services, and tourism are changing the narrative of regular business functions. For instance, Aworker is a blockchain-based platform that lets job seekers establish their qualifications instantly, thereby increasing their chances of landing job offers. Additionally, due to the transparent and decentralized nature of blockchain, such a system increases the speed and efficiency of assessing the candidates and determining the best competitive compensation packet in real time. Companies can therefore minimize their hiring and onboarding expenses in an impactful manner than the traditional way.[107]

The success of digital strategy implementations also depends on the problem(s) the digital strategy is attempting to solve. Specifically, firms must be clear in establishing what value is being created via the digital strategy and for whom.[108] For instance, the value created through a blockchain implementation could focus on (a) conducting transactions (e.g., Ripple for global payments through various financial institutions), (b) negotiating contracts (e.g., BitProperty allows anyone anywhere in the world (except the United States and Japan) to invest in real estate), (c) aggregation and/or dissemination of information (e.g., RiskBlock provides proof of insurance and notice of loss to insurers and insurance companies), (d) establishing authenticity (e.g., Provenance provides chain-of-custody and certification details of supply chains), (e) managing access control (e.g., MedRec provides secure access to patient records for patients and authorized medical professionals), (f) rights management (e.g., Monegraph enables artists to define their licensing terms and facilitate transactions with publishers or digital-art buyers) and (g) securing ownership control (e.g., Ubiquity records property information to ensure a clean record of ownership), among others. Further, such value can be created for one or more groups of users such as customers, firms, financial intermediaries, government, channel partners, and citizens, among others.

The Future of Blockchain in Marketing

The discussion thus far has focused on what blockchain can offer to individuals and organizations. To provide a brief recap, blockchain is a foundational technology that consists of an electronic, distributed ledger and creates an immutable database for securely transferring data. The decentralization of records ensures that no single point of weakness exists, which lowers the likelihood of hacking and data breaches. Additionally, the decentralization of the ledger implies that no single entity can make changes to the ledger without following a consensus protocol, in which most of the users on the network must agree with the change after authenticating themselves via mathematical algorithms. Further, the blockchain's security and automatic execution of transactions help hasten processes that would otherwise be dependent on the approval of intermediaries or transacting parties. In all, blockchain exemplifies the following three distinguishing elements: (a) decentralized electronic records secured by cryptography, implying greater security, (b) immutability of records and consensus-based system ensure the integrity of records through the blockchain, and (c) allows disintermediation rendering the middle-men unnecessary through automated execution of contracts.[109] Looking ahead, the future of blockchain for marketing purposes appears to be promising and varied. While we can expect progress in blockchain capabilities in many organizational areas, three areas that stand out are discussed here.

Data and Transaction Security

It is almost a given that newer technological innovations pay closer attention to making the usage experience safe and secure for all users concerning data and transaction security, compared to legacy technologies. This is also largely reflective of user needs and preferences in adopting newer technologies that stem from their concern about losing control over their data.[110] Yet, research among users has uncovered that when privacy is offered at the expense of loss of user experience, users are more likely to stay away from selecting the choice that would offer them greater protection.[111] Businesses must contend with and navigate this challenging paradox thereby requiring them to carefully balance business operations and security setting preferences. Even within companies, differences in attitudes towards security in the blockchain platform exist.[112,113]

In the future, blockchain offerings could increasingly focus on tapping newer sources of value for all the stakeholders involved, rather than be limited to serving functional benefits. In this regard, the following key guiding principles are expected to motivate companies to develop innovative business models and generate more value.[114] First, blockchain will not offer data and transaction security protection; instead, the appropriate security features will have to be decided based on the various business contexts. Second, no technology is perfect, and integrating a newer technology with existing systems may expose (new) security threats. Finally, there is a trade-off between security and efficiency, and determining levels of acceptable performance may be necessary to finalize the appropriate security settings.

Impact on Advertising Transparency

The US advertising industry has posted consistent performance in the past few years, with two notable outcomes. First, in 2018 digital advertising revenues crossed $100 billion for the first time to reach $107.5 billion.[115] Second, in 2019 the half-yearly advertising revenues crossed $50 billion for the first time to reach $57.9 billion.[116] These two impressive firsts indicate industry vitality and impactful changes that could continue in the future.

An industry development that has played a crucial role in this improved performance is the programmatic advertising model adopted by the industry. Programmatic advertising (PA) refers to the use of software, automated processes, machines, and algorithms to buy digital advertising. Here, advertisers buy targeted page views and audiences on a spot market through real-time auctions.[117] This contrasts with traditional advertising where proposals for ads are developed, tenders are called for, price quotes are generated, and price negotiation is involved before the ad spots are decided. The growth of PA is impressive and is estimated to account for 88 percent of all digital ads in the United States by 2021.[118, 119]

The quick growth and positive impact of PA can be observed through the major benefits it presents (especially over the traditional advertising models) to the ad ecosystem—that is, firms, ad agencies, and consumers.[120] First, the reach of PA is much wider. Since multiple ad exchanges are involved in the selection, firms can cast a wider net in terms of audience reach and potential ad spaces instantly. Essentially, this improves the scale of advertising while keeping the cost of advertising from going up. Second, firms and ad agencies have real-time access to data on ad placements and activity, thereby improving transparency of the process. Third, the real-time data on ad placements and activity is complemented with real-time data on ad insights. This allows firms and ad agencies to change the scope and content of the ad campaigns on short notice. Fourth, PA goes beyond just impressions and click-through rates. Specifically, it enables specific targeting, creating ideal user profiles, geo-targeting, and personalization to reach the right audiences. Finally, since automation is the key driver of this ad model, not only do firms get to decide on launching the campaigns immediately, but also avoid reaching out to users who are not their audiences. This instills efficiency and robustness in developing and running ad campaigns. Even though PA serves the ad ecosystem well, the inclusion of blockchain makes it even more appealing. In all the five major benefits, blockchain can potentially improve ad buying efficiency, ensure real-time access to the members of the eco-system, identify ad fraud, provide authenticity of information, and ensure that there are only authorized people involved in the ad campaign (see Image 10.3).

In this regard, Pepsico recently tested the viability of using blockchain to ensure advertisers only pay for ads served in environments deemed to be viewable, safe for the brand, and free of advertising fraud.[121] The trial test involved the comparison of ad campaigns with and without blockchain-based smart contracts, with initial results showing an improved ad efficiency of 28 percent because of using smart contracts. Similarly, for Super Bowl

Image 10.3 Blockchain for advertising effectiveness. Blockchain is used to improve efficiencies in ad buying and ad development
(*Source* Photo by *Scott Graham* on *Unsplash*)

2020, Avocados from Mexico developed a blockchain-powered campaign to recruit, register, reward, and track consumer engagement that resulted in the generation of 53,000 registrations for its loyalty program.[122] Demand Side Platforms (DSPs) and Supply Side Platforms (SSPs), which are middlemen in programmatic advertising, can be eliminated using blockchain, cutting costs and improving transaction efficiency. For instance, NYIAX (New York Interactive Ad Exchange) uses blockchain to provide a platform for trading future ad inventory and is based on the Nasdaq infrastructure.[123] Such early uses of blockchain in digital advertising show that the members of the ad ecosystem can be integrated more tightly while providing enhanced visibility of the transaction details to all members. While the promising results for PepsiCo, Avocados from Mexico, and NYIAX are only in early implementation, the future could see more uses of blockchain in the ad industry that can be truly transformative.

Online Marketing Campaign Management

Recent changes in technology have allowed consumers to interact with firms through a variety of touchpoints that subsequently lead to purchases and continued interaction. In this scenario, online channels are a critical component of the current marketing landscape. Particularly, WOM has increasingly taken a more primary role among marketers wherein, consumers provide information to other consumers who can become potential customers/marketers of the firm offerings they share information about. Consequently, firms are increasingly investing in social channels to rapidly create or propagate their brand through viral content, social media contests, and consumer engagement efforts. To this effect, firms develop and implement online campaigns to serve a set of established goals.

Formally, a campaign (online and offline) refers to a series of interconnected promotional efforts designed to achieve precise marketing goals. Typically, a campaign is composed of one or more promotions, each of which is an initiative, or a device designed to attract the customers' interest. Further, a campaign can be aimed at prospects or existing customers and usually is undertaken within a defined timeframe.[124]

In developing online campaigns, firms have always included social networks as an integral part of the campaign. By connecting three key dimensions—who, what, and when—social networks primarily operate through a wide range of media to enable functions such as exchanging ideas (e.g., blogs and microblogs), networking (e.g., job search), content sharing (e.g., news, video, audio and photo sharing sites), location services (e.g., local networking), promoting products (e.g., websites), providing feedback (e.g., review websites), conducting polls (e.g., online surveys), and so on.

With more firms paying attention to human connection, online campaigns almost always have some form of WOM and/or influencer marketing. The American Marketing Association refers to influencer marketing as "…leveraging individuals who have influence over potential buyers and orienting marketing activities around these individuals to drive a brand message to the larger market".[125] Further, the Marketing Accountability Standards Board defines an influencer as "a person whose views influence other members of the buying center in making the final decision".[126] In the social media setting, research has contributed two key metrics—customer influence effect (CIE) and customer influence value (CIV).[127] Whereas the CIE measures the net spread and influence of a message from an individual, the CIV calculates the monetary gain or loss realized by a firm that is attributable to a customer, through their spread of positive or negative influence. In tracking these two metrics for a company's social media campaign, Kumar et al.[128] demonstrated a 49 percent increase in brand awareness, an 83 per increase in ROI, and a 40 percent increase in sales revenue growth rate, thereby bringing accountability to social media marketing.

In recent times, blockchain has emerged as an attractive addition to a social media manager's toolkit. This is because influencers often recommend a firm's offering(s) that could win over new customers for the firm. That is, the right type of influencer could bring in impressive gains for a firm/brand. While research has devised a way to recognize, identify, and recruit influencers,[129] still operational challenges such as the influencer payment system (which is not often transparent) and customer trust issues in an influencer, among others.

In this regard, blockchain can, through smart contracts, help list the terms and prices of the influencer marketing services; set potential warranty conditions until the conditions of the influencer service have been met; serve as a transparent way for dispute resolution that is; speedily launch marketing campaigns; remove challenges in measuring campaign effectiveness; identify fraudulent messages that could mislead consumers; and integrate members within a single influencer marketing ecosystem (see Image 10.4). In this regard, blockchain-based companies such as SPIN Protocol and Boosto work to bring together marketers and influencers for influence marketing. Similarly, WOM Protocol enables brands, content creators, publishers, and social networks a way to monetize WOM recommendations on any app or platform. While such early implementations are only from digital natives that are built on the blockchain platform, more such implementations could see

Image 10.4 Blockchain for managing influencer marketing. Blockchain can be used to manage influencer marketing programs efficiently
(*Source:* Photo by *NordWood Themes* on *Unsplash*)

even established companies getting into blockchain applications for managing influencer marketing. Overall, the future looks promising for marketing with blockchain now gaining a firm place in a brand manager's toolkit.

Key Terms and Related Conceptualizations

Asset-backed tokens	Tokens that are tied to tangible or intangible assets, such as gold
Blockchain	A distributed ledger and immutable database for securely transferring data
Governance tokens	Tokens that allow token holders to vote on decisions regarding their host blockchain
Hybrid blockchain, or consortium blockchain	A blend of public and private blockchains wherein, the determination of what blocks get added to the chain and what the current state is, is controlled by a select group of participants
Influencer	A person whose views influence other members of the buying center in making the final decision
Influencer marketing	Leveraging individuals who have influence over potential buyers and orienting marketing activities around these individuals to drive a brand message to the larger market
Non-fungible token (NFT)	A token that is valued independently and is frequently used to represent digital assets like artwork or collectibles
Private blockchain, or permission blockchain	An invitation-only blockchain network governed by a central authority that decides the level and extent of read/write access participants get in the operations of the blockchain
Programmatic advertising	The use of software, automated processes, machines, and algorithms to buy digital advertising
Public blockchain, or permissionless blockchain	A blockchain where all participants in the network have access to all the ledgers, and no central agency/body manages the network, including approving or banning transactions
Security tokens	Represent ownership and are linked to physical assets, much like stock shares in a firm

(continued)

(continued)	
Tokens	Flexible tools in the blockchain that enable everything from straightforward transactions to intricate platform interactions
Utility tokens	Give users access to platform services or features

Notes and References

1. IDC. (2022). IDC FutureScape Webcast: Worldwide Blockchain, Crypto, NFT, and Web3 2023 Predictions. International Data Corporation. https://www.idc.com/getdoc.jsp?containerId=US49800122&pageType=PRINTFRIENDLY.
2. Deloitte. (2021). Deloitte's 2021 global blockchain survey. *Deloitte Insights*. https://www2.deloitte.com/content/dam/insights/articles/US144337_Blockchain-survey/DI_Blockchain-survey.pdf.
3. Nakamoto, S. (2008). Bitcoin: A peer-to-peer electronic cash system. www.bitcoin.org/bitcoin.pdf.
4. Crosby, M., Pattanayak, P., Verma, S., & Kalyanaraman, V. (2016). Blockchain technology: Beyond bitcoin. *Applied Innovation Review, 2*(June), 6–19.
5. Crosby, M., Pattanayak, P., Verma, S., & Kalyanaraman, V. (2016). Blockchain technology: Beyond bitcoin. *Applied Innovation Review, 2*(June), 6–19.
6. De Kruijff, J., & Weigand, H. (2017). Understanding the blockchain using enterprise ontology. In *International Conference on Advanced Information Systems Engineering* (pp. 29–43). Springer.
7. Lin, I. C., & Liao, T. C. (2017). A survey of blockchain security issues and challenges. *International Journal of Network Security, 19*(5), 653–659.
8. Zheng, Z., Xie, S., Dai, H., Chen, X., & Wang, H. (2017). An overview of blockchain technology: Architecture, consensus, and future trends. In *2017 IEEE international congress on big data (BigData congress)* (pp. 557–564).
9. Zīle, K., & Strazdiņa, R. (2018). Blockchain use cases and their feasibility. *Applied Computer Systems, 23*(1), 12–20.
10. Akcora, C. G., Gel, Y. R., & Kantarcioglu, M. (2017). Blockchain: A graph primer. *arXiv*. https://arxiv.org/pdf/1708.08749.pdf.

11. Akcora, C. G., Gel, Y. R., & Kantarcioglu, M. (2017). Blockchain: A graph primer. *arXiv*. https://arxiv.org/pdf/1708.08749.pdf; Griffith, K. (2014). A quick history of cryptocurrencies BBTC—Before Bitcoin. *Bitcoin Magazine*. https://bitcoinmagazine.com/articles/quick-history-cryptocurrencies-bbtc-bitcoin-1397682630.
12. Maslova, N. (2018). Blockchain: Disruption and opportunity. *Strategic Finance, 100*(1), 24–29.
13. Condos, J., Sorrell, W. H., & Donegan, S. L. (2016). Blockchain technology: Opportunities and risks. *State of Vermont*. http://www.gaingon.net/pdf2016/4301532863860983.pdf discuss the blockchain as a distributed, electronic database that can hold information—as records, events, transactions, etc. It is maintained through a distributed or shared network of participants using a group consensus protocol. As new blocks continue to be added, the chain grows continuously.
14. Yli-Huumo et al. (2016) offer that since the data is recorded in a public ledger, blockchain provides a decentralized solution for managing transactions without any third-party interference or mediation, implying that the public ledger cannot be modified or deleted after the data has been approved by all nodes, making it safe for use online.
15. Walch, A. (2016). The path of the blockchain lexicon (and the law). *Review of Banking & Financial Law, 36*(3), 713–765.
16. Nakamoto, S. (2008). Bitcoin: A peer-to-peer electronic cash system. www.bitcoin.org/bitcoin.pdf.
17. For instance, the SHA-256 hash function, which is frequently used in Bitcoin, always produces a 256-bit hash, regardless of whether the input is a single character or a whole book (Nakamoto, 2008).
18. Freni, P. & Ferro, E. & Moncada, R. (2022). Tokenomics and blockchain tokens: A design-oriented morphological framework. *LINKS Foundation*. https://www.sciencedirect.com/science/article/pii/S2096720922000094.
19. Aste, T., Tasca, P., & Di Matteo, T. (2017). Blockchain technologies: The foreseeable impact on society and industry. *Computer, 50*(9), 18–28; Clack, C. D., Bakshi, V. A., & Braine, L. (2016). Smart contract templates: Foundations, design landscape and research directions. *arXiv preprint arXiv:1608.00771*.
20. Kumar, V., Ramachandran, D., & Kumar, B. (2020). Influence of new-age technologies on marketing: A research agenda. *Journal of

Business Research. https://www.sciencedirect.com/science/article/abs/pii/S0148296320300151.
21. BMW Group. (2020). BMW Group uses Blockchain to drive supply chain transparency. https://www.press.bmwgroup.com/global/article/detail/T0307164EN/bmw-group-uses-blockchain-to-drive-supply-chain-transparency?language=en.
22. Morgan, N. (2023). JP Morgan Activates Euro Payment Settlement With Its JPM Coin. *Decrypt.* https://decrypt.co/146027/jp-morgan-using-jpm-coin-blockchain-to-settle-euro-payments.
23. Ledger Insights. (2022). MediLedger blockchain developer Chronicled raises $8.3m from True Global Ventures. https://www.ledgerinsights.com/mediledger-blockchain-founder-chronicled-raises-8-3m-from-true-global-ventures/.
24. Nelson, L. (2022). How Blockchain and Cryptocurrency Are Influencing the Real Estate Market. *National Association of Realtors.* https://www.nar.realtor/magazine/real-estate-news/technology/how-blockchain-and-cryptocurrency-are-influencing-the-real-estate.
25. Perez, S. (2017). Spotify acquires blockchain startup Mediachain to solve music's attribution problem. *TechCruch.* https://techcrunch.com/2017/04/26/spotify-acquires-blockchain-startup-mediachain-to-solve-musics-attribution-problem/.
26. Starbucks. (2022) Starbucks Brewing Revolutionary Web3 Experience for its Starbucks Rewards Members. https://stories.starbucks.com/press/2022/starbucks-brewing-revolutionary-web3-experience-for-its-starbucks-rewards-members/.
27. Sristy, A. (2021). Blockchain in the food supply chain—What does the future look like? *Walmart Global Tech.* https://tech.walmart.com/content/walmart-global-tech/en_us/news/articles/blockchain-in-the-food-supply-chain.html.
28. Kumar et al. (2020) discuss five key benefits that blockchain brings to firms—transparency in business operations, reduced processing time for transactions, ability to track the impact of marketing communications on consumers better, automation of the execution of contracts, direct compensation of customers and the ability to safeguard consumers' identities.
29. Owing to practitioner-led development, the underlying privacy and security settings of blockchain have not been entirely formalized, creating a lack of standardization in industry-accepted security measures (Zīle & Strazdiņa, 2018). The security settings are likely to be changed based on the individual choices of the developers and

the solutions developed (Halpin, H., & Piekarska, M. (2017). Introduction to security and privacy on the blockchain. In *2017 IEEE European Symposium on Security and Privacy Workshops (EuroS&PW)* (pp. 1–3). IEEE). This change is further compounded by issues in scripting language design and the lack of common vocabulary (Zīle & Strazdiņa, 2018).

30. Aravinthan, V., Namboodiri, V., Sunku, S., & Jewell, W. (2011). Wireless AMI application and security for controlled home area networks. In *2011 IEEE Power and Energy Society General Meeting* (pp. 1–8). IEEE; Karame, G. O., & Androulaki, E. (2016). *Bitcoin and blockchain security*. Artech House; Komninos, N., Philippou, E., & Pitsillides, A. (2014). Survey in smart grid and smart home security: Issues, challenges and counter- measures. *IEEE Communications Surveys & Tutorials, 16*(4), 1933–1954.
31. Kumar, V., Rajan, B., Venkatesan, R., & Lecinski, J. (2019). Understanding the role of artificial intelligence in personalized engagement marketing. *California Management Review, 61*(4), 135–155.
32. Salah, K., Rehman, M. H. U., Nizamuddin, N., & Al-Fuqaha, A. (2019). Blockchain for AI: Review and open research challenges. *IEEE Access, 7*, 10127–10149.
33. Dinh, T. N., & Thai, M. T. (2018). AI and blockchain: A disruptive integration. *Computer, 51*(9), 48–53.
34. As of March 2023, hackers stole nearly $3.7 billion in cryptocurrency crimes during 2022, a 58% increase over the $2.3 billion stolen from investors and exchanges in 2021. Illicit cryptocurrency activity hit a record high of $20.1 billion in 2022, up $2.1 billion from the previous year (Reed, J. (2023). Cryptocurrency-related crime boomed in 2022. *Security Intelligence.* https://securityintelligence.com/news/cryptocurrency-related-crime-boomed-2022/).
35. Achrol, R. S., & Kotler, P. (1999). Marketing in the network economy. *Journal of Marketing, 63*, 146–163; Glazer, R. (1991). Marketing in an information-intensive environment: Strategic implications of knowledge as an asset. *Journal of Marketing, 55*(4), 1–19.
36. Shaw, M. J., Subramaniam, C., Tan, G. W., & Welge, M. E. (2001). Knowledge management and data mining for marketing. *Decision Support Systems, 31*(1), 127–137.
37. Day, G. S. (1994). The capabilities of market-driven organizations. *Journal of Marketing, 58*(4), 37–52.
38. Day, G. S. (2011). Closing the marketing capabilities gap. *Journal of Marketing, 75*(4), 183–195.

39. Porter, M. E., & Millar, V. E. (1985). How information gives you competitive advantage. *Harvard Business Review*, *85*(July/August), 149–160.
40. Argote, L., McEvily, B., & Reagans, R. (2003). Managing knowledge in organizations: An integrative framework and review of emerging themes. *Management Science*, *49*(4), 571–582.
41. Carlile, P. R. (2004). Transferring, translating, and transforming: An integrative framework for managing knowledge across boundaries. *Organization Science*, *15*(5), 555–568.
42. Teece, D. J. (2000). Strategies for managing knowledge assets: The role of firm structure and industrial context. *Long Range Planning*, *33*(1), 35–54.
43. Dinh, T. N., & Thai, M. T. (2018). AI and blockchain: A disruptive integration. *Computer*, *51*(9), 48–53.
44. Graves, S. (2020). The decentralized ride-sharing disruptors taking on Uber. *Decrypt*. https://decrypt.co/18155/the-decentralized-ride-sharing-disruptors-taking-on-uber.
45. Ledger Insights. (2020). Blockchain ride-hailing firm raises $5 million. https://www.ledgerinsights.com/blockchain-ride-hailing-tada/.
46. Williams, M. (2023), "The end-to-end in sight at Volvo Cars," *Automotive Logistics*, March 21, accessed from https://www.automotivelogistics.media/supply-chain-management/the-end-to-end-in-sight-at-volvo-cars/44043.article.
47. Aura Blockchain Consortium (2022). Authenticating Luxury Goods with Blockchain. *Aura Blockchain Consortium*, August 23. https://auraluxuryblockchain.com/insight/authenticating-luxury-goods-with-blockchain.
48. Saunders, B. (2022). Diesel Announces D:VERSE NFT Collection. *Hypebeast*, March 10. https://hypebeast.com/2022/3/diesel-dverse-nft-collection-info.
49. Prabha, A. (2023). Crurated: reimagining the wine industry with blockchain and live auctions. *Inside Retail*. June 20. https://insideretail.asia/2023/06/20/crurated-reimagining-the-wine-industry-with-blockchain-and-live-auctions/.
50. Meisenzahl, M. (2023). Crurated's wine platform uses NFTs and memberships to find a younger market. *Digital Commerce 360*. February 6. https://www.digitalcommerce360.com/2023/02/06/crurated-wine-blockchain-nft-younger-market/.

51. Studies have investigated the impact of voter fraud on lowering voter confidence, while these studies have mixed results, blockchain and internet-based voting systems can help improve voter participation by enabling citizens to register to vote and caste their vote from anywhere in the world (Ansolabehere, S., & Persily, N. (2007). Vote fraud in the eye of the beholder: The role of public opinion in the challenge to voter identification requirements. *Harvard Law Review, 121,* 1737; Atkeson, L. R., Bryant, L. A., Hall, T. E., Saunders, K., & Alvarez, M. (2010). A new barrier to participation: Heterogeneous applica- tion of voter identification policies. *Electoral Studies, 29*(1), 66–73, Mearian, L. (2019). Why blockchain-based voting could threaten democracy. *Computerworld.* https://www.computerworld.com/article/3430697/why-blockchain-could-be-a-threat-to-democracy.html).
52. Kshetri, N., & Voas, J. (2018). Blockchain-enabled e-voting. *IEEE Software, 35*(4), 95–99; Ølnes, S., Ubacht, J., & Janssen, M. (2017). Blockchain in govern- ment: Benefits and implications of distributed ledger technology for information sharing. *Government Information Quarterly, 34*(3), 355–364.
53. Tatar, J. (2020). How blockchain technology can change how we vote. *The Balance.* https://www.thebalance.com/how-the-blockchain-will-change-how-we-vote-4012008.
54. Sinclair, S. (2020). West Virginia Ditches Blockchain Voting App Provider Voatz. *CoinDesk.* https://www.coindesk.com/policy/2020/03/02/west-virginia-ditches-blockchain-voting-app-provider-voatz/.
55. Changing Markets Foundation (2019), "Fishing for Catastrophe," *Changing Markets Foundation,* accessed from https://changingmarkets.org/wp-content/uploads/2019/10/CM-EX-SUMMARY-FINAL-WEB-FISHING-THE-CATASTROPHE-2019-.pdf.
56. Evans, M. (2023), "Can blockchain help you trace your food?" *Think Landscape,* April 19, accessed from https://thinklandscape.globallandscapesforum.org/60203/how-traceability-is-changing-supply-chains/.
57. Yiannas, F. (2018). A new era of food transparency powered by blockchain. *Innovations: Technology, Governance, Globalization, 12*(1–2), 46–56.
58. Daley, S. (2019). Five blockchain companies improving the food industry. *Built In.* https://builtin.com/blockchain/food-safety-supply-chain.
59. Kumar, V. (2021). *Intelligent Marketing: Employing New Age Technologies.* Sage Publications.

60. Caswell, J. A., & Mojduszka, E. M. (1996). Using informational labeling to influence the market for quality in food products. *American Journal of Agricultural Economics, 78*(5), 1248–1253.
61. Teisl, M. F., & Roe, B. (1998). The economics of labeling: An overview of issues for health and environmental disclosure. *Agricultural and Resource Economics Review, 27*(2), 140–150.
62. Kahneman, D., & Tversky, A. (1973). On the psychology of prediction. *Psychological Review, 80*(4), 237–251.
63. McCluskey, J. J., & Swinnen, J. F. (2004). Political economy of the media and consumer perceptions of biotechnology. *American Journal of Agricultural Economics, 86*(5), 1230–1237.
64. In today's highly connected world customers are very conscious about the origins of the products and services they consume—this helps them connect with the firms and form positive sentiments towards the firm and their offerings. Over time, this helps in building customer trust in the brands, and they become more inclined to share personal information with the brand, resulting in deeper levels of customer engagement (Harvey, C. R., Moorman, C., & Toledo, M. (2018). How blockchain can help marketers build better relationships with their customers).
65. Yakubowski, M. (2019). Alibaba Exec: E-commerce giant considering blockchain use in complex supply chains. *Cointelegraph.com.* https://cointelegraph.com/news/alibaba-exec-e-commerce-giant-con sidering-blockchain-use-in-complex-supply-chains.
66. High, M. (2020). Six world-leading blockchain and cryptocurrency firms. *FinTech.* https://www.fintechmagazine.com/blockchain/six-world-leading-blockchain-and-cryptocurrency-firms.
67. Everledger. (2022). To ensure ethical EV battery recycling, Everledger and Ford announced the beginning of a world-first battery passport pilot in October 2022. https://everledger.io/everledger-launches-bat tery-passport-pilot-with-ford/.
68. Win, T. L. (2020). Apps and blockchain help European supermarkets lure climate-conscious consumers. *Reuters.* https://www.reuters.com/article/us-europe-food-climate-change/apps-and-blockchain-help-eur opean-supermarkets-lure-climate-conscious-consumers-idUSKCN20 K0VN.
69. Carrefour. (2022). Carrefour is the first retailer to use blockchain technology with its own-brand organic products, providing consumers with more transparency. https://www.carrefour.com/sites/default/files/2022-04/CARREFOUR_bio_blockchain.pdf.

70. Muthoni, G. (2019). Adoption and usefulness of blockchain integration services. *CryptoNews*. https://www.crypto-news.net/adoption-and-usefulness-of-blockchain-integration-services/.
71. Renault Group. (2021). XCEED: a new blockchain solution for Renault plants in Europe. https://www.renaultgroup.com/en/news-on-air/news/xceed-a-new-blockchain-solution-for-renault-plants-in-europe/.
72. Kumar, V. (2021). *Intelligent Marketing: Employing New Age Technologies*. Sage Publications.
73. Yodanova, H. (2020). Blockchain in Bulgaria: Data storage and encryption. *Business Blockchain HQ*. https://businessblockchainhq.com/business-blockchain-news/blockchain-in-bulgaria-data-storage-and-encryption/.
74. Shabalala, Z. (2018). De Beers tracks diamonds through supply chain using blockchain. *Reuters*. https://www.reuters.com/article/us-anglo-debeers-blockchain/de-beers-tracks-diamonds-through-supply-chain-using-blockchain-idUSKBN1IB1CY.
75. The De Beers Group decided to install the Tracr blockchain at 100% scale in May 2022, ensuring provenances for all their diamonds from source to store (De Beers Group. (2022). De Beers group introduces world's first blockchain-backed diamond source platform at scale. https://www.debeersgroup.com/media/company-news/2022/de-beers-group-introduces-worlds-first-blockchain-backed-diamond-source-platform-at-scale#:~:text=The%20introduction%20of%20TracrTM,of%20De%20Beers'%20production%20possible). Such an initiative allows the company and other participating diamond manufacturers to trace their assets in real time.
76. Alexandre, A. (2020). Telecom giant Vodafone explores blockchain to verify suppliers. *Cointelegraph.com*. https://cointelegraph.com/news/telecom-giant-vodafone-explores-blockchain-to-verify-suppliers.
77. Ledger Insights. (2023). Vodafone's IoT blockchain used for cargo tracking with Aventus integration. https://www.ledgerinsights.com/vodafone-iot-blockchain-cargo-tracking-aventus/.
78. Kumar, V., & Ramachandran, D. (2020). *Developing a firm's growth approaches in a new-age technology environment to enhance stakeholder wellbeing* (Working Paper). Georgia State University.
79. Kumar, V., Ramachandran, D., & Kumar, B. (2020). Influence of new-age technologies on marketing: A research agenda. *Journal of Business Research*. https://www.sciencedirect.com/science/article/abs/pii/S0148296320300151.

80. Haig, S. (2020). Indonesian customs joins IBM's blockchain supply chain platform. *Cointelegraph.com.* https://cointelegraph.com/news/indonesian-customs-joins-ibms-blockchain-supply-chain-platform
81. Bhattacharya, A. (2018). Blockchain is helping build a new Indian city, but it's no cure for corruption. *Quartz India.* https://qz.com/india/1325423/indias-andhra-state-is-using-blockchain-to-build-capital-amaravati/.
82. Perez, E. (2019). Blockchain registers for recording ownership rights around the world. *Cointelegraph.com.* https://cointelegraph.com/news/blockchain-registers-for-recording-ownership-rights-around-the-world.
83. Hampton, L. (2019). Oil and gas majors sign deal to implement blockchain in Bakken oilfield. *Reuters.* https://www.reuters.com/article/us-blockchain-oil/oil-and-gas-majors-sign-deal-to-implement-blockchain-in-bakken-oilfield-idUSKCN1VV1SE.
84. Carson, B., Romanelli, G., Walsh, P., & Zhumaev, A. (2018). Blockchain beyond the hype: What is the strategic business value? *McKinsey.* https://www.mckinsey.com/business-functions/mckinsey-digital/our-insights/blockchain-beyond-the-hype-what-is-the-strategic-business-value.
85. McConaghy, T. (2023). Ocean Protocol Update II 2023. *Ocean Protocol.* https://blog.oceanprotocol.com/ocean-protocol-update-2023-44ed14510051.
86. Boulos, M. N. K., Wilson, J. T., & Clauson, K. A. (2018). Geospatial blockchain: Promises, challenges, and scenarios in health and healthcare. *International Journal of Health Geographics, 17*(1), 25.
87. Chiappinelli, C. (2019). Think tank: Blockchain evolves into geoblockchain. *ESRI.* https://www.esri.com/about/newsroom/publications/wherenext/geoblockchain-think-tank/; Dasgupta, A. (2017). The game changer of geospatial systems— Blockchain. *Geospatial World.* https://www.geospatialworld.net/article/blockchain-geospatial-systems/.
88. Kumar, V., Ramachandran, D., & Kumar, B. (2020). Influence of new-age technologies on marketing: A research agenda. *Journal of Business Research.* https://www.sciencedirect.com/science/article/abs/pii/S0148296320300151.
89. Cathay Pacific. (2018). Cathay Pacific Group leverages blockchain technology powered by Accenture to launch Asia Miles marketing campaign. https://news.cathaypacific.com/cathay-pacific-group-leverages-blockchain-technology-powered-by-accenture-to-launch-asia-miles-marketing-campaign#.

90. Zmudzinski, A. (2019). Unilever says its blockchain ad-buying pilot saved the company money. *Cointelegraph.com* https://cointelegraph.com/news/unilever-says-its-blockchain-ad-buying-pilot-saved-the-company-money.
91. Slefo, G. P. (2018). Toyota says it gets a boost when applying blockchain to digital ad buys. *Ad Age.* https://adage.com/article/digital/toyota-turns-blockchain-optimize-digital-ad-buys/315279?zd_source=mta&zd_campaign=12714&zd_term=chiradeepbasumallick.
92. Rao, V. (2017). With $3.3M in funding, Boostinsider bets on Social Book for YouTube influencer insights. *YourStory.* https://yourstory.com/2017/09/3-3m-funding-boostinsider-social-book-for-youtube-influencer-insights.
93. Tameez, H. (2020). Here's how The New York Times tested blockchain to help you identify faked photos on your timeline. *NiemanLab.* https://www.niemanlab.org/2020/01/heres-how-the-new-york-times-tested-blockchain-to-help-you-identify-faked-photos-on-your-timeline/.
94. Pansari, A., & Kumar, V. (2018). Customer engagement marketing. In R. W. Palmatier, V. Kumar, & C. M. Harmeling (Eds.), *Customer engagement marketing* (pp. 1–27). Palgrave Macmillan.
95. Dowling, N. (2020). Wine counterfeiters beware. *Cosmos.* https://cosmosmagazine.com/technology/wine-counterfeiters-beware.
96. Palmer, D. (2019). Miller Lite teams with blockchain firm for customer engagement game. *Coindesk.* https://www.coindesk.com/miller-lite-teams-with-blockchain-firm-for-customer-engagement-game.
97. Bijmolt, T. H., Krafft, M., Sese, F. J., & Viswanathan, V. (2018). Multi-tier loyalty programs to stimulate customer engagement. In
98. Lawlor, S. (2019). Blockchain technology is being used to lift the lid on false claims in the beauty industry and it's set to change the way we shop. *Glamour.* https://www.glamourmagazine.co.uk/article/what-is-blockchain-technology.
99. Vadino, J. (2019). Securing customer loyalty programs with blockchain for retail. *Retail Touchpoints.* https://retailtouchpoints.com/features/executive-viewpoints/securing-customer-loyalty-programs-with-blockchain-for-retail.
100. Conti, R. (2023). Guide To NBA Top Shot. *Forbes Advisor.* https://www.forbes.com/advisor/investing/cryptocurrency/nba-top-shot/.
101. Felin, T., & Lakhani, K. (2018). What problems will you solve with blockchain? *MIT Sloan Management Review, 60*(1), 32–38.

102. Kumar, V. (2021). *Intelligent Marketing: Employing New Age Technologies*. Sage Publications.
103. Kopalle, P. K., Kumar, V., & Subramaniam, M. (2020). How legacy firms can embrace the digital ecosystem via digital customer orientation. *Journal of the Academy of Marketing Science, 48*(1), 114–131.
104. Grigonis, H. K. (2018). KodakOne uses blockchain and web crawlers to spot stolen images. *Digital Trends*. https://www.digitaltrends.com/photography/kodakone-creates-photo-registry-blockchain-ces2018/.
105. Greene, T. (2018). Kodak is the latest company to jump on blockchain. And one of the few that make sense. *TNW*. https://thenextweb.com/hardfork/2018/01/09/kodak-is-the-latest-company-to-jump-on-blockchain-and-one-of-the-few-that-make-sense/.
106. Allison, I. (2019). Louis Vuitton owner LVMH is launching a blockchain to track luxury goods. *Coindesk*. https://www.coindesk.com/louis-vuitton-owner-lvmh-is-launching-a-blockchain-to-track-luxury-goods.
107. James, A. (2018) Aworker—Disrupting the HR industry through next-gen blockchain technology. *Bitcoinist*. https://bitcoinist.com/aworker-disrupting-hr-industry-next-gen-blockchain-technology/.
108. Felin, T., & Lakhani, K. (2018). What problems will you solve with blockchain? *MIT Sloan Management Review, 60*(1), 32–38.
109. Kumar, V., Ramachandran, D., & Kumar, B. (2020). Influence of new-age technologies on marketing: A research agenda. *Journal of Business Research*. https://www.sciencedirect.com/science/article/abs/pii/S0148296320300151.
110. Auxier, B., Rainie, L., Anderson, M., Perrin, A., Kumar, M., & Turner, E. (2019). Americans and privacy: Concerned, confused and feeling lack of control over their personal information. *Pew ResearchCenter*. https://www.pewresearch.org/internet/2019/11/15/americans-and-privacy-concerned-confused-and-feeling-lack-of-control-over-their-personal-information/.
111. Athey, S., Catalini, C., & Tucker, C. (2017). *The digital privacy paradox: Small money, small costs, small talk* (NBER Working Paper No. 23488). National Bureau of Economic Research. https://www.nber.org/papers/w23488.pdf.
112. A recent survey found that while existing companies that integrate blockchain into their operations (established enterprises) believe blockchain provides greater security than conventional IT solutions (71%), not many emerging disruptors feel the same way (48%). The survey also revealed that emerging disruptors found the opportunity

for new business models and the creation of new value chains to be significant benefits of blockchain (Pawczuk, L., Massey, R., & Holdowsky, J. (2019). Deloitte's 2019 global blockchain survey. *Deloitte Insights.* https://www2.deloitte.com/us/en/insights/topics/understanding-blockchain-potential/global-blockchain-survey.html).

113. While the two types of organizations have different attributes of blockchain technology, value can be brought in when the disruptor leads the way in identifying innovative solutions and the established enterprises can make it mainstream.

114. Zhang, R., Xue, R., & Liu, L. (2019). Security and privacy on blockchain. *ACM Computing Surveys (CSUR), 52*(3), 1–34.

115. IAB. (2019a). IAB internet advertising revenue report—2018 full year results. https://www.iab.com/wp-content/uploads/2019/05/Full-Year-2018-IAB-Internet-Advertising-Revenue-Report.pdf.

116. IAB. (2019b). U.S. digital ad revenue climbs to $57.9 billion in first half 2019, up 17% YOY, according to IAB internet advertising revenue report. https://www.iab.com/news/u-s-digital-ad-revenue-climbs-to-57-9-billion-in-first-half-2019/.

117. Cui, Y., Zhang, R., Li, W., & Mao, J. (2011). Bid landscape forecasting in online ad exchange marketplace. In *Proceedings of the 17th ACM SIGKDD International Conference on Knowledge Discovery and Data Mining* (pp. 265–273).

118. Fisher, L. (2019). US programmatic ad spending forecast 2019. *eMarketer.com.* https://www.emarketer.com/content/us-programmatic-ad-spending-forecast-2019.

119. The United States contributed more than $200 billion of the $418.4 billion in global programmatic ad spending in 2021, and this amount was expected to surpass $493 billion by the end of 2022 (Statista. (2023). Programmatic advertising in the United States. https://www.statista.com/topics/7912/programmatic-advertising-in-the-us/#topicOverview).

120. Brayer, M. (2020). What is programmatic advertising? *Outbrain.* Accessed from https://www.outbrain.com/blog/programmatic-advertising/.

121. Page, R. (2020). Can blockchain deliver on its big advertising promises? *CMO.com.* https://www.cmo.com.au/article/671101/can-blockchain-deliver-its-big-advertising-promises/.

122. Ellwanger, S. (2020). How blockchain fueled avocados from Mexico's super bowl campaign. *MediaPost.com.* https://www.mediapost.com/publications/article/346755/how-blockchain-fueled-avocados-from-mexicos-super.html.

123. Rogers, B. (2021). Carolina Abenante Cofounds NYIAX To Bring Nasdaq-Like Transparency To Digital Ads. *Forbes.* https://www.forbes.com/sites/brucerogers/2021/09/01/carolina-abenante-co-founds-nyiax-to-bring-nasdaq-like-transparency-to-programmatic-ads/?sh=2a0f1a3c1369.
124. Kumar, V., & Reinartz, W. (2018). *Customer relationship management—Concept, strategy, and tools* (3rd ed.). Springer.
125. AMA. (2020). Influencer marketing. https://www.ama.org/topics/influencer-marketing/.
126. MASB. (2020). Buying roles. https://marketing-dictionary.org/b/buying-roles/#cite_ref-1.
127. Kumar, V., Bhaskaran, V., Mirchandani, R., & Shah, M. (2013). Creating a measurable social media marketing strategy: Increasing the value and ROI of intangibles and tangibles for hokey pokey. *Marketing Science, 32*(2), 194–212.
128. Kumar, V., Bhaskaran, V., Mirchandani, R., & Shah, M. (2013). Creating a measurable social media marketing strategy: Increasing the value and ROI of intangibles and tangibles for hokey pokey. *Marketing Science, 32*(2), 194–212.
129. Kumar, V., Bhaskaran, V., Mirchandani, R., & Shah, M. (2013). Creating a measurable social media marketing strategy: Increasing the value and ROI of intangibles and tangibles for hokey pokey. *Marketing Science, 32*(2), 194–212.
130. Hileman, G., & Rauchs, M. (2017). Global blockchain benchmarking study. Cambridge Centre for Alternative Finance. https://cdn.crowdfundinsider.com/wp-content/uploads/2017/09/2017-Global-Blockchain-Benchmarking-Study_Hileman.pdf.
131. Tama, B. A., Kweka, B. J., Park, Y., & Rhee, K. H. (2017). A critical review of blockchain and its current applications. In *2017 International Conference on Electrical Engineering and Computer Science (ICECOS)* (pp. 109–113).
132. Zheng, Z., Xie, S., Dai, H., Chen, X., & Wang, H. (2017). An overview of blockchain technology: Architecture, consensus, and future trends. In *2017 IEEE international congress on big data (BigData congress)* (pp. 557–564).
133. Yli-Huumo, J., Ko, D., Choi, S., Park, S., & Smolander, K. (2016). Where is current research on blockchain technology?—A systematic review. *PloS One, 11*(10), e0163477.

134. Buterin, V. (2015). On public and private blockchains. *Ethereum Blog*. https://blog.ethereum.org/2015/08/07/on-public-and-private-blockchains/.
135. Wüst, K., & Gervais, A. (2018). Do you need a blockchain? In *2018 Crypto Valley Conference on Blockchain Technology (CVCBT)* (pp. 45–54). IEEE.
136. Buterin, V. (2015). On public and private blockchains. *Ethereum Blog*. https://blog.ethereum.org/2015/08/07/on-public-and-private-blockchains/.

11

Putting It All Together

Avant-garde. This book began with this term to characterize the changes occurring in the marketing world, and its subsequent impact on firms, consumers, and other stakeholders. We hope this book has effectively conveyed the revolutionary effect that new-age technologies, or NATs, are having on the state of marketing today. In particular, long-standing marketing strategies are changing dramatically regularly, redefining several aspects of our everyday lives. This is a result of the growing pressure on businesses to (a) outperform their rivals; (b) quickly adjust to shifting market conditions to stay in business; and (c) provide customers with timely offerings that genuinely meet their needs. More than ever, it seems like businesses are required to manage a multitude of constraints and factors at once, all the while needing to be agile and quick to respond to disruptions in the broader business environment.

Technology is the driving force behind this evolution of business, as it consistently demonstrates its capacity to fundamentally upend established business procedures and generate novel prospects for transformation. NATs offer both significant opportunities and difficulties to uphold the status quo in the current business environment.[1] Artificial intelligence (AI), generative AI, robots, machine learning (ML), drones, Internet of Things (IoT), blockchain, and metaverse are the eight NATs that are covered in this book. All eight of these NATs offer competent and practical opportunities for organizational activities that can benefit the organization as well as its other related stakeholders.

While each of the preceding chapters has focused on the individual NATs, this concluding chapter aims to tie in all the individual chapters into an overarching strategic framework—an integrated strategy for stakeholder engagement—that can be informative in understanding the power of transformative marketing using NATs. Figure 11.1 illustrates this framework.

As provided in Figure 11.1, each of the NATs, when adopted using the Marketing 5.0 concept, provides firms with opportunities to develop capabilities to perform better and to utilize technological advancements better. Subsequently, these capabilities will better prepare firms to deploy strategic and tactical marketing actions in a timely, efficient, and effective manner. These firm marketing actions would then result in the creation of a technology-based enhanced customer experience (CX). This is a crucial outcome for firms, as demonstrated by academic research as it leads to better customer engagement (CE).[2]

The connections up to this point have been covered in the previous chapters from each NAT's perspective. Benefits to all parties involved (customers, staff, community, channel partners, and government) can also be seen following the development of improved CX. In addition to discussing the advantages for the other stakeholders, this chapter will provide a summary of the framework that has been covered thus far in the book.

New-Age Technologies for Better Marketing: A Strategic Framework

As was previously established, technology is advancing quickly and is now widely present in practically every aspect of our lives. The convergence of NATs in a Marketing 5.0 world suggests a sophisticated, networked smart device ecosystem that can benefit both service providers and consumers. Although there are examples of businesses using NATs for marketing purposes on their own, new developments show that there is a need and desire to use these technologies as part of integrated marketing strategies. The continual gathering of data, continuous learning, and intuitive service delivery predicated on the acquired knowledge enables the ensuing generation of value from NAT-driven marketing strategies.[3] This section provides a discussion of the components described in Figure 11.1.

New-Age Technologies

Current business trends show that companies are becoming more interested in using data to inform regular business operations and the creation of targeted marketing campaigns. The usage of NATs has become apparent in

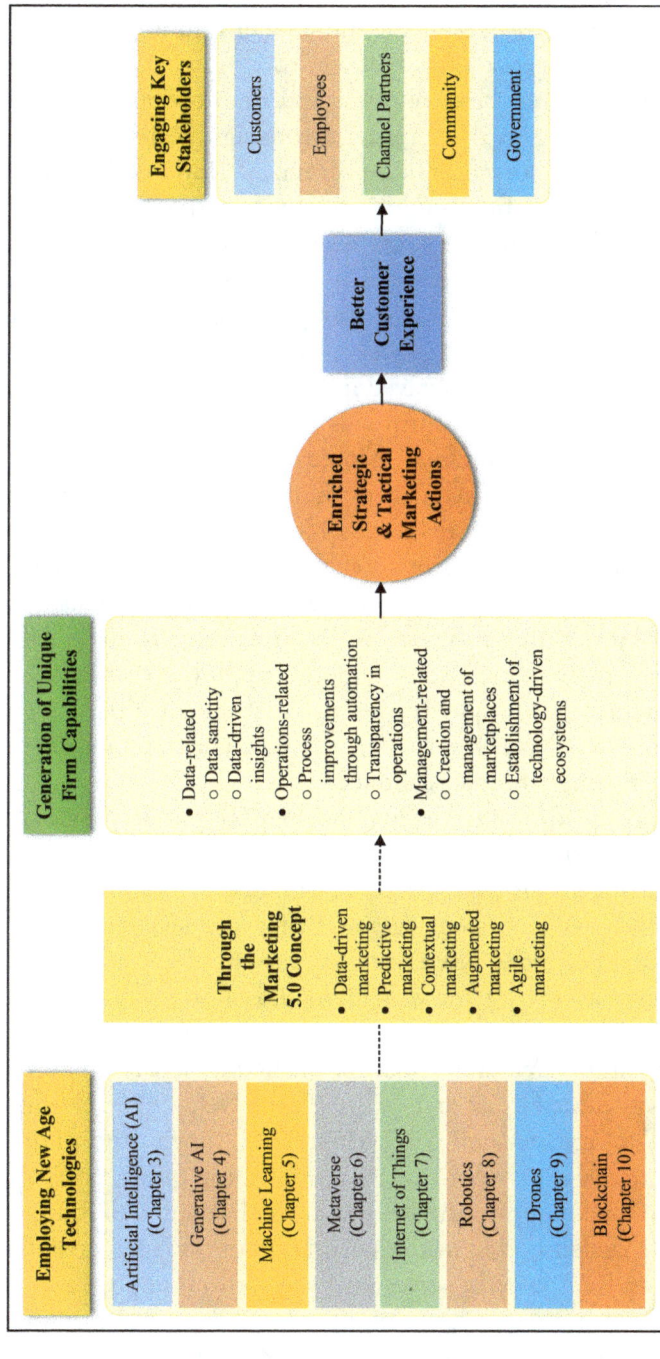

Fig. 11.1 NATs for transformative marketing: A strategic framework
(*Source* Adapted and extended from Kumar, V. (2021). *Intelligent Marketing: Employing New Age Technologies.* Sage Publications)

the process. Additionally, businesses are being encouraged to closely consider NATs due to their potential to streamline the tracking and integration of data from various sources as well as the subsequent mining of said data using advanced techniques to generate insights. Furthermore, the NATs' increased potential for creating innovative solutions and the new business opportunities they offer are adding to their appeal. More significantly, businesses can investigate the potential for combining several NATs to collaborate to find creative solutions that benefit all parties involved in the exchange ecosystem.

AI technology plays a crucial role in the marketing industry by enhancing intelligent searches, creating intelligent advertisements, personalizing offerings and content delivery, and transforming customer service through the use of bots, among other important actions. From a technical perspective, AI can automate various activities involved in collecting, storing, managing, and retrieving information, which in turn aids in the creation and management of valuable offerings for businesses.[4] Moreover, the success of AI initiatives relies on aligning them with the goals of the organization and making them a comprehensive effort that spans across hierarchies, functions, and stakeholders. The impact of AI on various stakeholders is evident through several factors, including the creation of personalized marketing campaigns to foster genuine relationships with customers (which adds value to firms), the emergence of new job roles (which adds value to employees), the development of additional technology ecosystem offerings that enhance the final product (which adds value to channel partners), the efficient handling of resource-limited settings through human-centered design (which adds value to the community), and the ability to deploy and manage public policy initiatives (which adds value to the government).

Generative artificial intelligence (GAI) models are made to recognize patterns and structures in current data and then produce new data samples that follow those patterns. These devices can produce a wide range of information, such as text, photos, audio, and more. Generating natural language, synthesizing images, creating content, augmenting data, finding drugs, and many more areas are just a few of the many uses for GAI. Particularly, GAI serves in activities such as product development & innovation, marketing & sales, and research & development, among others (a source of value for firms), enhancing work experience, boosting productivity via workflow automation, and empowering workers to achieve more (a source of value to employees), managing channel relationships, optimizing operations and collaborations, and empowering sales and support, among others (a source of value to channel partners), fostering positive change and improving lives across various sectors and user groups (a source of value to the community), and improving how governments operate, deliver services, and make decisions (a source of value to the government).

Machine learning deals with the process of training machines to learn over time. Firms are using ML for many functions that include personalizing content and offerings, developing dynamic pricing strategies, identifying counterfeit products, improving sales, and building and enhancing personal relationships with customers, among others. ML also serves stakeholders by its ability to aid customer management strategy initiatives (a source of value to firms), expediting customer segmentation, lead customization, and marketing element customization, thereby enabling employees to use their time productively for more meaningful actions (a source of value to employees), assisting in accurate sales forecasting and thereby efficient inventory management (a source of value to channel partners), assisting in environmental and natural resource conservation efforts (a source of value to the community), and monitoring and managing cyber security threats through specific, timely responses (a source of value to the government).

Metaverse is more than just a concept, but a concrete reality—an immersive place in which our online interactions transcend the constraints of traditional platforms. At the heart of the Metaverse is a web of interconnected technologies, including virtual reality (VR), augmented reality (AR), blockchain, artificial intelligence (AI), and others, all working together to create an immersive and unified digital experience. These technologies serve as the foundation for a new era, altering how we communicate, collaborate, and form communities in the digital sphere, thereby creating value for all parties involved. The metaverse also serves as a platform for businesses to interact with their audiences and learn more about them (a source of value to firms), a way for employees to collaborate in an interactive way (a source of value to employees), a way to bring together multiple brands and advertisers in one place to share an interactive space for customer courting (a source of value to channel partners), a place for community building, discussions, and interactions on matters of shared interest (a source of value to channel partners), and a way for governments to easily provide services and applications to citizens using a technology that simulates the three-dimensional world we live in (a source of value to the government).

IoT represents an interconnected web of devices that can collectively work in collecting, communicating, and processing information in real time through the internet to perform or aid in performing certain defined tasks. However, promising areas of IoT deployment such as smart cities and connected travel solutions indicate this NAT's increasing acceptance. Further, IoT continues to serve various stakeholders through their use in the development of an automation-driven ecosystem leading up to the term "Industry 4.0" (a source of value to firms), the accurate identification of when machinery parts/components may need replacements (a source of value to employees), its role in avoiding duplication of effort (a source of value to channel partners), its role in societal wellbeing functions such as ambient assisted living (a source of value to the community), and its ability in conducting governmental operations and managing national resources (a source of value to the government).

Robotics facilitates daily lives, while also learning and applying thought as they continue to work. This enables robotics to provide personalized service that uniquely matches the needs of every individual. The abilities of robots currently display a wide bandwidth to perform a variety of functions that range from basic (such as moving goods through a warehouse) to nuanced (such as responding to customer queries in a service setting and delivering healthcare services). Further, robots continue to serve various stakeholders through their versatility in being redesigned to accommodate changes in operations (a source of value to firms), their ability to work alongside humans to complete several consumer-facing tasks (a source of value to employees), their assistance in curation and personalization of offerings (a source of value to channel partners), their use in the distribution of essential services such as education, healthcare, and so on (a source of value to the community), and their use in the delivery of public utility offerings (a source of value to the government).

Drones provide firms with more access to users, more opportunities for customer interaction touchpoints, more avenues for operational efficiencies, and richer sources of information, among others. Drones also serve other stakeholders by assisting in business functions such as agricultural activities, construction, transportation, logistics, media, and so on (a source of value to firms), repurposing some aspects of jobs that can be replaced or directed towards critical and value-creating actions (a source of value to employees), being economical while being visually captivating and therefore of use in media (a source of value to channel partners), playing a vital role in emergency and humanitarian relief efforts (a source of value to the community), and serving as a critical asset of national security (a source of value to the government).

Blockchain refers to the distributed ledger technology that is based on creating a distributed consensus in the digital online world, thereby firmly establishing trust in actions even when operating in the online world. This technology contains salient features such as decentralized operation, security, immutability, transparency, and autonomy, among other properties.

Blockchain works on several consumer-facing applications such as ride-sharing apps, ensuring food safety, online payments, insurance services, and several more, thereby delivering real-time value to end users. Further, blockchain benefits other stakeholders by enhancing the efficiency of supply chain activities (a source of value to firms), authenticating candidate qualifications instantly to facilitate hiring processes (a source of value to employees), managing access control and rights management of supplier-related processes (a source of value to channel partners), addressing labor exploitation by ensuring workers' human rights (a source of value to the community), and optimizing information technologies for managing public digital services (a source of value to the government).

Generation of Firm Capabilities

The creation of firm capabilities was covered in great detail in each chapter, albeit from a particular NAT perspective. Upon delineating the comprehensive structure of the NATs and how they align within the Marketing 5.0 world, several distinct capabilities emerge. Furthermore, companies that frequently use multiple NATs for different organizational processes are specifically mentioned when discussing the significance of the identified capabilities. Combining several NAT deployments is anticipated to help businesses develop capabilities that will benefit all of their business divisions. As illustrated in Figure 11.1, these capabilities can be grouped as data-related, operations-related, and management-related and discussed here.

Data-related. These capabilities relate to how data can prepare firms for better performance. Whereas data-related capabilities may indicate several firm competencies, two specific capabilities are of interest—data sanctity, and data-driven insights.

Data sanctity refers to how "clean" the information being recorded is in the data. This suggests that the data thus obtained can be independently checked to confirm its accuracy. Additionally, the traceability and transparency of processes—which are frequently necessary for securing transactions—are also related to data sanctity. Blockchain, for example, can securely store all transaction records at every stage of the exchange process. Additionally, blockchain gives external stakeholders (like consumers, the government, etc.) access to data about the provenance of products, their ingredients and parts, and their supply chain journeys. This promotes trust in businesses, lessens counterfeiting, and establishes authenticity.

Data-driven insights pertain to the potential outcomes that businesses can achieve using "clean" data. Data-driven insights are essential for managing current and future firm offerings and customer expectations as businesses gather more detailed and up-to-date information about their customers and usage patterns. More significantly, businesses can create individualized offerings by learning about customers' preferences. In this sense, NATs like AI, ML, and IoT equip businesses to provide the anticipated offerings to the appropriate user at the appropriate moment. Businesses are also able to recognize changing market trends and plan pertinent reactions to deal with them. NATs also allow businesses to interact directly with their stakeholders. In this sense, smart contracts that use cryptocurrency to compensate CE can be created and managed using blockchain technology.

Operations-related. These capabilities have to do with how businesses can perform business processes more effectively and efficiently. Process improvements through automation and transparency in operations are two essential skills here.

The NATs allow firms to realize *process improvements through automation* which then prepares the firms to improve their product development and optimize their processes. Through NATs such as robotics, IoT, and ML, firms can monitor their operational assets and schedule proactive maintenance to increase productivity, improve efficiency, and reduce operating costs. Applications such as smart warehousing and smart transportation enable intuitive demand fulfillment, warehouse automation, and route optimization for maximum efficiency. Further, NATs such as generative AI and robotics allow firms to automate customer service actions that range from handling routine queries to addressing more complex issues.

The implementation of NATs greatly enhances *transparency in operations*, especially when it comes to determining the origin of products and their components. Furthermore, with increasing environmental concerns, both customers and companies feel the need to track the entire journey of products and components to evaluate how production practices align with their values. For instance, blockchain technology provides the necessary tools to trace the supply chain of products, allowing customers to develop greater trust in brands and make long-term decisions to support their offerings. By utilizing the Global Location Number, which serves as a unique identifier for a company's physical locations such as stores and warehouses, businesses can accurately track and share information about the production and harvesting of food items. This number plays a crucial role in supply chain exchanges and traceability programs, as it facilitates the precise capturing and sharing of data regarding the movement of products along the supply chain.[5]

Management-related. The management's ability to respond to and prepare for marketplace changes, whether influenced by technology or not, is crucial. This suggests that NATs can enhance organizational efficiencies at different levels and leverage technology to drive business activities. More specifically, capabilities such as the creation and management of marketplaces, and the establishment of technology-driven ecosystems can be developed to assist managements.

In addition to helping businesses get things done, the NATs' functionalities also help in the *creation and management of marketplaces*. In other words, management would be able to use NATs for purposes other than merely enhancing their technical capabilities, particularly to generate new business opportunities. Adoption of NATs can stimulate the development of new markets, including AI-powered eHealth/mHealth solutions, ML-powered online credit markets, blockchain-powered supply chain connectivity, crop information access, and IoT-powered connected devices. By putting data at the center of operations, these markets or offerings have completely changed several industries. In particular, businesses can protect and store their data, opening up a market for secure data sharing and monetization.

When NATs are implemented collectively and within the Marketing 5.0 context, they offer firms numerous benefits and can lead to the *establishment of technology-driven ecosystems*. As mentioned in previous chapters, AI, generative AI, and ML are often implemented together. Similarly, robotics and IoT have been combined to drive business transformation. Additionally, the joint implementation of AI and industrial IoT has resulted in impressive operational and efficiency gains for organizations. By connecting devices on a single platform, enabling them to exchange information with each other and with users, and integrating multiple functionalities, firms can gain a significant competitive advantage. This advantage allows firms to understand their users' behaviors and decisions, utilize these insights for new product development, improve service quality, manage customer experiences, and ultimately foster loyalty among stakeholders.

Strategic and Tactical Marketing Actions

When it comes to strategic marketing initiatives, NATs have the power to significantly alter how businesses are organized and run. Initiatives like customer relationship management (CRM), which entails tasks like bringing in new clients, keeping hold of current ones, and winning back former clients, may fall under this category of strategic actions. Moreover, among other things, NATs can help create profitable customer loyalty programs, valuable brands, and effective product development procedures. Businesses can use

AI/ML technology and specific customer data, for instance, to provide individualized goods and services. Additionally, NATs like AI, ML, and IoT can help managers improve the value proposition for customers over time and support real-time learning. By adopting a strategy that focuses on curated products delivering increasing value to customers, companies can achieve customer retention and establish a sustainable competitive advantage—a crucial outcome of strategic marketing actions.

When it comes to short-term tactical marketing actions, NATs can be used to target a particular behavior or result. Delivering superior brand experiences, service delivery initiatives, pricing, product management, distribution, and promotions, as well as targeted advertising and communications content, are a few examples of such tactical actions. For example, businesses can use drones and robotics to automate and streamline processes. Customers may receive better experiences from such effective actions. Technologies like blockchain and the Internet of Things can also help businesses with data and security management, which can lead to process economies and increased functional efficiency. These kinds of projects can create memorable customer experiences, automate, and optimize business procedures, create corporate equity, and eventually get companies ready to produce value for all parties involved.

Customer Experience

The strategic and tactical marketing actions adopted by firms using the NATs are expected to result in the creation of customer experience (CX). Research studies have advanced the concept of personalization, a distinct feature of NATs, to operate in the pathway to CX. These research findings suggest that NATs are well-suited to help firms establish CX that can subsequently add value to all the stakeholders involved.[6]

When clients receive communications and offerings that directly speak to their needs and preferences, the NATs guarantee that they will stay involved with the business. Developing curated offerings using AI and generative AI, creating personalized interactions in service settings using robotics, reducing variations in the service experience using IoT, identifying social topics important to customers using machine learning (ML), delivering mesmerizing experiences on metaverse that create conversations, providing functional benefits to consumers using drones (e.g., interactivity, faster delivery times, etc.), and fostering/building customer loyalty using blockchain are a few examples of enhanced CX initiatives using NATs.

Furthermore, social media interactions enable businesses to quickly assess the value of the different ways they choose to communicate and engage with their target audiences. In other words, consumers are vocal about their experiences and opinions with brands and businesses, fueled by digital communication options. When properly organized, these kinds of experiences can aid businesses in building stronger stakeholder engagement (SE). Consequently, the creation of SE benefits all parties involved in facilitating the exchange relationship, not just businesses and consumers. The NATs are essential in creating overall value for all stakeholders in such a situation.

Stakeholder Engagement/Benefits

In the multi-entity environment of business ecosystems, the members involved in coordinating, facilitating, and directing the exchange process are known as stakeholders, and the aim of the exchange process revolves around satisfying the mutual interests and expectations of the stakeholders. Several decades of academic research continue to investigate the role and impact of stakeholders in the overall exchange process, with a critical research area being stakeholder value and stakeholder engagement.[7]

Academic scholars and practitioners continue to be interested in the concept of stakeholder value because value is an obvious outcome of interest for the stakeholders (in any format of exchange). One important aspect of shareholder value is that it is best realized through a continuous exchange process.[8] The bidirectional flow of value between the related parties (i.e., stakeholders) in such a process allows the parties to continuously assess the value acquired. The relationship is frequently managed and tracked using the value that has been realized. For the association to be fruitful and fulfilling, stakeholders must continually assess the value that comes from their connections.

Ecosystems and business models are changing fundamentally as a result of NATs. Technology is still changing how businesses operate in NAT environments, but these changes are still very much in line with the idea of value. The benefits of NAT implementation for firms are substantial, as this book has demonstrated. The following discussion centers on five important stakeholders that are typically involved in a business environment: customers, employees, channel partners, the community, and the government.

Customers. As a stakeholder group, customers share a particularly close relationship with firms from a value standpoint. On the one hand, firms deliver value to customers through firm offerings that are intended to satisfy customers.[9] In return, customers provide value to the firm through their loyalty,[10] their contribution to firm profits,[11] and indirect engagement.[12] The NATs in a NAT environment deliver newer and innovative ways for users to modify or change their behavior. For example, IoT enables end users to integrate devices that were previously unattainable (e.g., smart locks, thermostats, etc.). Similar to this, AI enables ongoing learning of end users' usage patterns, which can then be applied to customize the user experience (personalization apps, for example). Furthermore, end users can now benefit from improved experiences (via metaverse), and personalized communication (e.g., health tips from wearables, personalized learning solutions, etc.) thanks to AI, ML's ongoing analysis of IoT data.

Because customers share their personal information, these advantages for the final user are made possible. In these situations, blockchain is used to protect personal information and give users more control over who can access it. Furthermore, by enabling end users to follow the path of products through the supply chain, blockchain will foster greater consumer engagement and brand trust (e.g., tracking foodborne outbreaks, detecting food counterfeiting, etc.). Ultimately, by improving physical movement-related tasks and providing functional support, robotics and drones improve end users' quality of life. End users who use these technologies continue to be drawn in by the benefits provided by NATs.

Employees. Internal marketing has been used to address the idea that employees are a company's "internal customers."[13] This kind of perspective shows how important employees are to the company. Workers are a vital component of all business sectors, performing tasks ranging from the regular, highly standardized physical transportation of goods to specialized services requiring a high level of customization. Employee criticality is most evident in service-oriented industries, such as financial consulting and medical services, where the caliber of the service offering is secondary to the caliber of the service personnel delivering it. The traditional view of how employees add value to companies has changed dramatically in a NAT environment. The implementation of NATs is frequently planned to overlap with regular staff duties to maximize value creation through the synergistic effects of technology and human interaction.

Studies regularly reveal that the concern of machines taking over human jobs is not a universal threat. While machines excel in simple and repetitive tasks, they are not suitable for tasks that require innovation and creativity, such as customer service and content creation. As a result, technology companies are now focusing on developing robots that can adapt to a wide range of job functions, rather than replacing humans altogether. This has led to collaborative efforts between robotics, drones, and humans in industrial settings, where they work together in tasks like picking and packing, ensuring employee safety, and even healthcare and surgical applications. Additionally, AI, generative AI, and ML applications are designed to enhance employee capabilities and assist in generating insights, managing customers, and handling knowledge management tasks. These advancements demonstrate that machines and humans can work together to create greater value for all stakeholders.

Channel Partners. Channel partners play a crucial role in maintaining the operations of a company. They are designed to work in harmony with the company to ensure that its products or services are produced, distributed, and made available to the target audience promptly, thereby creating value for customers. Additionally, channel partners also bring value to the company in their unique ways, particularly in the context of the NAT environment. With the integration of NATs, companies are increasingly focusing on integrating their supply chains to minimize resource wastage, eliminate redundant efforts, improve overall process efficiency, and streamline the exchange process. For example, the use of AI, generative AI, metaverse, and ML enables channel partners to deliver products and process enhancements that can generate valuable insights for subsequent decision-making by the company, such as product personalization and pricing strategies. Furthermore, IoT is also utilized by many channel partners to ensure smooth operations of routine tasks while adding value through actions like preventive maintenance, asset management, and smart energy systems.

Community. The communities that businesses operate in are an integral part of it. A company can operate in the middle of several communities at once. Communities are often built around company offerings (like product feedback, and technical support groups), consumer emotions (like love or rage), corporate governance (like privacy and human rights), causes (like the environment, and diversity), or a mix of the above. It is also critical to remember that not all communities are centered in the company's immediate vicinity. Because of the internet's energizing power, communities usually get stronger thanks to the advantageous network effects it provides. Communities have a clear influence on the generation of overall value even though they do not usually participate in the regular course of the firm's economic exchange.

NATs in the environment play a crucial role in helping firms minimize their environmental impact, adapt to changing environmental conditions, develop products and services that address the social and environmental needs of communities, and enhance transparency in their business operations. To achieve these objectives, firms need to closely monitor consumer sentiments expressed through various online and offline channels, covering a wide range of emotions from love to hate.

For instance, by leveraging AI and ML technologies, firms can analyze user sentiments, particularly related to societal issues, and take appropriate actions to align themselves and their offerings with the prevailing societal context. Further, companies are using metaverse to create environments that nurture community building by promoting inclusivity and openness. Additionally, drones are increasingly being utilized for valuable societal purposes such as disaster management, relief and recovery missions, and infrastructure assessment. Similarly, robots are being deployed in community-oriented activities like agriculture, healthcare, and public hygiene to contribute to the overall welfare of the public. These initiatives highlight the significant benefits that communities can derive from the implementation of NATs.

Government. Similar to communities, the government is an essential component of the business environment. Due in part to the uncertainty surrounding the predictors of firm success, determining how governments can add value to businesses is subjective. Businesses, for example, have traditionally defined success based on several factors, including offerings (e.g., novel products), size (e.g., market share), resources (e.g., human capital), strategic approach (e.g., customer-focused), and financial health (e.g., profitability). In light of this, the best way to gauge the value that the government adds to businesses is to look at the kind of business environment that it creates.

In this sense, technological advancements are ushered in by the NAT environment to create favorable business conditions. The use of AI, ML, metaverse, and IoT, for example, has consequences for the environment, energy use, and consumer privacy. As a result, governments are imposing stricter regulations on businesses (such as the General Data Protection Regulation (GDPR) in the European Union). Drones, robotics, and blockchain also support critical administrative procedures related to smart cities, e-governance, and collaborations between the public and private sectors. Drones, AI, and ML are examples of NATs that help governments ensure the welfare of the nation in times of national emergency.

The COVID-19 pandemic of late sufficiently illustrated government attempts to use NATs to obtain information and provide relief. We were able to recover from the pandemic thanks to several initiatives, including the use of drones to disinfect large areas, crowd surveillance to enforce social distancing, and the delivery of vital supplies to affected populations.[14] In a similar vein, governments are using AI and ML to help them plan future response measures like researching the virus, identifying illnesses, coming up with treatment plans, and comprehending the broad effects on the public.[15] These examples demonstrate how governments still gain from the use of NATs.

Value and Social Well-being in a New-Age Technology World

NATs, as described in the overall architecture, are now deeply embedded in our daily lives. The value that NATs add wherever they are employed is a distinguishing feature of their emergence. As more value is produced for all NAT users, a critical long-term implication becomes clear: the establishment of stakeholder well-being.[16] Several marketing studies have looked at well-being in the context of stakeholders. For example, the triple bottom line (a concept that reflects a corporation's economic, environmental, and social worth) considers the well-being of all stakeholders connected with the firm.[17] According to research, green actions by businesses drive not only the environmental but also the social and economic components of sustainability through recycling operations implemented by businesses.[18] Furthermore, the impact of corporations' corporate social responsibility (CSR) efforts on various stakeholders has been acknowledged as contributing to societal well-being.[19] Furthermore, the cause-related marketing concept has been demonstrated to include societal well-being in business actions, ensuring that commercial activity is more than just a financial venture.[20]

While the use of NATs is primarily a technological undertaking, it may and does help in ways other than technology. While existing knowledge on how NATs might contribute to the well-being of stakeholders is limited, the preliminary evidence of NATs' capacity to do so is both interesting (from the aspect of advancing knowledge) and enriching (from a practical and societal standpoint). In this regard, continuing research is looking into how enterprises' use of NATs might help to ensure the well-being of stakeholders while also discovering growth potential for the firms that utilize them.[21]

So far, the practical applications of NATs in numerous sectors of personal and economic actions have proven to be beneficial and valuable. Firms are always discovering fresh ways to use NATs to execute various corporate activities. These solutions generate "value in use," which means that the operations done utilizing NATs generate value through cost savings, efficiency, and better resource usage. NATs assist in how we do things when we do things, and how we get things done in our personal lives. The most significant advantage appears to be the time saved in executing each task. The value received from NATs varies greatly in our social life. This is mostly determined by the functional area of the application. That is, the value generated differs depending on whether NAT is used for nature protection, community relief, public governance, and so on. As a result, it is becoming increasingly clear that NATs can provide not only practical benefits to our everyday actions but also provide overall value and well-being.

One key idea that emerges from the book is the notion that technology serves as a powerful force for bringing people together. Throughout the various chapters, the discussion provides ample evidence to support this idea. As technology becomes more integrated into our lives, it permeates every aspect and becomes a permanent fixture. This permanence leads to repeated use and action, ultimately contributing to the creation of value and well-being for all stakeholders involved. Additionally, the widespread adoption of technology across different markets and geographical locations fosters collective growth and fosters a sense of shared value creation. By empowering both businesses and governments, technology has the potential to bridge gaps and unite people and resources, ultimately promoting harmony and purposeful action. In this context, the use of NATs can play a crucial role in unifying and enabling progress, rather than dividing and conquering. We hope that this book serves as a step towards achieving this goal.

Key Terms and Related Conceptualizations

Data sanctity	Refers to how "clean" the information being recorded is in the data
Data-driven insights	Refers to the potential outcomes that businesses can achieve using "clean" data

Notes and References

1. Kumar, V. (2021), *Intelligent marketing: Employing new age technologies*. Sage Publications.
2. To name a few, studies have found that CE: (a) functions as a critical success factor (Kumar, V., & Pansari, A. (2016), "Competitive advantage through engagement," *Journal of Marketing Research*, 53(4), 497–514; Verhoef, P. C., Reinartz, W. J., & Krafft, M. (2010), "Customer engagement as a new perspective in customer management," *Journal of Service Research*, 13(3), 247–252); (b) creates a value for firms

(Kumar, V., Aksoy, L., Donkers, B., Venkatesan, R., Wiesel, T., & Tillmanns, S. (2010), "Undervalued or overvalued customers: capturing total customer engagement value," *Journal of Service Research*, 13(3), 297–310); (c) informs firms about consumer behaviors (Van Doorn, J., Lemon, K. N., Mittal, V., Nass, S., Pick, D., Pirner, P., & Verhoef, P. C. (2010), "Customer engagement behavior: Theoretical foundations and research directions," *Journal of Service Research*, 13(3), 253–266); (d) supports the creation of interactive, co-creative customer experiences (Brodie, R. J., Hollebeek, L. D., Jurić, B., & Ilić, A. (2011), "Customer engagement: Conceptual domain, fundamental propositions, and implications for research," *Journal of Service Research*, 14(3), 252–271); and (e) manifests from the creation of positive service experiences (Kumar, V., & Rajan, B. (2017), "What's in it for me? The creation and destruction of value for firms from stakeholders," *Journal of Creating Value*, 3(2), 142–156).
3. Kumar, V. (2021), *Intelligent marketing: Employing new age technologies*. Sage Publications.
4. Kumar, V., Rajan, B., Gupta, S., & Dalla Pozza, I. (2019), "Customer engagement in service," *Journal of the Academy of Marketing Science*, 47(1), 138–160.
5. Fernandez, A. (2020), "The Three Drivers of Food Traceability Changes in 2020," *Food Safety Magazine*, June 2, [accessed from https://www.foodsafetymagazine.com/enewsletter/the-three-drivers-of-food-traceability-changes-in-2020/].
6. Personalization creates a connection between consumers and businesses (Murthi B. P. S., & Sarkar, S. (2003), "The Role of the Management Sciences in Research on Personalization," *Management Science*, 49(10), 1344–1362; Vesanen, J., & Raulas, M. (2006), "Building bridges for personalization—a process model for marketing," *Journal of Interactive Marketing*, 20(1), 1–16), and this connection is likely to strengthen the relationship that develops as a result (Simonson, I. (2005), "Determinants of customers' responses to customized offers: Conceptual framework and research propositions," *Journal of Marketing*, 69(1), 32–45). Furthermore, positive firm–customer relationships influence customer engagement behaviors (Van Doorn, J., Lemon, K. N., Mittal, V., Nass, S., Pick, D., Pirner, P., & Verhoef, P. C. (2010), "Customer engagement behavior: Theoretical foundations and research directions," *Journal of Service Research*, 13(3), 253–266), satisfied customer relationships with emotional bonding result in an enhanced customer experience (Pansari, A., & Kumar, V. (2017), "Customer engagement:

the construct, antecedents, and consequences," *Journal of the Academy of Marketing Science*, 1–18), and a personalized experience marketing approach, when carried out through the strategy of curation and the AI tool, can yield better marketing results in a NAT environment (Kumar, V., Rajan, B., Gupta, S., & Dalla Pozza, I. (2019), "Customer engagement in service," *Journal of the Academy of Marketing Science*, 47(1), 138–160).

7. For example, stakeholder value is defined as the difference between the accrued benefits (tangible and intangible) and the associated costs that firms and individuals/organizations realize in a commercial exchange process (Kumar, V., & Rajan, B. (2017), "What's in it for me? The creation and destruction of value for firms from stakeholders," *Journal of Creating Value*, 3(2), 142–156). In a multi-stakeholder setting, stakeholder engagement is defined as the attitude, behavior, the level of connectedness (1) among customers, (2) between customers and employees, and (3) of customers and employees within a firm (Kumar, V., & Pansari, A. (2016), "Competitive advantage through engagement," *Journal of Marketing Research*, 53(4), 497–514).
8. Kumar, V., & Rajan, B. (2017), "What's in it for me? The creation and destruction of value for firms from stakeholders," *Journal of Creating Value*, 3(2), 142–156.
9. Anderson, E. W. (1998), "Customer satisfaction and word of mouth," *Journal of Service Research*, 1(1), 5–17.
10. Dowling, G. R., & Uncles, M. (1997), "Do customer loyalty programs really work?" *Sloan Management Review*, 38(4), 71–82; Oliver, R. L. (1999), "Whence Consumer Loyalty?" *The Journal of Marketing*, 63, 33–44.
11. Reinartz, W. J., & Kumar, V. (2003), "The impact of customer relationship characteristics on profitable lifetime duration," *Journal of Marketing*, 67 (1), 77–99; Reinartz, W. J., & Kumar, V. (2000), "On the profitability of long-life customers in a noncontractual setting: An empirical investigation and implications for marketing," *Journal of Marketing*, 64 (4), 17–35.
12. Kumar, V., Aksoy, L., Donkers, B., Venkatesan, R., Wiesel, T., & Tillmanns, S. (2010), "Undervalued or overvalued customers: capturing total customer engagement value," *Journal of Service Research*, 13(3), 297–310.
13. Berry, L. L. (1981), "The Employee as Customer," *Journal of Retail Banking*, 3(1), 33–40; Grönroos, C. (1982), "An applied service marketing theory," *European Journal of Marketing*, 16(7), 30–41.

14. Banker, S. (2020), "Is the Future of Drones Now?" *Forbes*, June 11, [accessed from https://www.forbes.com/sites/stevebanker/2020/06/11/is-the-future-of-drones-now/#57855e7e3284]; Lewis, N. (2020), "A tech company engineered drones to deliver vital COVID-19 medical supplies to rural Ghana and Rwanda in minutes," *Business Insider*, May 12, [accessed from https://www.businessinsider.com/zipline-drone-coronavirus-supplies-africa-rwanda-ghana-2020-5].
15. Leong, B., & Jordan, S. (2020), "Artificial Intelligence and the COVID-19 Pandemic," *Future of Privacy Forum*, May 7, [accessed from https://fpf.org/2020/05/07/artificial-intelligence-and-the-covid-19-pandemic/].
16. Kumar, V. (2021), *Intelligent marketing: Employing new age technologies*. Sage Publications.
17. Elkington, J. (1994), "Towards the sustainable corporation: Win-win-win business strategies for sustainable development," *California Management Review*, 36(2), 90–100.
18. Crittenden, V. L., Crittenden, W. F., Ferrell, L. K., Ferrell, O. C., & Pinney, C. C. (2011), "Market-oriented sustainability: a conceptual framework and propositions," *Journal of the Academy of Marketing Science*, 39(1), 71–85.
19. Peloza, J., & Shang, J. (2011), "How can corporate social responsibility activities create value for stakeholders? A systematic review," *Journal of the Academy of Marketing Science*, 39(1), 117–135.
20. Ballings, M., McCullough, H., & Bharadwaj, N. (2018), "Cause marketing and customer profitability," *Journal of the Academy of Marketing Science, 46*(2), 234–251; Kumar, V. (2020), Global implications of cause-related loyalty marketing. *International Marketing Review*, 37(4), 747–772.
21. Kumar, V., & Ramachandran, D. (2020), "Developing a firm's growth approaches in a new-age technology environment to enhance stakeholder wellbeing," working paper, Georgia State University, GA.

Index

A

ABB 190
Accessibility 96, 161–163, 216, 261, 272, 315
Accountability 8, 307, 310, 328
Adaptability 9, 120, 151, 185, 226, 232, 273
Adidas 45
Adobe's Adobe Cloak 128
ADT 190
Advanced capabilities 255
Aerial photography 258, 263, 264
Aerodyne 270
Africarare 150
Agile marketing 13, 14, 21, 25, 42, 79, 117, 151, 185, 226, 273, 314
Agrimor 270
Aibo robotic dog 229
AI-powered chatbots 3, 31, 40, 73
AI-powered robots 222
Airbnb 119
Aircards 151
Aldi 314

Alexa 12, 31, 32, 34, 35, 71, 110, 131, 211, 279
Algorithms (develop, comprehend, evaluate) 103
Alibaba 315, 317
Allstate 283
Aloft hotels 219
Amaggi 117, 118
Amazon 12, 31, 34, 35, 53, 81, 87, 89, 110, 119–121, 123, 125, 126, 196, 228, 229, 232, 267, 278, 280, 282, 285
Amazon Bedrock 89
Amazon Echo 219
Amazon Fresh 121
Amazon Go stores 196, 197
Amazon Managed Blockchain 12
Amazon MTurk 131
Amazon Web Services (AWS) 12, 270
Ambient assisted living (AAL) 179, 198, 350
Ambiotex 191
American Express 120
Amgen 304

AMP Clarity 223
AMP Robotics 223
An Post 197
Apple 35, 37, 110, 121, 219, 273, 274
Apple Watch 37, 121, 177, 191, 192
Aquabot 219
Arcade City 311
Artificial intelligence (AI) vii, 3–5, 15, 16, 32, 39, 40, 43, 46, 54, 55
Artificial neural networks (ANNs) 33, 55, 104
ASOS 115
  Buy the Look 115
Asset traceability 318
Asset tracking and management 255
Atea 315
Atlanta Braves 142
Augmented marketing 13, 14, 21, 22, 25, 41, 78, 117, 151, 184, 225, 272, 314
Augmented reality (AR) 3, 5, 9, 12, 19, 20, 38, 78, 90, 124, 141, 142, 144, 151, 155, 156, 160, 167, 225, 239, 349
Augmenting capabilities 262
August 186
Aura Blockchain Consortium 312, 313
Authenticity 301, 302, 307, 311–313, 316, 319, 321, 323, 324, 326, 351
Autodesk 128
Automated customer interaction 31
Automatic systems 259
Automation 4, 5, 32, 71, 79, 80, 88, 119, 124, 128–131, 174, 179, 180, 185, 192, 203, 212, 222, 224, 229, 232, 273, 275, 279, 308, 310, 326, 333, 348, 350, 352
Automation technologies 212, 222

Autonomous Aircraft Inspection (AAI) program 272
Autonomous mobile robots 228
Autonomous systems 259, 260
Auto-tagging 110
AVA 156
Avatar realism 161
Aworker 323
AWS Robomaker 232
Azure AI Health Bot by Microsoft 74
Azure cloud 183, 304

B

Backpropagation 104
Balenciaga 153
Barcelona 194, 275
Bard 31, 32, 65, 72, 73
Basic Attention Token (BAT) 320
Bayer 74, 304
Bayesian networks 4
Bellabeat–Leaf Urban 38
Bestic 211
Bias 3, 6, 162, 223
Bidirectional flow of value 355
Biomechanical research 213
Biryani By Kilo 279
Bitcoin 142, 300–302, 305, 332
BitCongress 314
BitProperty 324
BizRate 230
Blockchain 3, 8, 9, 11–13, 15–17, 20, 23, 141, 145–147, 157, 159, 164, 299–327, 329–333, 336, 338, 341, 342, 345, 349–354, 356, 358
BloombergGPT 89
BMW 304
Boehringer Ingelheim 191
Boeing 46, 272, 273
Bon Viv Spiked Seltzer 151
Boosto 329
Bossa Nova 219

Brand experiences 3, 184, 222, 225, 354
Brand interactions 68, 184
Brand loyalty 19, 87, 159, 183
Brand outcomes 190
Brand positioning 153
Brand trust 356
Bransys 190
Brave browser 320
Brightspace insights 35
Broad Branch Market 231
Browsing behavior 12, 75, 85, 86
Budapest 275
Buddy 219
Burberry 126
Burger King 187–189
Business processes 9, 38, 128, 172, 196, 222, 234, 304, 352

C

Café X 211
California Farm Bureau Federation (CFBF) 266
Capabilities 2, 4, 6, 9, 14, 19, 20, 23–25, 27, 36, 40, 43–46, 54, 56, 74, 82, 87, 88, 90, 96, 108–110, 116–118, 120, 123–127, 129, 131, 134, 154, 156, 174, 175, 180–182, 185–190, 193, 198, 213, 219, 228, 229, 232, 233, 235, 236, 239, 241, 256, 258, 261, 262, 268, 272, 274, 276, 277, 279, 281, 282, 285, 286, 295, 310, 316, 317, 322, 323, 325, 346, 351–353, 357
  dynamic 24, 25, 187, 228, 240
  static 24, 26
Capability development 187, 277, 281, 295
Capgemini 190
Cardano 302
Carl's Jr. 86

Carmax 44
Carnegie learning 36
Carrefour 315, 317
Cartier 312
Cathay Pacific 320
Celebrity Beyond 158
Celebrity Cruises 158
Cellr 321
Center for Research on the Epidemiology of Disasters (CRED) 268
Change business methods 152
Changing user demographics 280
ChatGPT 31, 32, 65, 68, 72, 73, 92
Chick-fil-A 125
Chipotle 142
Circulor 312
Citymesh 271
Closed-loop supply chain 197
Coca-Cola 75, 76, 159, 285
Coca-Cola's GAI initiative 75
Codi 36
Collaboration 6, 9, 84, 108, 141, 145, 146, 152, 154, 164, 185, 187, 213, 217, 224, 226, 227, 270, 273, 321, 348, 358
Collaborative filtering 47
Community building 349
Community relief 360
Competition 3, 37, 70, 83, 85, 88, 117, 122, 148, 157, 163, 230, 235, 276
Competitive advantage 29, 38, 46, 83, 187, 192, 228, 233, 240, 275, 276, 295, 309, 353
Computational methods 5, 10, 103, 105
Computational resources 161
Computer intelligence 20
Confidentiality 307
Connected environments 172
Consensus protocol 324, 332
Consumer acceptance 256

Consumer behavior viii, 2, 19, 38, 42, 75, 76, 78, 122, 175, 270, 273, 361
Consumer well-being 178, 198
Content delivery 348
Contextually relevant content 41, 70, 181
Contextual marketing 13, 14, 20, 22, 25, 40, 77, 116, 150, 183, 224, 271, 312
Continuous learning 4, 5, 32, 308, 323, 346
CopyAI 47
Corporate agility 22
Cortana 31, 32, 38, 131
Crop health 266
Cross-functional teams 21, 25, 42, 79, 84
Crurated 313
Cryptocurrency 148, 300, 301, 307, 310, 322, 334, 352
Crypto loans 299
Crypto-spatial coordinate system 320
Cubelets 218
CultBeauty 322
Curation 48, 49, 124, 238, 240, 253, 350, 362
Customer care and back-office support 66
Customer-centric marketing strategies 23
Customer churn 127
Customer delight 128
Customer engagement (CE) 14, 23, 32, 47–49, 51, 87, 88, 97, 113, 122, 125, 130, 142, 148, 152, 177, 181, 190–192, 206, 222, 226, 232, 233, 235, 253, 256, 278–280, 296, 300, 310, 321, 322, 337, 346, 352, 360, 361
Customer experiences (CX) 6, 10, 12, 14, 19, 38, 40, 41, 75, 85, 87, 100, 101, 114, 157, 160, 171, 175, 181, 183, 190, 192, 198, 206, 226, 232, 234, 276–278, 282–284, 296, 346, 353, 354, 361
Customer feedback 40, 48, 81, 82, 185, 188, 233
Customer heterogeneity 124
Customer influence effect (CIE) 328
Customer influence value (CIV) 328
Customer journey 2, 14, 20, 25, 29, 68, 123, 310
Customer needs 14, 24, 31, 40, 44–47, 67, 81, 82, 84, 117, 119, 128, 153, 172, 181, 186, 188, 225, 227, 256, 275, 276, 300, 316, 323
Customer-oriented marketing 1, 11
Customer profiles 32, 47
Customer relationships 10, 47, 51, 52, 124, 237, 361
Customer response 32, 122, 126
Customer satisfaction 44, 47, 82, 87, 114, 115, 190, 224, 285
Customer segmentation 75, 126, 349
Customer sentiments 47, 52, 76, 81
Customer service 3, 6, 10, 52, 73, 75, 76, 80, 131, 219, 235, 236, 247, 276, 352, 356
Customer service transformation 348
Customer value 206, 234, 278
Customization 47, 68, 96, 120, 149, 158, 229, 232, 356
CVS 172, 268
Cybderyne's Hybrid Assisted Limbs 219
Cyberbullying and harassment 162

D

D:verse 313
Dall-E 32, 68, 71–73, 82
Dapper Labs 322

Dash 230
Dash & Dot 218
Data analysis 29, 34, 110, 223
Data augmentation 70, 104, 106
Data authentication 304
Data-based analytics 4
Data-driven insights 76, 84, 278, 351, 360
Data-driven marketing 3, 13, 14, 21, 25, 39, 51, 75, 114, 148, 181, 182, 223, 269, 310
Data ecosystem 21, 22, 120
Data granularity 174, 176
Data management 6, 24, 109, 304, 310, 316, 317
Data mining 104–106, 132
Data-oriented technology 174
Data processing 161
Data sanctity 351, 360
Data science techniques 116
Data variance 107
DeBeers 320
Decentraland 146, 148, 154, 156
Decentralized 11, 21, 25, 42, 79, 142, 145, 148, 152, 156, 159, 163, 302, 309, 310, 323, 324, 332, 350
Decision trees 105, 107
Deep Brew 41
Deep learning 4, 15, 31–34, 47, 65, 72, 77, 94, 104, 110, 120, 130, 223
Degree of autonomy 214, 240, 259
Delivery 9, 53, 59, 122, 128, 151, 161, 190, 213, 215, 227, 228, 232, 256, 260, 275, 276, 278–280, 294, 311, 318, 350, 354, 358
Demand forecasting 120, 128, 129
Demand Side Platforms (DSPs) 327
DHL 188, 228, 267, 278, 285
Diageo 188
Diesel 313
Digicash 302

Digital currency 300, 301
Digitalization 11–13, 22
Digital landscape 19, 88
Digital literacy 163
Digital strategies 14, 31, 48, 67, 88, 125, 126, 159, 160, 172, 191, 233, 234, 256, 280, 281, 300, 322–324
Digital trade finance transactions 299
Digital twins 6, 46, 142, 147
Digital world 4, 5, 10, 141, 145, 151, 180
Direct firm-customer interactions 318
Disaster response 256, 268, 288
Discreet Variational Auto-Encode (dVAE) 72
Discrimination 162
Disney 72, 125, 142
Disposable income 227
Disruption 174, 300, 345
Disruptive technology 83
Distributed ledger technology 299, 305, 350
Dolphin 219
Domino's Pizza 282
DoorDash 279
Drife 311
Driving customer engagement 14, 31, 47, 67, 87, 124, 158, 172, 190, 232, 256, 278, 321
Drone adoption 262, 287
Drone delivery 267, 275, 276, 279, 280, 285, 294
Drone-in-a-Box (DiaB) 271
Drones vii, viii, 3, 8, 9, 11–13, 15, 19, 20, 47, 255–285, 287, 288, 290, 292–294, 298, 345, 354, 356–358
DroneUp 269
DRONOS software 270
Dynamic capabilities 24, 187, 228
Dynamic customer experiences 171

Dynamic pricing 46, 271, 349

E

eBay 120, 231
Ecco 121
Echo 34, 229
Ecosystem-based innovation 299
Effective business models 187
Efficiency vii, 8, 9, 11, 22, 23, 26, 40, 42, 76, 79, 80, 84, 85, 89, 117, 126, 129, 130, 175, 180, 182, 201, 216, 218, 222, 224–226, 228, 229, 237, 256, 261, 274, 278, 306, 310, 315, 319, 320, 323, 325–327, 351–354, 359
Effie 219
E-gold 302
Ekso Bionic 219
Ekso NR 219
Elisa 232
ELIZA–chatbot 67
ElliQ 229
Emergency Events Database (EM-DAT) 268
Emergency response innovation 271
Employee criticality 356
Employee diversity 83
Enhanced customer experience 145, 283, 346, 361
Enhanced security 310
Enterprise drones 255
Environmental consciousness 227
Ethereum 148, 156, 302, 305
Ethical sourcing 304
ETS 111
Eufy 219
Everledger 317
Evo 174, 179
Evolutionary algorithms 4

F

Facebook 34, 110, 142, 192, 271
Facial recognition 34, 110
Fairness 307
Farfetch 89
Fasal 185
Fashion Innovation Agency (FIA) 87
Federal Aviation Administration (FAA) 263, 267, 270, 284
FICO 119, 126
Fifth age of virtual worlds 142
Financial services 29, 30, 66, 127, 304
Firm capabilities 13, 14, 31, 54, 67, 82, 120, 154, 172, 187, 188, 228, 256, 276, 300, 317, 322, 351
Firm-customer interaction 53
Firm response to market changes 187
First-mile delivery solution 267
Fitbit 37, 177, 191, 192
Flexible automated assembly lines 213
Flirtey 285
Fluid AI 131
FOAM 320
FoldiMate 219
Follow My Vote 314
Ford 317
Forecasting 32, 34, 40, 120, 129, 149, 349
Fortnite 142, 143, 146, 154
Fossil–Q Tailor 38
FreshAI by Wendy's 86
Friday 186
Functional benefits 193, 325, 354
Function-oriented technology 216, 229, 261, 277
FURO 230
Future-oriented technologies 238

G

Gaming industry 141
Gap 20, 84, 142, 281, 322, 360
Garmin 37
GE 188, 285
Genentech 304
General Data Protection Regulation (GDPR) 7, 9, 358
Generating new content 65
Generative artificial intelligence (GAI) 15, 65–71, 73–95, 97, 348
Generative design algorithms 46
Genetic algorithms 130
Gen Z 153, 167
Geo-blockchain 320
Geofencing 186, 187, 189
Georgia State University 35
Geospatial information 275
Giant Eagle 231
Gilead 304
Gladwell Gecko 219
GlaxoSmithKline 191
Global trade 319
Google
   Gmail 111, 125
   Search 125
   Search Generative Experience 44
Google's Duplex 35
Google ads 271
Google Assistant 34, 35
Google Cloud Robotics Platform 232
Google Glass 37
Google Home 178, 219, 229
Google Maps 111
GPS units 267
Grammarly 48, 111
Graphic visualization 105
Greater data security 318
Greenfence 315
Gucci 142, 153, 154, 156

H

Hamburg 275
Hamburg Port Authority 174
Hannah 159
Hanwa Life 159
Hardee's 86
HashCash 302
Haystack 131
Healthcare 1, 22, 30, 36, 38, 40–42, 66, 73, 74, 109, 134, 173, 175, 177, 178, 191, 199, 213, 215, 217, 218, 231, 233, 236, 237, 302, 319, 320, 350, 357, 358
Heathrow Airport 189, 236, 283, 318
HelloFresh 122
Heterogeneity 124, 173
High-quality cameras 263, 267
Hilton's Connie 124
Hitachi 110, 190
HOBOT 219
Honeywell 190
Horizon robotics 226
Hubert.ai 36
Human-centric marketing 2
Human intervention 13, 103, 106, 120, 179, 180, 216, 231, 234, 261, 303
Humanitarian relief efforts 350
Humanizing customer experience 41
Humanoid robots 213, 221, 253
HX2 230
Hybrid systems 258, 286
Hyper-connected digital universe 144
Hyper-localized offerings 189

I

IBM Watson 31, 48, 79, 139, 239
Ikea 155, 156
iLife 219
Illegal deforestation 282

Image classification 104
Immersive experience 3, 12, 15, 19, 145, 148, 151, 153, 162, 285
Immersive virtual environment 144
Immutable 11, 15, 302, 303, 324, 330
Immutable spatial context 320
Improve agility 274
Inclusivity 162, 358
Industrial automation 172, 179, 180, 203, 215, 240
Industrial IoT (IIoT) 180, 198, 353
Industrial revolution 1, 179, 180, 198
Industry 4.0 180, 198, 350
Inference 7, 34, 108, 309
Influencer payment system 329
Influencers 51, 52, 157, 264, 279, 321, 328–330
Information asymmetry 316
Information exchange 176, 208
Information fatigue 280
Information infrastructure 176
Information storage and retrieval 104
Infrared mapping 266
Innovation-friendly regulatory environments 175
Insight generation 192
Insights AI 85
Instantaneous 3, 232, 233, 303
Institute of Electrical and Electronics Engineering (IEEE) 180
Institutional performance 68
In-store navigation 215, 278
Instreamatic–audio marketing platform 77
Integrated strategy for stakeholder engagement 346
Integrity 24, 182, 307, 308, 310, 311, 316, 324
Intel 154, 285
Intel Drone Show 285

Intelligence amplification (IA) 117, 132
Intelligent advertisements 348
Intelligent automation 222, 223, 310
Intelligent driving technologies 226
Interaction orientation approach 190
Interactive experience 20, 78, 156, 181
Interactive robots 236, 237
Interactivity 5, 158, 236, 279, 354
Interconnectedness vii, viii, 10, 144
Interconnected virtual realms 141, 164
Internet connectivity 266
Internet of Things (IoT) viii, 2, 3, 8–10, 12, 13, 15, 17, 20, 22, 23, 41, 43, 47, 171–176, 179–201, 216, 317, 318, 345, 349, 352–354, 356–358
Intuitive service delivery 346
iPhone X–facial recognition 110
iRobot 219, 229
Istanbul Airport 190

J

JAMOR 219
Jasper 47, 71
Jet 53
Jet Blue 76
JPM Coin 304
JP Morgan Chase 304
Julia 219
June 17

K

Kanega 191
Kansas City Chiefs 123
Kashiwa-no-ha, Japan 194, 196
Keeko robot 53
KelaHealth 224
Kelkoo 231

Kenneth Cole 189
K-fold cross-validation, leave-one-out cross-validation 113
Kiki 220
Kiosk robot 230
K-nearest neighbors 107
Knowledge-driven strategic business decisions 106
Knowledge management 309, 357
KodakCoin 323
KodakOne 323
Kontakt 196
Kraft Foods 43
Kraft Heinz 43, 129
KrisFlyer 322
KrisPay 322
Kroger 172

L

L'Oréal 48
L'Oreal Modiface App 153
Labor-saving technology 266
Large language models for Dialogue Applications (LaMDA) 72
Large language models (LLM) 44, 72, 73
Last-mile delivery solution 267
Las Vegas, USA 194, 195
Latency 161, 233, 241
Lead customization 126, 349
Legal Robot 131
Lego WeDo 218
Leka 211, 218
Lenddo 131
Lenskart 114, 115
Levi Strauss 83
Lexical ambiguity 33
Liberty Mutual 283
Lighthouse 211
Lin by Seedtag 77
Litecoin 302
Liv 34, 131

Logistic regression 107
LogSentinel 317
London Heathrow Airport 189, 283
Loomo 211
Lowe's 215, 219
LoweBot 215, 236
Luna Lights 191
LVMH 312, 323
Lyft 111
Lyrebird 128

M

Machine learning capabilities 267
Machine learning (ML) vii, viii, 3–7, 10, 15, 25, 29, 33, 40, 44, 67, 70, 73, 103, 104, 110–112, 114–117, 130, 132, 225, 267, 345, 349, 354
Machine-to-human connectivity 176
Machine-to-human interaction capabilities 125
Machine-to-machine connectivity 176
Machine vision-enabled robot 213
Macy's On Call 124
Major League Baseball 189
MANA 148
Mapbox 184
Market expansion 20
Marketing 3.0 2
Marketing 4.0 2
Marketing 5.0 2, 13–15, 20–22, 25, 38, 75, 103, 114, 142, 145, 148, 181, 212, 222, 223, 269, 310, 346, 351, 353
Marketing element customization 126, 349
Marketing mix 14, 31, 46, 67, 83, 86, 121, 122, 132, 154, 155, 158, 172, 188, 229, 256, 277, 278, 300, 318, 319
Marketing strategy 46, 48, 53, 83, 90, 172, 277

Market trends 84, 117, 270, 352
Markov chains 67
Mars 93
Mass, segment-level and individual-level personalization 121
McCann, D. 48, 108
McCormick, Foods 48, 239
McDonald's 86, 116, 142, 189
Meal-time assistance 211
Mediachain 306
Medical robot 230
MediLedger 304
MedRec 324
Mercedes-Benz 46, 312
Merchandising and advertising platforms 172
Meta 154, 157
Meta (Facebook) Ads 142
Meta horizon worlds 154, 159
Metaverse viii, 3, 10, 19, 20, 141, 142, 144, 145, 147–165, 167–170, 299, 345, 349, 354, 356–358
Mezi 34, 131
Micro-electric-mechanic sensors (MEM) 36, 55
Micropayments 310
Microprocessor-controlled industrial robot 213
Microsoft 37, 43, 46, 74, 93, 142, 175, 182, 183, 201, 232, 304
Microsoft HoloLens 37
Midjourney by Midjourney Inc. 65
Milan 275
Miller Lite 321
Minecraft 154
Mitsui Chemicals, Inc. 79
Mobility 9, 163, 173, 215, 217
Model transparency, traceability 310
Moley 219
Mondelez 89, 91
Monegraph 324
Monetization 163, 310, 353

Moro 219
Morpheus 122
Multi-dimensional 178, 198
Multirotor drones 258, 260, 286
Multi-sensory solutions 128
Mystore-E 124, 239

N

Nala Robotics 225, 226
Nao 211, 218, 230
NASA 280
Natural language processing (NLP) 4, 15, 29, 31–33, 48, 56, 72, 73, 90, 111, 113, 118, 130
NBA collectible insights 322
Need for authenticity 227
Nespresso 320
Nest 34, 131, 191
Nestle 53, 89, 121, 171
Netflix 24, 25, 110, 123, 125, 128, 129
Network of sensors 10
Neural networks 4, 31–33, 55, 65, 67, 72, 89, 94, 103–105, 107, 110, 154, 221
New product development 353
New product ideation, generation, delivery 84
New York Interactive Ad Exchange (NYIAX) 327
New York Power Authority (NYPA) 284
NexTag 230
NextMeet 152
Nike 45, 84, 142, 155, 157, 191, 192
Nike Swoosh 157
Nivea 189
Nivea Sun Kids 189
NLP capabilities 77, 124
Non-fungible tokens (NFTs) 142, 303, 321, 330
Norwegian Seafood Trust 315

Nvidia Corporation 142

O

Ogilvy 53
Ogilvy Paris 88
Oklahoma Gas and Electric (OG&E) 284
Olivia 34, 131
Omnichannel engagement 90
Omnichannel models 122, 190
Open Web Application Security Project (OWASP) 308
Operational efficiency 86
Optimize harvesting process 273
Optimizing customer engagement behaviors 148
Optimizing operations 348
Optimus 221, 222
Oracle 116, 188
Order management, fulfillment, returns 121
Organizational efficiencies 353
Otto 120, 121
Oura Rings 38

P

Padova, Italy 194, 195
Pandora 34, 110, 131
Panera Bread 86
Patagonia 125
PathAI 135
Pattern recognition 6, 108
Payload 257, 258, 260, 261, 286
Payment frauds 112
PayPal 111, 112
Pay-per-click advertisements 48
Peer-to-peer network 299
Pepper 218, 219, 232
PepsiCo 91, 171, 326, 327
Pepsi Super Bowl LIII Halftime Show 285
Perceptive managerial judgment 108

Personalization 2, 5, 10, 39, 47, 49, 52, 53, 68, 75, 88, 90, 91, 115, 121–124, 132, 218, 361
Personalization elements 234
Personalized customer actions 29
Personalized customer engagement 3, 49
Personalized customer interaction 29
Personalized digital shopping experiences 148
Personalized offerings 6, 23, 49, 121, 234
Personal transporter 211
Pfizer 304
Phrasee 89, 100
Pillar Learning 36
Pillo 211
Pizzaiola 225
Playchess.com 117
Pokémon Go 142, 143
Poncho 128
Popeyes 86
Porsche 320
Pounce 35
Prada Group 312
Pragmatic ambiguity 33
Predicting customer behavior 82, 114
Prediction 5, 10, 33, 34, 36, 38, 52, 71, 103, 104, 108, 112, 113, 116, 117, 122, 124, 128, 129, 132, 185, 222, 224, 270, 299, 308
Predictive analytics 5, 22, 25, 32, 40, 108, 110, 115, 122, 149, 182, 224, 271, 309
Predictive marketing 13, 14, 20–22, 25, 39, 76, 115, 149, 182, 224, 270, 311
Pricerunner 231
Pricing trends, adjustments 46
Prime Air 282
PrimeAir packages 12

Privacy 3, 5, 7–9, 37, 77, 82, 92, 162, 163, 169, 171, 267, 282, 283, 300, 306, 309, 325, 333, 357, 358
Process efficiency 357
Process improvements 352
Procter & Gamble (P&G) 84, 182, 183
Product and service development 66
Product curation 44
Product delivery 49
Product development 41, 46, 74, 83, 84, 129, 188, 284, 348, 352, 353
Product-driven marketing 1
Productivity 10, 24, 25, 38, 43, 89, 96, 117, 118, 175, 180, 218, 227, 234, 270, 278, 348, 352
Product management 354
Product personalization 122, 357
Product segments 189
Programmatic advertising (PA) 326, 327, 330
Propy 304
Proximity sensor 216
Public governance 360
Public infrastructure 256
Purchase history 12, 32, 41, 46, 75, 85, 86, 114, 186

Q

QTrobot 218
Qualcomm Technologies 184
Quality control and testing 84
Querium Corporation, Stepwise 36
Quicker contract processing 318
QuillBot 47, 71
Quotient Health 135

R

Radio Frequency Identification (RFID) 172, 173, 176, 184, 197, 321
Ralph Lauren–Fortnite Item Shop 154
Rammas by the Dubai Electricity and Water Authority 87
ReCheck 317
Recommendation engines 87, 110, 119
Reconnaissance 256, 260
Red Bull 172, 285
Regulations 3, 6, 7, 9, 164, 283, 311, 358
Regulatory support 12, 256
Reinforcement learning 4, 39, 107, 113, 132
Renault 317
Repeatability 173
Resource allocation 270
Resource-based view (RBV) 23, 26, 228
Resource configuration 228, 229
Resource conservation 349
Retargeting 49
Returnable transport packaging (RTP) 196
Revolutionize customer experiences 152, 153
ReWalk's Exo-Suit 219
Ria 2.0 by Healthifyme 239
Ring 190
Ringly–Aries smart ring 38
Ripple 302, 305, 324
RiskBlock 324
Risk identification and mitigation 267, 283
RizzGPT 78
Roar, Volvo's robotic refuse collector 230
Roblox 146, 149, 154
Robomow 219
Robot butlers 219

Robotic capabilities 213, 221, 235
Robotic process automation (RPA) 216, 222, 231, 234, 240, 243, 257, 258, 261, 286
Robotics vii, 13, 19, 31, 211–214, 216, 219, 222–236, 238, 240, 241, 243, 245, 247, 252, 277, 310, 350, 352–354, 356–358
Robotics powered solutions 234
Robotic surgical systems 224
Robots 3, 8, 9, 11–13, 15–17, 20, 47, 72, 124, 128, 132, 211, 213, 215–222, 224, 225, 229–232, 236, 238, 240, 247
Roomba 211, 219, 229
Root 218
RTL Deutschland 91
Rule induction and refinement 105

S

Sainsbury's 314
Salesforce Einstein Analytics 39
Sales intent 49
Sales strategy 49
Samsung 37
Samsung Galaxy Fit 177
SAP 138, 188
SavorEat 232
Schnucks Markets 231
Search engine optimization 48, 52
Semantic ambiguity 33
Semi-supervised learning 107, 132
Semi-supervised machine learning 65, 94
SENSE by Citymesh 271
Sensors 5, 8, 22, 25, 36, 38, 55, 118, 171, 172, 174, 176–179, 182, 183, 185, 187, 188, 190–193, 195, 196, 198, 216, 221, 236, 257, 260–262, 270, 274, 281
Sensors–biological, chemical, meteorological 261

Sensory perception 90
Sentiment 40, 95, 113, 337, 358
Sentiment analysis 113
Sephora 186
Service operations 29, 30, 66
Service quality improvement 229, 234, 353
Service robots 11, 17, 215–220, 240, 253
Shipment visibility 319
ShopBot 230, 231
Shopify 109, 134, 146, 156
Simulation 35, 70, 154, 232
Singapore Airlines 322
Siri 16, 31, 32, 34, 35, 110, 131, 219
Slack 128
Slice Factory 225, 226
Smart bottles 188
Smart cities 2, 15, 172, 175, 176, 178, 194, 195, 208, 349, 358
Smart contracts 303, 309, 310, 316, 326, 329, 352
Smart home video surveillance system 211
Smart screens 171
Smart transportation options 129
Social and emotional reasoning 90
Social connectedness 227
Social media engagement 12
Societal wellbeing 350
Solana 302
Solutions-focused offerings 280
Spam filtering softwares 107
Specialized robots 211, 212
Speech recognition 279
Speech recognition software 107
SPIN Protocol 329
Spotify 39, 53, 110, 306
Spotify–AI DJ, Discover Weekly 39
Stanley, Morgan 82
Starbucks 40, 41, 306
Statistical model (SM) 65, 108, 114, 127

Stitch Fix 45, 82
Strategic flexibility 228
Strategic marketing actions 354
Streamlined communication 174
Superbowl 129, 326
Supervised machine learning 65, 94
Supply chain efficiency 310
Supply chain transparency 312, 319
Supply-side platforms (SSPs) 327
Surveillance 9, 11, 191, 215, 231, 255, 256, 261, 267, 288, 293, 358
Sustainability initiatives 22, 184
Sustainable competitive advantage 23, 26, 354
Sustainable marketing 20
Sustainable Skylines 270, 271
Syntactic ambiguity 33
Synthesia 71, 91

T

Taco Bell 120
Tactical marketing actions 346, 353, 354
Tactile internet (TI) 233, 241
TADA 311
Tailored experiences viii, 22, 25, 77
Target 3, 41, 42, 52, 54, 86, 106, 155, 160, 230, 256, 354
Target audience 2, 19, 38, 52, 75, 89, 114, 142, 148–150, 152, 157, 160, 223, 269, 312, 355, 357
Targeted marketing 12, 19, 25, 32, 76, 82, 346
Task-specific recommendations 177
Technological localization 226
Technology-backed strategy 108
Technology ecosystem offerings 348
Technology effectiveness 309
Technology efficiency 25, 309

Technology management 323
Technology-neutral 299
Telematics 187, 317
Temporary communications infrastructure 269
Tensor Processing Units of Google Cloud 74
Tesco 279, 314
Tesla 190, 221, 222, 229
Tevel 273, 274
Text categorization 104
Text-to-3D models 71
Text-to-image models 69, 71
Text-to-task models 71
Text-to-text models 71
Text-to-video models 71
The New York Times 321
Thermal sensors 267
The Sandbox 146, 159
The voice 124, 148, 149
3D vending machines 151
Tokenization 152, 160
Topic modeling 113
Toppr 121
Toyota 84, 320
Transformative marketing 3, 5, 15, 19, 20, 110, 141, 171, 255, 346, 347
Transparency 9, 195, 237, 300, 304, 306, 307, 309, 310, 314–317, 320, 322, 325, 326, 333, 350–352, 357
Transparent 11, 15, 40, 303, 315, 319, 320, 323, 329
Travel assistance 31
Travelers 158, 283
Trend analysis 118
Tug 230
Typeface 91

U

UAS Traffic Management 280
Uber 46, 111, 119, 121, 126
Uber Eats 53, 119, 121
Uber Freight 85
Ubiquity 324
Ubuntuland 150
Ugo 219, 229
Unacademy 121
Unilever 89, 172, 320
Unit load devices 318
Unmanned Aerial Vehicles (UAVs) 16, 17, 255, 256, 258, 269, 286
Unstructured data (UD) 105, 110, 132, 316
Unsupervised learning 107, 113, 132
Unsupervised machine learning 116
UPS 267, 268, 278, 285
UPS Flight Forward 267, 269
Urban city planning 175
Urchin Tracking Model (UTM) 271, 280
USAA 283
US Air Force 272
U.S. Cognitive Tutor 36
U.S. Department of Defense 42
User engagement 6, 157, 314
User experience 31, 41, 88, 123, 145, 161, 325, 356
User-facing interactions 31
User involvement 173
User sentiments 358
UVD Robotics 218

V

Value creating opportunities 80, 186, 227, 275
Value for firms 129, 282, 348, 360
Value growth for firms and customers 278
Value to channel partners 348–351
Value to employees 348
Value to the community 348–351
Value to the government 348–351

Vedantu 121
Vertex AI by Google Cloud 74
Virgin Voyages 91
Virtual assistance 211
Virtual reality headsets 169
Virtual reality technologies 12, 141, 164
Virtual reality (VR) 3, 5, 9, 10, 19, 38, 78, 128, 141, 144, 148, 151, 156, 160, 161, 169, 225, 263, 274, 276, 349
Voatz 314
Vodafone 318
Voice assistants 32, 35
Volkswagen 226, 227, 317
Volvo 129, 230, 312
VRIO framework 23

W

Walmart 123, 149, 172, 219, 228, 230, 231, 278, 279, 306, 315, 320
Walmart Land 149
Walmart Universe of Play 149
Wearable devices 36, 37, 171, 174, 177
Wearables 8, 22, 36, 37, 57, 172, 174, 176–179, 191, 199, 201, 219, 313, 356
Weather-dependent 266
Wendy's 86, 125, 230
Whisper by OpenAI 72
Whole Foods 125
Wing systems 257, 258
Wokker Noodles 285
WOM Protocol 329
Workhorse Group 269
WPP partnership with Nvidia 80

X

Xrana 219

Z

Zenbo 211

GPSR Compliance

The European Union's (EU) General Product Safety Regulation (GPSR) is a set of rules that requires consumer products to be safe and our obligations to ensure this.

If you have any concerns about our products, you can contact us on

ProductSafety@springernature.com

In case Publisher is established outside the EU, the EU authorized representative is:

Springer Nature Customer Service Center GmbH
Europaplatz 3
69115 Heidelberg, Germany